PUBLICATIONS
OF THE GREGORIAN RESEARCH CENTRE
ON CULTURES AND RELIGIONS

EDITED BY

ARIJ A. ROEST CROLLIUS S.J.

INTERRELIGIOUS AND INTERCULTURAL INVESTIGATIONS

VOLUME 1

PONTIFICIA UNIVERSITÀ GREGORIANA
CENTRO CULTURE E RELIGIONI

INTERRELIGIOUS AND INTERCULTURAL INVESTIGATIONS

VOLUME 1

GEORGE C. DECASA, SVD

THE QUR'ĀNIC CONCEPT OF *UMMA*

AND ITS FUNCTION IN PHILIPPINE MUSLIM SOCIETY

EDITRICE PONTIFICIA UNIVERSITÀ GREGORIANA
ROMA 1999

VIDIMUS ET APPROBAMUS AD NORMAM STATUTORUM UNIVERSITATIS

Romae, ex Pontificia Universitate Gregoriana

*Die **15** mensis **VI** anni **1998***

R.P. Prof. Arij A. Roest Crollius, s.j.

R.P. Prof. Thomas Michel, s.j.

ISBN 88-7652-812-1

EDITRICE PONTIFICIA UNIVERSITÀ GREGORIANA
Piazza della Pilotta, 35 - 00187 Roma

TABLE OF CONTENTS

CHAPTER TWO: *UMMA* IN THE CONTEXT OF THE *TĀFSĪR* 169

ACKNOWLEDGMENTS

It is my pleasant duty to express my gratitude to all those who have assisted me in the research that led to this study.

My deepest gratitude goes to Fr. Arij Roest Crollius, S. J., whom I had the privilege of having as director of this thesis. I say "privilege" because gradually I discovered that he belongs to that group of classical qurʾānic scholars who combine a profound respect for the written word with a vast knowledge of the exegetical tradition. I also discovered him as an Islamologist of international renown. Thus he guided me to various centers of Islamic learning and facilitated contacts with other Islamic scholars. A sincere thanks goes to Fr. Tom Michel, S. J., for his positive criticism and valuable remarks especially to the chapter concerning Islam in the Philippines and Southeast Asia.

I am grateful to the authorities and staff of Islamic libraries in different countries for making me feel welcome and for generously making available resources for research. A special word of appreciation goes to those of the University of Leiden, the Hebrew University of Jerusalem, the Bethlehem University, the Selly Oak Colleges of the University of Birmingham, the Institute of Islamic Studies in the University of the Philippines in Quezon City, the Gowing Memorial Research Center and the Mindanao State University - both in Marawi City, and the Notre Dame University and the Notre Dame College - respectively in Cotabato City and Jolo.

I will always remain indebted to my friends who helped me a lot during my studies and researches in various countries. I mention in a special way Ofra Hacohen of the Hebrew University of Jerusalem and Aida Kattan of Bethlehem. They not only taught me Arabic but also provided me generous guidance during my studies and researches in the Middle East. In the same way I mention the Jesuits at the Holy Family College of Cairo, Marawi Bishop Desmond Hartford and his staff, and the OMI communities both in Jolo and in Cotabato City.

I thank all the members of the SVD community in Rome for their support. I mention in a special way Fr. Mike Yasis, SVD, who generously helped with solving computer problems. In the same way I thank Fr. Bubi Scholz, SVD, for his encouraging attitude and especially for helping with translations of German texts. I equally thank my SVD confreres in Birmingham, England -- namely: Fr. Provincial Michael McPake, SVD and Fr. John Bettison, SVD - who made me feel most welcome in their small community and facilitated my researches in the libraries of Birmingham, Oxford and London.

Finally, I sincerely thank my SVD superiors -- namely: Fr. Henry Barlage, SVD - superior general, as well as Frs. Cornelio Alpuerto, SVD and Vicente de la Cruz, SVD - successive provincial superiors of the Philippine Central Province. They gave me the permission to do three successive studies: first, the licentiate studies at the Gregorian University, then the Arabic studies in Rome and in the Middle East, and, finally, the doctoral studies back in the Gregorian University, of which this dissertation is a fruit.

George Decasa, SVD

FOREWORD

It is a privilege to present this lucid and illuminating study on the Islamic concept of *umma* and its significance for today's Muslim population of the Republic of the Philippines. Very rare indeed it is to read, at this end of the century, a book by a Non-Muslim on Islam which is neither filled with "islamophobia," nor ingratiatingly attempting to ply to the canons of "dialogue." This book is simply an academic study. As such, it is made of research, of a report on the research, and of an evaluation of the report in its value for understanding Islam and Muslims.

Though the term *umma* is of central importance in the founding documents of Islam, a major study on this term in its employment in the Qur'ān and its interpretation by the *mufassirūn* was lacking. The work fills this gap. Because of the consistent use of comparative and historical linguistics, this study will serve as a model for future studies on similar Qur'ānic topics.

Fr. Decasa shows the political and universalistic potentialities of the term for defining the position of a Muslim community in a religiously pluralistic society. By showing the relevance of the word *umma* for other human societies, the study offers also material for a sociological study. Of particular interest are the derivative meanings the author registers among contemporary authors and also in the history of South-East Asian Muslim groups.

As the guide who has accompanied the research and writing of this thesis, and as the editor of the new series of "Inculturation": *Interreligious and Intercultural Investigations,* I am proud to welcome this work as the first one in this new series and express my firm conviction that it will be met with the critical appreciation it deserves. In this way, it will be a valuable pointer towards the new era of interreligious understanding of which, in our days, we perceive the first intimations.

Arij A. Roest Crollius, S. J.

Editor's Note

With the series "Interreligious and Intercultural Investigations," the Gregorian Research Centre on Cultures and Religions intends to create a new channel for the results of the interdisciplinary research for which it has been founded. The series "INCULTURATION" will be continued, accentuationg more its role as a collection of "Working Papers," as was its original intention.

aarc

System of Transliteration

The transliteration of Arabic words is according to the following alphabetical substitution:

ا = ʾ (omitted at the beginning of a word)

ب = b	ز = z	ف = f
ت = t	س = s	ق = q
ث = ṯ	ش = š	ك = k
ج = j	ص = ṣ	ل = l
ح = ḥ	ض = ḍ	م = m
خ = ḫ	ط = ṭ	ن = n
د = d	ظ = ẓ	ه = h
ذ = ḏ	ع = ʿ	و = w
ر = r	غ = ġ	ي = y

ة = a, when in construct - at

The dipthongs are written: ay [َيْ] and aw [َوْ]

The short vowels are represented by a for the *fatḥa*, i for the *kasra*, u for the *ḍamma*.

The long vowels are represented as follows:

اَ، ىَ = ā, وُ = ū, يِ = ī

The following system of bracketing has been used:

a) Transliteration and substitution of assumed material in translation: [. . .].

b.) Parenthetical comment: (. . .).

INTRODUCTION

Filipino Muslims describe the Muslim struggle in the Philippines as the struggle of the *umma*. Many of them see the present Philippine situation as a threat to their existence as an *umma*. This view has been underscored by the Filipino Muslim scholar Cesar Adib Majul.

> The fundamental question now facing individual Muslims in the Philippines is whether they still desire to have or preserve a Muslim community in the country - a community that will testify to the Oneness of Allah and the Prophethood of Muhammad and who will adhere to the fundamentals of Islam. This question is not the same as that as to whether the Muslims want to exist as individuals or not. The question, to be repeated, is whether the Muslims want to preserve their existence as an *umma*.... It is inconsistent and not canonically possible for an individual to claim that he can still be a Muslim and not advocate the existence of a Muslim community.... Moreover, Allah has commanded the believers to act as a community....[1]

This clarion call, sounded out many years ago, has up to now remained at the core of the Muslim struggle in the Philippines. However, Filipino Muslims differ among themselves in regard to how the *umma* is to be realized in today's world. While analyses of

---

[1] Cesar Adib Majul, *Muslims in the Philippines: Past, Present and Future Prospects* (Manila: Converts to Islam Society of the Philippines, 1971) 26-27.

the struggle from various perspectives have been done by Muslim and Christian scholars alike, no detailed study of the Filipino Muslim struggle from the perspective of the qurʾānic concept of *umma* has as yet been undertaken. It is with the purpose of filling this gap that this topic was chosen for the study. The present study seeks to understand and learn from the ideal of the Muslim community as it is described in its orginal source which is the Qurʾān and, in its light, to understand the Muslim situation in the Philippines. Thus it is entitled "The Qurʾānic Concept of *Umma* and its Function in Philippine Muslim Society." It is a modest attempt to propose that a proper understanding of the qurʾānic concept of *umma* is an important clue to the realization of the Islamic *umma* in today's world. This study is made with the desire to contribute to interreligious dialogue. Thus, it will be done in the context of the Islamic faith and exegesis; at the same time, we try to adhere to the standards of scholarly objectivity and honesty.

In the context of the Islamic faith, the subject of the *umma* concept may be approached in a number of different ways. We may start from the elaborate systems of theology, and find that we are led back to the Qurʾān as the original basis of the theological elaborations. Or we may start from the Muslim commentaries on the Qurʾān in order to see how the *umma* in the Qurʾān has been understood by Muslims through the centuries. We, however, have chosen to approach the subject by starting from the original source itself - the Qurʾān, in order to listen, firsthand, to what it says about the *umma*. This approach to the subject of *umma* has been inspired by the recommendations expressed by several respected Muslim scholars. Among them we cite, first of all, the renowned and respected scholar al-Suyūṭī[2] himself, who says that in the view of the *ʿulamāʾ*, whoever wants the true explanation of the Qurʾān should first search it in its own pages, for if the Qurʾān

---

[2] Jalāl al-Dīn al-Suyūṭī, *al-Itqān fī ʿulūm al-Qurʾān II* (Cairo: Maṭbaʿa Ḥijāzī, 1318/1900) 175.

mentioned a thing or a principle in one place, it is explained further in another (القرآن يفسر بعضه بعضاً). The modern Muslim scholar Mushir-ul-Haq of the Algerian Muslim University also recommends the same hermeneutical principle and explains that some Muslim views and practices in the past were not always consistent with the qurʾānic injunctions.[3] This hermeneutical principle made famous by respected scholars of old like al-Suyūṭī finds elaboration in the Islamic methodology of the Pakistani Muslim scholar Fazlur Rahman,[4] which elaboration may be summarized as follows: The Qurʾān, in terms of its overall teaching as well as in terms of its specific tenets, "has no inner contradiction" but coheres and gives an overall picture. In order to understand the meaning of the Qurʾān or the meaning of a qurʾānic concept, one must study all the verses concerned in the order of their revelation, analyze their specific applications, and, from these specifics the general principles must be discerned. To this task of understanding a study of the commentaries, especially the earlier ones, is helpful. But they must occupy a secondary place "since historical interpretations of the Qurʾān, although they will be of help, are also to be judged by the understanding gained from the Qurʾān itself."[5]

I have not found - whether in Muslim or non-Muslim scholarship - any full analysis and discussion of the term *umma* as used in the Qurʾān. In a recent paper which purports to discuss the origin of the Muslim *umma* and its integration, Ka-Ka Khel merely enumerates various usages of *umma* in the Qurʾān as his

---

[3] Mushir-ul-Haq, "Inter-Religious Understanding" in *Christian-Muslim Dialogue, Broumana 12-18 July 1972* (Geneva: WCC, 1973) 32.

[4] See Fazlur Rahman, *Islam and Modernity: Transformation of an Intellectual Tradition* (Chicago and London: The University of Chicago Press, 1984) esp. pp. 1-12 and 141-162.

[5] Ibid., 6.

main interest is in the post-qur'ānic Muslim application of the term.[6] Neither does Abdullah al-Ahsan's article "The Qur'ānic Concept of Umma"[7] take into consideration all the *umma* passages in the Qur'ān. It cites various meanings and usages of *umma* in the Qur'ān with the help of some of the classical commentaries, but does not analyze the connection between the various meanings and usages. Its main focus is on the post-qur'ānic historical Muslim community. Denny's[8] article focuses on the usages of *umma* in the Qur'ān. However, it is far from a comprehensive analysis of all the *umma* passages in the Qur'ān. Moreover, his study is not done within the context of the Islamic faith. Thus, first of all, not all of his assignments of the *umma* verses into either Meccan or Medinan find support in the writings of Muslim scholars. He makes only scant references to Muslim commentaries. Secondly, while he shows various meanings and usages of *umma* in the Qur'ān, he does not find out the logical connection between them. The various changes in the meanings and usages of *umma* are meant to support Denny's conclusion that Muhammad was able to create his *umma* only after much hard work which brought him from Mecca to Medina and then back to Mecca, and which process necessitated the changes in the meaning and use of the term *umma*.

---

[6] Muhammad Nazeer Ka-Ka Khel, "The Rise of *Umma* at Mecca and its Integration" in *Hamdard Islamicus* vol. 5 (Autumn 1982) 59-74.

[7] In *Journal Institute of Muslim Minority Affairs* 7/2 (July 1986) 606-622; also to be found as Chapter 1 of al-Ahsan's book which came out later and entitled *Ummah or Nation? Identity Crisis in Contemporary Muslim Society* (Leicester: The Islamic Foundation, 1992).

[8] Frederick M. Denny, "The Meaning of *Umma* in the Qur'ān" in *History of Religions* 15 (1975) 34-70. See also F. M. Denny, "Umma in the Constitution of Medina" in *Journal of Near Eastern Studies* vol. 36 (January 1977) 39.

Thus, following Fazlur Rahman's recommendation, first of all, we will study the qurʾānic verses in the order of their revelation[9] in order to arrive at an overall coherent picture of the qurʾānic concept of the *umma*. Consequently, in order to see how this concept has been interpreted or explained in various historical contexts, it will be followed, first, by a review of representative Muslim Qurʾān commentaries, and, secondly, by an inquiry into how the *umma* concept has been understood or translated in Philippine Islam. This is the original contribution that this dissertation wishes to make. Formulated thus, the main question that this study seeks to answer is: "What is the qurʾānic concept of *umma* and how has it been present or how has it been interpreted in divergent contexts through the centuries, and especially in the particular context of the Philippines?" Thus, our study follows a methodology of contextual reading within a threefold context, corresponding to the three main parts into which our work is divided.

---

[9] The presupposed conceptual framework here is that the qurʾānic revelation is primarily to be interpreted in light of biography, specifically the stages in the career of Muhammad. This framework within which to study the qurʾānic revelation is followed, with various nuances, also by most non-Muslim scholars of the Qurʾān. Other approaches attempted by some non-Muslim scholars have not met wide acceptance. For example, among others, John Wansbrough (*The Sectarian Milieu: Content and Composition of Islamic Salvation History* (Oxford University Press, 1978), has employed the biblical text to provide a paradigmatic view of salvation history, viewing the Qurʾān in terms of motifs developed within the Judaeo-Christian sectarian milieu. Two of Wansbrough's disciples, Patricia Cone and Michael Cook (*Hagarism: The Making of the Islamic World* (Cambridge University Press, 1977), tried to show that the religion of Muhammad's time was not Islam but *Hagarism*. Two other conceptual frameworks which either have not found acceptance by other scholars or have not been very fruitful in the interpretation of the Qurʾān are the use of the basic resources of archaeology and epigraphy as well as the attempt to see the qurʾānic text in literary terms.

Chapter One, which we call "*Umma* in the context of the Qur'ān," will be our reading of the Qur'ān in order to understand the qur'ānic concept of *umma*. First of all, we follow the Muslim community's division between the "Meccan" and the "Medinan" contexts within which to study the qur'ānic verses. Secondly, we confine our study to the verses or contexts in which the term *umma* appears. Thirdly, we then analyze the term *umma* in its various contexts and applications. Fourthly, according to the motifs that are detected, we then examine the development (if any) of the meaning of the term from the Meccan to the Medinan contexts. This is followed by a synthesis and a conclusion which will answer the question what then is the concept of *umma* in the Qur'ān? We complete this chapter with a consideration of other terms in the Qur'ān which are in some way related to *umma*. The first of these is *ummī*, which is a term closely related to *umma*, and thus will have to be discussed thoroughly. The rest are terms which the Qur'ān employs to refer to or to mean "group" or "community." They will be considered briefly in order to properly distinguish them from *umma*.

Our method of contextual reading of the *umma* verses in the Qur'ān can be called descriptive. We do our reading with the help of representative classical commentaries. Whenever in our contextual investigation we encounter important words which for us are "foreign words, embedded, that is, in a distant culture and epoch," it becomes imperative that we also "make use of philological investigations, which help us to understand the meaning the words have in themselves, and of historical considerations, which follow the development of the meaning of the words" in the Qur'ān "and open for us the meaning of the words such as they are used."[10]

[10] A. A. Roest Crollius, *The Word in the Experience of Revelation in Qur'ān and Hindu Scriptures* (Roma: Università Gregoriana Editrice, 1974) 12.

Chapter Two, which we call "*Umma* in the Context of the *Tafsīr*," will be a reading of representative Muslim commentaries on the *umma* verses which refer in an exclusive sense to the Muslims. The phenomenological method here may be specified as contextual historical reading. This means that representative Muslim commentaries on the Qurʾān throughout the centuries will be reviewed and examined in terms of how the *umma* verses were interpreted in relation to previous commentaries, and in terms of their reflection of the particular historical context in which each *mufassir* wrote. This will lead us to an appreciation of the complex and truly dynamic nature of the *umma*.

Chapter Three, which we call "*Umma* in the Context of the Philippines," is a reading of the particular Islamic context of the Philippines. Our source material here will be, first of all, the Filipino Muslim writings on the past and present of Islam in the Philippines. In addition, we will also make use of the works of other historians as well as of anthropologists on the Philippines and Southeast Asia. Through a descriptive analysis of Islam in the Philippines, we will discern how the concept of *umma* has been understood or has been at work in every particular context in Philippine history, and especially in the present situation. In this way, the forces at work in the Philippine Muslim situation today become more evident. We hope thereby to offer a contribution to a growth in mutual understanding among all citizens of the Philippines, and their claims for just and equitable forms of societal life.

At the concluding part of this thesis, the findings of each chapter are briefly summarized and compared. An attempt at interpretation of the Muslim Filipino struggle is made in light of the qurʾānic concept of *umma* and in light of the *umma* in the *tafsīr*. The thesis ends with a note on the importance of the qurʾānic concept of *umma* today, and on the clue to the realization of the *umma* in the particular context of the Philippines.

CHAPTER ONE

UMMA IN THE CONTEXT OF THE QURʾĀN

In this chapter we will try to clarify the meaning of *umma* in the Qurʾān. With the help of some of the classical commentaries[1] as well as of some philological and historical investigations whenever necessary, we will try to achieve our aim in a series of articulations. We will begin with an inventory of all the verses in the Qurʾān in which the term *umma* appears. We will classify them according to the Meccan and Medinan contexts of the qurʾānic revelation, and will try to identify the meanings which the term *umma* has in the Qurʾān. This will lead us to the discovery that, as used in the Qurʾān, the term *umma* is the kind of word that lends

---

[1] The principal commentaries referred to are: Abū Jaʿfar Muḥammad b. Jarīr al-Ṭabarī (224/839-310/923), *Jāmiʿ-al-bayān fī tafsīr-al-Qurʾān* (ed. Cairo 1321; abb.: Ṭabarī); Abū-l-Qāsim Maḥmūd b. ʿUmar al-Zamaḫšarī (467/1075-538/1144), *Al-Kaššāf ʿan ḥaqāʾiq-al-tanzīl wa ʿuyūn-al-aqāwīl* (ed. Tehran, no date; abbr.: Zamaḫšarī); Abū-ʿAbd-Allāh Muḥammad b. ʿUmar al-Rāzī (543/1149-606/1209), *Mafātīḥ-al-ġayb* (ed. Cairo 1352/1933; abbr.: Rāzī); ʿAbd-Allāh b. ʿUmar al-Bayḍāwī (d. ca. 690/1291), *Anwār-al-tanzīl wa asrār-al-taʾwīl* (abbr.: Bayḍāwī); Ismāʿīl b. ʿUmar abū-al-Fidāʾ b. Kaṯīr (701/1301-777/1373), *Tafsīr Ibn Kaṯīr,* 1393 AH; abbr.: Ibn Kaṯīr); Abū-l-Faḍl ʿAbd-al-Raḥmān b. Abī-Bakr Jalāl-al-Dīn al-Suyūṭī (849/1445-911/1505) and Al-Maḥallī Jalāl-al-Dīn (d. 864/1495), *Tafsīr al-Qurʾān* (Cairo: Dār al-maʿrifa, 1412/1992; abbr.: Al-Jalālayn). Whenever we quote from these works, the English rendering is our own, unless otherwise indicated.

itself to new shades of meaning; and even within a particular meaning, it is capable of a further subsequent development. We will then analyze the *umma* verses according to the meanings and motifs expressed by the term in its various contexts within the Qurʾān, in order to see the development (if any) in the meaning of the term from the Meccan to the Medinan contexts.[2] This will be followed by a synthesis of the various analyses and a conclusion which will answer the question what is the qurʾānic concept of *umma*? After we have done our study of the *umma* in the Qurʾān, we cannot avoid the inevitable question of the qurʾānic term *ummī*. As this term is in some way connected with the word *umma*, another section of this chapter will be a study of the qurʾānic term *ummī*, in order to clarify the meaning of the term and its relation to *umma*. A final section will deal briefly with other notable terms in the Qurʾān which either mean or describe human groups. This will

---

[2] The problem of the chronology of the Qurʾān was recognized and tackled by early Muslim scholars. A number of Medieval Muslim writers record varying ancient lists of the *sūras* in what is allegedly their correct chronological order, based chiefly on Traditions about Muhammad, especially those that deal with "the occasions of revelation" *(asbāb al-nuzūl)* and "the abrogating and abrogated" *(al-nāsiḫ wal-mansūḫ)* verses. The most widely-known of these lists is traced back to Ibn ʿAbbās - a celebrated companion of the prophet of Islam. Varying versions of Ibn ʿAbbās' list have come down to us. Although there is no universally accepted tradition about the precise order in which the *sūras* were revealed, there is a broad consensus in these lists about which *sūras* are Meccan and which Medinan, and about the approximate chronological order. Based on these earlier scholarships, a system of dating was established and gained some kind of imprimatur of orthodoxy only because it is carried in the first printed edition of the Qurʾān by and for Muslims, published in Egypt in 1925. This edition is to be referred to as the Standard Egyptian edition or the King Fuʿad edition or the Royal Egyptian edition. (A non-Muslim scholar, Gustav Flügel, had already published an Arabic Qurʾān in 1834, but this did not meet with the approval of the Muslims).

show that, although the Qurʾān employs numerous terms for human collectivities, the only single word and concept that comprehend whatever there is of a true religious community in the eyes of the Qurʾān is, *umma*.

After having done the above-mentioned fourfold inquiry, we shall have gained a better understanding of the concept of *umma* in the Qurʾān.

1. A General Survey of the *Umma* Verses

The term *umma* appears sixty-four times in the Qurʾān, in thirteen of these appearances the plural, *umam*, is used; forty-seven of the occurrences are Meccan while seventeen are Medinan.[3] As we shall see, the term *umma* covers a variety of realities. On the whole, however, *umma* is the term that the Qurʾān uses to refer to bodies of people who are the objects of

---

[3] It may be noted that, among non-Muslim theories of dating of the Qurʾān, the one that has gained wide acceptance not only among non-Muslims but also by some Muslims is the one proposed by T. Nöldeke in his *Geschichte des Qorans* in 1860, and revised later by his pupil F. Schwally and was first published in Leipzig in 1909. In the general classification of the *sūras* and verses into Meccan and Medinan, Nöldeke's chronology deviates from the Traditional Muslim chronology only in a very few points. Another theory of dating which has also gained wide acceptance is that of R. Blachère found in his *Introduction au Coran* (1947) and his *Le Coran* (1949-50). Blachère's chronology slightly modifies that of Nöldeke's, and, in so far as the chronology of the *umma* verses is concerned, the two are practically the same. A sometimes cited, though not a widely accepted theory of dating, is that incorporated in Richard Bell, *The Qurʾān: Translated, with a Critical Re-Arrangement of the Sūras*, 2 vols. (Edinburgh: T. and T. Clark, 1937). For a recent, useful discussion and critique of the various Muslim and non-Muslim chronologies, see, N. Robinson, *Discovering the Qurʾān* (London:SCM Press Ltd., 1996).

the divine plan of salvation. Following the Muslim classification of the qurʾānic verses into Meccan and Medinan, an overview of the *umma*-mentioning verses would be as follows.[4]

Meccan:

1.)	7:34	12.)	10:49	23.)	41:25	34.)	16:89
2-3.)	7:38	13.)	11:8	24.)	42:8	35-36.)	16:92
4.)	7:181	14-15.)	11:48	25.)	43:22	37.)	16:93
5.)	35:24	16.)	11:118	26.)	43:23	38.)	16:120
6.)	35:42	17.)	12:45	27.)	43:33	39-40.)	21:92
7.)	27:83	18.)	15:5	28-29.)	45:28	41.)	23:43
8.)	28:23	19.)	6:38	30.)	46:18	42.)	23:44
9.)	28:75	20.)	6:42	31.)	16:36	43-44.)	23:52
10.)	10:19	21.)	6:108	32.)	16:63	45.)	29:18
11.)	10:47	22.)	40:5	33.)	16:84	46-47.)	13:30

Medinan:

48.)	2:128	54.)	3:110	60.)	4:41
49.)	2:134	55.)	3:113	61.)	22:34
50.)	2:141	56.)	7:159	62.)	22:67
51.)	2:143	57.)	7:160	63.)	5:48
52.)	2:213	58.)	7:164	64.)	5:66
53.)	3:104	59.)	7:168		

---

[4] For the verse numbering that is used in all references to qurʾānic passages, we follow the one found in the Egyptian Standard Edition of the Qurʾān *(Al-Qurʾān al-Karīm,* Cairo Edition, 1342/1923). In our analysis and discussion of the *umma* verses, the text will be given, first in the Arabic original, followed by the English translation. For our English translation of every qurʾānic passage that is cited in this work, we have also consulted the existing English translations of the Qurʾān, especially Muhammad Marmaduke Pickthall's *The Meaning of the Glorious Qurʾān* (New York: Mentor Books, 1953) and Richard Bell's *The Qurʾān: Translated, with a Critical Re-Arrangement of the Sūras,* 2 vols. (Edinburgh: T. and T. Clark, 1937).

1.1 The Meccan Verses

The Meccan occurrences of *umma* show a development in the references of the term. First of all, the first and most frequent appearances of the term *umma* in the Meccan context are in reference to communities or nations in general. In connection with every *umma*, the Qurʾān speaks of a fixed term and a time for judgment (7:34, 7:38, 27:83, 28:75, 10:49, 15:5, 6:42, 6:108, 41:25, 45:28, 46:18, 16:84, 23:43, 23:44), as well as of a messenger of God sent to each *umma* (35:24, 35:42, 10:47, 11:48, 6:42, 40:5, 16:36, 16:63, 16:89, 29:18, 13:30[5]) to guide them to the right path. In connection with these universal themes, the Qurʾān relates a long history of God's relations with his peoples, marked especially by the rejection of God's messengers (35:42, 40:5, 43:22-23, 23:44, 29:18, 13:30). These messengers will appear on judgment day as witnesses against their respective *umam* (28:75, 16:84, 16:89), because each *umma* is brought to God's judgment (27:83, 28:75, 10:49, 15:5, 6:108, 45:28, 23:43). Thus, of the numerous *umam* that have passed away (7:38, 35:24, 11:48, 6:42, 40:5, 41:25, 46:18, 16:36, 16:63, 23:44), many whole *umam* are envisaged to be in hell (7:38), while a number within the individual *umam* followed God's guidance through his messengers (16:36).

At this stage, the term *umma* begins to be used more and

[5] In the Egyptian Standard Edition of the Qurʾān, 13:30 is listed as Medinan. However, in Nöldeke's and Blachère's chronologies, 13:30 is the last *umma*-bearing passage revealed in Mecca. In al-Yaʿqūbī's version of Ibn ʿAbbās' chronology - cited in N. Robinson, *Discovering The Qurʾān* (London: SCM Press, 1996) 70 - it is listed as Meccan while al Bayḍāwī (as cited in J. D. Pearson, "Al-Qurʾān" in *The Encyclopedia of Islam,* new ed., vol. 5, p. 416) considers it as one of the "disputed" passages. The British Muslim, M. Pickthall, also considers *sūra* 13 as Meccan in his chronological scheme. Cf. Muhammad Marmaduke Pickthall, *The Meaning of the Glorious Qurʾān* (New York: Mentor Books, 1953).

more to mean a religious community (7:181, 11:48). This usage of the term refers especially to the one religion preached by the prophets (21:92, 23:52), or to the original one religious community of the whole of humankind (10:19, 11:118, 42:8, 43:33, 16:93). In one verse, there is a particular reference to the one religious community formed by the prophet Abraham (16:120).

As regards the *umma* of Muhammad in particular, it also underwent changes or developments parallel to those of the concept of *umma* as such. Muhammad is seen as the latest in the succession of prophets or God's messengers who all brought the same universal message in the context of their respective communities. Thus, in the beginning of Muhammad's prophetic activity, his *umma* consisted of the Arabs in general as an ethnic community. Just as God had sent messengers to other *umam* in the past, Muhammad was now sent to his people in order to show them the way to salvation (35:24, 13:30). Like the other messengers to *umam*, Muhammad was also considered as a false prophet by his *umma* (35:42). However, like in other past communities, some people also accepted his message (16:89). In the logic of the Meccan verses, therefore, there should be only one community of believers as they are to believe in all the prophets and their identical universal message. Thus, those who accepted Muhammad's message represented an Arabian dimension of the one "spiritual" community of believers in the prophets who brought an identical universal message from God.

1.2 The Medinan Verses

When we turn to the occurrences of *umma* in the Medinan verses, we find that the term is now used only in the sense of religious community. It refers once more to the original one religious community of the whole of humankind (2:213). It applies once more to the religious community of Abraham as an *umma* that has gained its reward (2:134, 2:141). *Umma* is described as a community that surrenders (*umma muslima*) to God (2:128).

In the last instances of the usages of the term, *umma* is used to apply more and more, not in the sense of one religious community of the prophets, but to each particular group or religious tradition or some section of them, as a religious community or *umma* in an exclusive way. To each of these religious communities God has ordained a rite (22:34, 22:67) and a divine law as well as a traced-out way (5:48). On judgment day all will return to God who will tell them their differences (5:48b) and messengers will act as witnesses (4:41). Thus, some section of the people of the Scripture (Jews and Christians) is an *umma* (7:159, 7:160,[6] 7:164, 7:168, 3:113 and 5:66). Of these separate *umam*, it is the *umma* of Muhammad which is exclusively described as *umma wasaṭ* or "middle community" (2:143), the "best community" (3:110), with the task of inviting others to that which is good (3:104), and of vying with others in good works (5:48). Thus, in the logic of the Medinan verses, while various religious groups are recognized as separate *umam* or religious communities, the *umma* of Muhammad is in truth the continuation and the standard-bearer of the *umma* in the prophetic tradition.

Our overview of the *umma* verses has shown that the *umma* concept underwent several variations and changes. There is a

---

[6] In the Traditional Muslim chronology, 7:159-160 are classified as Meccan verses. However, R. Blachère (*Le Coran III* (Paris: Maisonneuve, 1950, p. 642f), like many other Muslim and non-Muslim scholars, see 7:157-7:175 as not belonging to the main flow of thought of *sūra* 7 because, while most of *sūra* 7 belong to the Meccan period, in this group of inserted or revised verses we see, among other things, a pressing attitude to bring Jews and Christians to recognize the message of Muhammad and we find the terms "Tora" and "Gospel" - both elements, many Muslim and non-Muslim scholars are agreed, belong to the Medinan period. See, among others, N. Geagea, *Maria Nel Messaggio Coranico* (Roma: Edizioni del Teresianum, 1973) 23f. In one of the varying versions of the list of the chronological order of the *sūras* attributed to Ibn ʿAbbās, these verses are also listed as Medinan. See N. Robinson, *Discovering The Qurʾān* (London: SCM Press, 1996) 71.

marked difference between its earlier meaning of "community under judgment" and its later usage with the exclusive sense of "religious community." Furthermore, in the context of this final meaning of "religious community," the designation of Muhammad's community as the best *umma* has made the term almost an exclusive property of Islam as a world historical movement.

1.3 A Note on the Etymology of the Term *Umma*

Some older scholars claimed that *umma* was derived from *umm*, which is the Arabic term for "mother," because of the similarity of the two terms. However, the *umma-umm* linkage is not supported by any qurʾānic usage of *umma*.[7] More recent scholarship instead sees *umma* as a loan-word. It was Horovitz who first presented the "loan-word theory" as regards the origin of *umma*, saying that the term appears to have been borrowed from the Hebrew *ummā* or the Aramaic *umetha*, but that it cannot be ascertained whether the Arab language received it through Jewish or Christian mediation inasmuch as the Syrians employ the Aramaic term as well.[8] Jeffery contends that as the word

---

[7] The *umm* - *umma* linkage was explained by Robertson Smith in his discussion of matriarchy as the original model of kinship among the Semitic people. Accordingly, *umma* means a "community" with a common *imām*, or leader. W. Robertson Smith, *Kinship and Marriage in Early Arabia*, ed. Stanley A. Cook (London: Adam and Charles Black, 1907 reprint of 1885 original) 32. Smith's view was followed by, among others, L. Massignon, "L'umma et ses synonymes: Notion de 'communauté sociale' en Islam" in *Revue des études islamiques* (1947) 152, and L. Gardet, *La Cité Musulmane* (Paris: Librairie Philosophique J. Vrin, 1954) 61.

[8] J. Horovitz, "Jewish Proper Names and Derivatives in the Qurʾān" in *Hebrew Union College Annual*, vol. 2 (Hildesheim: Georg Olms,1964) 190; cfr. also the following work by the same author, *Koranische Untersuchungen* (Berlin/Leipzig: Walter De Gruyter & Co., 1926) 52.

apparently is not a native Semitic word at all, the ultimate origin could be Akkadian *ummatu*, whence Hebrew, Aramaic and Syriac seem all to have derived it.[9] Accordingly, the possibility that the Arabic *umma* is an ancient borrowing from the Akkadian *ummatu* could be evidenced by a Ṣafā inscription in Northern Arabia if its translation "at the expense of the community"[10] can be depended on. Other than this very old inscription, the word *umma* does not seem to have been widely used; researchers have not found any examples from pre-Islamic poetry, except the one by the Christian poet Al-Nābiġa al-Ḏubyānī, in which the term is used in the sense of a religious community.

حَلَفْتُ فَلَمْ أَتْرُكْ لِنَفْسِكَ رِيبَةً. وَهَلْ يَأْثَمَنْ ذُو أُمَّةٍ وَهْوَ طائِعُ

I swear it and leave behind no suspicion in your soul. Can a man belonging to a religious community go astray if he is pious?[11]

We concur with most of today's scholars in preferring Horovitz's position, although the issue is by no means closed. *Ummā* in biblical and talmudic Aramaic or *ummāta* in talmudic, means tribe, people, nation. The People of Israel are referred to

---

9 A. Jeffery, *The Foreign Vocabulary of the Qurʾān* (Baroda: Oriental Institute, 1938) 69.

10 Ibid., and J. Horovitz, *Koranische Untersuchungen* (Berlin/Leipzig: Walter De Gruyter & Co., 1926) 52, where Horovitz translates it into German as "auf Kosten der Gemeinde."

11 Arabic text quoted from *Ṭabarī* (on 2:213) 335. Robertson Smith (*Kinship And Marriage*, 32, note 2) has noted that "for religion pure and simple, Nābiġa says دين."

as *ummata qedišta* (Shabb. VI, 8d) i.e., as "the Holy Nation," while the peoples of the earth, i.e., all nations that do not belong to Israel, are referred to as *ummōt ha-ʿōlām*.[12]

2. Analysis and Discussion of the Main Motifs Expressed by *Umma*

In this section, we will examine and discuss the *umma* verses grouped together according to references and motifs that they express in connection with *umma*. In this study according to a particular motif, the Meccan verses will be analyzed first, followed by an analysis of the Medinan verses that express the same motif, in order to see the change or development (if any) in the meaning or application of the term from the Meccan to the Medinan contexts. This procedure in our analysis will lead us to a better understanding of the final sense of *umma* which is "religious community," and especially its special sense of "Muslim community."

2.1 A Community Under Judgment, with an *Ajal*

We group together under one heading the closely associated early themes of "fixed term," "judgment," and "perishing and punishment." Chronologically speaking, the first appearance of *umma* in the Qurʾān is in connection with the term *ajal* "appointed time, period." All the appearances of *ajal* in connection with *umma* are Meccan, and the first verse (7:34) also marks the first appearance of *umma* in the Qurʾān.

---

[12] J. Levy, *Wörterbuch über die Talmudim und Midrashim*, I (Berlin/ Wein, 1924) 95.

وَلِكُلِّ أُمَّةٍ أَجَلٌ فَإِذَا جَاءَ أَجَلُهُمْ لَا يَسْتَأْخِرُونَ سَاعَةً
وَلَا يَسْتَقْدِمُونَ.

To every *umma* is an appointed time. When their appointed time comes, they cannot delay [it] nor anticipate [it] (7:34)

قُل لَّا أَمْلِكُ لِنَفْسِي ضَرًّا وَلَا نَفْعًا إِلَّا مَا شَاءَ اللَّهُ لِكُلِّ أُمَّةٍ
أَجَلٌ إِذَا جَاءَ أَجَلُهُمْ فَلَا يَسْتَأْخِرُونَ سَاعَةً وَلَا يَسْتَقْدِمُونَ.

Say: I have no power/control over any harm or benefit to myself, except that which Allah/God wills; for every *umma* there is an appointed time; when their time comes, they cannot put it back an hour nor put it forward (10:49).

مَا تَسْبِقُ مِنْ أُمَّةٍ أَجَلَهَا وَمَا يَسْتَأْخِرُونَ.

No *umma* anticipates its appointed time, nor do they postpone [it] (15:5 and 23:43).

The employment of the term *ajal* denotes a contact between the qurʾānic language and that of the existent literary traditions.[13] At the same time, the Qurʾān gives a new meaning to the word. In pre-Islamic poetry, *ajal* was a concept which meant a pre-determined "appointed time," and when applied to human life meant nothing other than "death" as the ultimate end. For the pre-Islamic poet it is simply a brute fact of life that each human being

[13] In his book, *God and Man In the Qurʾān* (Tokyo: The Keo Institute of Cultural and Linguistic Studies, 1964) 123-130, T. Izutsu discusses in detail the transformation of the pre-Islamic concept of *ajal* into an Islamic religious concept.

has a term fixed for him somehow.[14] The qurʾānic *ajal*, on the other hand, is appointed by God.[15] The occurrences of *ajal* in connection with *umma* belong to passages which are God's admonitions, in which either it is God himself who pronounces the verse (7:34, 15:5, 23:43) or the messenger is told to announce it (10:49). Secondly, the *ajal* of an *umma* is the end of its earthly

---

14 For the pre-Islamic Arabs, it was the course of Time or of temporal happenings which was regarded as determining their lives. They could not be said to have personified Time but to have thought of it as an impersonal force, not a deity to be worshipped. The Qurʾān itself also expresses this pre-Islamic idea of the inevitable working of Time when it quotes the pagans in 45:24: "They (the pagans) say: 'There is nothing but this present life of ours; we die and we live; and only Time *(dahr)* destroys us." Connected with the belief that Time determines the events of man's life was the somewhat different belief that these events were pre-determined. There was no explanation for this pre-determination, while Time was seen as the efficient cause through which the pre-determined events were brought into existence. "Two points that are specially mentioned are the date of a man's death (the "term" or *ajal* of his life) and his food or provision (his *rizq)."* W. M. Watt, "Pre-Islamic Arabian Religion in the Qurʾān" in *Islamic Studies* XV (1976) 73-79; cfr. also Toshihiko Izutsu, *God And Man in the Qurʾān* (Tokyo: The Keo Institute of Cultural and Linguistic Studies, 1964) 124f.

15 In the Qurʾān, the word *ajal* can be applied in various ways: to any fixed date in a business contract, such as the date for the repayment of a loan (2:282), or for the completion of Moses' service for his wife (28:28f), or to the fixed date for the birth of the embryo in the womb (22:5). Elsewhere *ajal* means the date for the termination of existence. In regard to human beings, the Qurʾān says, for instance, in 6:2 - "It is He who created you of clay, then determined an *ajal* for you; an *ajal* for you is fixed with Him;" or in 63:11 - "God will not defer [the death of] any person when his *ajal* comes; God is well-informed of what you do." Not only human beings but even the sun and the moon have each an *ajal* (35:13-14). Thus, every existence or every creature of God has an *ajal*.

existence; and, in the face of unbelieving people, its being the time of punishment for unbelief is emphasized: the context of 7:34 is a warning to all children of Adam (all people) that every *umma* has an *ajal*;[16] in the passage in which 15:5 occurs, it is mentioned that no township was ever destroyed without its time written in the Book of God's decrees;[17] while in the passage in which 23:43 occurs, *ajal* is mentioned in connection with the destruction of a wrongdoing people in the past. Thirdly, *ajal* is not the terminal point of existence but the gateway to the hereafter. It goes together with the Day of Judgment - as an instant before the summoning - as can be gauged in the passage where 10:49 occurs,[18] as well as in the following "judgment" and "perishing and punishment" passages which are all Meccan.

وَيَوْمَ نَحْشُرُ مِن كُلِّ أُمَّةٍ فَوْجًا مِّمَّن يُكَذِّبُ بِئَايَاتِنَا
فَهُمْ يُوزَعُونَ.

On the day when We shall round up from each *umma* a

---

[16] In another place the Qurʾān says: "If God were to take the people to task for their wrongdoing, He would not leave upon it [referring to the custom of burying female infants] a living creature, but He is postponing them to an appointed time, and when their term comes, they cannot put it off an hour nor advance (it)." (16:61). Thus, Ṭabarī has commented that if unbelievers seem not to be punished by God, it is because their *ajal* has not yet been reached. See Ṭabarī on 7:34.

[17] Cf. 15:4.

[18] In the wider context to which belong the *umma* verses 10:47 ("messenger" verse) and 10:49, the Qurʾān says: "On the day when we gather them, [when it will seem] as though they had not remained [in the grave] but an hour of the day, mutually recognizing each other, those will indeed have perished who have counted false the meeting with God, and have not been guided" (10:45).

troop of those who have counted Our signs false, they will be set in array (27:83).

قَالَ ٱدْخُلُواْ فِي أُمَمٍ قَدْ خَلَتْ مِن قَبْلِكُم مِّنَ ٱلْجِنِّ وَٱلإِنْسِ فِي
ٱلنَّارِ كُلَّمَا دَخَلَتْ أُمَّةٌ لَّعَنَتْ أُخْتَهَا حَتَّىٰ إِذَا ٱدَّارَكُواْ فِيهَا
جَمِيعًا قَالَتْ أُخْرَاهُمْ لِأُولَاهُمْ رَبَّنَا هَٰؤُلَاءِ أَضَلُّونَا فَئَاتِهِمْ
عَذَابًا ضِعْفًا مِنَ ٱلنَّارِ قَالَ لِكُلٍّ ضِعْفٌ وَلَكِن لَا تَعْلَمُونَ.

He (God) will say: Enter into the fire among *umam* of the *jinn*[19] and humankind who passed away before you. Every time an *umma* enters, it curses its sister *(umma)*, till, when they have all been made to follow one after another there,

---

[19] In the Qurʾān, *jinn*, like humankind, were created by God to serve Him (51:56): while humankind was created out of clay and mud (cf. 15:28, 16:4, 38:71, 55:14), the *jinn* were created of smokeless fire (cf. 15:27, 55:15); there are good and bad *jinn* (46:29, 72:11); some of them heard the Qurʾān and believed (cf. 46:29, 72:1f); and the believers among them are called Muslims too (72:14). The relation of the *jinn* to Iblīs the Šayṭān and to the Šayṭāns in general is obscure: in 18:50 Iblīs is said to be a *jinn* but in 2:34, 7:11, 15:31, etc. he is said to be an angel. The existence of *jinn* is accepted in official or orthodox Islam and it occupies an important place in Muslim folklore. T. Izutsu has a good discussion of the concept of *jinn* in pre-Islamic Arabia and in the Qurʾān in his *God and Man in the Qurʾān* (Tokyo: The Keio Institute of Cultural and Linguistic Studies, 1964) 169-175 and other places. On the same theme, confer also the following: J Wansbrough, *The Sectarian Milieu* (Oxford: Oxford University Press, 1978) 4f; P. Voorhoeve, "Djinn" in *Encyclopedia of Islam,* new ed., vol. II, pp. 546-550. In the attempt to demonstrate that the Qurʾān is too elevated to be contradicted by modern science, M. ʿAbduh - a Muslim exegete of modern time, has suggested that the *jinn* are to be interpreted in present-day terms as microbes. Cf. *Tafsīr al-Manār* vol. 3 (Cairo, 1954-1961) 94-96 as cited in J. J. G. Jansen, *The Interpretation of the Qurʾān in Modern Egypt* (Leiden: E. J. Brill, 1980) 34 & 43.

the last of them will say to the first of them: Our Lord! These led us astray, so give them double torment of the Fire. He wil say: Unto each a double [torment], but you know not (7:38).

وَنَزَعْنَا مِنْ كُلِّ أُمَّةٍ شَهِيدًا فَقُلْنَا هَاتُوا بُرْهَانَكُمْ فَعَلِمُوٓاْ أَنَّ
ٱلْحَقَّ لِلَّهِ وَضَلَّ عَنْهُمْ مَا كَانُواْ يَفْتَرُونَ.

And We shall draw out from each *umma* a "witness," and say: "Produce your proof;" and they shall know that the truth belongs to God; and astray from them will go what they have been inventing (28:75).

وَلَا تَسُبُّواْ ٱلَّذِينَ يَدْعُونَ مِنْ دُونِ ٱللَّهِ فَيَسُبُّواْ ٱللَّهَ عَدْوًا
بِغَيْرِ عِلْمٍ كَذَٰلِكَ زَيَّنَّا لِكُلِّ أُمَّةٍ عَمَلَهُمْ، ثُمَّ إِلَىٰ رَبِّهِمْ
مَرْجِعُهُمْ فَيُنَبِّئُهُمْ بِمَا كَانُواْ يَعْمَلُونَ.

Abuse not those [idols] to whom they pray, apart from God, or they will abuse God in revenge without knowledge. Thus we have decked out fair to every *umma* their deeds, then to their Lord is their return, and He shall announce to them what they have been doing (6:108).

كَذَّبَتْ قَبْلَهُمْ قَوْمُ نُوحٍ وَٱلْأَحْزَابُ مِنْ بَعْدِهِمْ وَهَمَّتْ كُلُّ أُمَّةٍ
بِرَسُولِهِمْ لِيَأْخُذُوهُ وَجَادَلُواْ بِٱلْبَاطِلِ لِيُدْحِضُواْ بِهِ ٱلْحَقَّ
فَأَخَذْتُهُمْ فَكَيْفَ كَانَ عِقَابِ.

The people of Noah and the factions after them counted [their messengers] as false, and each *umma* had it in mind to lay hold of their messenger, and argued with falsehood that by it they might refute the truth. Then I took hold of them, and how [terrible] was my punishment (40:5).

وَقَيَّضْنَا لَهُمْ قُرَنَاءَ فَزَيَّنُوا لَهُم مَّا بَيْنَ أَيْدِيهِمْ وَمَا خَلْفَهُمْ
وَحَقَّ عَلَيْهِمُ الْقَوْلُ فِي أُمَمٍ قَدْ خَلَتْ مِن قَبْلِهِم مِّنَ الْجِنِّ
وَالْإِنسِ إِنَّهُمْ كَانُوا خَاسِرِينَ.

And We assigned them comrades, who made it seem fair to them that which is before them [their present] and that which is behind them [their past]. So against them has been realized the word concerning *umam* that have passed away before them, *jinn* and humans alike; surely they were losers (41:25).

وَتَرَى كُلَّ أُمَّةٍ جَاثِيَةً كُلُّ أُمَّةٍ تُدْعَى إِلَى كِتَابِهَا الْيَوْمَ
تُجْزَوْنَ مَا كُنتُمْ تَعْمَلُونَ.

And you shall see every *umma* kneeling, every *umma* being summoned unto its Scripture. "Today you shall be recompensed for that which you were doing" (45:28).

أُولَئِكَ الَّذِينَ حَقَّ عَلَيْهِمُ الْقَوْلُ فِي أُمَمٍ قَدْ خَلَتْ مِن قَبْلِهِم
مِّنَ الْجِنِّ وَالْإِنسِ إِنَّهُمْ كَانُوا خَاسِرِينَ.

Such are those on whom had effect the Word concerning *umam* that passed away before them, *jinn* and humans alike; they were the losers (46:18).

تَاللَّهِ لَقَدْ أَرْسَلْنَا إِلَى أُمَمٍ مِّن قَبْلِكَ ، فَزَيَّنَ لَهُمُ الشَّيْطَانُ
أَعْمَالَهُمْ ، فَهُوَ وَلِيُّهُمُ الْيَوْمَ وَلَهُمْ عَذَابٌ أَلِيمٌ.

By God, We sent [messengers] to *umam* before you, but Satan made their conduct seem fair to them; he is their patron today, and in store for them is painful punishment (16:63).

وَيَوْمَ نَبْعَثُ مِنْ كُلِّ أُمَّةٍ شَهِيدًا ، ثُمَّ لا يُؤْذَنُ لِلَّذِينَ كَفَرُوا
وَلا هُمْ يُسْتَعْتَبُونَ.

On the day when We shall raise up from every *umma* a witness, then no permission [to speak] is given to those who have disbelieved, and they are not asked for their approval (16:84).

وَيَوْمَ نَبْعَثُ فِي كُلِّ أُمَّةٍ شَهِيدًا عَلَيْهِمْ مِنْ أَنْفُسِهِمْ ، وَجِئْنَا
بِكَ شَهِيدًا عَلَى هَؤُلاءِ ، وَنَزَّلْنَا عَلَيْكَ الْكِتَابَ تِبْيَانًا لِكُلِّ
شَيْءٍ ، وَهُدًى وَرَحْمَةً وَبُشْرَى لِلْمُسْلِمِينَ.

On the day when We call forth a witness from every *umma* to testify against it, We shall call you [Muhammad] to testify against these. And We have sent down to you the Scripture as an explanation of everything and as guidance and mercy and good tidings to those who have surrendered (Muslims) (16:89).

In the above-listed passages, verse 27:23 stands out as an example of the connection between *ajal* and the Day of Judgment. It conveys the same meaning as *ajal*, although it does not specifically mention the term, and at the same time says that it happens "on the day," i.e., the Day of Judgment. The *ajal* is the end of an earthly existence which is the first of the moments that make up the Day of Judgment, i.e., "on the day" when all will "return to the Lord," when all who have died will be resurrected and tried (27:83, 28:75, 6:108, 45:28, 16:84, 16:89). The Day of Judgment seems to happen in only one day, and yet all are gathered together at the same time. It's as though those who had reached their *ajal* ahead of the others "did not remain in the grave but an hour of the day." While each *umma* has its term, for some, historically early (7:38a, 40:5, 41:25, 46:18) and for others, late

(7:38b, 27:83, 16:63), they will all return to or be summoned together by God (28:75, 6:108, 45:28). Thus, *umma* means "community under judgment, with an appointed time, an *ajal*." This is the earliest meaning of *umma* in the Qurʾān according to the Muslim chronological arrangement of the *sūras*.[20] It is the dominant meaning of the term *umma* before it comes to mean "religious community" and, especially in the Medinan period, to refer rather exclusively to the *ahl al-kitāb* and the Muslims. In connection with this primitive meaning of the term *umma* we can further note the following.

First, along with the occurrences of the verses where the Qurʾān emphasizes the *ajal*, appointed time of every *umma*, we find two verses where *umma* is used homonymously, i.e., where the term *umma* itself is equated with "time." "And if we delay the chastisement from them until a reckoned time/moment (*umma*)..... وَلَئِنْ أَخَّرْنَا عَنْهُمُ ٱلْعَذَابَ إِلَى أُمَّةٍ مَعْدُودَةٍ ... ." (11:8) and "Then said the one of them who was saved, remembering after a time (*umma*) ...وَقَالَ ٱلَّذِى نَجَا مِنْهُمَا وَٱدَّكَرَ بَعْدَ أُمَّةٍ..."(12:45). There seems to be no relation between *umma* as "community, people, nation" and *umma* as "time or period." Classical commentators[21] explain that time may be referred to as *umma* since every *umma* has a fixed time.

Second, when the Qurʾān emphasizes that all and every *umma* will be brought to judgment, we also find isolated cases of references to non-people, i.e., to the *jinn* in three instances (7:38,

---

[20] According as well to the chronologies followed by Nöldeke and Blachère. Bell, on the other hand, classifies 15:5 and 23:43 as Medinan.

[21] Cf. Rāzī, vol 17:189 and Ṭabarī (on 11:8) 6-7 where *umma* is translated as *ḥīn*, propitious time, or *awqāt*, period of time. See also Al-Jalālayn, p. 285, Bayḍāwī, p. 291 and Zamaḫšarī, Book 2 260. In the case of 12:45, Bayḍāwī and Zamaḫšarī cite also some variant readings: *immatin*, "favor," i.e., after favor had been shown him; and *amahin*, "forgetting." Cf. Zamaḫšarī Book 2, p. 324 and Bayḍāwī p. 316.

41:25, 46:18 - all quoted above) and to every living species.

وَما مِنْ دابَّةٍ فِي ٱلأَرْضِ وَلا طائِرٍ يَطِيرُ بِجَناحَيْهِ إِلاَّ أُمَمٌ أَمْثالُكُمْ، مَّا فَرَّطْنا فِي ٱلْكِتابِ مِنْ شَيْءٍ، ثُمَّ إِلى رَبِّهِمْ يُحْشَرُونَ.

> There is not an animal in the earth nor a flying creature flying on its two wings, that [do not form diverse] *umam*, in the same way as you. We have neglected nothing in the Scripture; then unto their Lord they will be gathered (6:38).

These usages illustrate the pervasiveness of the judgment idea in the Qurʾān. No creature escapes the divine scheme of salvation. All are liable to God's judgment.

Third, in almost all the passages that we have gathered under the present heading, the punishment that is reserved for the Last Day is for unbelief in God by association of partners with Him, although trials and hardships may be inflicted upon an *umma* during its earthly existence (6:42). In some passages, however, especially in those which belong to the last occurrences of *umma* in the Meccan period, the ethical aspect of belief is also emphasized. One such a verse is 46:18. Its context is the Qurʾān's recommendation of kindness to parents (46:15-17); which recommendation stands on the same line as doing what is acceptable to God, and which together are put on the same level as surrendering *(muslim)* to God (46:15); doing such an act makes one enter Paradise (46:16), and the opposite of the act is put on the same level as unbelief (46:17). Thus, of those who don't show kindness to their parents the Qurʾān says: "Such are those upon whom has come true the Word about *umam* of *jinn* and human beings who have passed away *(qad ẖalat)* before them; verily they have become losers" (46:18).[22] We shall see

[22] Cf. the wider contexts of 7:34, 45:28, 16:89.

that in the definitive sense of *umma*, the doing of what is acceptable put on the same level as belief in God, constitutes an *umma muslima*.

As we now go to the Medinan verses, we find, first of all, two identical passages sharing the same formula of "passed away" *(qad ḫalat)* that are found in three Meccan verses (7:38, 41:25, 46:18) which refer to the punishment of *jinn* and human beings.

تِلْكَ أُمَّةٌ قَدْ خَلَتْ لَهَا مَا كَسَبَتْ وَلَكُمْ مَّا كَسَبْتُمْ وَلَا تُسْأَلُونَ عَمَّا
كَانُوا يَعْمَلُونَ.

> That is an *umma* that has passed away; to it what it has earned and to you what you have earned; and you will not be asked about what they used to do (2:134 which is identical with 2:141).

In these Medinan passages, however, *qad ḫalat* does not include the idea of punishment. Rather, it speaks of the fulfillment of an *umma*'s term and the independence of a succeeding *umma* from the debt or reward of its predecessors. In particular, it speaks of an *umma* that has earned its reward.[23] The reference

---

[23] As can be discovered by examining the wider contexts of the "punishment in hell" verses that we have studied, the result of the Judgment is either everlasting bliss in heaven or everlasting torment in hell. Thus, as regards the punishment in hell, the context of 7:34,7:38 shows that the unbelievers are the "heirs of the fire or hell" *(aṣḥāb al-nār)* , wherein they shall remain forever *(ḫālidūna)* (7:36); that of 41:25 speaks of hell as the unbelievers' "immortal home" *(dār al-ḫuld)* (41:28). Such an idea is also found in another place in the Qur'ān: "Those whose balances are light are those who lose their souls in hell *(jahannam)* remaining there forever *(ḫālidūn)* (23:103). Elsewhere, however, the Qur'ān says: "The damned shall be cast into the fire/hell *(nār)* ..... they remain *(ḫālidūna)* there as long as the heavens and the earth remain, unless God wills otherwise..." (11:106-107).

here, as can be discovered by examining the contexts, and as interpreted too by the commentators, is to Abraham and his kindred. In the Medinan period, it becomes clear that in the Qurʾān's eye, a true *umma* can only be one that follows in the footsteps of the *umma* of Abraham - a model of an *umma* that is not punished but rewarded. It is the *umma muslima*.

The judgment idea is pervasive in the Qurʾān. While it is especially marked in the Meccan period, it also occurs in the usages of *umma* in 7:164, 4:41 and in the context of 5:48 - Medinan *umma* verses which will be discussed in the following sections of our study. "Under judgment"[24] is a universal aspect of *umma* and should be seen as standing behind the term in all its references to nations or communities, whether religious or not.

[24] As regards the view in Islam on the issue of punishment in hell, Carra de Vaux reports: "Al-Ašʿarī has reproached the Muʿtazilīs and the Qadarīs with making men despair of the mercy of God, by teaching that sinners are condemned to eternal fire. This, according to him, is contrary to the words of the Qurʾān, IV:116: 'Except idolatry, God will pardon all else to whom He will' and to this traditional saying of the Prophet: 'He shall make men come out of hell after they have been burned and reduced to cinders.' This Imām's view is that which has prevailed in Islam." B. Carra de Vaux, "Djahannam" in *Shorter Encyclopedia of Islam*, ed. H. A. R. Gibb and . H. Kramers (Leiden and New York: E. J. Brill, 1991) 82. See also L. Gardet, "Djahannam" in *TheEncyclopedia of Islam*, new edition. Volume II (1965) 381-382. See also T. Fahd, "Nār" in *Encyclopedia of Islam*, new edition. Volume 7 (1993) 957-960.

2.2 *Umma:* A Community with a Personal Agent of God

This is a prominent theme, closely connected with the preceding motif as both are predicates of *umma* in general. We treat this present theme separately in order to understand *umma* from the viewpoint of its having a messenger of God. Several of the verses in which an agent of God is mentioned in connection with *umma* have been quoted in the immediately preceding section. We quote here the remaining ones of the Meccan verses.

إِنَّا أَرْسَلْنَاكَ بِٱلْحَقِّ بَشِيرًا وَنَذِيرًا وَإِنْ مِّنْ أُمَّةٍ إِلاَّ خَلا
فِيهَا نَذِيرٌ.

Indeed we have sent (*arsalnā*) you (Muhammad) with the Truth, as an announcer *(bašīr)* and a warner *(naḏīr)*; there is not an *umma* but a warner has passed among them (35:24).

وَأَقْسَمُواْ بِٱللَّهِ جَهْدَ أَيْمَانِهِمْ لَئِنْ جَاءَهُمْ نَذِيرٌ لَّيَكُونُنَّ
أَهْدَى مِنْ إِحْدَى ٱلأُمَمِ فَلَمَّا جَاءَهُمْ نَذِيرٌ مَّا زَادَهُمْ إِلاَّ نُفُورًا.

They swore by God as solemnly as they could, that if a warner came to them they would be better guided than one of the *umam;* but when a warner came to them, it only aroused in them nothing but repugnance (35:42).

وَلِكُلِّ أُمَّةٍ رَّسُولٌ فَإِذَا جَاءَ رَسُولُهُمْ قُضِيَ بَيْنَهُمْ بِٱلْقِسْطِ
وَهُمْ لا يُظْلَمُونَ.

And for every *umma* there is a messenger, and when their messenger comes, judgment is given between them with justice, and they are not wronged. (10:47).

وَلَقَدْ أَرْسَلْنَا إِلَى أُمَمٍ مِّنْ قَبْلِكَ فَأَخَذْنَاهُمْ بِالْبَأْسَاءِ وَالضَّرَّاءِ
لَعَلَّهُمْ يَتَضَرَّعُونَ.

We have sent [messengers] unto *umam* before your time, and We have afflicted them with misery and hardship that they might be humble (6:42).

كَذَّبَتْ قَبْلَهُمْ قَوْمُ نُوحٍ وَالْأَحْزَابُ مِنْ بَعْدِهِمْ وَهَمَّتْ كُلُّ أُمَّةٍ
بِرَسُولِهِمْ لِيَأْخُذُوهُ وَجَادَلُوا بِالْبَاطِلِ لِيُدْحِضُوا بِهِ الْحَقَّ
فَأَخَذْتُهُمْ فَكَيْفَ كَانَ عِقَابِ.

The people of Noah and the groups *(aḥzāb)* after them disbelieved, and each *umma* had it in mind to lay hold of its messenger, and brought vain arguments to refute the truth; then I took hold of them, and of what nature was my punishment? (40:5).

وَلَقَدْ بَعَثْنَا فِي كُلِّ أُمَّةٍ رَسُولًا أَنِ اعْبُدُوا اللَّهَ وَاجْتَنِبُوا
الطَّاغُوتَ ، فَمِنْهُمْ مَنْ هَدَى اللَّهُ وَمِنْهُمْ مَنْ حَقَّتْ عَلَيْهِ
الضَّلَالَةُ.

We raised up in every *umma* a messenger, saying: "Serve God and shun idolatry (*Ṭāġūt*)." Some of them there were whom God guided, and some there were upon whom error was justly laid (16:36).

ثُمَّ أَرْسَلْنَا رُسُلَنَا تَتْرَا كُلَّ مَا جَاءَ أُمَّةً رَسُولُهَا كَذَّبُوهُ
فَأَتْبَعْنَا بَعْضَهُمْ بَعْضًا ، وَجَعَلْنَاهُمْ أَحَادِيثَ ، فَبُعْدًا لِقَوْمٍ لَا
يُؤْمِنُونَ.

Then we sent Our messengers, one after the other; whenever a messenger came to an *umma*, they considered him a false one; so We caused them to follow each other, and made them stories; away with people who do not believe (23:44).

وَإِنْ تُكَذِّبُوا فَقَدْ كَذَّبَ أُمَمٌ مِنْ قَبْلِكُمْ وَما عَلى الرَّسُولِ إِلاَّ
الْبَلاغُ الْمُبِينُ.

If you deny, *umam* have denied before you; it is only for the messenger to deliver the clear message (29:18).

كَذالِكَ أَرْسَلْناكَ في أُمَّةٍ قَدْ خَلَتْ مِنْ قَبْلِها أُمَمٌ لِتَتْلُوَا
عَلَيْهِمُ الَّذي أَوْحَيْنا إِلَيْكَ وَهُمْ يَكْفُرُونَ بِالرَّحْمانِ ، قُلْ: هُوَ
رَبّي ، لا إِلاهَ إِلاَّ هُوَ ، عَلَيْهِ تَوَكَّلْتُ وَإِلَيْهِ مَتابِ.

Thus we have sent you [Muhammad] unto an *umma* before which other *umam* have passed away, that you may recite to them that which we have revealed to you; and yet they disbelieve in the All-Merciful. Say: "He is my Lord - there is no god but He. In Him I have put my trust,and unto Him is my recourse" (13:30).

We will first deal briefly with the agents of God which are of an impersonal type. *Kitāb*, "scripture, writing," appears a few times within the same context as *umma* but only once do they appear in direct connection with each other. This is in a Meccan passage that pictures the Judgment scene, when each *umma* is called to its *kitāb* or scripture (45:28). Scripture here may refer to the record in heaven of each *umma*'s performance by which God judges them.[25] In the context of 6:38 which speaks of every creature being recorded, *al-kitāb* may refer to the "Preserved

---

[25] Thus in another place in the Qurʾān, also Meccan, where a more detailed picture of the Judgment scene is presented, it is said: "... and the scripture will be set, and the prophets and the witnesses will be brought, and judgment will be given between them with the truth..." (39:69).

Tablet" in heaven which contains God's decrees[26]; while in 16:89, *al-kitāb* refers to the Scripture that is revealed through God's messenger as an exposition of the truth, and as guidance and mercy from God to those who have surrendered.[27] Another impersonal type of agent, *āyāt*, appears also once, in 27:83, where it refers to God's signs or tokens.[28] Also once we find

---

[26] Cf. 85:21-22 in which is said: "Nay, but it is a Glorious Qur'ān, on a guarded tablet .(بَلْ هُوَ قُرْءَانٌ مَّجِيدٌ فِي لَوْحٍ مَّحْفُوظٍ)

[27] In his analysis and discussion of "Scriptures and Writings" in qur'ānic revelation, Ary Roest Crollius (*The Word In The Experience of Revelation In Qur'ān and Hindu Scriptures* (Roma: Università Gregoriana Editrice, 1974), among other considerations, has pointed out that the qur'ānic use of the word *kitāb* is not limited to the meaning which the English word "book" has which is the end result of writing or what has been written. He explains: "As a *maṣdar* the word *kitāb* has the sense of a *nomen actionis*: an abstract noun expressing the action of the verb without relation to time. When used in a more verbal sense, *kitāb* should be rendered by "writing." From this meaning of "writing" it develops in a more nominal sense to indicate the product of the writing: "writ," or "scripture." Hence it is used finally to indicate the end result of the writing, the collection of what has been written: a "book.....When *kitāb* is used for the revealed Scripture, its form is not specified. This uncertainty as to its concrete form makes it preferable to render *kitāb* not with "book," which conveys the idea of a very characteristic type of a written text, but rather with a more neutral term, such as "scripture," or "writing." (Ibid., 89-90).

[28] Roest Crollius (*The Word in the Experience of Revelation in Qur'ān and Hindu Scriptures*, p. 142, note 203), has pointed out that "in the qur'ānic language, *āya* (pl. *āyāt*) means both "sign" and "verse [of a *sūra*] "for which "token" may be the nearest possible English rendering of the word. "The *āyāt* are the "tokens" or "coins" of the *kitāb*, both as signs of the heavenly Scripture and as parts, verses of the Scripture in the hands of men." See also Ahmad von Denffer, *'Ulūm al- Qur'ān* (Leicester: The Islamic Foundation, 1994) 67f.

*quranā*ʾ, "contemporaries, comrades" (41:25), which, according to some, indicates here the satans.[29] Among the Medinan verses, 22:34 and 22:67 - which will be treated under the category "religious community" - relate *umma* to "creed, rite." What we will analyze further under the present heading are the passages that relate to personal agents of God to *umam*.

The agents of God to *umam* are designated in the Meccan verses as follows: 1) warner (*naḏīr*) in 35:24, 35:42, 43:23; 2) announcer of good news (*bašīr*) in 35:24; 3) witness (*šahīd*) in 28:75, 16:84, 16:89; 4) messenger (*rasūl*) in 10:47, 40:5, 16:36, 16:63, 23:44, 29:18. Each of the above denominations describes a particular office or function of God's personal agent to an *umma*. The generic term for all of them would be *mursal*, that is, "one who is sent," although the term *mursal* as such is not used in the *umma*-mentioning verses; instead, the active verbal form "We sent" (*arsalnā*) is employed in 35:24, 6:42, 43:23, 16:36, 16:63, 23:44, 13:30.

Chronologically speaking, the first passage that shows a direct connection between a personal agent of God and *umma* is 35:24, which marks the fifth appearance of the term *umma* in the Qurʾān. Verse 35:24 speaks of an announcer (*bašīr*), a warner (*naḏīr*), and, within the context, also messengers (*rusul*).

> We have sent (*arsalnā*) you [Muhammad] with the Truth, as announcer (*bašīr*) and warner (*naḏīr*); there is not an *umma* but a warner has passed among them. If they consider you a false one, those before them have also considered [messengers] false, to whom the messengers (*rusul*) came with the Evidences (*al-bayanāt*), the writings/psalms (*al-zubur*) and the light-giving Scripture (*al-kitāb al-munīr*) (35:24-25).

---

[29] Cfr. F. Denny, "The Meaning of Umma in the Qurʾān" in *History of Religions* 15 (1975) 52; Ṭabarī (on 41:25) 111; Al-Jalālayn (on 41:25) 633. Cfr. also sūra 43:36.

Spoken of in this passage is, of course, Muhammad. His role as one "sent" is basically as a "warner" (*nadīr*) as well as an "announcer" (*bašīr*) to his people, just as other past communities had their warners. The denomination "messenger" is also mentioned but only in relation to past communities.

Only in two other Meccan *umma* passages is "warner" also mentioned, always in connection with Muhammad's role as God's agent among his people. One occurs in a passage describing the attitude of the Meccan antagonists of Muhammad. We quote them again here.

> They swore by God as solemnly as they could, that if a warner came to them they would be better guided than one of the [other] *umam*; but when a warner came to them, it only aroused in them nothing but repugnance (35:42).

In the following and last one, a more universalized association of *umma* with warner is implied as the Qur'ān speaks of unbelieving people in general:[30] "Thus we never before you (Muhammad) sent a warner to any town, but the affluent of it said: 'We found our fathers following an *umma*, and we on their footsteps do follow close (43:23)."

From these "warner-to-*umma*" passages, we cannot decipher the exact object of the warning, especially as (surprisingly!) "warner" or "warning" is not associated with the *umma*-mentioning passages on the theme of "punishment." It could include both temporal as well as eschatological punishment. In Bell-Watt's analysis of all "warner" passages in the Qur'ān, it is

---

[30] This verse is quoted here in so far as it speaks of "warner." The term *umma* here as well as the full meaning of this verse will be discussed under the category *ahl al-kitāb* and other particular communities. See below.

shown that both types of punishment are included.[31] Welch, who also has made an analysis of all "warner" passages in the Qurʾān, has discovered that "the most frequent designation of Muhammad's role in Meccan parts of the Qurʾān is "warner."[32]

Bašīr is mentioned only once, in 35:24 (quoted above) together with *naḏīr* or warner. The term *bašīr* has usually been rendered in most English translations of the Qurʾān as an "announcer of good news" which displays a contrast with *naḏīr* (a warner of impending punishment and the urgency of an action to take in order to avoid it). The corresponding verb *baššara* is supposed to mean "to announce good news;" and in Christian Arabic the noun *bišāra* is used for "good news" or "gospel." However, in a number of places the Qurʾān uses *baššara* to speak of punishment too.[33] The original meaning of *baššara*, however, is the announcement of something which produces a change in one's *bašara* or complexion, and that something may be good news or bad news.[34] Thus, as has been suggested by

---

[31] "Sometimes the word 'warn' is used absolutely without an object, though one may gather from other passages the object implied; in 92:14 it is the fire, that is, Hell, and in 78:40 it is punishment in the life to come. There are also passages in which a messenger has to warn his people that they will be punished by a temporal calamity (as Hūd warned ʿĀd in 46:21). W. M. Watt, *Bell's Introduction to the Qurʾān* (Edinburgh: Edinburgh University Press, 1977) 26.

[32] A. T. Welch, "Muhammad's Understanding of Himself" in *Islam's Understanding of Itself*, ed. R. G. Hovannisian and S. Vryonis, Jr. (Malibu, California: Undena Publications, 1983) 41.

[33] Cf. 3:21, 4:138, 9:3, 9:34, 31:7, 45:8 and 84:24.

[34] Cfr. E. W. Lane, *Arabic-English Lexicon*, vol. 1 (Cambridge: The Islamic Texts Society, 1984) 207.

Bell-Watt,[35] we find "announcer" a sound English rendering of the Arabic *bašīr*. Bell-Watt is of the opinion that the word *bašīr* also indicates that the function of Muhammad is not limited to warning.[36] What is clear though from these verses is that "announcer-warner" is the first role that we come to know of God's personal agent (that is, following the Muslim chronology as well as those of Nöldeke-Schwally and Blachère). Contextually, it is the first designation of Muhammad being "sent" to his people.

The denomination "messenger" is described in the context of 35:24 as one who comes with clear evidences or miracles and with the Scripture. In 10:47 the messenger is mentioned in the context of the Day of Judgment,[37] as the one who comes (as witness) when God judges each community:

> And for every *umma* there is a messenger, and when their messenger comes [on the Day of Judgment] judgment is given between them with justice, and they are not wronged. (10:47).

In 40:5, 16:36, 16:63, 23:44, and 29:18, *rasūl/rusul* is mentioned in reference to earlier messengers and is described as one who announces: "Serve God and shun false gods (16:36);" or one who "delivers the clear message, *al-balāġ al-mubīn*" (29:18). Only in the last Meccan *umma* passage, it is mentioned with reference to Muhammad, in the form *arsalnā* (We sent):

> Thus we have sent you [Muhammad] unto an *umma* before which other *umam* have passed away, that you may recite to them that which we have revealed to you; and yet they

---

35 W. M. Watt, *Bell's Introduction to the Qur'ān* (Edinburgh: Edinburgh University Press, 1977) 27.

36 Ibid.

37 As can be gauged from the passage where this verse is found, and as interpreted too by the commentators, especially Ṯabari (on 10:47, p. 121).

> disbelieve in the All-Merciful. Say: "He is my Lord - there is no god but He. In Him I have put my trust, and unto Him is my recourse" (13:30).

An agent of God designated as *šahīd* or "witness" occurs in three Meccan passages, all of which speak about the Day of Judgment and emphasizes doom for the unbelievers. The first is as follows:

> On the day when He will address them and say: "Where are my associates whom you used to assert?" And We shall draw out from each *umma* a "witness" *(šahīd)*, and say: "Produce your proof;" and they shall know that the truth belongs to God; and astray from them will go what they have been inventing (28:74-75).

God's agent on judgment day is a "witness," *šahīd.* In the context of the above passage, it seems that it is the community that the *šahīd* represents primarily, "although it may be said that he indirectly acts as God's agent as a most damaging witness, who represents not what God Himself disposes but what man has proposed."[38] The two other Meccan *šahīd* passages in connection with *umma* are as follows:

> On the day when we raise up from every *umma* a *šahīd* (witness), then no permission [to speak] is given to those who have disbelieved, and they are not asked for their approval. (16:84).

> For those who disbelieve and debar [people] from the way of God, We add doom to doom because they wrought corruption. On the day when We call forth a witness from every *umma* to testify against it, We shall call you

---

[38] F. Denny, "The Meaning of *Umma* in the Qurʾān" in *History of Religions* 15 (1975) 54.

[Muhammad] to testify against these [your people].[39] And We have sent down to you the Scripture as an explanation of everything and as guidance and mercy and good tidings to those who have surrendered [Muslims] (16:88-89).

Like in 28:75, the context of the use of *šahīd* in the above two passages is eschatological, i.e., the Day of Judgment. Unlike in 28:75, however, in the above two passages (especially in 16:89) it is emphasized that the witness is God's agent raised up from among the people to witness against them. The *šahīd* is that agent to whom the Scripture has been entrusted.

Looking now at all the above Meccan passages which mention agents of God in connection with *umma*, we make the following observations: 1) "Messenger," *Rasūl*, seems to be the highest function of God's personal agent to an *umma*. A *rasūl* is, first and foremost, one to whom the Scripture is given. He announces the "clear message" and may function as a *naḏīr* or *bašīr* but not necessarily vice versa, the possession of the Scripture being the distinguishing mark of a *rasūl*. On the Day of Judgment, the *rasūl* acts as a "witness," *šahīd*, for or against his people. 2) Muhammad's first common designation is as "warner" to his people. "Messenger" is mentioned several times but refers to God's earlier agents, i.e., to messengers before Muhammad's time. Towards the end of the Meccan period, however, Muhammad is referred to, not just as a warner but this time as a messenger, who will then witness for or against his *umma* on Judgment Day.

There are only three Medinan *umma* passages that mention God's agent (namely: 2:143, 2:213 and 4:41), but they are the most important ones for a proper understanding of the God's agent-*umma* connection. The first is as follows:

---

[39] Ṭabarī (on 16:89 p. 161) says that *ʿalā hāʾulāʾ* here means *ʿalā qawmika wa ummatika;* cfr. also Al-Jalālayn (on 16:89) 358.

وَكَذَٰلِكَ جَعَلْنَاكُمْ أُمَّةً وَسَطًا لِّتَكُونُوا شُهَدَاءَ عَلَى ٱلنَّاسِ
وَيَكُونَ ٱلرَّسُولُ عَلَيْكُمْ شَهِيدًا وَمَا جَعَلْنَا ٱلْقِبْلَةَ ٱلَّتِي كُنْتَ
عَلَيْهَا إِلَّا لِنَعْلَمَ مَنْ يَتَّبِعُ ٱلرَّسُولَ مِمَّنْ يَنْقَلِبُ عَلَى عَقِبَيْهِ.

Thus We have made you an *umma* in the middle *(ummatan wasaṭan)*, that you may be witnesses in regard to the people, and the messenger be in regard to you a witness. We appointed the *qibla* [the direction to be faced at prayer] which you have been observing only that We might know those who would follow the messenger from those who would turn on their heels (2:143).

In this verse, we note the following new points: First of all, the term *umma* coincides with "witness." In the Meccan verses, we saw that the messenger was a witness in regard to the *umma*. While that also remains true here, the *umma* in turn becomes a witness in regard to the rest of the people. In its being witness the *umma* is described as *wasaṭ*. The concept of *umma wasaṭ* is to be found only in the Medinan period, when the concept of *umma* reached its most developed stage. If in the past an *umma* could reject its messenger, in the Medinan period *umma* becomes a purely religious community; and, in the context of 2:143, it applies to the community of Muhammad. The *umma wasaṭ* is witness in regard to the rest of the people and Muhammad is witness in regard to the *umma wasaṭ*. Secondly, it is only in this appearance of the term "witness" or *šahīd* that the context does not appear to be clearly the Day of Judgment. The context seems to speak of temporal witnessing first of all and, consequently, also of the eschatological one. Thirdly, "messenger" in the present passage - which passage is the only *umma*-mentioning Medinan passage which speaks of "messenger" - clearly refers to Muhammad and in a manner not familiar in the Meccan usage of the term. If in the Meccan period *rasūl* occurs in reference to messengers in their capacity as "sent" by God, in the Medinan period the term *rasūl* takes on something of a technical meaning as a title for Muhammad, "the messenger."[40] Since this present verse refers in an exclusive sense to the Muslim community, it will be fully discussed in a later section under the category *umma muslima*. It will also be among those verses which will be dealt with in the next chapter in order to see how they have been explained throughout the centuries by the *mufassirīn*. The second Medinan verse to be studied is as follows:

كَانَ ٱلنَّاسُ أُمَّةً وَاحِدَةً ، فَبَعَثَ ٱللَّهُ ٱلنَّبِيِّينَ مُبَشِّرِينَ
وَمُنْذِرِينَ وَأَنْزَلَ مَعَهُمُ ٱلْكِتَابَ بِٱلْحَقِّ لِيَحْكُمَ بَيْنَ ٱلنَّاسِ
فِيمَا ٱخْتَلَفُوا۟ فِيهِ.

> Humankind used to be one *umma*; then God raised up prophets as announcers and warners, and with them He sent down the Scripture with the truth to judge among the people regarding that in which they had differed... (2:213).

In the above passage, the office of *nabī* or "prophet," - which is clearly delineated as that of an "announcer," "warner" and

[40] The designation of "The Messenger" to Muhammad is not limited to the occurrence of the term "messenger" in the passage presently under consideration, but, also in most of the occurrences of the term in non *umma*-mentioning Medinan verses. Welch's study of all the "messenger" or *rasūl*-mentioning passages in the Qur'ān has shown that in the number of times that the term occurs in the Meccan period, it rarely if at all referred to Muhammad but to earlier messengers (thus corroborating the result of our narrower area of study), while "by far the most common designation for Muhammad in Medinan parts of the Qur'ān is *rasūl*, "messenger," usually in the expressions "God and His messenger" (about eighty times) and "the messenger" (about sixty times). A. T. Welch, "Muhammad's Understanding of Himself" in *Islam's Understanding of Itself*, ed. R. G. Hovannisian and S. Vryonis, Jr. (Malibu, California: Undena Publications, 1983) 42.

"custodian of the Scripture" - coincides with what we have already seen as belonging to the *rasūl* or messenger. As this is the first and only time that the term *nabī* is encountered in connection with *umma*, let us briefly consider the appearances of this term in the Qurʾān.

First of all, it is generally accepted by modern scholars that the term *nabī* was taken over from the Jews or the Christians and transformed into an Arabic word.[41] Bell-Watt has pointed out that, with the exception of Muhammad, *nabī* in the Qurʾān is not applied to any of the messengers in the Arabian tradition (such as Ḥūd and Ṣāliḥ) but only to personages mentioned in the Old or New Testaments - which application relates Muhammad to the Judaeo-Christian tradition. According to the chronology which we follow, *nabī* occurs already in the Meccan parts of the Qurʾān although we do not find explicit references to Muhammad there. The references are either to earlier prophets or indirectly only to Muhammad in some verses which speak of prophets in general.[42] On the other hand, in the Medinan parts references to Muhammad as *nabī* occur about thirty-five times. As applied to Muhammad this term usually occurs as a title with the definite article, *an-nabī*,

---

[41] In the process of transformation the word *nabī* was made to depend on the Arabic *nabaʾa*, "to bring news," though some thought it was from the meaning of that root "to be high." Horovitz has noted that "as the plural form *nabiyūn* has the preponderance, only in a few passages belonging to the Medinan period the broken plural *anbiyāʾ* occurs and this fact likewise is an indication that it took Muhammad quite a long time to forget the foreign derivation of the word." J. Horovitz, "Jewish Proper Names And Derivatives In The Qurʾān" in *Hebrew Union College Annual* vol. 2, 1924 (Hildesheim: Georg Olms, 1964 reprint) 222-223 and A. Jeffery, *The Foreign Vocabulary of the Qurʾān* (Baroda: Oriental Institute, 1938) 276.

[42] For instance, in 6:112 and 25:31 where the Qurʾān says: "We appointed for every prophet an opponent."

"the prophet."[43] Fourteen times Muhammad is addressed "O Prophet...... *(yā'ayyuhā nnabī).*"[44]

The relationship between the two terms *rasūl* and *nabī* has been very much discussed, both in Islamic theological treatises and in modern non-Muslim literature on Islam. The discussion centers on whether the rank of *nabī* or *rasūl* was higher, and whether every prophet had to be a messenger or vice versa, or whether Muhammad saw a distinction between his role as *rasūl* and as *nabī*.[45] Our study shows that these two terms are not identical in their usage in the Meccan period but become synonymous in the Medinan period. *Rasūl* occurs earlier and much more frequently and has a more general usage, while *nabī* seems to be more closely associated with the Biblical characters of the Qur'ān. This is corroborated by the conclusion arrived at by Welch,[46] who has analyzed all the *rasūl* and *nabī* passages of the Qur'ān. He says that

> . . . . . those who have argued that these two terms designate two different lists of men, with distinct function,

---

[43] Cfr., among others, the following: 3:68, 5:81, 7:157, 7:158, 9:61, 9:113, 9:117.

[44] Cfr. 8:64, 8:65, 8:67, 8:70, 9:73, 33:1, 33:28, 33:45, 33:50, 33:59, 60:12, 65:1, 66:1, 66:9.

[45] Lists of Muslim and non-Muslim works on this may be found in A. Jeffery, "The Qur'ān As Scripture" in *The Muslim World* 40/1 (January 1950)116 and W. Bijlefeld, "A Prophet And More Than A Prophet?" in *The Muslim World* 59/1 (January 1969)1. See also A. T. Welch, "Muhammad's Understanding of Himself" in *Islam's Understanding of Itself*, ed. R. G. Hovannisian and S. Vryonis, Jr. (Malibu, California: Undena Publications, 1983) 43f.

[46] A. T. Welch, "Muhammad's Understanding of Himself" in *Islam's Understanding of Itself*, ed. R. G. Hovannisian and S. Vryonis, Jr. (Malibu, California: Undena Publications, 1983) 42-46.

> are either reading later ideas into the Qur'ān or placing too much emphasis on differences that happen to occur in the contexts of the two terms. *Rasūl* is simply the general Arabic term for a "messenger," which is also used in the specific sense, "God's messenger," while *nabī* came into the Qur'ān as a borrowed, technical term for "God's messenger."....There is no reason to assume that Muhammad distinguished between his identity and function as a *rasūl* and his identity and function as a *nabī*. He saw himself as continuing a long line of prophet-messengers that went back to Noah (see 33:7 and 42:13).[47]

In Ṭabarī's commentary on this verse (2:213), the office of prophet is the same as the office of messenger: "God's saying 'Then God sent forth the prophets ......' means that 'He sent messengers *(arsala rusulan)*......"[48]

The last Medinan *umma* verse that mentions God's agent is as follows:

> فَكَيْفَ إِذَا جِئْنَا مِنْ كُلِّ أُمَّةٍ بِشَهِيدٍ، وَجِئْنَا بِكَ عَلَى هَاؤُلَاءِ شَهِيدًا.

> How then shall it be, when we bring forward from every *umma* a witness, and we bring you [Muhammad] as a witness against these? (4:41).

This verse repeats 16:89 - the last Meccan verse mentioning God's agent. Muhammad is God's final witness on the Day of Judgment. The commentators have explained the full meaning of this verse in the following way.[49] On the Day of Judgment the

---

47 Ibid. This is the view held - with varying nuances - by more recent scholars.

48 Ṭabarī (on 2:213) 337.

49 Cf. Ṭabarī (on 4:41) 92; Zamaḫšarī (Book 1) 537; Rāzī (vol. 10) 105.

prophet of every age will stand as a witness before God against his people; he will testify that he conveyed to them the revelation he had received from God. Each prophet's witness will be limited to his own period. Thus Jesus is mentioned in the Qurʾān (5:117) as having reported to God: "I was a witness of them while I dwelt among them - وَكُنْتُ عَلَيْهِمْ شَهِيداً مَا دُمْتُ فِيهِمْ." Muhammad will stand as a witness to the period beginning with his coming as a prophet right up to the Day of Judgment. From Muhammad's time until the Last Day, the *umma* that he founded is a witness to what the prophets had communicated. On the Day of Judgment itself, Muhammad will witness to the witness of his *umma*. For this task of witnessing, the *umma* of Muhammad has been made *umma wasaṭ*.

We are now in a position to summarize what we have learned from our consideration of the God's agent-mentioning *umma* verses. First of all, the denominations: prophet *(nabī)*, messenger *(rasūl)*, announcer *(bašīr)*, warner *(naḏīr)*, and witness *(šahīd)*, each describes a particular office or function of God's personal agent in connection with His plan of salvation for humankind. Thus, although different messengers have been sent to different peoples and nations at different times, their messages are universal and identical. To believe in God's revelation is to believe in all His personal agents. Of all the various functions of God's personal agent, the office of prophet *(nabī*, and by extension *rasūl)* is distinguished especially by the custody of the Scripture.

Secondly, the last of the prophets sent by God was Muhammad. The message he brings is universal and identical with what each of the previous prophets brought. He is called "the messenger" or "the prophet" in the context of the period which is his area of witness, i.e., the period beginning with his arrival right up to the Last Day. In the present age, therefore, a true following of the previous prophets means recognizing the prophet of Islam - Muhammad. Thus the *umma* founded by Muhammad is (called to be) today's witness to what the prophets brought from God. On

Judgment Day, Muhammad himself will witness to the witness of his community.

Finally, the development in the role of Muhammad as God's personal agent (from warner to the messenger or the prophet) as laid out in the Qurʾān, does not constitute an "essential change" but is a gradual unfolding of the true nature of Muhammad as a messenger and prophet of God. In the face of an idolatrous people, he was more of a warner and announcer of God's message; in the face of divided groups of believers, he was "the messenger," "the prophet."

2.3 *Umma*: Humankind as One Community

The reference to humankind as one community provides the most general usage of the term *umma* in the Qurʾān. There are six passages in the Qurʾān in which *umma* and humankind as a whole appear in direct connection with each other. Five of these passages are Meccan and one is Medinan. They constitute the tenth, sixteenth, twenty-fourth, twenty-seventh, thirty-seventh and fifty-second appearances of *umma* in the Qurʾān. They are thus so spread out in the whole chronological range that they serve as a refrain as the Qurʾān connects *umma* with other motifs of particular character. In the order of chronological appearance, the Meccan passages that refer to the whole of humankind as *umma wāḥida* are as follows:

وَمَا كَانَ ٱلنَّاسُ إِلَّآ أُمَّةً وَاحِدَةً فَٱخْتَلَفُواْ وَلَوْلَا كَلِمَةٌ سَبَقَتْ مِن رَّبِّكَ لَقُضِيَ بَيْنَهُمْ فِيمَا فِيهِ يَخْتَلِفُونَ.

Humankind *(al-nās)* was only one *umma (umma wāḥida)*; but they went different ways; and had it not been for a word that had already gone forth from your Lord, it would have been judged between them in regard to that in which they differ (10:19).

وَلَوْ شَآءَ رَبُّكَ لَجَعَلَ ٱلنَّاسَ أُمَّةً وَاحِدَةً وَلَا يَزَالُونَ مُخْتَلِفِينَ.

If your Lord had willed, He would have made humankind one *umma;* but they don't cease differing (11:118).

وَلَوْ شَآءَ ٱللَّهُ لَجَعَلَهُمْ أُمَّةً وَاحِدَةً وَلَكِن يُدْخِلُ مَن يَشَآءُ

فِي رَحْمَتِهِ وَالظَّالِمُونَ ما لَهُمْ مِّنْ وَلِيٍّ وَلا نَصِيرٍ.

If God had so willed, He would have made them one *umma*, but He brings whom He will into His mercy, and the wrongdoers have neither patron nor helper (42:8).

وَلَوْ لا أَنْ يَكُونَ ٱلنَّاسُ أُمَّةً واحِدَةً لَّجَعَلْنا لِمَنْ يَكْفُرُ بِٱلرَّحْمانِ لِبُيُوتِهِمْ سُقُفًا مِّنْ فِضَّةٍ وَمَعارِجَ عَلَيْها يَظْهَرُونَ.

Were it not that humankind would have become one *umma*, We might well have appointed, for whoever disbelieves in the Merciful, roofs of silver for their houses, and stairs by which to ascend (43:33).

وَلَوْ شاءَ ٱللَّهُ لَجَعَلَكُمْ أُمَّةً واحِدَةً، وَلَكِنْ يُضِلُّ مَنْ يَشاءُ، وَيَهْدِي مَنْ يَشاءُ، وَلَتُسْئَلُنَّ عَمَّا كُنْتُمْ تَعْمَلُونَ.

If God had so willed, He would have made you one *umma*, but He leads astray whom He wil and guides whom He will, and assuredly you will be asked about what you have been doing (16:93).

10:19 occurs in the context of the Qur᾿ān's exposition of the vital truths of creation. The One God who created the universe and sustains it is the master of all mankind; He is the only Lord of heaven and earth and thus should be the only One to be worshipped. In fact, according to the Qur᾿ān, this was the original situation of the whole humankind: one community because of one religion, i.e., submission to the One God,[50] or, "they were all

[50] Cfr., among others, Ṭabarī (on 10:19) 98; Al-Jalālayn (on 10:19) 268; Zamaḫšarī (Book 1) 355.

originally monotheists in religion."[51] Only afterwards did differences arise, i.e., people started to associate other gods with God. The immediate occasion for the pronouncement of this universal principle was the early Meccan period of Muhammad's prophetic activity. Very few people accepted his preaching of the One God while numerous others remained idolaters. 11:118 occurs in a context where the Qur᾿ān emphasizes the moral aspect of a community. Given the actual situation of people differing in religion, corruption and wrong-doing must be restrained and just dealings preserved. "Never would your Lord destroy a community for wrong [beliefs alone][52] so long as their people behave righteously [toward one another] - وَمَا كَانَ رَبُّكَ لِيُهْلِكَ الْقُرَى بِظُلْمٍ وَأَهْلُهَا مُصْلِحُونَ (11:117)." Thus, seen in connection with 10:19, God allows that people may have different beliefs but He does not tolerate injustice in the relationships among people in this world. And, seen in connection with what we have seen above, under the theme of community under judgment, punishment for unbelief will take place in the afterlife but punishment for harm done to God's messenger or to other people as a

---

[51] R. Bell, *The Qur᾿ān: Translated, with a Critical Re-Arrangement of the Sūras,* 2 vols. (Edinburgh: T. and T. Clark, 1937) 193, note 4.

[52] *Ẓulm* (lit. "wrong" or "evildoing,") in this context, according to commentators, is synonymous with "wrong beliefs." Thus, Ṭabarī (on 11:117 p. 140), says: "He does not destroy them for their associating partners with God *(biširkihim billāhi)*; and that is God's saying *biẓulmin,* i.e., *biširkin."* Rāzī (vol. 18, p. 76 on 11:117) also says: "God's chastisement does not afflict any people merely on account of their holding beliefs amounting to associating partners *(širk)* and unbelief *(kufr)*, but afflicts them only if they persistently commit evil in their mutual dealings, and deliberately hurt [other human beings] and act tyranically [towards them]"- this translation is based on that one of Muhammad Asad in his *The Message of the Qur᾿ān* (Gibraltar: Dar Al-Andalus, 1980) 334, note 149.

whole may be punished in this world.[53]

42:8 and 16:93 correspond respectively to 10:19 and 11:118. The qurʾānic context of 42:8 speaks about differing beliefs and about what is in store in the afterlife for those who prefer to associate others with God, with emphasis on the omnipotence of the One God and the powerlessness of "other gods" on Judgment Day. On the other hand, 16:93 occurs in a context which speaks about God's injunction of justice and about differing moral values of people, the truth of which will be known on Judgment Day.

43:33 occurs in a context in which the Qurʾān speaks about the "religion" of unbelievers in the One God; the immediate reference is to the "religion" of Muhammad's antagonists in Mecca who did not accept him and his message because neither came up to what was for them the highest of values - i.e., wealth and power - which values the present verse devaluates. This ironic passage thus explains the "religious center" of *umma wāḥida* by emphasizing that wealth is of no account in the eyes of God who would have bestowed it upon all in untold measure, only it might have resulted in all humans being unbelievers.

Looking now at all the above Meccan passages together, we note the following points: First, all the above instances clearly carry the meaning of *umma* as "religious community." *umma wāḥida* is set in opposition to *al-nās*. *Al-nās*, i.e., humankind, is a generic term which applies to human creatures, while *umma wāḥida*, on the other hand, is "not equivalent to *al-nās* as 'all humankind'; rather, here *umma* is a special way of describing a human collectivity, even the totality of humankind, but in a special religious way."[54] This shows that in the early stage of the

[53] This idea in the Meccan period may be seen in connection with 16:125 and 29:46, and may be summed up in the Medinan verse which says "there is no compulsion in religion" (2:256).

[54] F. Denny, "The Meaning of *Umma* in the Qurʾān" in *History of Religions* 15 (1975) 48.

occurrences of the term *umma* a strong sense of its being a religious community was already present. Second, the passages would seem to present the original one community of humankind in two contradictory ways: one that was realized and at the same time one that remains a possibility, and which has never been realized. However, when the above texts are seen together as well as in their contexts, it becomes clear that it is 10:19 that speaks of the original one religious community of humankind while the other passages speak of the possibility or ideal of one religious community of humankind since the time when people started going different ways. In other words, the Qur'ān is saying that the first religion of humankind was monotheism before it degenerated into polytheism. Third, there is a sense in these passages that God both wills that some people go astray and break up any potential unity and allows people to will it on their own as well. This ambiguity appears often throughout the Qur'ān, the most representative of which appearances is the oft-recurring phrase يُضِلُّ مَنْ يَشاءُ ، وَيَهْدِي مَنْ يَشاءُ which can be understood either as meaning that God *leads astray whomever He wills and guides whomever He wills* or that He *leads astray whoever wills [to be led astray] and guides whoever wills [to be guided].* This ambiguity has become the core of the question of "free will" and "predestination" in the Qur'ān.[55] We shall see in the next chapter that this question plays a big role in the classical commentators' views regarding what it means to be the "best

---

[55] In several other places, the Qur'ān supports both free will (e.g., 41:44, 53:38-39, 18:29) and predestination (e.g., 11:34, 76:30, 35:8, 13:27). The issue of free will versus predetermination became a major issue in Islamic theology. Among the chief advocates of free will were the Muʿtazila. On the other hand, the idea of a divinely determined universe was spearheaded by Al-ʿAšarī who was the father of the Asharite school of theology and whose position became accepted by the majority of Muslims as the school he founded came to dominate Sunnī Islam.

umma." Fourth, the various contexts of the above passages picture three possible descriptions of an *umma*: one which is composed of believers and unbelievers (43:33) which is not pleasing to God; a religious community with emphasis on its religious dimension i.e., belief in God (10:19 & 42:8); a religious community with emphasis on its ethical dimension, i.e., being just or righteous in dealing with others (11:118 & 16:93). We shall see that, when *umma* in the Medinan period becomes a term that exclusively applies to Muslims, the ethical and the religious dimensions form two inseparable aspects of *umma* as a concept and a social reality.

As we now turn to the Medinan period, we must bear in mind that in Mecca the people whom Muhammad was immediately dealing with in connection with God's revelations, were his followers as well as the Meccan idolaters *(mušrikūn)* or unbelievers *(alla<u>d</u>īna kafarū)*. In the Medinan period he came into personal contact with other groups in addition, namely: the Jews and later the Christians (together referred to as People of the Scripture or *ahl al-kitāb*), as well as the hypocrites or *munāfiqūn*, i.e., (Medinan) converts to Muhammad's religion not out of true conviction but out of the need to safeguard their interests. Such circumstances occasioned a further unfolding or development of the qurʾānic concept of *umma* as "religious community," as well as the arriving at its most developed stage, i.e., when the term came to be applied to Muslims in an exclusive sense. It is within this general Medinan context that the Qurʾān once more speaks of *umma* with reference to the whole of humankind.

كانَ ٱلنّاسُ أُمَّةً واحِدَةً ، فَبَعَثَ ٱللّهُ ٱلنَّبِيِّينَ مُبَشِّرِينَ
وَمُنْذِرِينَ ، وَأَنْزَلَ مَعَهُمُ ٱلْكِتابَ بِٱلْحَقِّ لِيَحْكُمَ بَيْنَ ٱلنّاسِ
فِيما ٱخْتَلَفُوا فِيهِ ، وَما ٱخْتَلَفَ فِيهِ إِلاَّ ٱلَّذِينَ أُوتُوهُ مِنْ بَعْدِ
ما جاءَتْهُمُ ٱلْبَيِّناتُ بَغْياً بَيْنَهُمْ ، فَهَدَى ٱللّهُ ٱلَّذِينَ ءامَنُوا
لِما ٱخْتَلَفُوا فِيهِ مِنَ ٱلْحَقِّ بِإِذْنِهِ ، وَٱللّهُ يَهْدِي مَنْ يَشاءُ إِلَى
صِراطٍ مُسْتَقِيمٍ.

> Humankind was one *umma;* then God raised up the prophets as announcers and warners and with them He sent down the Scripture with the truth to judge among the people regarding that in which they had differed; it was only those to whom it had been given who differed in regard to it after clear proofs had come to them, because of jealousy among themselves; And God by His permission guided those who believe unto the truth of that concerning which they differed; God guides whom He will unto a straight path (2:213).

Of all the texts where *umma* occurs with reference to humankind as a whole, the one quoted above has been the most commented on by the *mufassirūn.* There are two main views of the various exegetes regarding the meaning of *umma* in this verse: 1) There are those who say that *umma* in this context means a community *(jamāʿa)* unified by a single religion. They cite, as support for this view, the pre-Islamic usage of the term to mean religion or religious community by the Christian poet al-Nābiġa al-D̲ubyānī: "Can a man belonging to a religion (or religious community) err if he is pious?" - وَهَلْ يَأْثَمَنْ ذُو أُمَّةٍ وَهْوَ طائِعُ - so that then one spoke of 'the *umma*' instead of 'the religion' because the latter indicated the former."[56] Thus, according to this view which is claimed to have been reported by Ibn ʿAbbās, when the Qurʾān says "the people were a single *umma,*" it means they were adherents of a single religion, but then came to disagree. 2) There are also those authorities who, citing 16:120 as support, maintain that in the phrase "humankind *(al-nās)* was one *umma,*" *al-nās* means Adam, i.e., Adam is an *umma* of one because the virtues found dispersed in his descendants before their disagreement were embodied in the person of Adam; or in an eponymous sense, i.e., Adam represents the one religious community consisting of himself and his descendants until the latter came to a disagreement.

---

[56] Ṭabarī (on 2:213) 335.

The majority of the classical commentators[57] follow the first of the two interpretations above, and add that the religion or faith of that original one community *(jamāʿa)* was the true faith of Adam. They explain 2:213 in the following way. "The people were a single community with a single religion *(dīn)* and a single creed *(milla)*"[58] and "they followed the faith and the religion of truth and there was with them no unbelief in God and no association of partners with Him."[59] Later they began to differ, separating and following different gods.[60] "Then God raised up prophets as announcers and warners, and with them He sent down the Scripture with the truth to judge among the people regarding that in which they had differed," i.e., the prophets - each with a Scripture - were sent to call men back to the original religion. "It was only those to whom it

---

[57] Cfr. Ṭabarī (on 2:213) 336-339; Zamaḫšarī (on 2:213, Book 1) 355; Ibn Kaṯīr (on 2:213, Book 1) 187; Al-Jalālayn (on 2:213) 44.

[58] Ṭabarī (on 2:213) 336.

[59] Ṭabarī (on 2:213) 337. As to the question "When were all people one community and when did they begin to differ," the commentators cite several opinions: There are authorities who say that it was the time from Adam till Abel was murdered by Cain, or, till the days of Noah, or the time in Arabia from Abraham to that of ʿAmrū ibn-Luhayy - supposed to be the great introducer of idolatry in the country. However, most of the authorities cited by commentators are of the opinion that it was the time from Adam till Noah and Noah was the first prophet to be sent after the disunity. Ṭabarī, however, after enumerating the opinions of authorities, makes it clear that he leaves the matter open as he sees no clear answers indicated whether in the Qurʾān or in the *ḥadīṯ* (Ṭabarī on 2:213, p. 336). Among other places, cfr. Ṭabarī (on 2:213) 334-339; Zamaḫšarī (on 2:213) 355 and (on 10:19, Book 2) 230; Al-Jalālayn (on 10:19) 268.

[60] "That is the frequent and almost general meaning of the phrase *mā iḫtalafū fīhi*, "that in which they had differed," which refers to paganism and not to disputes among Christians." R. Bell, *The Origin of Islam In Its Christian Environment* (London: Frank Cass and Co. Ltd., 1968) 181, note 1.

(i.e., the Scripture)[61] had been given who differed in regard to it after clear proofs had come to them, because of jealousy among themselves," i.e., those who have received the Scripture, i.e., People of the Scripture like the Jews and Christians. "And God by His own permission guided those who believe unto the truth of that concerning which they differed; God guides whom He will into a straight path," i.e., God by His guidance leads to the truth those who believe in Muhammad and his message.

> . . . then this guidance lies in His assisting them to [return to] the truth, according to which the people lived before the disunity that God describes in this verse existed. For those people were one *umma*, namely the religion *(dīn)* of Abraham, the *ḥanīf* who was surrendered to God and the friend of the compassionate. [Those who believe] have been made a community in the middle *(umma wasaṭ)* - as their Lord describes them [in 2:143] - in order to be witnesses to the people.[62]

In other words, what the commentators on this Medinan verse are saying is that the religion preached by Muhammad restores the underlying truth of the religion of the Jews and of the Christians. This means that, because the Jews and Christians have gone apart as separate religious communities, they have not lived the truth of the one religion of the prophets. It is now through the religion of Muhammad that they will be guided back to the straight path. This is indeed a new idea since the Meccan "humankind as one *umma*" verses do not speak of separate religious communities but of one religion with its various prophetic traditions. Also in related Meccan passages the Qur'ān says: "If

---

[61] For Ṭabarī, "Scripture" here is the Torah given to the Jews of the Children of Israel who then differed in regard to it. Cfr. Ṭabarī (on 2:213) 337.

[62] Ṭabarī (on 2:213) 339, as quoted in H. Gätje, *The Qur'ān and Its Exegesis* (London: Routledge & Kegan Paul, 1976) 99.

you (Muhammad) are in doubt concerning what We sent down to you, ask those who read the Scripture before you (10:94)."[63] The Meccan verses speak of one religion and/or original one religious community as the original situation of humankind and as the ideal to be restored. The Medinan verse speaks of this original situation of oneness as well as of the division within the one religious community founded by the prophets for the restoration of the original situation.

Thus, by way of conclusion, all the "humankind as one *umma*" passages, when viewed together, convey the qurʾānic view of religion: In the beginning, the whole of humankind was one religious community, i.e., all had the same religion of submission to the One God (monotheism). Later, people began to associate other gods with God (polytheism). Thus God raised up prophets, each with a Scripture, with the identical message and mission of calling all human beings back to the original religion, i.e., of restoring the original one religious community of humankind, characterized by faith in God and by justice and righteousness. Thus, the followers of the various prophets sent by God should recognize all prophets, should recognize the oneness of their religion and, consequently, should not consider themselves as separate, exclusivist religious communities but, at most, as "various dimensions" of the one religious community. The Meccan and Medinan periods of Muhammad's preaching were the historical contextualizations of this qurʾānic principle in Muhammad's time.

Based on the foregoing, in the eyes of the Qurʾān, the message brought by Muhammad was of universal character right from the beginning, although preached in the context of the Mecca of his time. The Meccan period was a case of the one religion and one religious community of the prophets in its mission to unbelievers and idolaters. On the other hand, the Medinan verse under the present heading speaks especially of an actual,

[63] Cfr. also, 25:59, 16:43, 21:7, 17:101.

historical situation of division among people that the Qur'ān says, were supposed to have received the same revelation through the prophets. In such a situation of differences and division, the Qur'ān declares that the truth which the previous prophets had communicated is now preserved in God's revelation through Muhammad who, as we have seen in the preceding section, is "the Messenger" and "the Prophet."

2.4 *Umma*: *Ahl al-Kitāb* and other Particular Communities

Under the present heading, we will discuss the *umma* passages that refer to a group within a larger group, or to particular groups, especially the *ahl al-kitāb*. References to religious groups in general fall under this heading because they are particular references as compared to the most general references to nations or communities or groups in general whether religious or not, or to the whole of humankind as a religious community. Thus some of the passages that will be considered under the present heading refer at the same time to Abraham and the Muslims. The passages that refer in an exclusive sense to these two latter ones will be discussed separately as they are the most important components for the qurʾānic doctrine of the *umma* in its fullest form. The Meccan passages gathered under this heading are 7:181, 35:42, 27:83, 28:23, 11:48, 43:22-23, 16:92, 21:92, and 23:52. We will first discuss the first five of these verses.

وَمِمَّنْ خَلَقْنَا أُمَّةٌ يَهْدُونَ بِٱلْحَقِّ وَبِهِ يَعْدِلُونَ.

And of those that We created is an *umma* that guides by the truth and by it acts with justice (7:181).

وَأَقْسَمُواْ بِٱللَّهِ جَهْدَ أَيْمَانِهِمْ لَئِنْ جَاءَهُمْ نَذِيرٌ لَّيَكُونُنَّ
أَهْدَىٰ مِنْ إِحْدَى ٱلْأُمَمِ فَلَمَّا جَاءَهُمْ نَذِيرٌ مَّا زَادَهُمْ إِلَّا نُفُورًا.

They swore by God as solemnly as they could, that if a warner came to them they would be better guided than anyone of the [other] *umam;* but when a warner came to them, it only aroused in them nothing but repugnance (35:42).

وَيَوْمَ نَحْشُرُ مِنْ كُلِّ أُمَّةٍ فَوْجًا مِّمَّنْ يُكَذِّبُ بِئَايَاتِنَا فَهُمْ
يُوزَعُونَ.

On the day when We shall round up from each *umma* a troop of those who have considered Our signs false , they will be led in groups..... (27:83).

وَلَمَّا وَرَدَ مَاءَ مَدْيَنَ وَجَدَ عَلَيْهِ أُمَّةً مِّنَ ٱلنَّاسِ يَسْقُونَ
وَوَجَدَ مِنْ دُونِهِمُ ٱمْرَأَتَيْنِ تَذُودَانِ

When he (Moses) came unto the water of Midian, he found by it an *umma* of the people, watering. And he found, apart from them, two women, keeping back [their flock] (28:23).

قِيلَ يَانُوحُ اهْبِطْ بِسَلَامٍ مِّنَّا وَبَرَكَاتٍ عَلَيْكَ وَعَلَى أُمَمٍ مِّمَّنْ
مَّعَكَ وَأُمَمٌ سَنُمَتِّعُهُمْ ثُمَّ يَمَسُّهُمْ مِّنَّا عَذَابٌ أَلِيمٌ.

It was said [unto him]: "O Noah, disembark with peace from Us, and blessings upon you and upon [some] *umam* of those who are with you; [To other] *umam* We shall give enjoyment a long while and then painful punishment will affect them from Us. (11:48).

The first of the passages quoted above, i.e., 7:181, is certainly Meccan according to traditional Muslim chronology as well as that of Nöldeke-Schwally. Its actual location, however, may not be its original place as it has a variant reading in 7:159 and as it does not necessarily fit in the main flow of thought in the text. Bell[64] considers the date of this verse uncertain. Blachère

---

[64] R. Bell, *The Qur'ān: Translated, with a Critical Re-Arrangement of the Sūras*, 2 vols. (Edinburgh: T. and T. Clark, 1937) 156.

sees this verse as Meccan with 7:159 as a Medinan variation.[65] The classical commentators are unanimous in saying that *umma* in 7:181 refers to the *umma* of Muhammad, i.e., the Muslims.[66] They cite authorities who were supposed to have reported that when Muhammad recited this verse to his followers, he added, "This is for you, and the race [of Moses] before you was given one like it: Of the people of Moses is an *umma* guiding by the truth and thereby acting fairly كان يقول إذا قرأها: هذه لَكُمْ وَقَدْ أُعْطِيَ القومُ بينَ أيدِيكُمْ مِثْلَها، (وَمِنْ قَوْمِ مُوسى أُمَّةٌ يَهْدُونَ بِٱلْحَقِّ وَبِهِ يَعْدِلُونَ). (7:159)." This passage then sets the pattern for the Qurʾān's presentation of the Muslims as the Muhammadan or Arabian dimension for what we will shortly see as the one religion and religious community of the prophets, which guides by the truth and acts with justice.

35:42 speaks about the Meccans who did not believe in Muhammad; and, according to the commentators,[67] *umam* in this passage refers in general to people who do not accept their messengers. In particular, it makes known the similar situations encountered by Muhammad, Moses and Jesus in their respective times.[68] 27:83 speaks of an *umma* of good and bad people, the bad ones being distinguished as a *fauj*, "troop" or "dense company;" and *umma* here is not limited to the *ahl al-kitāb* (i.e., Jews and Christians) or Muslims, as Ṭabarī also confirms when

---

[65] See R. Blachère, *Le Coran III* (Paris: Maisonneuve, 1950) 642 and 644.

[66] Ṭabarī (on 7:181) 135; Ibn Kaṯīr (on 7:181, Book 2) 70; Zamaḫšarī (on 7:181, Book 2) 133. Cfr. also Al-Jalālayn (on 7:181) 222.

[67] Cfr. Ṭabarī (on 35:42) 145; Ibn Kaṯīr (on 35:42, Book 3) 153; Zamaḫšarī (on 35:42, Book 3) 31; Rāzī (on 35:42, vol. 12) 24; Al-Jalālayn (on 35:42) 577.

[68] Rāzī, Ibid.

he paraphrases this verse thus: "And on the day when we gather (نجمع) from every generation (قرن) and religion (ملّة) a troop (فوج) ..."[69] *Umma* in 28:23 has the basic meaning of community as a natural group of people with a unifying trait (in this case, "waterer" or "drawer of water") not shared by the rest of the society to which it belongs; it may be noted that in this verse the "two women keeping back" are not considered together (i.e., too few to be considered!) as an *umma*, "community." 11:48 refers to Noah and the good communities *(umam)* that followed him and the bad communities *(umam)* which did not follow him and thus will suffer damnation.

Viewing together all the above passages - which, chronologically speaking, are the first passages that refer to particular groups - we note that while in an isolated case *umma* is applied to a group of people according to profession (28:23), in all other cases it is used as a generic term for people grouped according to their attitude towards God and His agent. Thus, a community of religious people is an *umma* and a community of irreligious people is also called an *umma*. The usage of the term to refer to religious people is not necessarily limited to the *ahl al-kitāb* or the Muslims. In other words, the first usages of the term *umma* to refer to a group within a bigger group or to particular groups is to cite their unifying trait whether that trait is one of common profession or common irreligiosity or religiosity. In the rest of the passages that are gathered under the present heading, we will see that the use of the term *umma* is narrowed down to its reference to religion or religious community. The next passage that we will consider would serve as end point for the foeregoing type of the use of the term *umma*, and at the same time as a starting point for its exclusive reference to "religious community."

---

[69] Ṭabarī (on 27:83) 17. Zamaḫšarī explains that the use of *fauj* here shows that the bad ones are the majority group. Zamaḫšarī (on 27:83, Book 3) 160.

بل قالوا إنّا وجدنا ءاباءنا على أمّة وإنّا على ءاثارهم
مهتدون. وكذالك ما أرسلنا من قبلك في قرية من نذير
إلاّ قال مترفوها إنّا وجدنا ءاباءنا على أمّة وإنّا على ءاثارهم
مقتدون.

> Nay, they say: "Lo, we found our fathers following an *umma*, and in their footsteps/traces do we guide ourselves." Thus we never before you (Muhammad) sent a warner to any town, but the affluent of it said: "We found our fathers following an *umma*, and we on their footsteps do follow close" (43:22-23).

Translators differ in the rendering of *umma* in this place. Pickthall renders it "religion" and Bell renders it "common religion" with a note which says "literally 'a community' - a community in Muhammad's view being always founded on religion."[70] Arberry and Blachère render it "on a community."[71] Most of the classical commentators[72] say that *umma* here is religion (دين وملة) which in this case is the religion of the pagans, i.e., their worship of idols (عبادتهم الأوثان). It refers to the religion of Muhammad's pagan Meccan opponents in particular (43:22) and to pagan religions in general (43:23). Without contradicting what the commentators

---

[70] In their translations, M. M. Pickthall, *The Meaning of the Glorious Qurʾān* (New York: Mentor Books, 1953) and R. Bell, *The Qurʾān: Translated, with a Critical Re-Arrangement of the Sūras*, 2 vols. (Edinburgh: T. and T. Clark, 1937).

[71] In their translations, Arthur J. Arberry, *The Qurʾān Interpreted* (Oxford: Oxford University Press, 1983); and Règis Blachère, *Le Coran* (Paris: Maisonneuve, 1950).

[72] Ṭabarī (on 43-22-23) 59; Al-Jalālayn (on 43:22-23) 649; Ibn Kaṯīr (on 43:22-23, Book 3) 288. Zamaḫšarī (on 43:22-23, Book 3) 484) reads *umma* here as *imma* and interprets it as *ṭarīqa* or way (of life).

have said, an explanation is needed in order to understand the complete meaning of the pagan religion of the Meccans. As we have noted in our discussion of *Ajal*,[73] for the pre-Islamic Arabs, the only world that existed was the present world. We learn from the poets of *jāhilīya* that the highest value for the pre-Islamic Arabs was to belong to a tribe which could boast of notable deeds of bravery and generosity, and to have some share in this oneself. Thus tribal solidarity dictated one's actions as well as how one had to obey the categorical imperative of tribalism.[74] There was of course the traditional pagan religion of the desert but by the time of Muhammad it showed signs of degeneration and tribalism had practically become the effective religion of the Arabs, from which standpoint,

> the realization of human excellence in action is an end in itself, and at the same time usually contributes to the survival of the tribe, which is the other great end of life. This is humanism in the sense that it is primarily in human values, in virtuous and manly conduct, that it finds significance. But it differs from most modern humanism in that it thinks of the tribe rather than the individual as the locus of these values.[75]

In light of the foregoing, what 43:22-23 means is that the Arabs were following their ancient customs, traditions and values which included what could be called "religious concerns" but also kinship ties, military prowess, veneration of old tribal hunts, fond recollec-

---

[73] See our discussion of "Community under judgment, with an *ajal*," above, page 20 f.

[74] The spirit of tribal solidarity of the pre-Islamic Arabs has been analyzed and discussed thoroughly by T. Izutsu in his *Ethico-Religious Concepts in the Qur'ān* (Montreal: Mc Gill University Press, 1966) 55-73.

[75] W. M. Watt, *Muhammad at Mecca* (Oxford: Clarendon Press, 1953) 24.

tion of past successes, etc. "What the tribal spokesmen are saying, in short, in reply to the invitation to Islamic life is that they prefer and revere their customary ways."[76] Thus, "religion" may not really fit as a rendering of *umma* in 43:22-23. Perhaps it is more appropriate to translate *ʿalā ummatin* in this passage as "on a community," like Arberry and Blachère have done,[77] but with the understanding that it contains a "pagan" religious dimension.

The next passage speaks about relationships between *umam*.

وَلَا تَكُونُوا۟ كَالَّتِى نَقَضَتْ غَزْلَهَا مِنۢ بَعْدِ قُوَّةٍ أَنكَٰثًا ، أَن تَكُونَ أُمَّةٌ هِىَ أَرْبَىٰ مِنْ أُمَّةٍ تَتَّخِذُونَ أَيْمَٰنَكُمْ دَخَلًۢا بَيْنَكُمْ إِنَّمَا يَبْلُوكُمُ ٱللَّهُ بِهِۦ ، وَلَيُبَيِّنَنَّ لَكُمْ يَوْمَ ٱلْقِيَٰمَةِ مَا كُنتُمْ فِيهِ تَخْتَلِفُونَ.

> And be not like unto her who breaks her thread into untwisted strands after it was firmly spun, making your oaths a deceit among you that you may be an *umma* more numerous than (another) *umma*. However, God only tries you thereby, and verily He will make clear to you on the Day of Judgment that on which you have been differing (16:92).

This verse has reference to the preceding verse which speaks of covenant *(ʿahd)* and oaths *(aymān)*: "Fulfil the covenant *(ʿahd)* of God when you have taken [it], and do not violate *(lā tanquḍū)* oaths *(aymān)* after their confirmation (16:91)." The term *naqaḍa*,

---

[76] Cfr. F. Denny, "The Meaning of *Umma* in the Qurʾān" in *History of Religions* 15 (1975) 58.

[77] Denny, who also accepts the translation of Blachère and Arberry, remarks thus: "It is an awkward and curious construction, perhaps, but so is the Arabic." Ibid., 61.

which is the usual term for the breaking of covenants,[78] is used in both 16:91 and 16:92. The imagery, therefore, of the woman who loosens what she has made strong is a potent metaphor of divided, and thus weakened, *umam*.[79] At the same time, covenants[80] among groups should not be concluded for the sole purpose of becoming a community more powerful than another, for such a covenant is only a deception.[81] As this passage (i.e., 16:91-92) is Meccan (i.e., according to the Muslim chronology as well as that of Nöldeke-Schwally; Bell is undecided), its complete meaning does not become clear since the circumstances to which they refer are obscure.[82] First, there is the question of the woman referred to in the verse. Classical commentators say that a particular Meccan lady is meant, but the significance of this

---

[78] Cfr. 2:27, 8:56, 13:20, 13:25, 4:155, 5:13.

[79] F. Denny, "The Meaning of *Umma* in the Qur᾿ān" in *History of Religions* 15 (1975) 51.

[80] *ʿAhd* is one of two words (the other is *mīṯāq*) used in the Qur᾿ān for "covenant." *ʿAhd* is related to the verb *ʿahida* "to enjoin," "to stipulate," which in Form III is used to mean "to make a covenant with;" on the other hand, *mīṯāq* is related to the verb *waṯiqa* "to enter into a compact or treaty with anyone." Both *ʿahd* and *mīṯāq* are used also with reference to compacts or contracts between people; generally, however, both are used for the covenant relation entered into by communities with God through the messages sent to them by the messengers. For a thorough discussion of the usages of these two terms in the Qur᾿ān see Arthur Jeffery, "The Qur᾿ān as Scripture" in *Muslim World* 40/2 (April 1950) 119-121.

[81] Cfr. Ṭabarī (on 16:92) 167 and Ibn Kaṯīr (on 16:92, Book 2) 345.

[82] Cfr. W. M. Watt, *Companion to the Qur᾿ān* (London: George Allen and Unwin Ltd., 1967) 132.

reference is not clear.[83] Secondly, there is the question of the *umma* or *umam* referred to in this passage as "in competition." Buhl[84] is of the opinion that the above verses might have originated in Medina, since it is impossible to construct a situation during the Meccan period in which that kind of competition between different *umam* could have taken place, whether or not by *umma* one understands different tribes or different religious groups. Zamaḫšarī says that the *umma* which is greater in number refers to the Qurayš who outnumber the believers;[85] but,

---

[83] Cfr. Ṭabarī (on 16:92) 165f; Rāzī (on 16:92, vol. 20) 108 where the Meccan lady meant here is specified as Rāyta or Rīta; Ibn Kaṯīr (on 16:92, Book 2) 345; Al-Jalālayn (on 16:92) 359. Bell also says that the phrase ought to refer to a definite person. He is silent about what the classical commentators say. Instead, he considers as rather improbable Margoliouth's suggestion of Penelope (faithful wife of Ulysses in Greek legend) - the lady who used to undo at night what she had done in the day. See R. Bell, *The Qur'ān: Translated, with a Critical Re-Arrangement of the Sūras,* vol. 1 (Edinburgh: T. and T. Clark, 1937) 258, note 3.

[84] "....aber jedenfalls betrachte ich es als wahrscheinlich, daß diese Verse erst in Medina entstanden sein können, da es mir unmöglich scheint, in der mekkanischen Periode eine Situation zu konstruieren, worauf ein derartiger Wettkampf zwischen verschiedenen *ummât* passen könnte, mag man nun bei *"umma"* an verschiedene Stämme oder an verschiedene religiöse Gemeinschaften denken." F. Buhl, "Zur Kurânexegese" in *Acta Orientalia,* vol. 3 (1924) 105. Buhl says that his "Medinan theory" is reinforced by some Medinan passages which are most likely directed against the Jews, like 33:76-77 = "Nay, but [the chosen of God is] he who fulfills his pledge and wards off [evil]; for lo! God loves those who ward off [evil]. Lo! those who purchase a small gain at the cost of God's covenant and their oaths, they have no portion in the Hereafter." Ibid.

[85] Zamaḫšarī (on 16:92, Book 2) 426.

Denny[86] points out that this argument is merely circumstantial, based on the meaning of *arbā*, "greater in power and wealth," and thus, who but the Qurayš. Buhl concludes that what is meant by the above verses will probably remain a mystery forever.[87] Ṭabarī and Ibn Kaṯīr seem to be aware that the circumstances to which the above verses refer are difficult to know, so that for them, whether or not such a woman in Mecca actually existed does not matter since the message is clear that it is a metaphor of one who breaks his covenant after its confirmation;[88] and whether or not there were actually competing *umam* in Mecca does not matter either since the second part of this verse may refer to competing groups in general.[89] Thus, following this view, this passage should be seen as a warning and reminder to all believers not to break their bond of faith in God, nor to break up into sects, but to maintain being *umma wāḥida*.

The last two Meccan passages under this heading are related to each other. Both speak of the unity of a religious community.

إِنَّ هَذِهِ أُمَّتُكُمْ أُمَّةً واحِدَةً ، وَأَنا رَبُّكُمْ فَاعْبُدُونِ (٢١:٩٢)
وَتَقَطَّعُوا أَمْرَهُم بَيْنَهُمْ كُلٌّ إِلَيْنا راجِعُونَ (٢١:٩٣)

> Verily, this *umma* of yours is one *umma* and I am your Lord, so serve me (21:92). But they cut up their affair among them; all are going to return to Us (21:93).

---

86 See F. Denny, "The Meaning of *Umma* in the Qurʾān" in *History of Religions* 15 (1975) 51.

87 "Was damit gemeint ist, wird wohl immer ein Geheimnis bleiben." F. Buhl, "Zur Kurânexegese" in *Acta Orientalia*, vol. 3 (1924) 105.

88 Cfr. Ibn Kaṯīr (on 16:92, Book 2) 345.

89 Cfr. Ṭabarī (on 16:92) 167.

وَإِنَّ هَذِهِ أُمَّتُكُمْ أُمَّةً وَاحِدَةً ، وَأَنَا رَبُّكُمْ فَاتَّقُونِ (٢٣:٥٢)
فَتَقَطَّعُوا أَمْرَهُم بَيْنَهُمْ زُبُراً كُلُّ حِزْبٍ بِمَا لَدَيْهِمْ فَرِحُونَ
.(٢٣:٥٣)

> Lo, this *umma* of yours is one *umma* and I am your Lord, so show piety towards me (23:52). But they cut their affair to pieces among them in the matter of Scriptures *(zuburan)*,[90] each group in what is with them rejoicing (23:53).

These two passages are each preceded by an enumeration of earlier prophets that were sent to people by God. We agree with the majority of the classical *mufassirūn*[91] who consider the *umma* in both verses as referring to the religion or religious community of these prophets. They are the orthodox or true believers, i.e., the prophets who each brought a Scripture with an identical message from God, which in essence is the true faith of Islām which is the worship of the One God without associating

---

[90] *Zubur*, the plural of the Arabic word *zabūr*, which means "writing," is used in the Qurʾān of Scriptures in general. For a thorough discussion of *zubur* and its cognates, see: A. Jeffery, *The Foreign Vocabulary of the Qurʾān* (Baroda: Oriental Institute, 1938) 148-149; J. Horovitz, "Jewish Proper Names and Derivatives in the Qurʾān" in *Hebrew Union College Annual*, vol. 2 (Hildesheim: Georg Olms, 1964) 205-206; A. Roest Crollius, *The Word in the Experience of Revelation in Qurʾān and Hindu Scriptures* (Rome: Università Gregoriana Editrice, 1974) 82.

[91] Ibn Kaṯīr (on 21:92, Book 2) 520 and (on 23:52, Book 2) 567; Zamaḫšarī (on 21:92, Book 2) 583 and (on 23:52, Book 3) 34. Cfr. also Rāzī (on 21:92, vol. 22) 219 and (on 23:52, vol. 23) 103-104; Ṭabarī (on 21:92) 85 and (on 23:52) 29; and Al-Jalālayn (on 21:92) 430 and (on 23:52) 451.

partners with Him.[92] The main difference between the two verses is that the *umma* verse 21:92 comes immediately after the reference to Mary and Jesus (21:91) while, on the other hand, between the enumeration of earlier messengers and the *umma* verse 23:52, there is an intervening verse directed to the messengers: "O you messengers, eat of the good things and do right. Lo! I am aware of what you do (23:51)."[93] The classical *mufassirūn*, as well as Bell and Watt[94] have suggested that the succeeding verses 21:93 and 23:53 refer to the division between Jews and Christians. Such a suggestion seems to be a narrow or incomplete interpretation. An interpretation of these verses which is truer to their qurʾānic contexts may be the following one by Asad.

> In the first instance, this verse refers to the various religious groups as such: that is to say, to the followers of one or the other of the earlier revelations who, in the course of time, consolidated themselves within different "denominations," each of them jealously guarding its own set of tenets,

---

92 Islām as the "religion of God" is not to be confused with Islam as a historical movement. Islām as the "religion of God" is *tawḥīd*, i.e., faith in the One God and the Last Day. This is the religion proclaimed by all the prophets. Thus, in this sense, all religious communities, whatever names they may bear as historical existences, are Muslims if at the core of their religion is submission to the One God and thus, Islām. Cfr. 3:18-19, 83-85; 4:125.

93 Paret makes a case of this and says that, while *umma* in 23:52 refers to the community of orthodox or true believers (Rechtgläubigen), i.e., the prophets who all professed the true faith of Islam, *umma* in 21:92 may refer to the *umma* of Jesus in particular. See R. Paret, *Der Koran, Kommentar und Konkordanz* (Berlin: Verlag W. Kohlhammer, 1986) 345-346.

94 Cfr., respectively, R. Bell, *The Qurʾān: Translated, with a Critical Re-Arrangement of the Sūras,* vol. 1 (Edinburgh: T. and T. Clark, 1937) 312, note 4 and 330, note 2, and W. M. Watt, *Companion to the Qurʾān* (London: George Allen and Unwin Ltd.,1967) 151 and 159.

> dogmas and rituals and immensely intolerant of all other ways of worship. In the second instance, however.....[it] applies to the breach of unity *within* each of the established religious groups; and since it applies to the followers of all the prophets, it includes the latter-day followers of Muhammad as well, and thus constitutes a prediction and condemnation of the doctrinal disunity prevailing in the world of Islam in our times - cfr. the well-authenticated saying of the Prophet quoted by Ibn Ḥanbal, Abū Dāʿūd, Tirmidī and Dārimī: "The Jews have been split up into seventy-one sects, the Christians into seventy-two sects, whereas my community will be split up into seventy-three sects."[95]

At any rate, verses 21:92 and 23:53, even in their wider contexts do not mention Jews or Christians or various *umam* or communities. Instead, they speak of one *umma* and of *ḥizb,* i.e., party, sect. What can be deduced from these verses would be the following: 1) First of all, *umma* in these two passages is clearly and exclusively a religious community. It means the religious community of the prophets. There is only one religious community (one *umma*) of the prophets. Prophets were sent by God each with a Scripture and with one, identical, universal message to proclaim, namely, the religion of submission to the One God, without associating partners with Him. 2) Particular religious traditions in respect of the one religion are formed and based on the specific revelation or Scripture of each prophet. They are

---

95 Muhammad Asad, *The Message of the Qurʾān* (Gibraltar: Dar al-Andalus, 1980) 524, note 30. "It should be remembered that in classical Arabic usage the number "seventy" often stands for "many" - just as "seven" stands for "several" or "various" - and does not necessarily denote an actual figure; hence, what the Prophet meant to say was that the sects and divisions among the Muslims [i.e., the community of Muhammad] in later days would become many, and even more numerous than those among the Jews and the Christians." Ibid.

various dimensions for the one *umma*. 3) Thus, the followers of each prophet must maintain the unity[96] within its own religious tradition as well as its essential unity in religion *(dīn)* with all other religious traditions.[97] Thus, while Jews and Christians may be referred to in these verses, they are referred to not as separate *umam* but as *al-aḥzāb* or "sectarians, partisans, people who are divisive of the unity of religion and disruptive of the line of prophetic succession."[98]

We now recapitulate our discussion of the Meccan verses under the present heading. First of all, in the first usages of the term *umma*, in reference to a group within a bigger group or to particular groups, it means a group with a common trait not shared by the others within the bigger group, whether that common trait is profession or irreligiosity or religiosity. Thus a group of drawers of water is an *umma* (28:23) or a group of irreligious people within a bigger group is also called an *umma* while the religious group within the same bigger group is also called an *umma* (11:48). Secondly, when the term is used to mean religious group within a bigger group, its scope is not necessarily limited to the Muslims or the *ahl al-kitāb* (7:181, 11:48, but see

---

[96] In the further context of 21:92, as long as a breach of religious unity does not involve a worship of false gods (cfr. 21:94) or false moral values (cfr. 21:98-99) but the doing of good deeds, it is not totally unforgivable (cfr. 21:94).

[97] As we have cited in our discussion of "humankind as one community," the essential unity among religious traditions may also be inferred from other Meccan passages like the following: "So if you [Muhammad] are in doubt as to what We have sent down to you, ask those who recite the Scripture before you [i.e., Jews or Christians] (10:94)." Cfr. also 16:43, 17:101, 21:7, 25:59.

[98] Fazlur Rahman, "The People of the Book and the Diversity of Religions" in *Christianity through Non-Christian Eyes*, ed. Paul J. Griffiths (New York: Orbis Books, 1990) 103.

27:83). At this stage, the use of the term to mean religious community, also applies to the religion of the pagans (43:22-23). Thirdly, in the last two Meccan usages of the term, it means the one religion and the one community of the prophets (21:92, 23:52), i.e., that the various traditions or communities formed by each prophet are not considered as separate communities or *umam* but as various dimensions of the one *umma* of the *ahl al-kitāb* or people of the Scripture. Finally, the doing of good deeds or justice (7:181 and the context of 21:92) goes together with or is seen as the expression of, religiosity or responsiveness to God.

When we now turn to the Medinan passages gathered under this heading, we find that the use of the term *umma* refers to the various groups of the *umma* of the prophets or to some of them, in addition to references of the term to religious communities in general. We begin with those verses which refer explicitly to the Jews. They are as follows.

وَمِن قَوْمِ مُوسَى أُمَّةٌ يَهْدُونَ بِالْحَقِّ وَبِهِ يَعْدِلُونَ (٧:١٥٩)
وَقَطَّعْنَاهُمُ اثْنَتَيْ عَشْرَةَ أَسْبَاطًا أُمَمًا (٧:١٦٠)

Of the people of Moses is an *umma* guiding by the truth and thereby acting fairly (7:159). And We cut them up into twelve tribes as *umam*...(7:160).

وَإِذْ قَالَتْ أُمَّةٌ مِّنْهُمْ لِمَ تَعِظُونَ قَوْمًا اللَّهُ مُهْلِكُهُمْ أَوْ
مُعَذِّبُهُمْ عَذَابًا شَدِيدًا قَالُوا مَعْذِرَةً إِلَى رَبِّكُمْ وَلَعَلَّهُمْ
يَتَّقُونَ.

And when an *umma* among them said: "Why do you admonish a people whom God is going to destroy or punish with a violent punishment, they said: "As an excuse to your Lord; and maybe they will be God-fearing" (7:164).

وَقَطَّعْنَاهُمْ فِي ٱلأَرْضِ أُمَمًا مِنْهُمُ ٱلصَّالِحُونَ وَمِنْهُمْ دُونَ
ذَالِكَ وَبَلَوْنَاهُمْ بِٱلْحَسَنَاتِ وَٱلسَّيِّئَاتِ لَعَلَّهُمْ يَرْجِعُونَ.

> And we cut them up in the land as *umam;* some of them upright and some of them [falling] short of that, and We put them to the test with good things and evil things that haply they might return (7:168).

On the whole, these passages speak of the divisions among the supposed to be one people of Moses. In 7:159 *umma* refers to a group of Moses' people who followed the truth and guided by it. Seen within the wider Meccan context of *sūra* 7 to which this verse most probably belonged originally, here *umma* could refer in particular to those who repented after the worship of the calf (7:149-153), as has also been suggested in Geiger's statement: "This seems to refer to the tribe of Levi and especially to their behavior about the calf, although possibly it may also refer to their belief in Moses' mission to Pharaoh."[99]

The commentators themselves give various explanations regarding the reference of *umma* in verse 7:159. They are enumerated in Rāzī as follows:

> 1) "They were the Jews in the time of the Prophet who believed [became Muslims] like ʿAbdu b. Salām and Ibn Ṣūriyā, but the objection to it is that they were few in number, and the term *umma* requires a large number. The

---

[99] A. Geiger, *Judaism and Islam* (New York: KTAV Publishing House, Inc., 1970 edition of the 1898 original) 132. Geiger adds that "in the biblical account a statement is made [in Exodus 32:26] which is explained by the Rabbis as follows: "From Exodus 32:26, it is clear that the tribe of Levi was not implicated in the matter of the golden calf." The Arabian commentators produce the most unedifying fables about this passage." Ibid.

answer can be that since they were those who disagreed in the religion, the application of the term *umma* to them is allowed, just as it is said "Abraham was an *umma*..... (16:120)."

2) "They were a tribe that observed the true religion that Moses brought, and they called people to it and defended it against the distortion and substitution in the time of the division of the Children of Israel with their innovations. It is possible that they were abiding by it until the Messiah came because they would enter his religion. It is also possible that they had perished before that."

3) "When the Children of Israel disbelieved and killed the Prophets, a tribe from the twelve groups stayed back for what they did and asked God to save them from the others. Then God opened a tunnel for them through which they walked until they reached beyond China. Then these disagreed: some of them were those who said that they remained adherents of the Jewish religion up to this day, while some of them were those who said that they now observed the religion of Muhammad and face the *Kaʿba*, disregarded the Sabbath and adhered to Friday."[100]

Umam in 7:160 as also in 7:168 is a neutral, generic usage which means "communities" or "tribes." They refer to the twelve tribes of Israel. The commentators assert that the division into

---

[100] Rāzī on 7:159, vol. 15, p. 31; Cfr. also Ṭabarī (7:159, p. 88) as well as Zamaḫšarī (7:159, Book 2, p. 123f) and Bayḍāwī (7:159, p. 225) who both add that these people became Muslims when the angel Gabriel introduced them to Muhammad on the latter's night journey *(laylatu-l-isrāʾi)* or the night of Muhammad's ascension [to the seven heavens], i.e., *laylatu-l-miʿrāji*. Cfr. also Ibn Kaṯīr (on 7:159, Book 2, p. 57) who says in addition that the *umma* referred to in this verse is the same as that one referred to in 3:113 as well as those people referred to in 2:121 or 28:52.

twelve tribes is in connection with religion.[101] *Umma* in 7:164 is one such Jewish community speaking about their differences in religion, in this case, regarding the Sabbath. This verse refers to the previous passage (7:163) which speaks about a township by the sea many of whose people would break the Sabbath in order to fish because the fish would come to the shore on the Sabbath but would keep away on other days. Accordingly, the *umma* in 7:164 would refer to those who strictly observed the Sabbath and admonished in vain those among them who would break it in order to catch the fish; there are also those who say that *umma* here refers to the Sabbath-breaking fishermen.[102] As a verse retouched in Medina, *umma* here would refer to the religious group among them. At any rate, by these Medinan verses that specifically refer to the Jews, the Qur'ān shows that the people who were intended by God to be one in following the Torah, broke

---

[101] Rāzī (on 160, vol. 15, p. 32) says that they were divided into twelve tribes "because they were from the twelve men of the children of Jacob, and He (God) separated them and did that to them so that they would not envy each other; however, disorder and confusion have taken place among them." In Ṭabarī, *umam* refers to the people of Moses of the Children of Israel whom God cut into different groups of Jews because of their differences in religion. See Ṭabarī on 7:160, p. 88f and on 7:168, p. 104. Watt has noted that "the tribal character of the Israelites was not clear to the Arabs." W. M. Watt, *Companion to the Qur'ān* (London: George Allen and Unwin Ltd.,1967) 93.

[102] Cfr. Ṭabarī (on 7:164) 92f; Rāzī (on 7:163-164, vol 15) 36-38; Ibn Kaṯīr (on 163-164, Book 2) 58-59; Al-Jalālayn (on 7:163-164) 218. Most classical commentators identify this township as Eilat *(Ayla)* by the Red Sea. Accordingly, the incident referred to in this verse happened in the days of David who at length cursed the referred-to Sabbath breakers who then were turned into apes and after three days were swept into the sea by a wind. "This story has not been traced in Jewish legend." W. M. Watt, *Companion to the Qur'ān* (London: George Allen and Unwin Ltd.,1967) 21f.

their unity. The cause of the division, in the Qurʾān's eye, was religion.

The next passage refers to the People of the Scripture.

لَيْسُواْ سَوَاءً مِّنْ أَهْلِ الْكِتَابِ أُمَّةٌ قَائِمَةٌ يَتْلُونَ ءايَاتِ اللهِ
ءَانَاءَ الَّيْلِ وَهُمْ يَسْجُدُونَ (٣:١١٣) يُؤْمِنُونَ بِاللهِ وَالْيَوْمِ
الأخِرِ وَيَأْمُرُونَ بِالْمَعْرُوفِ وَيَنْهَوْنَ عَنِ الْمُنْكَرِ وَيُسَارِعُونَ
فِي الْخَيْرَاتِ ، وَأُولَائِكَ مِنَ الصَّالِحِينَ (٣:١١٤).

They are not [all] alike. Among the People of the Scripture there is an *umma* which stands in prayer: during the night they recite the verses of God and prostrate themselves (3:113). They believe in God and in the Last Day, they order equity, forbid iniquity and hasten to good works. They belong to the righteous (3:114).

The term *qāʾima* in the above verse has been rendered by most classical commentators as "upright" or "just," that is, by the terms *mustaqīma* or *ʿādila*.[103] Rāzī, however, renders it as *qāʾima fī-ṣṣalāti*, "standing in prayer."[104] We follow Rāzī's interpretation because it fits the context; it is also followed by scholars like Paret[105] and especially by Roest Crollius who points out that this interpretation is justified not only by the context but also by

---

103 Cfr. Ṭabari (on 3:113) 53; Zamaḫšarī (on 3:113, Book 1) 456; Ibn Kaṯīr (on 3:113 Book 1) 312; Bayḍāwī on (3:113) 86; Al-Jalālayn (on 3:113) 82.

104 Rāzī (on 3:113, vol. 8) 188.

105 "Eine Gemeinschaft, die andächtig im Gebet," i.e., a community which devoutly in prayer stands. R. Paret, *Der Koran, Kommentar und Konkordanz* (Berlin: Verlag W. Kohlhammer, 1986) 77.

several other places in the Qur'ān.[106]

Passage 3:113-114 occurs in a section which criticizes the *ahl al-kitāb* or People of the Scripture and comes after two verses which deal with the evildoers among the People of the Scripture (3:111-112). These two verses follow the declaration of the Qur'ān that the *umma* of Muhammad was the best community ever brought forth for mankind (3:110). As the text is, *umma* in passage 3:113-114 refers to a group of the People of the Scripture, the immediate reference of which could be either to the Jews, particularly to the Banī Qurayẓa as Bell[107] has suggested; or, to the Christians with an allusion to the Christian monks who had nightly prayers, a view which was pointed out by earlier scholars like Rudolph[108] and Bell who has suggested for its argument - without carrying it out - a comparison of the present verse with 24:35-37.[109] Roest Crollius has convincingly carried out this interpretation, particularly by demonstrating that it is also echoed in other places in the Qur'ān as well as confirmed by

---

106 A. Roest Crollius, "Mission and Morality: *Al-amr bi-l-maʿrūf* as expression of the communitarian and missionary dimensions of Qur'ānic ethics," in *Missionalia* vol. 27 (Roma: Università Gregoriana Editrice, 1978) 263. Roest Crollius cites as support for the above interpretation, the following qur'ānic passages, among others: 39:9, 73:2-4, 22:26, 25:6. Ibid.

107 R. Bell, *The Qur'ān: Translated, with a Critical Re-Arrangement of the Sūras,* vol. 1 (Edinburgh: T. and T. Clark, 1937) 56, note 1. Torrey had earlier mentioned that whether the Qur'ān refers to Jews or Christians or both together is difficult to know especially as both had nocturnal devotions. He did not, however, go through the other passages in the Qur'ān to resolve his difficulty. C. C. Torrey, *The Jewish Foundation of Islam,* new ed. (New York: KTAV Publishing House, 1967) 45-46.

108 W. Rudolph, *Die Abhängigkeit des Qorans von Judentum und Christentum* (Stuttgart: W. Kohlhammer, 1922) 8.

109 R. Bell, *The Origin of Islam in its Christian Environment* (London: Frank Cass and Co. Ltd., 1968) 115-116.

other Muslim *tafsīrs* like *al-Manār*.[110]

The passage as it is, shows two things about *umma*. First, it shows the religious and ethical dimensions as two inseparable aspects of the *umma* concept in its fullest form, i.e., the worship of God and belief in Him and in the Last Day, and the ordering of equity *(maʿrūf)*,[111] forbidding of iniquity *(munkar)* and hastening to good works *(ḫayrāt)*. We saw in the Meccan passages that an *umma* is described as believing in God as well as doing justice or showing kindness to kindred. In this Medinan passage 3:113-114, we find these descriptions summed up, gathered together and put on the same line as the distinctive mark of a true *umma*. In his thorough study of all the *maʿrūf* passages in the Qurʾān, Roest Crollius has also shown that, as used in the Qurʾān, *maʿrūf* has two connotations, namely: "its religious character and its referring to the way of disposing of one's property in behalf of others."[112] Secondly, the text as it is, affirms that among the People of the Scripture there is an *umma* which possesses these religious and ethical characteristics. We will see in our discussion of the Muslim *umma* that the same religious and ethical characteristics make up the distinctive mark of the *umma* of Muhammad as it is described by the Qurʾān as the best community ever brought forth for humankind.

---

[110] A. Roest Crollius, "Mission and Morality" in *Missionalia* vol. 27 (Roma: Università Gregoriana Editrice, 1978) 263, and, by the same author, "The Prayer of the Qurʾān" in *Studia Missionalia* 24 (1975) 223-252.

[111] *Maʿrūf* and *munkar* have been rendered with "equity" and "iniquity," respectively. *Maʿrūf* literally means "what is known" and thus "what is according to the acknowledged norm, what is accepted;" while *munkar* literally means "what is unkown" and thus is disavowed, rejected. See A. Roest Crollius "Mission and Morality" in *Missionalia*, vol. 27 (978)257-283.

[112] Ibid., 261.

Traditional Muslim commentators,[113] however, do not accept the sense of passage 3:113-114 as it is and interpret *umma* here as referring to those of the People of the Scripture who have converted to Islam, i.e., the religion of Muhammad. However, as Watt has pointed out, the few names of such converts hardly justifies "community/*umma*."[114] Not a few Muslim scholars of today have decried the unwillingness of classical and some later commentators to admit the obvious meaning of the passage.[115] The next Medinan *umma* passage that we will discuss is 5:66, because it has a similar context as the preceding one. It also speaks of "some" of the *Ahl al-kitāb*.

وَلَوْ أَنَّهُمْ أَقَامُوا التَّوْرَاةَ وَالإِنْجِيلَ، وَمَا أُنْزِلَ إِلَيْهِمْ مِنْ
رَبِّهِمْ لأَكَلُوا مِنْ فَوْقِهِمْ، وَمِنْ تَحْتِ أَرْجُلِهِمْ مِنْهُمْ أُمَّةٌ
مُقْتَصِدَةٌ وَكَثِيرٌ مِنْهُمْ سَاءَ مَا يَعْمَلُونَ.

If they had abided by the Torah and the Gospel and what has been sent down to them from their Lord, they would have eaten from above them and from beneath their feet;

---

[113] Ṭabarī (on 3:113) 53; Rāzī (on 3:113, vol.8) 187; Ibn Kaṯīr (on 3:113, Book 1) 312; Al-Jalālayn (on 3:113) 82.

[114] W. M. Watt, *Companion to the Qurʾān* (London: George Allen and Unwin, Ltd., 1967) 54. See also, R. Bell, *The Qurʾān: Translated, with a Critical Re-Arrangement of the Sūras,* vol. 1 (Edinburgh: T. and T. Clark, 1937) 104, note 3.

[115] Among others, see M. M. Ayoub, *The Qurʾān and Its Interpreters*, vol. 2 (New York: State University of New York Press, 1992) 298-299; Fazlur Rahman, "The People of the Book and the Diversity of Religions" in *Christianity through Non-Christian Eyes,* ed. Paul J. Griffiths (New York: Orbis Books,1990) 106; and Mushir-ul-Haq, "Inter-Religious Understanding" in *Christian-Muslim Dialogue, Broumana 12-18 July 1972* (Geneva: WCC, 1973) 32. See our discussion of 5:48 and 5:66, below.

among them is an *umma* that aims at doing right, but most of them - evil is what they do (5:66).

This passage occurs also in a section criticizing the People of the Scripture. As the text is, *umma* in this passage refers to a certain section of the People of the Scripture which is described as *muqtaṣida*, "one that aims at doing right" or "one that follows the middle and just way."[116] As in the case of 3:113-114, most classical commentators take *umma* here to mean those of the People of the Scripture who have embraced Islam,[117] with the explanation that the phrase وَمَا أُنْزِلَ إِلَيْهِمْ refers to the Qurʾān which was brought by Muḥammad.[118] Rāzī gives two interpretations for *umma muqtaṣida* here:

---

[116] According to commentators, this is the meaning of *muqtaṣida* as it is used here. Otherwise, a usage of the term in another place in the Qurʾān can be cited (for instance, 31:32) about which commentators say "middle course" or "intermediate position" may be understood as not being wholeheartedly devoted to God. Cfr. H. Ringgren, "The Pure Religion" in *Oriens* 15 (1962) 96.

[117] In the many examples given by Ṭabarī, *ummatun muqtaṣidatun* is rendered either as *muslimatu ahli-l-kitābi* (Muslims of the People of the Scripture) or *muʾminatun* (believers). Ṭabarī explains that by *muqtaṣidatun* is meant that they are "moderate *(muqtaṣidatun)* in their speaking about Jesus son of Mary, speaking the truth about him, that he is the messenger of God and His word which He delivered to Mary and the spirit from Him; no exaggerated saying that he is son of God after what they have said about that, and no neglectful speech which is beyond forthrightness" Ṭabarī (on 5:66) 306. Zamaḫšarī once more specifies these people of the *Ahl al-kitāb* as ʿAbd-Allāh b. Salām and his companions and 48 of the Christians. Zamaḫšarī (on 5:66, Book 1) 630; Cfr. also Bayḍāwī (on 5:66) 156.

[118] Ṭabarī (on 5:66) 304; Zamaḫšarī (on 5:66) ibid; Ibn Kaṯīr (on 5:66, Book 1) 533; Al-Jalālayn (on 5:66) 149.

First, it means those who believe [Muslims] among the People of the Scripture (الذين آمنوا من أهل الكتاب) , like ʿAbd-Allāh b. Salām of the Jews and Negus (النجاشى) [the emperor of Ethiopia] of the Christians, because they are on the moderate side (على القصد) of their religion, and on its right way (على المنهج المستقيم) , neither tending to the side of exaggeration nor to negligence. Second, it means the unbelievers [non-Muslims] among the People of the Scripture (الكفار من أهل الكتاب) who are just (عدول) in their religion; in them there is no strong willfulness nor is there total rudeness as God says: "Among the People of the Scripture there is he who, if you trust him with a weight of treasure, will return it to you" (3:75).[119]

If we look once more at the classical commentaries on *umma* in passages 113-114 and 5:66, several possible interpretations can be made. The explanation that *umma* in both passages refers to the Muslims or to those from among the People of the Scripture who have accepted Muhammad's message, can be interpreted in two ways: 1)*umma* in the Medinan period only refers to the members of Muhammad's community; 2) however, seen in light of 21:92 and 23:52 (which we discussed earlier) as well as of 5:48 (which we will discuss shortly), "Muslims of the People of the Scripture" may immediately refer to "some" of the People of the Scripture who have accepted the religion of Muhammad but can also at the same time mean those of the People of the Scripture who, without leaving the fold of their respective religious traditions, recognize the oneness of the religion preached by the prophets and thus recognize and respect Muhammad and his message as representing a separate religious tradition. Rāzī's explanation of *umma muqtaṣida* can also be interpreted in this way, for he also

119 Rāzī (on 5:66, vol. 12) 47.

sees an *umma muqtaṣida* among the People of the Scripture as such, except that for him it is inferior - but nevertheless an *umma* - compared with that of the Muslim community, which latter, as we shall see, will be described not only as *muqtaṣida* but as *wasaṭ* or "best."

At any rate, the interpretation that the text as it is refers to a group of the People of the Scripture as such, is supported by the wider context of the verse and confirmed by not a few modern Muslim scholars: After 5:66 comes the verse in which Muhammad is urged to convey the message (5:67). He is told to tell the People of the Scripture to observe the Torah (التَّوْراة) and the Gospel (الإِنْجِيل) (5:68). Then comes 5:69 which says: "Lo! those who believe [the Muslims], and those who are Jews, and Ṣābians,[120] and Christians, whosoever believes in God and the Last Day and works righteousness - no fear shall be on them, neither shall they grieve."[121] Among Muslim scholars who do not agree with the classical commentators in their interpretation of the passage under consideration, we cite Fazlur Rahman who says:

> The vast majority of Muslim commentators exercise themselves fruitlessly to avoid having to admit the obvious meaning... They either say that by Jews, Christians, and Sabaeans here are meant those who have actually become "Muslims" - which interpretation is clearly belied by the fact that "Muslims" constitute only the first of the four groups of "those who believe" or that they were those good Jews,

---

[120] "The Sabaeans were the people of Saba (biblical Sheba) in what is today Yemen. They are mentioned often in the Qur'ān, which enumerates them, along with Christians and Jews, as people who worship Allah in their own way but who should nevertheless be ready to receive the message brought by Muhammad." F. Rahman, "The People of the Book and the Diversity of Religions"... 254, note 4.

[121] إنَّ الذينَ آمَنُوا وَالذينَ هادُوا وَالصَّابِئُونَ وَالنَّصارى مَنْ آمَنَ بِاللّه وَاليَوْمِ الآخِرِ وَعَمِلَ صَالِحًا فَلا خَوْفٌ عَلَيْهِمْ وَلا هُمْ يَحْزَنُونَ.

> Christians and Sabaeans who lived before the advent of the Prophet Muhammad - which is an even worse *tour de force*. Even when replying to Jewish and Christian claims that the hereafter was theirs and theirs alone, the Qurʾān says, "On the contrary, whosoever surrenders himself to God while he does good deeds as well, he shall find his reward with his Lord, shall have no fear, nor shall he come to grief (2:112)."[122]

Thus far, our discussion in the present section has shown a development in the usage of *umma* in the sense of a religious community. In the Meccan verses, *umma* as religious community refers to the one community of the prophets; the followers of prophetic traditions that would cut their bond of basic oneness with the other prophetic traditions are referred to not as *umma* or *umam* but as *aḥzāb* or sects. In the Medinan verses, on the other hand, these different traditions are recognized as each being an *umma*. In the remaining *umma* verses that we shall take up in the present section, the reference of the term *umma* is to each of these religious communities. (Like we mentioned earlier, the *umma* verses which refer only and exclusively to the Muslims will be taken up separately). The first is as follows:

وَلِكُلِّ أُمَّةٍ جَعَلْنَا مَنْسَكًا لِّيَذْكُرُوا اسْمَ اللَّهِ عَلَى مَا رَزَقَهُمْ
مِّنْ بَهِيمَةِ الأَنْعَامِ ، فَإِلَاهُكُمْ إِلَاهٌ وَاحِدٌ ، فَلَهُ أَسْلِمُوا ، وَبَشِّرِ
الْمُخْبِتِينَ.

> For every *umma* we have appointed a sacred rite, that they should make mention of the name of God over such beasts of the flock as He has provided them with; your God is One God, so to Him surrender yourselves, and give good tidings to the humble (22:34).

---

[122] F. Rahman, "The People of the Book and the Diversity of Religions"... 106.

In the above-quoted passage, *umma* appears in direct connection with *mansak*. As this is the first time that the term *mansak* is encountered in our study, we will begin our discussion of this passage with an explanation of *mansak*, as well as a brief overview of the appearances of the term in the Qurʾān.

Mansak, which we have rendered as "sacred rite," is from the root *nasaka*, which means, among other related things, "to lead a devout life; to live the life of an ascetic; to be pious, devout, otherworldly." Ibn Kaṯīr[123] says that in its original Arabic usage *mansak* meant a place *(mawḍiʿ)* where people would go regularly. Accordingly, later the term was used to refer to the rites and ceremonies of the *hajj (manāsik-l-hajj)*, or to the places of performance of those rites.[124] In the Qurʾān, the term *mansak* (plural, *manāsik)* is not common. Of its six qurʾānic occurrences, five are Medinan and only one Meccan. Of the five Medinan occurrences, three are in connection with *umma*: 2:128 *(manāsik)* which refers to the Muslims in a special way; 22:34 and 22:67 which refer directly to the Muslims but also to all other religious communities. In addition to the *umma*-related passages, a form of the term occurs in 2:196 *(nusuk)*, 2:200 *(manāsik)* and in the Meccan passage 6:162 *(nusuk)*. The *mansak* verses are closely related to the Qurʾān's doctrine of the *hajj*. In 6:162 "ritual sacrifice" is the specific meaning as well as similar ceremonies performed even outside the *hajj*,[125] all of which should be done for the sake of God only.[126] In 2:196, the meaning is the sacrifice of

---

123 Ibn Kaṯīr, (on 22:67, Book 2) 554; Cfr. also Ṭabarī (on 22:67) 198.

124 See also E. W. Lane, *Arabic-English Lexicon*, vol. 2 (Cambridge: The Islamic Texts Society, 1984) 3032.

125 Al-Jalālayn (on 6:162) 192.

126 Ibn Kaṯīr (on 6:162, Book 1) 639.

an animal (sheep, "*šā*").[127] In 2:200 the *hajj* ceremonies as a whole are meant, after the performance of which, a remembrance of God should take place.[128]

Verse 22:34 occurs in a *hajj* or pilgrimage passage where the sacrifice of old in the ancient House or the *Kaʿba* in Mecca (22:33), is discussed. As it is, the text states that God has appointed a sacred rite for each religious community.[129] And the passage points out the particular pious rite for the Muslims as one which is to be performed in connection with the *kaʿba* in Mecca. Here the Qurʾān reinterprets the sacrifice of old in the *Kaʿba*: God does not consider as lawful the shedding of the blood of animals unless it is a turning of one's face to Him,[130] a devotion of the hearts (22:32). Ibn Kaṯīr[131] - as well as the other commentators - specify an aspect of the reinterpretation by citing a tradition by Imām Ahmad b. Hanbal which may be summarized as follows:

> The slaughter of animals for food for the poor which is one of the ceremonies of the Muslim pilgrimage is not a propitiatory sacrifice, but is in commemoration of the sacrifice of Abraham which marked the end of human sacrifices for the Semitic race, and which made it clear that the only sacrifice which God requires of man is the Surrender of his will and purpose - i.e., Al-Islām.[132]

---

127 Zamaḫšarī (on 2:196, Book 1) 344; Ibn Kaṯīr (on 2:196, Book 1) 174; Al-Jalālayn (on 2:196) 41.

128 Zamaḫšarī (on 2:200, Book 1) 349; Ibn Kaṯīr (on 2:200, Book 1) 181.

129 Cfr. Zamaḫšarī (on 22:34, Book 3) 14; Ṭabarī (on 22:34) 161.

130 Zamaḫšarī, Ibid.

131 Ibn Kaṯīr (on 22:34, Book 2) 543.

132 M. M. Pickthall, *The Meaning of the Glorious Qurʾān* (Cairo: Dar al-kitab al-masri, no date) 437.

It is in the Medinan period that rites which are connected with Mecca, are spoken of in connection with *umma*. In the present passage, the pre-Islamic tradition of animal sacrifice is continued but given an Islamic meaning, i.e., as a commemoration of the sacrifice of Abraham which includes a strong remembrance *(d̲ikr)* of God. The proclamation that God has prescribed for each religious community a *mansak*, is repeated in the later part of the same *sūra*, when the Qur'ān speaks about everything on the earth as God's blessings for man, and about God's power over the heaven and earth as well as His power to take away and restore life (22:61-66).

لِّكُلِّ أُمَّةٍ جَعَلْنَا مَنْسَكًا هُمْ نَاسِكُوهُ ، فَلَا يُنَازِعُنَّكَ فِي الْأَمْرِ
، وَادْعُ إِلَى رَبِّكَ ، إِنَّكَ لَعَلَى هُدًى مُسْتَقِيمٍ

> Unto every *umma* We have appointed a sacred rite which they are to perform; so let them not dispute with you on the matter, but summon to your Lord; surely you are upon a straight guidance (22:67).

Based on the context, the immediate occasion for this revelation must have been the fact that some Muslim practices differed from those of the Jews (cfr. 22:67b-69). *Mansak* here refers to religious rituals or ceremonies as a whole which every religious community has and which may include sacrifice, feast, etc.,[133] and, in this passage, the Muslims are assured that with their particular rites, they are upon straight guidance *(ʿalā hudan mustaqīm)*.[134]

Thus our consideration of the *mansak* verses shows that *mansak*, as an aspect of the religion of a religious community, refers to formal ritual and in the strictest sense refers to sacrifice. If God sent a messenger to every *umma* from whom the

---

[133] Ṭabarī (on 22:67) 198.

[134] See especially Ibn Kat̲īr (on 22:67, Book 2) 554.

community hears and receives God's Word, God also appointed a rite for each *umma* for the community's disciplined performance of His Word. The inward and spiritual states of submission *(islām)*, remembrance *(ḏikr)* and thankfulness must be reinforced and expressed by set forms. The possession of *mansak*, which is part of God's providence, helps to ensure that an *umma* is upon a straight guidance *(ʿalā hudan mustaqīm)*. The last passage under the present heading is 5:48.

وَأَنْزَلْنَا إِلَيْكَ ٱلْكِتَابَ بِٱلْحَقِّ مُصَدِّقًا لِّمَا بَيْنَ يَدَيْهِ مِنَ
ٱلْكِتَابِ وَمُهَيْمِنًا عَلَيْهِ ، فَٱحْكُمْ بَيْنَهُمْ بِمَا أَنْزَلَ ٱللَّهُ ، وَلَا
تَتَّبِعْ أَهْوَاءَهُمْ عَمَّا جَاءَكَ مِنَ ٱلْحَقِّ ، لِكُلٍّ جَعَلْنَا مِنْكُمْ
شِرْعَةً وَمِنْهَاجًا ، وَلَوْ شَاءَ ٱللَّهُ لَجَعَلَكُمْ أُمَّةً وَاحِدَةً وَلَكِنْ
لِيَبْلُوَكُمْ فِي مَا ءَاتَاكُمْ ، فَٱسْتَبِقُوا ٱلْخَيْرَاتِ ، إِلَى ٱللَّهِ
مَرْجِعُكُمْ جَمِيعًا ، فَيُنَبِّئُكُمْ بِمَا كُنْتُمْ فِيهِ تَخْتَلِفُونَ.

And We have revealed to you the Scripture with the truth, confirming the Scripture that was before it, and assuring it. So judge between them according to what God has sent down; and do not follow their caprices as a substitute for that which has come to you of the truth. For each one of you [religious communities] We have appointed a religious law *(širʿa)* and an open way *(minhāj)*. If God had willed, He would have made you one *umma* but [He has not done so] in order that He might try you in regard to what has come to you, so vie with one another in good works *(ḫayrāt)*; unto God you will all return; and He will inform you of that in which you have been differing (5:48).

As can be discovered by examining the context, the immediate reference of this passage is to the Jews, Christians and Muslims, although it may also refer to all other religious communities. The context begins with the Qurʾān stressing that the prophets were surrenderers to God and specifies the role of the Scripture for each religious tradition - with a warning after every reference to the Scripture that those who judge not according to what God has revealed are unbelievers (5:44b, 5:47b). Thus, the Torah is guidance for the Jews (5:44), the Gospel is guidance for the Christians (5:46-47), and the revelation to Muhammad is guidance for him and his community (5:48a). According to this teaching of the Qur'ān, all those who are true adherents respectively of the Torah, the Gospel and the Qur'ān are "submitters" to God. Each of these Scriptures confirms the truth of the one that it succeeded (5:44, 5:46). The latest-arrived - the Qur'ān - also confirms whatever Scripture was before it and is the custodian *(muhaymin)* of the previous Scriptures (5:48a). Thus the *umma* verse that we have quoted above follows as a conclusion, bringing home the point that while the essence of religion is identical, to each community is given its respective religious law *(šir'a)* and manifest way *(minhāj)*[135] on the basis of which, they should vie with one another in good works. Ṭabarī cites many explanations from various authorities as regards this verse which may be summarized as follows: God could have made all communities into one community of Muhammad, whose

[135] The term *šir'a* or *šarī'a* literally means a watering-place, a place to which men come to drink therefrom and to draw water - an element indispensable to their life or the path or way to the water. Thus it can also signify religion *(dīn)* because it is a way to the means of eternal life. As used in the Qur'ān, it means God's ordaining of the right way for His faithful creatures, a way that includes actual law. The term *minhāj*, on the other hand, denotes an "open road," usually in an abstract sense, that is, "a way of life." The terms *šir'a* or *šarī'a* are more restricted in their meaning than the term *dīn*, which comprises not merely the laws relating to a particular religion but also the basic, unchanging spiritual truths which, according to the Qur'ān, have been preached by every one of God's prophets, while the particular body of laws *(šir'a)* promulgated through them, and the way of life *(minhāj)* recommended by them, vary. Cfr. E. W. Lane, *Arabic-English Lexicon*, vol. 2 (Cambridge: The Islamic Texts Society, 1984) 1535 and 2856; Ṭabarī (on 5:48) 269; Bayḍāwī (on 5:48) 152.

community is one (not divided); but it is clear that God had sent other prophets like Moses and Jesus, each with a religious law to be followed; but when God sent Muhammad, he told him that his community was different and better than the other communities.[136] Other classical commentators have interpreted this verse as follows:

> If God had willed, He would have made you one *umma*, i.e., a group agreeing upon one religious law *(šarīᶜa wāḥida)*..... but that He might try you in regard to what has come to you of the various religious laws, whether you put it into practice, submitting to God, humbling before the commandments of God, or whether you strive after that which is ambiguous and neglect the practice (Rāzī).[137]

> But that He might try you in regard to what has come to you of the various religious laws, as to whether you put it into practice obediently, convinced that they are matters that have varied depending on the years and the times, knowing that God does not intend their disparity [as such] but that which wisdom demands (Zamaḫšarī).[138]

> We have made for each of you, O People, a religious law *(šarīᶜa)* and a clear path *(ṭarīq wāḍiḥ)* in religion (dīn) on which you may walk. If God had willed, He would have made you one community following one religious law, but He divided you into groups that He may test you in that which has come to you of the various laws, in order to see the obedient and the disobedient among you (Al-Jalālayn).[139]

---

[136] Cfr. Ṭabarī (on 5:48) especially 270f; Cfr. also Ibn Kaṯīr (on 5:48, Book 1) 524.

[137] Rāzī (on 5:48, vol. 12) 13.

[138] Zamaḫšarī (on 5:48, Book 1) 618.

[139] Al-Jalālayn (on 5:48) 145.

The Medinan verse 5:48, therefore, basically explains the existence of various religious communities. While it remains a divine mystery that with the prophets' preaching of one religion various "exclusivist" communities (of prophetic traditions and within a tradition itself) were allowed to emerge, 5:48 explains the positive value of such a situation. The positive value is that they may then compete with each other in goodness. A true religious community, therefore: 1) is one whose religion is essentially a submission to the One God which it shares in common with other religious communities; 2) has its particular law *(šarīʿa)* and way of life *(minhāj)* on the basis of which, it has to compete with the others in good works. In other words, according to this verse, what God willed was, in the final analysis, "one community of goodness or of good people," because if all communities vie with one another in goodness, then the world will consist of various communities characterized by goodness, thereby making this world one world of goodness - thus a community of communities of goodness. They will all return to God on the Last Day; on that Day, God will gather them together, inform them of that in which they had differed, and bring unity among them (5:48, cf. 42:13-15).

Our interpretation of 5:48 is shared by several modern Muslim scholars of the Qurʾān. Among others, we cite here Asad who says that "the Qurʾān impresses upon all who believe in God - Muslims and non-Muslims alike - that the differences in their religious practices should make them vie with one another in doing good works rather than lose themselves in mutual hostility."[140] Another scholar, Azad Faruqi, in discussing the qurʾānic view of other religions, cites 5:47-71 and concludes that "the Qurʾān is perfectly willing to allow everybody to be judged by the standards contained in the Scripture of his own tradition"; moreover, he cites 5:69 and 71 as exhorting followers to be faithful to the teachings of

---

[140] Muhammad Asad, *The Message of the Qurʾān* (Gibraltar: Dar al-Andalus, 1980) 154, note 68.

their particular traditions.[141]

By way of concluding, we now outline the main points that we have seen in our analysis and discussions of the various Meccan and Medinan *umma* verses gathered under the present heading.

In the Meccan verses, first of all, except for 28:23 which shows *umma* in its neutral, basic meaning of a group of people, from the viewpoint of the use of the term to refer to particular groups or communities, *umma* is used as a generic term for people grouped according to their attitude towards God: thus a community of religious people is called an *umma* and a community of unbelievers is also called an *umma* (e.g., 11:48); and in its first references to religious groups, *umma* is not necessarily limited to the *ahl al-kitāb* or the followers of Muhammad (e.g., 27:83). Religiosity is expressed as belief in God together with being truthful and just in dealing with others. Later in the Meccan period, however, the term begins to be used to refer exclusively to mean a religious community, and even the "religious" community of pagans (43:22-23). In its last two occurrences (21:92, 23:52), the term is used exclusively to refer to the one *umma* of the prophets, with the prophetic traditions forming its various dimensions. Those in these various traditions who have not lived up to the basic vocation of oneness of the People of the Scripture are not referred to as separate religious communities or *umma*, but as sects or divisive groups within the one *umma*. Here the Qur᾽ān speaks of one *umma* with the accompanying warning and reminder to those who follow this *umma* not to break the unity and to act rightly and justly towards others. (16:92, 21:92, 23:52). This one *umma* is best exemplified during the time of the prophet Abraham (in

---

[141] I. H. Azad Faruqi, "The Qur᾽ānic View of Other Religions," *Islam and the Modern Age* 18/1 (February 1987) 47-48. Syed Barakat Ahmad also expresses the same view in his "Non-Muslims and the *Umma*," *Studies in Islam* 17/2 (April 1980) 116f.

16:120, which we will discuss in detail separately) and characterized by submission *(islām)* to the One God.

In the Medinan verses, the term *umma* always means religious community. Its distinctive mark consists of two inseparable dimensions, namely: belief in God and the Last Day, and the ordering of what is good or acceptable, and the forbidding of what is evil or unacceptable. Here, however, the Qurʾān speaks not of one *umma* but of various *umam* or religious communities. Those who were referred to in the Meccan verses as *al-aḥzāb*, i.e., sects or divisive groups within the one *umma* are now recognized as each an *umma*, i.e., each a separate religious community. Thus here the term *aḥzāb* is dropped and the terms Jews, Christians and Ṣābians are mentioned and recognized as communities. Here in the Medinan period, any community which is characterized by the two inseparable dimensions mentioned above (i.e., worship of the One God together with ordering what is good and forbidding what is evil), is an *umma*. What distinguishes one *umma* from another is its particular *širʿa* and *minhāj* (5:48) as well as *mansak* (22:34, 22:67). Every particular *umma* is called to be united in the particular way of belief or tradition that God has provided for it to follow. The reason God has allowed the existence of various *umam* is that they may compete with one another in good works (5:48b). In the final analysis, therefore, what God has willed is "one community of goodness or of good people," because if all communities (i.e., not only Muslim, Jewish, Christian or Ṣābian but also any other that has the same religious and ethical dimensions described in the foregoing) vie with one another in goodness, then the world will consist of various communities characterized by goodness, thereby making this world one world of goodness - hence, a community of communities of goodness. It is in the hereafter that God will inform them of that in which they had differed and will bring about perfect unity among them (5:48, 42:13-15).

2.5 *Umma*: Abraham

Abraham is of the People of the Scripture[142] but is discussed here separately because of his central role in the final or fullest development of the concept of the *umma*. There are three passages that directly connect Abraham and/or his people with the *umma* concept: 16:120 (Meccan), 2:134 and 2:141(Medinan). The Meccan verse is as follows.

إِنَّ إِبْرَاهِيمَ كَانَ أُمَّةً قَانِتًا لِلَّهِ حَنِيفًا ، وَلَمْ يَكُ مِنَ
ٱلْمُشْرِكِينَ.

> Verily, Abraham was an *umma* obedient to God, a *ḥanīf* and not of the idolaters (16:120).

The text as it is, would seem to show that Abraham was an *umma* or community of one man. Can *umma* in this context then be translated as "nation" or "community"? Our discussion of this verse then will have to begin with an explanation of the meaning of *umma* here. Indeed, there has been a good deal of disagreement among scholars (Muslim and non-Muslim alike) regarding the right interpretation of the word *umma* in this context. Some translators render *umma* in this passage as nation[143] or community;[144] others

---

[142] As we have seen in our earlier discussions, every prophet is sent by God with a Scripture (cfr., for instance, 2:213). The Qurʾān, however, also explicitly makes mention of a Scripture given to Abraham (4:54, 87:19).

[143] For instance, M. M. Pickthall, *The Meaning of the Glorious Qurʾān* (New York: Mentor Books, 1953) and A. Arberry, *The Qurʾān Interpreted* (Oxford: Oxford University Press, 1982).

[144] For instance, R. Bell, *The Qurʾān: Translated with a Critical Re-Arrangement of the Sūras*, 2 vols. (Edinburgh: T. & T. Clark, 1937) and Sayyid Abul Aʿlā Mawdūdī, *Towards Understanding the Qurʾān*, vol. IV (Leicester: The Islamic Foundation, 1993).

render it as "paragon" or "exemplar," i.e., of virtue or piety (e.g., Dawood and Khan).[145]

The "paragon" interpretation which is homonymous to *umma* as "community" or "nation," finds support in the many examples given by Ṭabarī who renders *umma* here as *muʿallim al-ḫayr* i.e., "one who teaches the good."[146] Zamaḫšarī and Rāzī also prefer the "exemplar, paragon" interpretation although they both render *umma* in this place as "community," which, accordingly, is one which Abraham forms all by himself as he combines within himself all the good qualities of the religious nations.[147] Izutsu also finds "paragon" a more reasonable interpretation than "nation" or "community," because the latter, according to him, gives "a very odd meaning."[148] However, Paret explains the probability of the "community" interpretation by referring to "Abraham" here as an eponym, i.e., he represents the community established by him (thus already Horovitz),[149] which community was the prototype of the true Muslim community, independent of the later Jews and other religious groups but connected to them in so far as the latter ones would share in the same belief of submission to God.[150]

---

145 N. J. Dawood, *The Qurʾān* (London: Penguin Books, 1956/1974); M. Zafrulla Khan, *The Qurʾān* (London: Curzon Press, 1991).

146 Cf. Ṭabarī (on 16:120) 190-191; In Al-Jalālayn, (on 16:120) 362 and in *Ibn Kaṯīr* (on 16:120 Book II) 351, it is glossed by *imāman qudwatan*, i.e., "model leader."

147 Zamaḫšarī (on 16:120, Book II) 433 and Rāzī (on 16:120, vol. 20) 134.

148 T. Izutsu, *Ethico-Religious Concepts in the Qurʾān* (Montreal: McGill University Press, 1966) 191, note 6.

149 J. Horovitz, "Jewish Proper Names and Derivatives in the Koran" in *Hebrew Union College Annual*, vol. 2 (Hildesheim: Georg Olms, 1964) 190.

150 R. Paret, *Der Koran: Kommentar und Konkordanz* (Berlin: Verlag W. Kohlhammer, 1986) 294.

Denny,[151] who follows Paret, rightly cites passages 2:134 and 2:141 as corroborating this interpretation: "That is a community (*umma*) which has passed away; to it what it has earned and to you what you have earned... تِلْكَ أُمَّةٌ قَدْ خَلَتْ لَهَا مَا كَسَبَتْ وَلَكُمْ مَا كَسَبْتُمْ (2:134 and 2:141)." *Umma* in these two identical passages, according to the commentators,[152] refers to Abraham and his kindred, i.e., Ismael, Isaac, Jacob and their sons. Passages 2:134 and 2:141 would thus clarify the meaning of *umma* in 16:120, i.e., that Abraham there is an eponym for the religious community of his time. That Abraham, mythically or theologically, is a paragon or exemplar is not questioned here; it is just that it is not the meaning of *umma* in 16:120.

This verse then shows that the *umma* founded by the prophets was, "*umma wāḥida.*" Like the other Meccan *umma* verses which refer to the *ahl al-kitāb* (which we have discussed in the preceding section), this present verse speaks of the one *umma* of the *ahl al-kitāb*. *Ḥanīf* is a fundamental characteristic of Abraham and should be understood as of all the other prophets. We will now survey briefly the qurʾānic usages of this term in order to understand its meaning in the Qurʾān.

In the Qurʾān, the term *ḥanīf* occurs twelve times. Most of the occurrences are Medinan, though some may belong to the late Meccan period. From these passages, we note the main points. First of all, the term *ḥanīf* is used to indicate a religious attitude as opposed to that of the idolaters or polytheists in the *umma* verse 16:120, quoted above (also in 2:135, 3:67, 3:95, 6:79, 6:161, 10:105, 16:123, 22:31). It is identified with the religious attitude of

---

151 F. Denny, "Meaning of UMMA in the Qurʾān" in *History of Religions* 15 (1975) 38-39.

152 Ṭabarī (on 2:134 and 2:141, respectively) 563 and 575; Zamaḫšarī (Book I) 314; Al-Jalālayn (on 2:134) 27.

submission or Islām (3:67, 4:125).[153] It is further identified as the religious attitude originally intended by God, given with the human nature, before men went different ways in religion (30:30-31). At the same time it is not to be identified with being a Jew or Christian (2:135-140, 3:67, 16:123, 98:5, etc.).

Ḥanīf thus, is basically a spiritual attitude, not identified with a religious tradition but with the basic religious impulse in humanity towards dedication to God. This is best expressed in the following passage.

> So set your face to the religion as a *ḥanīf (fa aqim wajhaka li-ddīni ḥanīfan)*, God's original creation, according to which He originated mankind *(fiṭrata-l-llāhi allatī faṭara an-nāsa ʿalayhā)*: There is no alteration of the creation of God *(lā tabdīla liḫalqi-l-llāhi)*: That is the upright religion, but most of the people do not know *(ḏālika al-dīnu al-qayyimu wa lākinna akṯara al-nāsi lā yaʿlamūna)*. Turning repentantly to Him *(munībīna ilayhi)*, show piety towards Him and perform the prayer *(waʾttaqūhu wa aqīmū aṣ-ṣalawāta)* and don't be among the idolaters *(wa lā takūnū min al-mušrikīna)* (30:30-31).

The idea of *ḥanīf* is thus, "the negation of any sectarian particularism."[154] This is further elaborated in the following verse which is part of another *ḥanīf* passage:

> Say: "We believe in God and in what has been sent down to us, and in what has been sent down to Abraham and Ismael and Isaac and Jacob and the [Twelve] Tribes, and in

---

153 Bayḍāwī (on 3:67) 77, emphasizes that the phrase "Abraham was not a Jew or a Christian" does not mean that Abraham belonged to the *milla* of Islam.

154 A. Roest Crollius, *The Word in the Experience of Revelation in Qurʾān and Hindu Revelation* (Roma: Università Gregoriana Editrice, 1974) 129.

> what has been given to Moses and to Jesus - in what has been given to the prophets from their Lord; we do not make distinction between any one of them" (2:136).

Thus, the religious attitude of the *ḥanīf* is described as one which recognizes the fundamental equality of all revelations or religious traditions and identifies itself with what is essentially the same in all these revelations, i.e., the natural religion laid down by God for which humankind was created. And, as mentioned in verse 16:120, Abraham is the great example of the true *ḥanīf* (also mentioned in 2:135,3:67, 3:95, 4:125, 6:79, 6:161, 16:123).

Furthermore, being *ḥanīf* is put on the same level as performing prayer (30:31) and practising charity, which, all together are described as *dīn al-qayyimati* or "religion of the true" (98:5). Thus when in 16:120 Abraham is described as an *umma*, he is one who displays a *ḥanīf* attitude which is associated with religious ritual and good work. As we have already seen earlier, so here we see once again the description of a true *umma*, that is, one in which the religious and the ethical dimensions inseparably make up its distinctive character; here the religious dimension consists in the *ḥanīf* attitude.

The other two passages with certain references to Abraham belong in the wider context of one of the *ḥanīf* passages (2:135) that mention Abraham.

تِلْكَ أُمَّةٌ قَدْ خَلَتْ لَهَا مَا كَسَبَتْ وَلَكُمْ مَّا كَسَبْتُمْ وَلَا تُسْأَلُونَ
عَمَّا كَانُوا يَعْمَلُونَ.

> That is an *umma* that has passed away; to it what it has earned and to you what you have earned; and you will not be asked about what they used to do (2:134, identical with 2:141).

Here it is emphasized that the *umma* of Abraham is one "that has passed away," i.e., that to be an *umma* patterned on the

Abrahamic model is not to be earned automatically by ethnical connection or ascendancy but by following the religion of Abraham who was a *ḥanīf*. This is elaborated in the context which connects these two verses: in order to be rightly guided there is no need to become Jew or Christian but to follow the religion *(milla)* of Abraham, who was a *ḥanīf* and not one of the idolaters (2:135). Such a religion consisted in belief in God and belief in the equality of the revelation received by each of the prophets (2:136). Thus a rightly guided community will not dispute with the others regarding God for He is the same One God for all of them (2:137-139), but concentrates on its deeds with the knowledge that it is God who is the most knowledgeable and most just (2:139-140).

2:134 and 2:141 immediately refer to the *umma* of Abraham as one which has received its reward and therefore is a model for all other *umam* to follow; hence, they also refer to the Muslim community as a community which does not have to connect with the Jewish and the Christian communities in order to have access to the grace of God. These passages, therefore, are a declaration of the independence of each religious community and of the equal chance of access to God's grace. All three passages - i.e., 16:120, 2:134 and 2:141 - are Medinan according to Nöldeke-Schwally and Bell; traditional Muslim chronology says the same of 2:134 and 2:141 but places 16:120 in the Meccan period. The last verses of *sūra* 16 (i.e., the verses that come after 16:120), however, would be Medinan, as they emphasize the separateness or independence of the religion of Muhammad. The Meccan verses, as we have seen, emphasize the nearness or oneness of his religion with those of the People of the Scripture, i.e., oneness of religion and thus of the community formed by the prophets. As a Meccan verse, therefore, 16:120 states the oneness of the religion of the prophets; and the idea conveyed is that during the time that Abraham was the latest-arrived prophet, those who had received God's message through prophets before him (i.e., Noah and others) as well as those who received it through him, recognized the oneness of their religion. They were distinct prophetic traditions but not separate *umam*. They were *ḥanīfs*, and the Qur'ān mentions Abraham as an eponym for people of the Scripture for that period. Would the mention of such a verse in the Meccan period only be a belaboring of the obvious if the Meccan verses emphasize only one *umma* of the prophets? Precisely such a verse is mentioned in the late Meccan period, as a reminder and warning, when some groups of the people of the Scripture started to lose the *ḥanīf* attitude and to acquire a sectarian one *(hizbī)*. Thus when in Medina the Qur'ān recognizes these various sects as separate religious communities, the *umma* of Abraham became a model to be followed (2:134, 2:141).

Summarily, our consideration of the *umma* passages with explicit references to Abraham reveals the following about *umma*: 1) a true *umma* is one with no ethnicity or nationality apart from religion (2:135, etc.), one which is described with the quality of *ḥanīf*, the outward expression of which involves the performance of a religious ritual and good deeds (30:31, 98:5) and the ideal example of which is the *umma* of Abraham. 2) The relationship among *umam* that we have seen in our discussion of *ahl al-kitāb* and other religious communities, is further elucidated here: all religious traditions are accepted - each worship the same God in their own respective ways (5:48, 22:34, 22:67). 3) Finally, the whole context of the Abraham passages shows that in the competition among *umam*, the one of Muhammad is far ahead of the others because, in following the *umma* of Abraham, it restores the *ḥanīf* attitude which expresses the sense of the original impulse, *fiṭra* (30:30) in humanity of submission to the One God. Thus the *umma* of Muhammad is the one closest to the "origin of things." As such, it believes in the equality of the revelation received by all the prophets and becomes the preserver of the original *umma wāḥida* of the prophets.

2.6 *Umma*: The Muslim Community

The *umma* of Muhammad or Muslim community has been referred to in many of the passages that we have considered thus far, either implicity or explicitly but together with other religious communities.

In the Meccan period, the *umma* of Muhammad runs parallel especially to the *umma* of the people of Moses, and also to all other *umam* under God's plan of salvation. Thus, like other *umam* to each of whom a messenger is sent, Muhammad is sent to his *umma* (13:30); since every *umma* will have a witness against it on the day of judgment, Muhammad will also be a witness against his *umma* (16:89), etc. In other words, the Meccan passages which apply to Muhammad and his community establish them as having essentially the same religion as the other religious groups, especially the *ahl al-kitāb* (cfr. 16:92, 16:120, 21:92, 23:52). The *umma* of Muhammad is the Arabian dimension for the one *umma* formed by the prophets.

In the Medinan passages, we find that the various dimensions of the one *umma* of God's messengers are now recognized as separate communities, in which the essential sameness of religious communities continues to be recognized but the independence of each tradition, and especially that of the Muslims, is emphasized (3:113, 5:48, 5:66 22:34, 22:67, etc.). There are four *umma* verses that we have not yet discussed. They are all Medinan (2:128, 2:143, 3:104 and 3:110). We discuss them separately here because they speak of the specialness of the Muslim community: the first one (2:128) refers to the Muslim community in a special way, while the other three (2:143, 3:104, 3:110) refer to it not only in a special way but also in an exclusive sense. The first one speaks of an *umma muslima* as that which Abraham prayed for.

رَبَّنا وَاجْعَلْنا مُسْلِمَيْنِ لَكَ وَمِنْ ذُرِّيَّتِنا أُمَّةً مُسْلِمَةً لَكَ
وَأَرِنا مَناسِكَنا وَتُبْ عَلَيْنا إِنَّكَ أَنْتَ التَّوّابُ الرَّحِيمُ.

> O Our Lord, make us submissive *[muslimīn]* to you, and of our descendants an *umma* submissive to you, and show us our rites, and relent towards us; You are the forgiving one, the compassionate (2:128).

This verse belongs to an Abraham passage. To properly understand it, let us outline the ideas in the other verses which are parts of its wider context. Verse 124 emphasizes that, what was bestowed on Abraham, is not to be gained by future generations through claims of descent; they have to earn it, because God excludes from His covenant whoever does wrong. Verses 125 to 127 speak about the House of worship *(Kaʿba)* which Abraham and Ishmael were commanded to purify and the foundations of which they raised. Then the *umma* verse 128 which follows is the prayer for a muslim (submitting to God) *umma* and proper rites, and verse 129 is the prayer for a messenger for their descendants. Verses 130 to 132 speak of the surrender or submission of Abraham to God and his enjoining upon his sons and Jacob to do the same. Verse 133 speaks of Jacob's enjoining his sons to do the same, emphasizing that the latter answered him: "We shall worship your God, the God of your fathers, Abraham and Ishmael and Isaac, One God, and unto Him we have surrendered." Then follows the Qurʾān's declaration (2:134 which we have quoted in the preceding section) that the *umma* of Abraham has passed away and has earned its reward, and whoever follows the same religion of submission will also earn a reward.

Verse 2:128 is the clearest connection between *umma* and *islām* that we have encountered in our survey of the *umma* passages in the Qurʾān. A true *umma* in the posterity of Abraham is an *umma muslima,* that is, one which is submissive to God. A look at the classical commentaries on this verse reveals varied interpretations of *min ḏurriyyatinā*, "of our descendants." Ṭabarī says it means "some of the offspring" and by that is meant the Arabs.[155] Rāzī, on the other hand, explains as follows:

> ".... *min* here is partitive and singles out some of them because God informs the two [Abraham and Ismael] that among their descendants are wrongdoers, as God said; *My covenant will not extend to the wrongdoers* (2:124). And among the people there are those who say that by it is meant the Arabs because they are among the children of the two; and it is said that *umma* here is the *umma* of Muhammad by the indication of the phrase *And raise among them a messenger from among themselves* (2:129).[156]

Ibn Kaṯīr[157] also mentions the foregoing interpretations and concludes that "the correct one is that it includes the Arabs and others - والصواب أنه يعم العرب وغيرهم" but that in the context, it specifies the Arabs because no messenger was sent to them as yet. Thus 2:129 follows which is a prayer for a messenger for the Arabs, the intention of which is Muhammad. He was sent among them as it is said in 62:2 - "He it is Who sent among the *ummiyyīn* a messenger of their own, to recite to them His revelations..."[158]

The explanation given by Ibn Kaṯīr is one which is true to the qurʾānic context which shows that the *muslim* in Abraham's prayer does not refer to a historical movement of people who should call themselves *muslims* but to the spiritual attitude of submission or *islām* which, as we have seen in the preceding section, is given with the human nature and which should be the

---

155 Ṭabarī (on 2:128) 553.

156 Rāzī (on 2:128, vol. 4) 61. Cfr. also Zamaḫšarī (on 2:128, Book 1) 311 and Al-Jalālayn (on 2:128) 27.

157 Ibn Kaṯīr (on 2:128, Book 1) 128.

158 Ibid.

soul of every religious community, whatever historical name it may carry. To be an *umma muslima* is, in the eyes of the Qurʾān, to be earned and not to be claimed by descent or ethnical connection (cfr. 2:124, 2:134, 2;141). This passage then in the first place delineates once more the religious aspects of the *umma* concept which we have already seen earlier, namely: the spiritual attitude of submission, exemplified by Abraham, which should be commonly shared by every true *umma*, and its expression in rites which vary from *umma* to *umma*. The context at the same time establishes these two religious aspects in so far as the community of Muhammad is concerned. There is no need to follow the religious ritual of other religious groups like the Jews because, after all, it was Abraham who founded the *Kaʿba* (2:127) in Mecca. Thus, the *Kaʿba* which had for a long time been the center of Meccan idolatrous worship, was resacralized and became the center to which the religious practices and beliefs of Muhammad's community became connected. As the *Kaʿba* plays a central role in the ritual aspect of Muhammad's religion, let us deal briefly with the qurʾānic data as well as with some extra-qurʾānic data about it.

In the Qurʾān, the references to the sanctuary in Mecca are all to be found in the Medinan period of the qurʾānic revelation. It is referred to as the *Kaʿba* (5:95, 5:97) or The House (in all the other passages that are cited in this paragraph). In 2:125, Abraham and Ismael are commanded to purify the House as the sanctuary for those who go around and meditate therein and who bow down and prostrate themselves (cfr. also 22:26 and 22:29); and the *maqām Ibrāhīm*, the place where Abraham stood, is indicated as the suitable place for the prayer. In 2:127 it is mentioned that it was Abraham together with Ismael who raised the foundations of the House. It is the first sanctuary (House) to be built for humankind (3:96), appointed by God to be the sacred House (5:97), the ancient House (22:29, 22:33), the place for pilgrimage and sacrifice (5:95, 22:27, 22:33).

The *Kaʿba*[159] in Mecca was an object of idolatrous worship prior to the coming of Islam.[160] However, outside of Muslim traditions,[161] practically nothing is known of its history. The geographer Ptolemy's mention of Mecca under the name Macoraba - which the German scholar Glaser interpreted as the South Arabian or Ethiopian *mākrāb*, "temple," - is the sole reason for presuming that the *Kaʿba* was already in existence in the second century AD.[162] The accounts of the expedition against Mecca by Abraha[163] - the Abyssinian ruler of Yaman - which expedition is also referred to in the Qurʾān (*sūra* 105), also suggest the existence of the *Kaʿba* in the sixth century but tell us nothing of its appearance or equipment. However, that the worship of the sanctuary had developed into a carefully-regulated cult several generations before Muhammad is probable.[164] On the other hand, scholars say that all that tradition relates regarding

---

159 For a detailed description of the *Kaʿba* and its surroundings, see, U. Rubin, "The Kaʿba" in *Jerusalem Studies in Arabic and Islam* 8 (Jerusalem: Hebrew University Magnes Press, 1986) 97-131 and A. J. Wensinck and J. Jomier, "Kaʿba" in *Encyclopedia of Islam,* new edition, vol. 4: 317-322.

160 A. J. Wensinck and J. Jomier, "Kaʿba," 321.

161 For an exhaustive collection of Muslim traditions about the "Kaʿba," see R. Firestone, *Journey in Holy Lands: The Evolution of the Abraham-Ishmael Legends in Islamic Exegesis* (Albany: State University of New York Press, 1990) especially Chapter 11.

162 Cfr. A. J. Wensinck and J. Jomier, "Kaʿba" in *Encyclopedia of Islam,* new ed., vol. 4: 318 where are cited, among other data, the following references: Ptolemy, *Geography*, vol. 6, p. 7 and Glaser, *Skizze der Geschichte und Geographie Arabiens* vol. 2 (Berlin, 1890) 235.

163 An analytical account of the Muslim traditional presentation of this event is done by R. Bell, *The Origin of Islam in its Christian Environment* (London: Frank Cass & Co., Ltd., 1968) 39ff.

164 See A. J. Wensinck and J. Jomier, op. cit., 319-322.

the origin of the *Kaʿba* and its connection with biblical personages belongs to Islamic legend which attached itself to the qurʾānic statements and spun them out, so that "it is incontrovertible that an entire pre-Islamic ritual, previously steeped in paganism, was adopted by Islam [i.e., the Muhammadan religion] after it had been purified and given a strictly monotheistic orientation."[165] The basis for the adoption is in religious history, i.e., the revelation in Medina that the *Kaʿba* was, after all, raised by Abraham and Ismael. The pilgrimages to the *Kaʿba* and ritual progressions around the building were continued, but were now for the glorification of the One God.

Passage 2:128 is the Qurʾān's account of the prayer of Abraham of long ago that he be one who submits to God and that his descendants be submitters as well. We learn from the Abraham *umma* verses that the community of Abraham in his time was one *umma* (16:120); that it was a *ḥanīf umma*, i.e., consisting essentially in submission to God and the recognition of the equality of all revelations. With the foundation of Muhammad's community in connection with this prayer for all people, the Qurʾān makes it clear that such a community is the continuation of the mission of the prophets not only to call humankind back to their original dedication to the One God, but also and especially to recognize the equality of all revelations through the prophets. This appointment distinguishes this community from the rest of the religious communities among whom it has to compete in good works. The physical distinction of this community is established by the Qurʾān with the adoption of the *Kaʿba* as the *qibla* (i.e., the place towards which the face is turned at prayer) of this

165 Ibid., 320.

community.[166] This brings us to the next *umma* passage.

وَكَذَٰلِكَ جَعَلْنَاكُمْ أُمَّةً وَسَطًا لِّتَكُونُوا شُهَدَاءَ عَلَى النَّاسِ
وَيَكُونَ الرَّسُولُ عَلَيْكُمْ شَهِيدًا وَمَا جَعَلْنَا الْقِبْلَةَ الَّتِي كُنتَ
عَلَيْهَا إِلَّا لِنَعْلَمَ مَن يَتَّبِعُ الرَّسُولَ مِمَّن يَنقَلِبُ عَلَىٰ عَقِبَيْهِ
وَإِن كَانَتْ لَكَبِيرَةً إِلَّا عَلَى الَّذِينَ هَدَى اللَّهُ وَمَا كَانَ اللَّهُ
لِيُضِيعَ إِيمَانَكُمْ إِنَّ اللَّهَ بِالنَّاسِ لَرَءُوفٌ رَّحِيمٌ

> Thus We have established you an *umma wasaṭ*, that you may be witnesses in regard to the people, and the messenger be in regard to you a witness. We appointed the *qibla* which you have been observing only that We might know those who would follow the messenger from those who would turn on their heels, though it was a big thing [a hard test] except to those whom God guided. God is not one to let your faith go lost; indeed, God is with the people gentle and compassionate (2:143).

Umma in this passage clearly refers to the community of Muhammad in an exclusive sense. The immediate context of this verse is the change of the *qibla* (from Jerusalem to the *Kaʿba* in Mecca), by which it is implied that no *qibla* is inherently more

---

166 "From very early times the direction at prayer and divine service was not a matter of choice among the Semitic peoples. There is already an allusion to this in 1 Kings 8:44 and it is recorded of Daniel (Daniel 6:11) that he offered prayer three times a day in the direction of Jerusalem (which has remained the Jewish *qibla* to this day). As is evident from the names of the quarters of the heavens, the whole life of the Semitic peoples was turned eastwards. The Essenes prayed in the direction of the rising sun and the Syriac Christians also turned eastwards at prayer." A. J. Wensinck, "Qibla" in *Encyclopedia of Islam,* new edition, volume V (1986) 82.

suited than any other,[167] but that which makes a *qibla* the proper one for a community is God's guidance (cfr. 2:142b) and the faith of the community (2:143b). The change of the *qibla* completes the establishment of the physical identity of Muhammad's community which distinguishes it as a separate community distinct from other communities, like the Jewish and the Christian. As such this community is described as *wasaṭ*.

As a description of the *umma* of Muhammad, *wasaṭ* has been much debated. The term *wasaṭ* as it is can mean "middle," "center," "means," "average," "medium quality," and the like.[168] *Umma wasaṭ* can mean middle community or community in the middle which could also merely be a geographical middle position on the earth or a moderation in ethical terms which refuses the extreme either way. Among the further meanings of *wasaṭ* are "best" because the best part of a thing is in the middle, surrounded by the edges; and "just," "equitable" because it is midway between the lack and the excess. Thus *umma wasaṭ* can also mean a community conforming, or conformable, to the just mean, or a just community.[169] Cragg has pointed out that "these conjectures do not readily fit the context which adds ".... in order

---

167 There is no existing verse in the Qurʾān prescribing Jerusalem as *qibla* for Muhammad's community, but it is certain that in the period immediately following the *hijra*, the *qibla* taken by the Jews was also used by Muhammad's community. Tradition dates the alteration in the *qibla* to 16 or 17 months after the arrival of Muhammad in Medina, in February 624 (Rajab or Šaʿbān of the Muslim year 2), which period also marked the important change in Muhammad's attitude to the Jews. There are various opinions as regards the reason for the Prophet's using of Jerusalem as *qibla*. Cfr. A. Wensinck, Ibid., and M. Ayoub, *The Qurʾān and its Interpreters*, vol. 1 (Albany: State University of New York Press, 1984) 167f.

168 Cf. the usages in 2:238; 5:89; 68:28.

169 Cfr. E. W. Lane, *Arabic-English Lexicon*, vol. 2 (Cambridge: The Islamic Texts Society, 1984) 2941-2942.

that you may be witnesses to the people,"[170] it must mean more than just the sense of being different from or being independent of the other religions. One of the explanations given by Ṭabarī, i.e., "middle in religion,"[171] has been the usual sense accepted and further interpreted by some scholars.[172] (Like we have mentioned earlier, this passage, and two others - namely, 3:104 & 3:110 - refer to the Muslims in an exclusive sense and have been most extensively commented on by the *mufassirīn*. In the next chapter, we will deal at some length with the more important of these commentaries).

The qur'ānic context shows that both the appointment of the *qibla* and being *wasaṭ* serve to distinguish - although each on a different level - the Muslim community from the rest of the communities. The *qibla* as a physical direction establishes the physical identity of the Muslim community, marking them off as a separate community distinct from others, like the Jews and the Christians (2:143b) - it is a physical, constant marker of the Muslim community as it is, so to say. Being *wasaṭ*, on the other

---

170 K. Cragg, *The Event of the Qur'ān: Islam in its Scripture* (London: George Allen and Unwin Ltd., 1971) 183, note 1.

171 Ṭabarī (on 2:143) 7.

172 Thus, for instance, Bell writes: ... "he [Muhammad] changed the *qibla* to the direction of the *Ka'ba*, thus making his community a "middle people," i.e., one which avoided following either Jews or Christians in points in which they differed. The same idea may appear in the adoption of Friday as the day of special service instead of either the Jewish or Christian Sabbath; as also in the call to prayer by means of the human voice. Tradition indeed asserts that the use of the wooden clapper by which Christians were summoned to service in the East was suggested to the Prophet, but rejected by him. So he also rejected the trumpet because it was Jewish." R. Bell, *The Origin of Islam in its Christian Environment* (London: Frank Cass & Co., Ltd., 1968) 144. See also, J. Wellhausen, *The Arab Kingdom and its Fall* (London: Curzon Press, 1927) 18-19.

hand, distinguishes the Muslims from the others in the whole of their religious and ethical life. Its precise meaning may be deduced from the wider context of the passage under discussion: After the appointment of the Muslim community as *wasaṭ*, as well as the announcement of the change in the *qibla* from Jerusalem to Mecca, the Qur'ān says, "Every one has his direction (وِجْهَةٌ) to which he turns; so vie with one another in good works (2:148)." Later in the same *sūra*, the Qur'ān says, "It is not piety that you turn your faces to the East and to the West. True piety is this: to believe in God and the Last Day, the angels, the Scripture, and the prophets, to give of one's wealth, however cherished, to kinsmen and orphans, the needy, the traveler, beggars, and to ransom the slave, to perform the prayer, to pay the alms ... (2:177)." This is followed by the prescription of religious practices like fasting on the month of Ramaḍān and the *hajj*, after which the Muslims are told (in 2:185, cf. also 2:195): "God desires for you ease; He desires not hardship for you يُرِيدُ اللّهُ بِكُمُ اليُسْرَ وَلاَ يُرِيدُ بِكُمُ العُسْرَ.

Umma wasaṭ, therefore, is one whose religious practice is done with ease or *yusra*, and one for whom the *qibla* means more than just the physical direction in prayer but, more importantly, the vying with others in good works (as the direction to be followed).

Thus when we now turn to the next passage which applies to the Muslims in an exclusive sense, they are an established community and are given a task which is an emphasis on this direction to be followed.

وَلْتَكُنْ مِّنْكُمْ أُمَّةٌ يَدْعُونَ إِلَى الْخَيْرِ، وَيَأْمُرُونَ بِالْمَعْرُوفِ
وَيَنْهَوْنَ عَنِ الْمُنْكَرِ وَأُولَائِكَ هُمُ الْمُفْلِحُونَ.

That of you be [formed] an *umma* inviting to the good, ordering equity and forbidding iniquity; such are the prosperous (3:104).

Here the ethical aspect of a true *umma* is emphasized and refers to the Muslims. However, it is not clear who exactly of the Muslims is referred to by *umma* in this verse, whether it refers to the whole Muslim community or to some of them. Neither is it clear to whom the inviting, ordering and forbidding are to be directed. Muslim commentators differ in their interpretations of this verse.[173] The text may be interpreted in two ways. In its literal sense, the task of ordering belongs to some of the Muslims. However, it may also be read "That of you may be [formed] a community..." - thus explicative - i.e., that you Muslims may become a community that invites to the good, orders equity and forbids iniquity. Such an *umma* which maintains its oneness in hearing, upholding and enforcing God's revealed Will, is destained for success. This second interpretation may fit the context in which the preceding verse (3:103),[174] as well as the succeeding one (3:105), both emphasize the oneness of the Muslims while the others are divided and going different ways. Most of all, it fits in connection with the final *umma* passage which refers to the Muslims in an exclusive sense and which is the climax of them all, almost immediately following the preceding one, and which speaks of the task mentioned in 3:104 as the distinctive character of the entire community.

---

[173] Representative Muslim commentaries on this verse will be treated in the next chapter.

[174] "And hold you fast to God's bond/cable, together,and do not scatter; remember God's blessing upon you when you were enemies, and he brought your hearts together, so that by His blessing you became brothers. (3:103)." One may note the similarity in the formulation of this verse and that of Paul's Letter to the Colossians 1:21-23: "You were foreigners and enemies... but now he has reconciled you, by his death and in that mortal body... as long as you persevere and stand firm on the solid base of faith, never letting yourselves drift away from the hope promised by the Good News." See also Paul's Letter to the Ephesians 2:13ff.

كُنْتُمْ خَيْرَ أُمَّةٍ أُخْرِجَتْ لِلنَّاسِ، تَأْمُرُونَ بِالْمَعْرُوفِ وَتَنْهَوْنَ
عَنِ الْمُنْكَرِ وَتُؤْمِنُونَ بِاللَّهِ.

> You are the best *umma* ever brought forth for humankind: you order equity, you forbid iniquity and you believe in God (3110).

Here, the ordering of equity and the forbidding of iniquity together with belief in God[175] become the distinctive mark of the Muslim community. It is the fulfillment of the recommendation in 3:104. The religious and the ethical - which are the inseparable aspects of the true *umma* as a concept and as a social reality - are fully realized in, and thus become the distinctive mark of, the whole Muslim community. Thus in the Qurʾān's eye they are the best community, the *umma* par excellence. As we have seen in our earlier discussions, according to the words of the Qurʾān such a distinctive mark applies also to some of the People of the Scripture (although as we also have shown, most classical Muslim commentators do not quite agree with our interpretation in this regard).

Looking now at all the four *umma* verses that we have just discussed, we very briefly summarize the main points. The Muslim community has been established as an *umma* patterned on the Abrahamic model (2:128). This means that, as a continuation of the *umma wāḥida* of the prophets, the Muslim community recognizes the equality of all revelations. Its existence

---

[175] Katsh has noted the similarity of this and an idea expressed in the Bible and in the Midrash: "It has been told thee, O man, what is good, and what the Lord requires of thee: Only to do justly, and to love mercy, and to walk humbly with thy God" (Micah 6:8); R. Eliezer said: "To do justly refers to the execution of justice: to love kindness refers to acts of benignity and to walk humbly refers to the acts of burying the dead and the dowering of brides." A. I. Katsh, *Judaism in Islam* (New York: New York University Press, 1954) 212.

is characterized by being *wasaṭ*, i.e., its religious practices are meant to be convenient or easy, and the direction the community follows is one of commitment to call others to what is good, to order that which is *maʿrūf* and to forbid that which is *munkar* (3:104). Such an appointment of this whole community makes it the best community ever brought forth for humankind (3:110). Seen in the whole context of these verses, this highest praise of the Qurʾān is to be understood as a praise for the appointment received, and as a reminder that it is something that has to be merited.

By way of concluding our discussions under this section, we may cite here the modern Muslim scholar I. H. Azad Faruqi. He says that the privileged position of the Muslim community expressed in 3:110 as well as in other similar verses in the Qurʾān,

> is not a particularism produced by religious groupism or monopolization of salvation by a particular religious community. But, rather, it is the particularism adopted by a universal message and its earlier followers as a necessary requirement for an organized and collective community life. It is the particularism rendered necessary to defend the universal vision and the religious freedom in face of the sectarian forces.......... In spite of all their universalistic beliefs and spirit, the early Muslims could not but have a particular mode of worship, if they were going to worship at all, and could not but have a particular style of life, if they were going to live in this world.... Islam in essence is a message of universal brotherhood and fellowship of all men in the worship of one God and in practice of a moral behavior. But in form and body, it appears in a particular mode and a specific tradition. The latter is not a negation of the former, but, a necessary condition of its physical existence.[176]

---

[176] I. H. Azad Faruqi, "The Qur'anic View of Other Religions," *Islam and the Modern Age* 18/1 (Feb 1987) 49-50.

2.7 ReligiousTerms Constitutive of the *Umma* Concept in its Definitive Sense

We have seen that the term *umma* in the Qurʾān has a variety of meanings and applications. Its fully developed meaning is that of a religious community while its most important application is to the Muslims as a religious community in a special sense. In this section, we will briefly highlight some important religious terms that are constitutive or specificative of the *umma* in its fully developed meaning of a religious community. In this way, we understand more about the qurʾānic teaching concerning the *umma* in its definitive sense. We limit our treatment of these terms to the most important ones, namely: the special terms *ḥanīf/ ḥunafāʾ* and *milla*, and the names of groupings, *muslimūn* (those who submit) and *muʾminūn* (believers).

2.7.1 *Ḥanīf*

We have discussed the qurʾānic use of the term *ḥanīf* under the heading "Abraham." Thus here we shall repeat only the main points. Instead, we will devote more pages to a consideration of the origin of the term as it is a very important clue for the proper understanding of the Islamic religion and the circumstances surrounding its birth.

The term *ḥanīf*, as we have seen earlier, is intimately linked with the teaching of the Qurʾān concerning Abraham. The term expresses the sense of the original religious impulse in humanity of submission to the One God, which, according to the Qurʾān, was originally intended by God (see especially 30:30). It is in contrast to the particular religions which arose later, polytheism on the one hand and then in part the extremist or neglectful religions of some of the possessors of the Scriptures. It recognizes the fundamental equality of all revelations.

The origin of the qur'ānic term *ḥanīf* has been the subject of much controversy among Muslim[177] as well as non-Muslim scholars.[178] It is now generally agreed upon, that, as used in the Qur'ān, *ḥanīf* is not to be derived from the Arabic root *ḥ-n-f* but

---

[177] Early interpretations quoted in the classical commentaries vary. Ṭabarī (in his comments on 2:128-9 and 2:135), for instance, quotes an authority who says that *ḥanīf* is one who makes a pilgrimage to the *Ka'ba* (also in Rāzī on 16:120, vol. 20, p. 135), while another says *ḥanīf* is one who follows the practice of circumcision established by Abraham. Ṭabarī himself refutes these views saying that the Jews, who are circumcised, are not considered *ḥanīfs*, and the pagans who used to make the pilgrimage before the coming of Islam were not called *ḥanīfs*. (Margoliouth has suggested that the reference to circumcision would show the influence of a Jew who interpreted *milla Ibrāhīm* as the Hebrew "circumcision of Abraham" while the reference to pilgrimage would merely be an inference from *sūra* 22:28. Cf. D. S. Margoliouth, "On the Origin and Import of the Names Muslim and *Ḥanīf*" in *The Journal of the Royal Asiatic Society* vol. 5 (1903) 483.) Ibn Kaṯīr (on 2:135, Book 1, p. 132), says that a *ḥanīf* is one who believes in all the messengers, from the first to the last. Most authorities cited by classical commentators would explain *ḥanīf* as being derived from the Arabic root *ḥ-n-f* with the sense of "to incline," "to turn, *(mā'il)*, so that a *ḥanīf* was supposed to be one who turned from false religion to the true. Cfr. Ṭabarī (on 16:120)190; Zamaḫšarī (on 16:120, Book 2) 434; Rāzī (on 16:120, vol. 20) 135; Ibn Kaṯīr (on 16:120, Book 2) 351; Bayḍāwī (on 16:120) 369; Al-Jalālayn (on 16:120) 362.

[178] A long list of literature on *ḥanīf* (from the previous century until 1940), classified according to their views on the matter, are found in N. A. Faris and H. W. Glidden, "The Development of the Meaning of Koranic *ḤANĪF*" in *The Journal of the Palestine Oriental Society*, vol. 19 (Jerusalem: Palestine Oriental Society) 1-2; cfr. also F. Denny, "Some Religio-Communal Terms and Concepts in the Qur'ān" in *Numen*, vol. 24 (1977) 26-59.

from the Aramaic *ḥānèfā* or the Syriac *ḥanpā*.[179] In Syriac *ḥanpā* means pagan. In the Christian world, however, the word *ḥanpā* came to be used in two senses: in the Syriac translation of the Bible, it is the term for "pagan;" at the same time, Christian authors used the term to indicate those Christian heretics, like Mani and the Ṣābians, whose ideas were so influenced by Hellenistic paganism that one could consider them as apostates. Roest Crollius has demonstrated the probability that the qurʾānic use of the term was occasioned by contact with these people to whom the second sense of the term was applied.[180]

---

[179] Cfr., among others, A. Roest Crollius, *The Word in the Experience of Revelation in Qurʾān and Hindu Revelation* (Roma: Università Gregoriana Editrice, 1974) 124, note 112; W. M. Watt, "Ḥanīf" in *The Encyclopedia of Islam,* new edition, vol. III (1971) 165-166; F. Denny, "Some Religio-Communal Terms and Concepts in the Qurʾān" in *Numen,* vol. 24 (1977) 26-59; A. Rippin, "RḤMNN And The Ḥanīfs" in *Islamic Studies Presented To Charles Adams,* W. B. Hallaq and D. P. Little, eds. (Leiden/New York: E. J. Brill, 1991) 158-159. Among ancient Muslim scholars, Masʿūdī represents the opinion that, as used in the Qurʾān, *ḥanīf* was a foreign word: *"wa hāḏ̱hi kalimatun suryāniyyatun ʿurribat"* - "This is a Syrian word which has been Arabicized." Quoted in A. Jeffery, *The Foreign Vocabulary of the Qurʾān* (Baroda: Oriental Institute, 1938) 114, note 7. As regards the transfer from *hanpā* to *ḥanīf,* Bell explains: "The long vowel of the second syllable of *ḥanīf* is fatal to its derivation from Syriac *ḥanpā* in its singular form; but this objection vanishes at once when we look at the plurals. For the Arabic *ḥunafāʾ* is as close a reproduction of the Syriac *ḥanephē* as there is any need to demand. We may therefore assume that the word was borrowed in its plural form, and that the singular *ḥanīf* was formed from that in accordance with one of the rules of correspondence between singular and plural forms in Arabic." R. Bell, "Who Were The *Ḥanīfs?"* in *Muslim World* 20/2 (1930) 121.

[180] A. Roest Crollius, *The Word in the Experience of Revelation in Qurʾān and Hindu Revelation* (Roma: Università Gregoriana Editrice, 1974) 127-132.

In the Qurʾān, the Ṣābians[181] are mentioned in three Medinan verses[182] as a community of believers distinct from but on the same level as the Muslims, Jews and Christians. By inference from what we have learned about religious communities, the Ṣābians must have had their own messenger and their own Scripture; although none of this is explicitly mentioned in the Qurʾān, the Ṣābian revelation has been identified via an external evidence, in the *Fihrist*:

> I have interpreted this book from the book of the *ḥanīfs* who are the Ibrahimitic Ṣābians, who believed in Ibrāhīm - peace upon him - and brought from him the pages which God sent down upon him.[183]

Although nothing is known about these "pages of Abraham," in an early Meccan passage the Qurʾān makes mention of such pages:

إِنَّ هَٰذَا لَفِي ٱلصُّحُفِ ٱلْأُولَىٰ؛ صُحُفِ إِبْرَاهِيمَ وَمُوسَىٰ.

"Verily this is in the ancient pages, the pages of Abraham, and Moses (87:18-19).

---

[181] "We do not repeat here Andrae's arguments that Muhammad, in his quest for religious independence, has been influenced by the Gnostics and Manichaeans. It is enough to recall that the contemporaries of Muhammad have remarked the affinity between him and the Gnostics: they called Muhammad and his followers Ṣābians." A. Roest Crollius, *The Word in the Experience of Revelation in Qurʾān and Hindu Revelation* (Roma: Università Gregoriana Editrice, 1974) 127.

[182] 2:62, 5:69, 22:17.

[183] Al-Nadīm, *Al-Fihrist*, ed. Flügel, S. 22. As quoted by A. Roest Crollius, op. cit., 127.

As Roest Crollius and Widengren[184] have done, we can assume "that on Arabian soil there may have existed at the time of Muhammad's appearance certain Gnostic sects with baptismal rites, Ṣābians, claiming to possess a heavenly Scripture, given by God to Ibrāhīm, whom they counted as their Apostle, the bringer of revelation to them." Consequently, the religious attitude of the *ḥanīf* was for Muhammad and his followers not an abstract idea but a creed incarnated in a religious community other than Jewish or Christian. Historical researches have not as yet been able to identify with certainty this particular Gnostic sect but have demonstrated its association with the earlier Elchasaites.[185] However, as we have seen in our discussion of *ḥanīf* in the Qurʾān, the idea of *ḥanīf* is larger than that of any particular sect; thus, "the link that exists between the *ḥunafāʾ* and the Elchasaites does not imply that they are to be simply identified."[186]

---

[184] G. Widengren, *Muhammad, the Apostle of God, and his Ascension* (Uppsala/Wiesbaden, 1955) 135. As cited in A. Roest Crollius, op. cit., 128.

[185] Of the Elchasaites, Bell reports: "Their founder Elchasai was an Arab and may illustrate the effect of mingled Jewish and Christian ideas upon the Arab mind. His activity fell in the time of Trajan. He was the revealer of a book which was held by his followers to have come down from heaven. There were also other points of similarity between the religion of the Elchasaites and that of the Prophet of Arabia. They believed in one God and in the Last Judgment. In prayer they turned towards Jerusalem, as Muhammad at one stage did, though probably in his case it was due to direct Jewish influence. What is said to have been the secret watchword of Elchasai, "I am a witness over you on the day of judgment," is found almost in so many words in the Qurʾān.... the Ṣābians were some remnant of the Elchasaites who had maintained themselves in the north-west of Arabia, where they would be known to the Meccans, and may have exercised some influence upon Muhammad." R. Bell, *The Origin of Islam in its Christian Environment* (London: Frank Cass & Co., Ltd., 1968) 59-60.

[186] A. Roest Crollius, op. cit., 129.

As regards Manichaeism, we learn from Arabian historiography that it was known in Mecca. It is impossible to find precise indications as to the contacts between Muhammad and the Manichaeists; however, the elements of the Manichaeian doctrines which were known in Muhammad's environment may be pointed out as follows:

> 1) God sent to various peoples, at various times, their own prophets. 2) These former revelations all had a part of the truth. Mani's revelation completes the former revelations. 3) This revelation corrects what has been corrupted in the former ones. 4) Mani was thus "the seal of the Prophets." 5) He also considered himself as the *paraklêtos* promised by Christ.[187]

Thus, to conclude, *ḥanīf,* as used in the Qurʾān,[188] indicates a religious attitude which, at the time of the appearance of Muhammad, was embodied in religious movements like the Manichaeian or Ṣābian, which adopted in Arabia and in a good sense, the Syriac term *ḥanʾphê* which was applied to them by Christian authors in regarding them as heretics, and which

---

[187] Ibid., 131, note 170, with all the references to original sources.

[188] Attempts have been made to interpret the word *ḥanīf* when used in the Qurʾān by referring to persons who were supposedly called *ḥanīfs* in pre-Islamic times as told in the *Sīra* or by referring to Epigraphical South Arabian inscriptions which convey the idea of monotheism. These are supposed to be evidences of an organized monotheistic movement called *ḥanīfiyya* in pre-Islamic Arabia which would be the historical referent of the term when used in the Qurʾān. The most recent research and evaluation of previous studies on the epigraphical South Arabian inscriptions was done by A. Rippin ("RḤMNN and the ḤANĪFS" in *Islamic Studies Presented to Charles Adams,* W. B. Hallaq and D. P. Little, eds. (Leiden: E. J. Brill, 1991) 153-168) where he concludes, like many other scholars did before him, that the inscriptions do not provide evidence for the existence of *ḥanīfiyya.*

element, among others, came to be assimilated in an original way by the Qur'ān. It became the basis of the qur'ānic ideology of belief which is embodied in Abraham and captured in the word *muslim*.

2.7.2 *Milla*

Milla is a qur'ānic word which may be roughly translated as "religion." Recent scholars are generally agreed that it is a loan-word. It may stem from the Hebrew and Jewish and Christian Aramaic *millā* which means "utterance, word," which could also be used figuratively for the religious beliefs of a person.[189] Jeffery considers the Syriac *melltā* as the more likely source, "for besides meaning *word*, it is also used to translate *logos* and is used technically for religion," and he cites the suggestion of Horovitz that the meaning was also influenced by the sense of "way," which may be derived from the Arabic root itself.[190] Roest Crollius agrees that "Hebrew *(millā)* or Syriac *(melltā)* origin cannot be excluded" but it is "impossible to read the qur'ānic word in the meaning of *Logos*."[191] Jeffery sees no evidence which could attest to a pre-Islamic use of the term in its qur'ānic sense and

---

[189] F. Buhl, "Milla" in *The Encyclopedia of Islam*, vol. 7, new edition, ed. C. E. Bosworth, etc. (Leiden: E. J. Brill, 1993) 61. Following the view of most Arab philologists, Nöldeke had earlier suggested an Arabic origin of the word by referring to the fourth form *amalla* or *amlā*, "to dictate" but, as Buhl has noted, the signification of the Arabic root is very far-fetched from the meaning of "religion" which the word has in the Qur'ān. Ibid.

[190] A. Jeffery, *The Foreign Vocabulary of the Qur'ān* (Baroda: Oriental Institute,1938) 268f.

[191] A. Roest Crollius, *The Word in the Experience of Revelation in Qur'ān and Hindu Scriptures* (Roma: Università Gregoriana Editrice, 1974) 125, note 153.

concludes that Muhammad must have borrowed the word himself, which word must have been intelligible to his audiences who were more or less acquainted with the Jews and Christians.[192]

The term *milla* appears fifteen times in the Qurʾān. It is most often found in connection with Abraham, especially in the phrase مِلَّةَ إِبْرَاهِيمَ (2:130, 2:135, 3:95, 4:125, 6:161, 12:38, 16:123, 22:78); it is also used to refer to the religion of the Jews and Christians (2:120, 38:7[193]); and to pagan beliefs (18:20, 7:88-89,14:13 and 12:37). *Milla* as "religion" would properly mean an attitude towards religion, "a way of belief and practice in respect of religion."[194] To distinguish it from *dīn* - the other qurʾānic term which explicitly means religion, Izutsu says that while *dīn* is basically religion as a personal existential act of faith and obedience to God, *milla* "is religion as an objective 'thing' in the full sense of the word, a formal system of creeds and rituals which constitute the principle of unity for a particular religious community and works as the basis of its social life.[195] *Milla* is thus

---

192 Ibid. Horovitz (*Koranische Untersuchungen* (Berlin and Leipzig: Walter de Gruyter & Co., 1926, pp. 62-63) has mentioned the use of the *milla* of God or the *milla* of *ar-raḥmān* by poets contemporary with Muhammad, and also noted by Jeffery, Ibid., 269.

193 In this particular case, the reference of *milla* is not very clear. The text reads: "We have not yet heard of this in the very last [form of] religion" = 'مَا سَمِعْنَا بِهَذَا فِى الْمِلَّةِ الأَخِرَةِ' . Of this verse, Bell (*The Qurʾān: Translated with a Critical Re-Arrangement of the Sūras,* 2 vols. (Edinburgh: T. and T. Clark, 1937) 451, note 1) says: "The sense is uncertain, probably "in any religion whatever." Al-Jalālayn and Bayḍāwī say it refers to the religion of Jesus = 'مِلَّة عِيْسَى'. Jalālayn (on 38:7) 598 and Bayḍāwī on (on 38:7) 600.

194 E. Lane, *Arabic-English Lexicon*, vol. 2 (Cambridge: The Islamic Texts Society, 1984) 3023.

195 T. Izutsu, *God and Man In the Koran* (Tokyo: The Keio Institute of Cultural and Linguistic Studies, 1964) 228.

synonymous with such phrases as "tradition of faith" or "religious tradition." *Dīn* is basically shared by all true religious communities.[196] *Milla,* on the other hand, is a neutral term and applies to the system of beliefs and rituals in respect of *dīn* and which is particular to every religious community. The distinctiveness of the *milla* of Abraham does not lie in its being a *milla* but in its being a *milla* in a certain or particular sense: *ḥanīfan, musliman,* a *milla* of submission which recognizes the essential equality of all true religions. Thus, while Jews and Christians may look to Abraham as "father of faith," it is the Muslim *umma* that lives the *milla* of Abraham.

Islamic literature follows the qurʾānic usage of *milla.* "With the article, *al-milla* means the true religion revealed by Muhammad and is occasionally used elliptically for *ahl al-milla,* the followers of the Islamic religion, just as its opposite *al-d̲imma* is an abbreviation for *ahl al-d̲imma,* the non-Muslims who are under the protection of Islam."[197] In more recent and modern Arabic, *milla* still maintains its qurʾānic meaning, although the word is largely obsolete. However, whether or not because of the influence of the elliptical

---

196 In his study of *dīn* as religion, Izutsu (Ibid., 219-229) distinguishes two aspects of *dīn* depending on how it is used in the Qurʾān. Its first aspect is its being religion in the sense of a personal existential act of faith and obedience to God (as mentoned above). Its second aspect is bound up with a more rigidly defined concept including notions like doctrines, rites and creeds. He calls the first a "non-reified sense" and the second a "reified sense" - a distinction used earlier by W. C. Smith (*The Meaning and End of Religion* (Minneapolis: Fortress Press, 1991, chapter 4) and also cited by Izutsu. *Dīn* in the Qurʾān is first used to mean non-reified religion, but develops steadily from lesser to greater reification, until in Medina definitively it comes to mean reified religion, and Islam as this reified religion par excellence, in which case, *dīn* is used as a synonym for *milla.*

197 F. Buhl, *"Milla"* in *The Encyclopedia of Islam,* new edition, vol. 2, p. 61, with citations from Ṭabarī and others.

use of the term, in Persian and Turkish the term has undergone a semantic change,[198] that is, it developed into meaning a particular religious community, i.e., the followers of one religious tradition as distinct from others and considered as a systematic group, rather than the tradition of faith that they followed.

2.7.3 *Muʾmin/Muʾminūn*

Muʾmin/Muʾminūn is one of the terms that designate the members of a true *umma*. The fourth form *āmana*, meaning "to believe," and its derivatives occur very frequently in the Qurʾān. The term *īmān*, "faith," itself occurs forty-five times. Compared with *aslama*, "to submit, to surrender" and its derivatives, *āmana* and its derivatives occur a lot more times in the Qurʾān and begin to appear fairly early in the Meccan verses; while the *aslama*-group appears later.

Many modern scholars (Muslim and non-Muslim) agree that the use in the Qurʾān of the fourth form *āmana*, meaning to believe, is new. Jeffery says that while the primitive verb *amina*, "to become secure, to feel free from fear" with its derivatives is pure Arabic, the fourth form *āmana*, "to put one's trust in something or someone" with its derivatives *muʾmin*, "a believer"

---

[198] "In modern Persian, *millat* means 'people, nation,' and the adjective from it, *millī*, means 'national.' In Ottoman Turkish, *millet* became a technical term latterly to denote internally autonomous religious groups within the Ottoman empire." There were then five *millets:* the Islamic, the Greek Orthodox, the Armenian, the Latin and the Jewish. In 20th century Turkish, however, *millet* has come rather to mean (as in Persian) "nation, people," with *millī* meaning "national," *milliyet* "nationality" and *"milliyetci* "nationalist." Cfr. M. O. H. Ursinus, "Millet" in *Encyclopedia of Islam*, new edition, vol. 7, pp. 61-64; C. E. Dawn, *From Ottomanism to Arabism* (Chicago/London: University of Illinois Press, 1973) and K. Karpat, *Turkey's Politics* (Princeton: Princeton University Press, 1959).

and *īmān,* "believing, faith," is a technical religious term which seems to have been borrowed from the older faiths.[199] Horovitz[200] says that the derivation could be either from the Hebrew *he'emīn,* or, citing an earlier suggestion by Sprenger, from the Ethiopian, which employs the word *mā'men* in the sense of "believing" (adjective).[201]

Only in a few instances is *umma* used in close connection with any of the fourth form derivatives, but these instances are very important references. They are used in passages that refer to Muslims and the People of the Scripture (in 2:143, 2:213, 3:110, 3:113-114). For a true *umma,* faith is basic; and faith is found not only in the Muslim community but also in other religious

---

[199] A. Jeffery, *Foreign Vocabulary of the Qur'ān* (Baroda: Oriental Institute,1938) 70.

[200] J. Horovitz, "Jewish Proper Names and Derivatives in the Qur'ān" in *Hebrew Union College Annual,* vol. 2 (1964) 191.

[201] A typical Muslim explanation and resolution of a case of a new usage of a word in the Qur'ān is the following one by A. K. Kazi: "...the expression is new, there being no background to its usage in this or a similar sense in the pre-Islamic Arabic language. The only authenticated pre-Islamic usage of *āmana* is in the sense of giving protection. When, therefore, the theologians of the second and third centuries and the lexicographers later on tell us that *āmana* literally means *taṣdīq* [belief], they in fact are telling us what became the literal meaning of *āmana* under the impact of its characteristic usage in the Qur'ān. *Lisān al-ʿArab* quotes no example from the pre-Islamic Arabic poetry to corroborate that *al-īmān* is *taṣdīq.* ... The meaning of *āmana* in the Qur'ān should, indeed, be sought in the Qur'ān itself, in its characteristic usage in a variety of places expressing a complex of ideas." Abdul Khaliq Kazi, "The Meaning of *Īmān* and *Islām* in the Qur'ān" in *Islamic Studies,* vol. 5, no. 3 (September 1966) 233. What Kazi says here is true, but what distinguishes him especially from non-Muslim scholars is his reluctance to venture into the possibility of a foreign origin of the term.

communities like the People of the Scripture.[202] In the case of the People of the Scripture, faith is found only in some of them. The connection between *umma* and faith is strongest in those passages in which *umma* refers exclusively to the Muslim community. We have seen in 2:143 that the middle community is a community of faithfulness. The middle ground of witness is had because of faith, which in turn is had because of God's guidance. This community of faithfulness is described in 3:110 - the climax of all *umma* passages - as the best community, i.e., the faith of the whole community, and not just of a part of it, is an indispensable aspect of its being the best community.

2.7.4 *Muslim/muslimūn*

Like *muʾmin/muʾminūn, muslim/muslimūn* is used in close connection with *umma* in only very few instances. We have seen in our earlier discussions in this chapter that the religion of submission or *islām* was the common denominator of the religion

[202] Muslim traditional commentators, as we have seen earlier, have interpreted the phrase "believers among the People of the Scripture" as referring to those who have converted to Islam, but the contexts do not prove it. Kazi (op. cit., p. 234f) says that *āmana* as used in the Qurʾān would specifically mean to follow Muhammad and enter his experience. He cites as the clearest proof of this those verses where *allaḏīna āmanū* is used for followers of Muhammad in contradistinction to Jews and Christians such as in 5:69 (also 2:62). However, while it is true that many passages where *āmana* is employed refer to the followers of Muhammad, it is not true in all cases, and this is precisely demonstrated in 5:69 (cfr. 2:62): the first occurrence, *āmanū*, refers to the followers of Muhammad, while the second occurrence, *āmana*, refers to all believers in general. It would seem that in many cases of the appearances of *allaḏīna āmanū* the reference is to the followers of Muhammad, but when the phrase "in God and in the Last Day" is added, the reference is to all believers, Muslim or not.

of the prophets, and thus, of the religious traditions followed by the People of the Scripture; however, as could also be seen, submission is not linked in a necessary way with the actual religious communities or *umam* like those of the People of the Scripture, that claim to follow the religious traditions of their prophets. The most important use of *islām* or *muslim* in connection with *umma* is when *umma* refers to the community of Muhammad in a special way, though not necessarily exclusively, in 2:128f, for there the two terms are linked with each other in a necessary way. Passage 2:128 is the prayer of Abraham. We have seen that Abraham is the great example of the true *ḥanīf*.[203] His prayer for an *umma muslima* contains exactly the basic elements that we saw are constitutive of the *ḥanīf* attitude, namely: submission to God together with a ritual dimension. Verse 2:128 is the Qur'ān's clear association between the religion of Abraham and Muhammad's community. The whole context of 2:128 shows, first of all, that the community of Muhammad is a properly guided community; it is patterned on the Abrahamic model, an *umma muslima*. The establishment of the Muslim community, however, does not mean the election of a people by God or one that is earned by claims of descent but the fruit of God's guidance and the community's acts of goodness and justice (2:120 and 2:124).

---

[203] Watt is of the opinion that in early times, the Muslims called themselves the *ḥanīfs* to distinguish themselves from the Jews and Christians. However, since the Christians continued to use the term for 'pagan' and to taunt the Muslims with it, it passed out of favor with the Muslims who eventually preferred *'muslim'*. See the following works by W. M. Watt: *Muhammad, Prophet and Statesman* (London: Oxford University Press, 1961)117; *Islamic Political Thought* (Edinburgh: University Press, 1968) 60; "Ḥanīf" in *Encyclopedia of Islam,* second edition. For a summary of other views on this, see F. Denny, "Some Religio-Communal Terms and Concepts in the Qur'ān" in *Numen*, vol. 24 (1977) 31, note 20.

As also pointed out by Fazlur Rahman,[204] the whole mystique of election is undermined by statements of the Qur'ān in this context, i.e., that the tenor of the whole context is against election and exclusivism. In verse 2:124, to Abraham's question of the fulfillment of God's promise to his progeny, the reply is "My promise does not extend to the unjust ones." After mentioning biblical prophets and their people, the Qur'ān repeatedly says: "That community is by-gone: to them belongs what they earned and to you [Muslims] will belong what you will earn, and you will not be asked for what they had done (2:134 and 2:141)." Finally, while the Jews and the Christians may be seen as not having provided the high example praised in this passage, yet "in conformity with this strong rejection of exclusivism and election, the Qur'ān repeatedly recognizes the existence of good people in other communities - Jews, Christians and Ṣābians - just as it recognizes the people of faith in Islam: 'Those who believe (Muslims), the Jews, the Christians, and the Ṣābians - whosoever believe in God and the Last Day and do good deeds, they shall have their reward from their Lord, shall have nothing to fear, nor shall they come to grief (2:62, cfr. 5:69)."[205]

In fact, exclusivism is not a quality or attitude of the *ḥanīf*. The *ḥanīf* recognizes the equality of all revelations or of all religions except that of the idolaters. Thus, the establishment of the Muslim community patterned on the model of Abraham, the true *ḥanīf*, is a "missioning" of this community to live the original one religion of humankind; and thus, at the same time, a continuation of the mission of the prophets to call back humankind to the original *umma wāḥida*. In other words, the prayer of Abraham in 2:128 is for all of humankind, for the *umma wāḥida*, that all may be one.

---

[204] F. Rahman, "The People of the Book and the Diversity of Religions" in *Christianity through Non-Christian Eyes*, ed. Paul Griffiths (New York: Orbis Books, 1990) 105-106.

[205] Ibid., 106.

2.8 Summary and Conclusion

We are now in a position to summarize and conclude our survey and analysis of the *umma* verses in the Qurʾān. We have seen that the term *umma* usually refers to human community in a religious sense, to ethnical, linguistic or religious bodies of people who are the objects of God's plan of salvation. The isolated cases of homonymous and quasi-homonymous usages of the term or the non-people references, form part of the "emphasis points" in the different stages in the unfolding of the final meaning of *umma* in the Qurʾān: when the Qurʾān repeatedly says that every *umma* will be gathered and brought to judgment, we find references as well to the *jinn* (7:38, etc.) and to every species of living creatures (6:38); when the Qurʾān repeatedly says that every *umma* has an appointed time, we find instances where *umma* is equated with time (11:8, 12:45); when the Qurʾān emphasizes the oneness of a true religious community, we find a passage where *umma* refers to an eponym for a religious community (16:120). We shall now briefly review the conclusions in our analysis of *umma* according to the main motifs expressed in its usages in the Qurʾān. Based on these findings, we shall then trace the history of the *umma* according to the Qurʾān, in order to arrive at a proper understanding of the *umma* in its final, special sense.

<u>A Community under judgment, with an appointed time</u>: This is a universal message which is written in the Scripture of God's decrees (15:4-5), announced through God's messengers in their respective times, and now announced in the context of Mecca. Unbelief will be punished on the Day of Judgment. Kindness to parents is put on the same level as belief. The theme of judgment is unrelenting in the Meccan and Medinan periods, although it is more marked in the former. It should be regarded as standing behind the use of *umma* in most contexts.

To every umma is a messenger of God: God sends messengers to different peoples and nations at different times, with identical, universal messages, functioning either as warner, announcer, bringer of Scripture, depending upon the situation of the people he is sent to. In the Meccan verses, Muhammad is mentioned always in relation to the fact that other messengers were sent before him; he is one of God's messengers. In the Medinan period, the emphasis is on the period of his being God's messenger or prophet - i.e., the period beginning with his arrival right up to the Last Day. Thus he is "The Messenger," "The Prophet" of the present age.

Humankind as one community: Here, *umma* begins to be used in the sense of a religious community. It has two aspects: belief in God and being just and righteous in dealing with others. In the context of Mecca where the immediate addressees are polytheists, i.e., people who associate other gods with God, the verses emphasize that in the beginning humankind was one religious community, adoring One God (monotheism); afterwards, many people started to associate other gods with God (polytheism). In the context of Medina the people consisted not only of idolatrous worshippers but also of separate, exclusivist communities of followers of past prophets. The verses thus emphasize that the prophets were sent to preach one religion. The separate, exclusivist communities of the followers of various prophetic traditions are supposed to be only various dimensions of the essentially one community of the prophets, and thus ought to recognize the equality of all revelations and all prophetic traditions.

Ahl al-kitāb and other communities: When the term *umma* comes to mean the religious or good group within a larger group, the first reference(s) may not be only to the People of the Scripture. *Umma* is characterized as a community guiding with the truth and establishing justice in dealing with others. In the Meccan verses, when *umma* comes to refer to the people who have accepted the message of the prophets, it refers to them as one *umma*. Divisive groups within the one *umma* are referred to as sects, *aḥzāb*, but not as separate communities or *umam*. In the Medinan verses, the *umma* concept is very clearly presented as having two inseparable dimensions, namely: 1) belief in the One God and the Last Day, and 2) ordering of what is good and forbidding of what is evil, and acting justly. The reference of *umma* is to each of the divided communities within the one *umma* of the prophets. In other words, the *aḥzāb* in the Meccan verses are here recognized as separate communities *(umam)*, each with a particular rite and way of life. God allows this separation into various communities in order that they compete in works of goodness and righteousness. In this way, the original one community of humankind will be restored in the form of a community of communities of righteousness and goodness.

Abraham: In the late Meccan period, in the same period that the Qurʾān speaks about some divisive groups, sects in the one community of the prophets, the image of Abraham, the *ḥanīf* is recalled as an *umma wāḥida*, as a model *umma*. The *ḥanīf* attitude is one which is identified with the basic religious impulse in humanity of submission to the One God, created by God in man to be followed in obedience and purity. It recognizes the essential equality of all revelations. Its outward expression includes the performance of a religious rite and good deeds. Abraham is the example of the true *ḥanīf*. In the Medinan verses, it is emphasized that Abraham has earned his reward and that whoever follows him will also earn a reward.

The Muslim community. The *umma* verses in which the Muslims are referred to in a special way and also in an exclusive sense all belong to the Medinan period. In the actual situation of various separate religious communities that resulted from the various dimensions of the one *umma* of the prophets, the Muslim community is established as a separate community patterned on the Abrahamic model, as a restoration of the one *umma* of the prophets. Like the original one *umma* of the prophets, the mission of this community is to call idolaters and unbelievers back to the original worship of the one God. At the same time, like the original one *umma* of the prophets, the Muslims recognize the fundamental equality of all revelations contained in the traditions followed by various religious communities. In relation to these religious communities, they are to compete in works of goodness and righteousness. The Qur᾽ān praises the formation of the Muslim community as "the best" and thus challenges the Muslims to actualize their mission to be front runners and standard-bearers in the pursuit of the Qur᾽ān's vision for humankind of a community of communities of goodness.

The above conclusions would all together present an overall view of the *umma* as the one religious community of humankind which existed in the beginning of humanity but which has now become an ideal to be achieved. The historical situations in Mecca and Medina of the seventh century provided the context for the Qur᾽ān's teaching on how the ideal is to be achieved. The Muslim *umma*, founded in Medina, is the Qur᾽ān's restoration of the original one *umma* in a world of many *umam*. It is an *umma* in a special sense: it is an *umma* among other separate *umam* of followers of various prophets; at the same time, it is also the restoration of the one, undivided *umma* of the prophets. In order to understand better the specialness of this community, we conclude by presenting it in the context of the history of the *umma* according to the Qur᾽ān, as can be gathered from the above outlined findings.

The whole of humankind was originally one religious community *(umma wāḥida)*. Everyone followed the basic impulse *(fiṭra)* to submit to the One God, which impulse God himself created in man to be followed in obedience and purity. For some time the human race remained on the right way, until people started to invent other gods, thus breaking the original unity.

Then God sent prophets to different nations and peoples at different times, in order to call idolaters and unbelievers back to the original one religion and one religious community of humankind. These prophets or messengers preached the same original religion and thus constituted a community that was a continuation of the original one which used to be of the whole of humankind. Various religious traditions developed based on each prophet's historically contextualized preaching. These religious traditions constituted the various dimensions for the one religion and the one religious community of the prophets. True followers of these traditions would recognize the equality of the prophetic traditions.

Muhammad was raised from among the Arabs to whom no prophet had as yet been sent, in order to preach to them the same message that the other prophets before him had brought. His prophetic activity started in Mecca and the mission then was to form a Muhammadan or Arabian dimension for the one religion and one religious community of the prophets. Thus, when in doubt at the beginning of his preaching, the Qur'ān (in 10:94, 16:43, 17:101, 21:7, 25:9) advised Muhammad to consult those who had received the Scripture (Jews and Christians). It is expected that, the other religious groups (immediately Jews and Christians) while continuing to follow their respective traditions, would recognize Muhammad as an Arabian prophet who would preach to the Arabs a message essentially identical to the one that their respective prophets had preached to them. For all the prophets preached to the idolaters and pagans of their respective times the same message of a return to the original religion of submission to the One God. However, already in the Meccan context of the qur'ānic revelation, the Qur'ān notes the existence of divisive groups within the one community of the prophets. These groups are neither identified nor considered by the Qur'ān as separate communities but as sects, *aḥzāb*. For the existence of separate, exclusivist communities among those who have received the

Scripture would be a contradiction to the reason for which the prophets were sent. The one *umma* at the time of Abraham is thus cited by the Qurʾān as a model of the unity of the *umma*.

In the Medinan context of the qurʾānic revelation, the *aḥzāb* in the Meccan context are recognized as separate religious communities, each with a particular rite and way of life. The presence in Medina of Jewish and Christian groups, who were not only mutually exclusive but would neither recognize Muhammad as the prophet for his group, occasioned the unfolding of the Qurʾān's teaching on how the ideal of one community of humankind may be achieved in such and similar situations. Religious groups that are now considered independent communities are to vie with one another in good works. It is in the context of a multi-religious community world that the Muslim community is established as a separate community.

The Muslim community is an *umma*, just as the other religious communities (Jews, Christians, Ṣābians, etc.) are each an *umma* too. The specialness of the Muslims does not necessarily consist in their submission to the One God. The other religious communities are precisely each an *umma* too because of this basic submission to God. Neither does their specialness lie in their having particular rites in connection with the *Kaʿba* because God has provided for each religious community a proper rite. What makes the Muslim community an *umma* in a special sense is their *ḥanīf* way, i.e., the religious attitude originally intended by God, given with the human nature, the expression of which includes or results in the recognition of the equality of all revelations. Thus they recognize the equality of the revelations received by Jesus, Moses and all the other prophets. This is something which the Jews and Christians lack and for which reason the one *umma* of the prophets has been ruptured. It is in its being *ḥanīf* that the Muslim community becomes the preserver of the original *umma wāḥida* of the prophets. Thus in a world of various *umam*, the Muslim community is The *Umma*. Its existence is a constant invitation to the other religious communities to adopt the *ḥanīf* way of submitting to the One God, so that they may recognize all the prophets, including Muhammad, while they continue with the worship or rituals particular to their respective communities.

The Qurʾān postpones the final resolution of the differences of these religious communities to the day when all will return to God, for then God Himself will inform them regarding that in which they had differed (5:48) and will bring unity among them (42:13-15). What the Qurʾān emphasizes is the task of calling back all the worshippers of idols and unbelievers, to the worship of the One God. In this regard, all religious communities, being now recognized as each an *umma*, are asked to vie with one another in works of goodness and righteousness, so that the whole of humankind may become a community of communities of goodness, worshipping the One God each in its own particular way. In this competition, the Muslim *umma* is to be distinguished from the others by their being *ḥanīf*, i.e. not exclusivist, and by their being *wasaṭ*, i.e., not extremist. For their faith in God and their works of goodness and righteousness, the Qurʾān, consequently, has described the Muslims as the best *umma*. (Statements like this enabled *umma* to come to mean almost exclusively the Muslim community, although the term in the Qurʾān is not limited to the best religious community). This eminence of the Muslims, as we have seen in our study of the *umma* verses, is based only and exclusively on God's guidance met with their faith and obedience. Also in other places in the Qurʾān (47:38; 9:38; 5:54), the Muslims are warned that If they turn their backs on this teaching, God will substitute another people for them.

The overall picture, therefore, that the *umma* verses of the Qurʾān present, may be summarized as follows: (1) A true religious community or *umma* is one which adores the One God and commits to works of justice and righteousness, i.e., it is an *umma muslima*. (2) *Umma* does not apply only to the Muslim, Jewish and Christian communities but also to any other which bears the same Islamic values of adoring the One God and committing to works of justice and righteousness (as is also echoed in other places in the Qur'ān, i.e., 2:62; 2:112; 5:69). (3) The Qur'ān thus presents an "interreligious" project of bringing out these Islamic values in all religions. (4) The Muslim community has been established as the standard-bearer of this "inter-religious" project of the Qur'ān. (5) The carrying out of this project does not necessarily mean one has to adopt the institutionalized religion of Islam but to adopt the Islamic values, i.e., to adore and serve the One God and to commit to works of goodness and justice. In this way, one is a *muslim*, not in the sense of being a follower of the historical Islamic religion but in the sense of one who lives the basic sense of *islām* or submission to God. The Qur'ān itself testifies that before the institutionalized religion of Islam, there were already *muslims*: Abraham was a *muslim* (2:131; 3:67; 4:125) and the disciples of Jesus were *muslims* (5:111).

3. *Ummī* - A Related Qur᾿ānic Term

The qur᾿ānic term *ummī* is difficult to interpret precisely. The traditional Muslim interpretation of this term has been much questioned by modern scholars. As this term is in some way connected with the word *umma*, we have to deal with it here. We will first take the qur᾿ānic texts as they are and see what they tell us about *ummī*; next we will see how this term has been interpreted by the classical commentators; and, finally, we will look into how this term has been interpreted by modern scholars.

3.1 The *Ummī* Verses

The term *ummī* appears six times in the Qur᾿ān, twice as an epithet of Muhammad as *nabīy*, "prophet" (in 7:157-158), and four times in the form *ummīyūn* (in 2:78, 3:20, 3:75 and 62:2). All these verses are Medinan.[206]

وَمِنْهُمْ أُمِّيُّونَ لا يَعْلَمُونَ ٱلْكِتَابَ إِلا أَمَانِىَّ وَإِنْ هُمْ إِلا
يَظُنُّونَ.

Some of them are *ummīyūn* who do not know the Scripture except from hearsay. They but guess. (2:78)

....وَقُل لِّلَّذِينَ أُوتُوا۟ ٱلْكِتَابَ وَٱلْأُمِّيِّينَ ءَأَسْلَمْتُمْ فَإِنْ أَسْلَمُوا۟
فَقَدِ ٱهْتَدَوا۟ ...

Say unto those who have received the Scripture and the *ummīyūn*: "Have you surrendered yourselves?" If they have

---

[206] For the explanation of our classification as Medinan of 7:157 &158, see above, page 17, note 6.

surrendered themselves, then they have let themselves be guided...(3:20).

وَمِنْ أَهْلِ الكِتَابِ مَنْ إِنْ تَأْمَنْهُ بِقِنطَارٍ يُؤَدِّهِ إِلَيْكَ وَمِنْهُم مَنْ إِن تَأْمَنْهُ بِدِينَارٍ لا يُؤَدِّهِ إِلَيْكَ إِلا مَا دُمْتَ عَلَيْهِ قَائِماً ذَالِكَ بِأَنَّهُمْ قَالُوا لَيْسَ عَلَيْنَا فِي الأُمِّيِّنَ سَبِيلٌ وَيَقُولُونَ عَلَى اللَّهِ الكَذِبَ وَهُمْ يَعْلَمُونَ.

Among the People of the Scripture there is he who, if one entrusts him with a talent, will pay it back; but among them there is he who, if one entrusts him with a *dīnār*, will not pay it back, except so long as one remains standing over him. That is because they say: "We have no duty in regard to the *ummīyūn*." They speak falsehood about God, knowingly. (3:75).

هُوَ الَّذِى بَعَثَ فِي الأُمِّيِّنَ رَسُولاً مِنْهُمْ يَتْلُواْ عَلَيْهِمْ ءَايَاتِهِ.....

He it is who has raised up among the *ummīyūn* a messenger, one of themselves, to recite to them His signs....(62:2).

الَّذِينَ يَتَّبِعُونَ الرَّسُولَ النَّبِيَّ الأُمِّيَّ الَّذِي يَجِدُونَهُ مَكْتُوباً عِنْدَهُمْ فِي التَّوراةِ وَالإِنْجِيلِ.

Those who follow the messenger, the *ummī* Prophet, whom they find mentioned [written] in the Torah and the Gospel [which are] with them. (7:157).

فَـَٔامِنُواْ بِاللَّهِ وَرَسُولِهِ النَّبِيِّ الأُمِّيِّ...

So believe in God and His messenger, the *ummī* Prophet (7:158).

An analysis of the above-quoted passages, without a preconceived idea of what *ummī/ummīyūn* means, will give us the following data: in 2:78 the *ummīyūn* are those who do not know the Scripture except through hearsay and conjecture; in 3:20 and 3:75 they are contrasted with the People of the Scripture; in 62:2 God has sent to the *ummīyūn* their prophet who is from among themselves; in 7:157-158, this prophet is described as the *ummī* Prophet. In accordance with most of these passages, *ummīyūn* is the antithesis of "People of the Scripture." But the occurrence in 2:78 makes one ask in what sense is it an antithesis. Thus the question is how to explain *ummī* in such a way that it becomes relevant to all its occurrences.

3.2 *Ummī* in Classical Muslim Exegesis

Ṭabarī's collection of interpretations on the meaning of *ummī/ummīyūn* can be grouped as follows. The first interpretation - which is traced back to Ibn ʿAbbās on the authority of Ibn Jubayr - is that "the *ummīyūn* are those who have no Scripture."[207] In line with this interpretation, *ummīyūn* in 2:78 - also according to Ibn ʿAbbās, as transmitted by al-Ḍaḥḥāk and quoted by Abū Rawq - is seen as referring to people among the Jews who did not accept the Scriptures of God and His messengers:

عن أبى روق، عن الضحاك، عن إبن عباس (ومنهم أميون) قال:
الأميون قوم لم يصدّقوا رسولا أرسله الله، ولا كتابا أنزله الله...
سماهم أميين لجحودهم كتب الله ورسله.

Among them are *ummīyūn* - the *ummīyūn* were people who did not believe any apostle sent by God, nor any Scripture revealed by God... [God] called them *ummīyūn*

207 Ṭabarī (on 3:20, vol. 3) 215 = ".الذين لا كتاب لهم"

because of their rejection of the Scriptures of God and His messengers.[208]

In the rest of the passages the reference is to all non-Jew, non-Christian, and in particular the pagan Arabs, to whom no Scripture has been given from heaven.[209] A second interpretation, also traced back to Ibn ʿAbbās on the authority of Ibn Jurayj, says that the *ummīyūn* are those who do not write[210] (الذين لا يكتبون) or who do not write well,[211] (منهم من لا يحسن ان يكتب) which refers to some of the Jews in 2:78 and to the Arabs in the other passages. A third interpretation is that the *ummīyūn* are those who do not read the Scripture[212] (لا يقرءون لاكتاب) which again refers to some among the Jews in 2:78 and to the Arabs in the other passages.[213] A fourth interpretation, which Ṭabarī says is his interpretation, is that the *ummīyūn* are those who can neither read nor write.[214] To support his view, Ṭabarī says that the Prophet himself said: ."إنّا أمّة أمّيّة لا نكتب و لا نحسب". It is for this reason, Ṭabarī concludes, that Muhammad is designated as the "*Ummī* Prophet."[215]

---

208 Ṭabarī (on 2:78, vol. 1) 374.

209 Cfr. Ṭabarī (on 3:20, vol. 3) 214f; (on 3:75, vol. 3) 319; (on 62:2, vol. 28) 94; (on 7:157-158, vol. 9) 83f.

210 Ṭabarī (on 3:20, vol. 3) 215.

211 Ṭabarī (on 2:78, vol. 1) 373.

212 Ibid., and (on 62:2, Book 1) 94.

213 Cfr. Ibid., and (on 62:2, vol. 28) 94.

214 Ṭabarī (on 2:78, vol. 1) 373.

215 Ibid.

In his analysis of the authority statements contained in the *tafsīr* of Ṭabarī, together with works of *tafsīr* from the first century not used by Ṭabarī in connection with the illiteracy interpretation, Goldfeld[216] has shown that

> . . . none of the scholars of the first century referred to the illiteracy of the Arabs or of the Prophet at all, while this concept gradually evolved during the first half of the second century, especially around the figures of Ibn Jurayj and Saʿīd b. Abū ʿArūba, as well as al-Kalbī and Muqātil b. Sulaymān. We have also shown that well to the end of the second century of the *Hijra* the lexical definition of *ummīyūn* was not absolutely and univocally "illiterates," putting forward the assumption that the noun acquired this sense during the third century of the *Hijra*.[217]

The significance of this finding may lie in the fact that independent source material from the first phase of Muslim exegetical activity is virtually non-existent, that what we know about them is from works from the middle of the second century AH at the earliest,

---

216 I. Goldfeld, "The Illiterate Prophet (Nābī Ummī): An Inquiry into the Development of a Dogma in Islamic Tradition" in *Der Islam* 57 (1980) 58-67.

217 Ibid., 67. Ibn Jurayj and Saʿīd b. Abū ʿArūba are quoted by Ṭabarī in connection with the *ummī/ummīyūn* verses. N. Calder, "The *Ummī* in Early Islamic Juristic Literature" in *Der Islam* 67 (1990) 111-124, tries to show that the idea of illiteracy did not dominate the exegesis of the *ummī* passages starting in the third century AH and mentions as counter examples, Zamaḫšarī and Al-Jalalāyn, among others, on 3:20 and 3:75. (Ibid., 112, note 2). It seems to me, however, that Calder does not distinguish between the meaning and the reference of the word. Al-Jalalāyn for instance, as will be shown in our subsequent analysis, indicates the references of the term in all its occurrences but he explains its meaning in 62:2 (i.e., illiterate).

that claim to contain the exegesis of earlier authorities.[218]

In Zamaḫšarī, *ummīyūn* in 2:78 are those of the Jews who cannot write well, so that they consult the Torah to verify its contents[219] - "لا يحسنون الكتب فيطالعوا التوراة ويتحققوا ما فيها". In 3:20 the term refers to the pagan Arabs who don't have a Scripture.[220] On 62:2, Zamaḫšarī writes:

> {بَعَثَ فِي الأمِّيِّينَ رَسُولاً مِنْهُم} بعث رجلا أميا فِي قوم أميين كما جاء في حديث شعياء. إنى أبعث أعمى في عميان وأمى في أميين ، وقيل منهم كقوله تعالى – من أنفسكم – يعلمون نسبه وأحواله .... {يتلوا عليهم آياته} يقرؤها عليهم مع كونه أميا مثلهم لم تعهد منه قراءة ولم يعرف بتعلم ، وقراءة أمى بغير تعلم آية بينة.

> He has sent to the *ummīyūn* a messenger from among themselves," i.e., He has sent an *ummī* man among a tribe of *ummī*, just as it is said in *ḥadīṯ šaʿyā*.[221] "I am sent as a blind [messenger] to the blind, and an *Ummī* [Prophet] to the *ummī* people." And it is said "one of them" as in God's saying - "one of yourselves (9:128)" - i.e., they know his origin and his status......."to recite to them His signs," i.e., to recite it to them in spite of his being an *ummī* like them.

---

218 See below, page 173, note 3.

219 Zamaḫšarī (on 2:78, Book 1) 291.

220 Zamaḫšarī (on 3:20, Book 1) 438.

221 Lazarus-Yafeh, in her inquiry into the biblical texts read by Muslims as predictions of the coming of Muhammad, points out the employment of linguistic play, between *aʿmā* ("blind") and *ummī*, in this *ḥadīṯ* which seems to be a Muslim reading of Isaiah 42:7. Cfr. H. Lazarus-Yafeh, *Intertwined Worlds* (Princeton: University Press, 1992) 108-109.

> Reading was not familiar to him and he did not have education. Thus a reading/recitation of clear verses by an *ummī*, without education.[222]

For Zamaḫšarī, therefore, *ummīyūn* when used to refer to some of the Jews (2:78) means partial illiteracy, i.e., those who cannot read nor write well; and when used to refer to the Arabs, means those who don't have a Scripture (3:20) and, more essentially, absolutely illiterate (62:2). Accordingly, despite being an *ummī* himself like the rest of the Arabs, the Prophet Muhammad was able to recite the Qurʾān to his people - he is thus called صاحب المعجزات or "the master of miracles."[223]

Rāzī follows Ṭabarī closely in his interpretation of *ummīyūn* as absolutely illiterate whether in reference to some of the Jews or to the Arabs as a whole *umma*. Thus, in reference to some of the Jews in 2:78, he says:

> الذين لا معرفة عندهم بقراءة ولا كتابة وطريقتهم التقليد وقبول ما يقال لهم.

> They are those who don't possess the knowledge of reading or of writing, and their way is a blind following of tradition and acceptance of whatever is said to them.[224]

In reference to the Arabs, Rāzī says,

> الأمي منسوب إلى أمة العرب، لما أنهم أمة أميون لا كتاب لهم، ولا يقرأون كتاباً ولا يكتبون.

---

[222] Zamaḫšarī (on 62:2, Book 4) 102.

[223] Zamaḫšarī (on 7:157, Book 2) 122.

[224] Rāzī (on 2:78, vol. 3) 138.

ummī is a description of their *umma* since they were an *umma* of illiterate people: they had no Scripture, they could not read a scripture nor could they write.[225]

Thus, because of his origin, the Prophet is described as an *ummī*, "illiterate" Prophet. To support his view, Rāzī quotes the same saying of the Prophet about the illiteracy of the Arab *umma* that is quoted by Ṭabarī (see above).[226]

Ibn Kaṯīr also says:

والأميون جمع أمي وهو الرجل الذي لا يحسن الكتابة.

Ummīyūn is the plural of *ummī*, that is, the man who is not familiar with writing.[227]

Accordingly, in 2:78 this refers to some of the Jews while in the other passages the Arabs are referred to.[228]

Al-Jalālayn's very brief commentary mentions the references of the term in the different passages: the common people (العوام) among the Jews in 2:78; the Arabs in 3:20, 3:75 and 62:2; and Muhammad in 7:157-8, and explains that

ولأمي: من لا يكتب ولايقرأ كتاباً

225 Rāzī (on 62:2, vol. 30) 3.

226 Rāzī (on 7:157, vol. 15) 23.

227 Ibn Kaṯīr (on 2:78, Book 1) 81.

228 Cfr. Ibn Kaṯīr (on 2:78, Book 1) 81 and (on 3:20, Book 1) 272; (on 3:75, Book 1) 292; (on 7:157, Book 2) 55.

ummī is one who cannot write and cannot read a scripture.[229]

Based on our foregoing considerations, we agree with Goldfeld that the general tendency[230] (especially among commentators who are highly esteemed by Sunnī Muslims) since the time of Ṭabarī, has been to interpret *ummī/ummīyūn* as illiterate[231] and to emphasize the illiteracy of the Prophet. Generally, Muslim scholars derive *ummī* from *umm* (mother). The explanations for this are found in most of the commentaries that are primary references for our study.[232] They are summarized in Rāzī's *tafsīr* as follows:

---

[229] Al-Jalālayn (on 62:2) 741.

[230] The Muslim scholar K. ʿAthamina, "Al-Nabiyy al-Umiyy: An Inquiry Into the Meaning of a Qurʾānic Verse" in *Der Islam* 69 (1992) 61-80, has also pointed out several early scholars within the Sunnī circle, who did not share the "illiterate" interpretation of *ummī*. Within the Šīʿī tradition, on the other hand, the "illiterate" interpretation is rejected especially as an epithet of Muhammad because, according to them, this argument contradicts the teachings of the Qurʾān. For them, *ummī/ummīyūn* simply refers to the inhabitants of Mecca which in the Qurʾān (see 6:92 and 42:7) are referred to as "umm al-qurā" (the mother of the cities).

[231] Of the Muslim English translations of the Qurʾān, an example of the illiterate interpretation is the translation by M. Asad (*The Message of the Qurʾān* (Gibraltar: Dar Al-Andalus, 1980) where he renders *ummī* in all its occurrences as "unlettered." On the other hand, A. A. K. Jullundri (*The Glorious Holy Qurʾān* (Lahore: Ripon Press, 1962) renders *ummī* in 2:78 as illiterate while in all the other occurrences he interprets it *[ummīyūn]* as referring to the inhabitants of Mecca, thus including Muhammad, who were not illiterate and ignorant. Ibid., p. 314, note 157.

[232] Cfr., for instance, Ṭabarī (on 2:78, Book 1) 374 and Ibn Kaṯīr (on 2:78, Book 1) 81.

[الأمى] منسوب إلى الأم ، وسمى النبى صلى اللّه عليه وسلم أمياً قيل لأنه كان لا يكتب وذلك لأن الأم أصل الشئ فمن لا يكتب فقد بقى على أصله فى أن لا يكتب ، وقيل : نسب إلى مكة وهى أم القرى.

> The *ummī* is ascribed to the mother, and the Prophet is called *ummī*. It is said that it is because he could not write and that is because the mother is the origin of the thing [i.e., of the illiteracy]. Thus "he who cannot write" remains within this basic meaning in that he cannot write. It is also said that it refers to Mecca because it is the mother of cities.[233]

Looking at our considerations thus far, we see two positions regarding the meaning of *ummī* according to the Muslims. First, and the main one, is that it means illiterate; this position is supported by the *ummī-umm* connection as well as by a *ḥadīṯ* attributed to the Prophet. The second one is that the term simply means Meccan by reference to 6:92 and 42:7 in which Mecca is referred to as *umm al- qurā*. This second one may sound logical but it cannot explain the usage of the term in 2:78. The *ummī-umm* explanation hardly needs any careful examination, "it is not only groundless; it is also arbitrary."[234] The "illiterate" interpretation is not confirmed by the qurʾānic usage of *ummī/ummīyūn* nor by the situation which existed both in Mecca and in the other settled and nomadic sectors of the Arabian peninsula on the eve of Islam. "The situation of the Arabs *vis-à-vis* their literacy was no different during the *jāhilīya* period preceding Islam than it was after the advent of Islam. The Qurayš, the inhabitants of Mecca, were

---

233 Rāzī (on 3:75, vol. 8) 102.

234 K. ʿAthamina, "Al-Nabiyy al-Umiyy: An Inquiry into the Meaning of a Qurʾānic Verse" in *Der Islam* 69 (1992) 67.

generally literate in comparison with the inhabitants of Medina."[235] In regard to the saying attributed to the Prophet which says "we are an *umma ummīya,*[236] we do not write and we do not count *[naḥsib]*" (see above, in Ṭabarī and Rāzī) it seems to have been quoted out of context. On the other hand, *sīra* works[237] that are cited to support the "illiterate" interpretation have been discovered to be reworks of the original with additional explanations and interpretations based on the exegetical position of "illiteracy." Thus they do not really provide external evidence of the exegetical finding but a promulgation of the exegetical position.

---

[235] Ibid., pp. 68-69. ʿAthamina cites here al-Suyūṭī, *al-Muzhir*, ed. M. Jād al-Mawlā et al. (Cairo: n. d.) II, 344 and Ibn Saʿd, *Kitāb al-ṭabaqāt al-kabī r*, ed. E. Sachau (Leiden, 1917) II (part 1) 14.

[236] This saying is found in al-Bukhari, *Ṣaḥiḥ* (ed. Beirut, 1978) III, p. 35, and the context is the calculation of dates for commencement and termination of the month-long fast of Ramaḍān. "The impression from the context of this *ḥadīṯ*, however, is that the verb *naktub* has nothing whatsoever to do with the art of writing; rather the interpretation is that we as Muslims must not fix the fast to begin on a fixed date.... Evidence for this interpretation may be found in the denotation of the root "k-t-b" in the classical lexicons. The latter include for this root the meaning of "to tie," as in tying the legs of an animal. The verb is used in the sense in various forms of classical Arabic poetry." K. ʿAthamina, "Al-Nabiy Al-Ummiy" in *Der Islam 69*, p. 68.

[237] For a discussion on this, see K. ʿAthamina, Ibid., 72-74 and I. Goldfeld, "The Illiterate Prophet" in *Der Islam* 57, 62-63. Here we cite one of the many examples cited by ʿAthamina: "As for the first revelation of the Prophet, Ibn Ishaq reports that the angel Gabriel commanded the Prophet, saying: 'Recite/Read!', and the Prophet replied: 'What shall I read'?" In a later *sīra* work al-Sīra al-ḥalabiyya, I, 384, this is quoted with addition as follows: "...Gabriel said: 'Read! and I said: 'I do not know how to read,' i.e., 'I am *ummī* who do not know how to read,' i.e., the written document,' I do not read at all." K. ʿAthamina, op. cit., 72-73.

3.3 *Ummī/ummīyūn* in Modern Scholarship

Early non-Muslim scholarship tended to accept without careful examination the interpretation "*ummī* = illiterate" which was dominant in Sunnī Muslim circles.[238] However, since non-Muslim scholars began to apply modern criticism to qurʾānic studies, it is generally agreed that the *ummī* verses in the Qurʾān do not convey the meaning of "illiterate" and the discussion centers on the correct interpretation of the verses and the origin of the term. The starting point of the ensuing debate may be said to be the interpretation proposed in Nöldeke-Schwally which says that *ummī* cannot mean illiterate but, rather, indicates those who do not have (or know) the ancient Scriptures.[239] Thus, in this case, when referring to Jews in 2:78 it means ignorant insiders and in the other passages, it means pagan outsiders. It is suggested that *ummī* was derived from *umma* in the same manner that in Greek *laikos* (lay) is derived from *laos* (people) or the Aramaic *ʿālmāyā* (secularis) from *ʿālma* (mundus, seculum) with the explanation: "The Jews call the people who are ignorant of the Scriptures and of the Law, or who are not sufficiently well-versed therein, *ʿam hā-*

---

[238] It is, for instance, the interpretation followed by George Sale in his English translation of the Qurʾān (*The Koran: commonly called the Al-Koran of Mohammed*) which first appeared at London in 1734; it is based on the Muslim commentators, especially al-Bayḍāwī, and accompanied by a Preliminary Discourse which includes, among other topics, a summary of previous non-Muslim scholarship on the Qurʾān. T. Nöldeke, basing himself on the interpretation by the Muslim Tradition as well as the prevailing low estimate of the Arabian culture, also accepted the "illiterate" interpretation in his prize-winning work *Geschichte des Qorans*, published at Gottingen in 1860. A revised edition of this book by Nöldeke's pupil F. Schwally, appeared in 1909.

[239] T. Nöldeke/F. Schwally, *Geschichte des Qorans* (Leipzig: Dieterich'sche Verlagsbuchhandlung, 1909) 14.

āreṣ."[240] Several scholars have demonstrated the unsatisfactoriness of the Nöldeke/Schwally interpretation[241] but the ones worth mentioning here would be, first of all, Horovitz who says: "We are not concerned with a contrast between the "ḥābêr" or the "talmid ḥākām" and the "ʿam hā-āreṣ" but with a contrast between Israel and the "ummōt hā-ʿōlām."[242] Thus he explains:

In 62:2 God is praised for having raised among the *ummī-*

---

[240] "Die Juden nennen das der Schrift und des Gesetzes unkundige oder nicht genügend kundige Volk *ʿam hā-āreṣ.*" Ibid. Prior to Nöldeke/Schwally, A. Geiger *(Was hat Mohammed aus dem Judenthume aufgenommen?* (Bonn: F. Baaden, 1833, p. 28) had already suggested the *laikos* interpretation and was criticized by Fleischer who, instead, proposed the interpretation "communal" because for him the distinction within the *umma* is not between the religiously learned and the others but between the ignorant common people and the learned aristocracy or leaders, so that "communal" for him would be a simple member as distinguished from the leader. For him the parallel to *umma-ummī* would be "Gemeinde" = *umma* and "gemein" = *ummī.* H. L. Fleischer (*Kleinere Schriften* (Leipzig: Verlag von S. Hirzel, 1888) 115. People in the sense of "laity" or "layman" is not conveyed neither by the Arabic *umma* nor by the Hebrew *ummā* nor by the Aramaic *ummetā.* Fleischer's view on the other hand falls out of the qurʾānic context as it fails to explain the contrast with the People of the Scripture nor does the term *umma* convey the distinction he proposes.

[241] For instance, Torrey *(The Jewish Foundation of Islam* (New York: Jewish Institute of Religion Press, 1933) p. 38), criticizes Nöldeke/Schwally saying, among other things, that *ummī* cannot be derived from *ʿam hā-āres,* and that *ummī* is simply a transfer into Arabic of the Hebrew *gôi, gôyīm;* but this scholar does not explain the etymology of *ummī.* A. Geiger had suggested the semantic similarity of *ummī* and *gôi* in his *Judaism and Islam* (New York: KTAV Publishing House, Inc., 1970 edition) 20.

[242] J. Horovitz, "Jewish Proper Names and Derivatives in the Qurʾān" in *Hebrew Union College Annual,* vol. 2 (Hildesheim: Georg Olms, 1964) 190.

yūn a prophet who was from among them, and for this reason Muhammad calls himself *"an-nabī al-ummī"* in 7:157-158, because he came from the ranks of the Arabs, i.e., from one of the *ummōt hā-ʿōlām,* and not from Israel. In 3:20 and 3:75 likewise the *ummīyūn,* i.e., the adherents of the *ummōt hā-ʿōlām,* are contrasted with those whose communities had in previous times already been deemed worthy of divine revelation (الّذين أوتوا الكتاب).[243]

When sūra 2:78 refers to the *ummīyūn min ahl al-kitāb,* the reference is most probably to originally pagan Arabs who had adopted Judaism.[244]

Thus for Horovitz, the derivation of *ummī* from *ummōt hā-ʿōlām* fits all the qurʾānic passages. The term refers to non-Jews and more, to peoples, in this particular case the Arabs, who have not received a messenger and a Scripture.

Wensinck sees a very close relation between the terms *umma* and *ummī. Umma* means "people" and, seen in a purely religious sense, means "community." When *umma* is used in the profane sense, it means *ethnos*[245] and *ummī* means *ethnikos.* "When Muhammad called himself *ummī,* he meant thereby that he was the Arabian prophet of the Gentiles, speaking to the Gentiles

---

243 Ibid., 190-191.

244 J. Horovitz, "Nabī" in *Shorter Encyclopedia of Islam*, ed. H. A. R. Gibb and J. H. Kramers (Leiden/New York: E. J. Brill, 1991) 428. This explanation for 2:78 is a later idea of Horovitz. The first time he proposed the *ummōt hā-ʿōlām* explanation for *ummī,* he regarded *ummīyūn* in 2:78 as an exception and explained it as perhaps based on *ʿam hā-āreṣ.* Cfr. . Horovitz, "Jewish Proper Names..., 191.

245 Thus, already A. Sprenger *(The Life of Muhammad* (Allahabad, 1851) 101.

to whom no Apostle had ever been sent before."[246]

Post Horovitz comments[247] by scholars show a distinct tendency to assume that *ummī* is more likely to be related to *ummōt hā-ʿōlām* than to *ʿam hā-āreṣ*, although the interpretations of 2:78 vary. Guillaume, like Horovitz, sees the usage of *ummīyūn* in 2:78 as in line with its use in the rest of the passages.[248] He sees *ummīyūn* in 2:78 as not Jews in the full sense of the word but Jewish proselytes or gentiles, particularly pagan Arabs, who had converted to Judaism and who knew nothing about the Torah

---

[246] A. J. Wensinck, *The Muslim Creed: Its Genesis and Historical Development* (Cambridge: Cambridge University Press, 1932) 6. Wensinck adds: "His [Muhammad's] feelings are the same as those of St. Paul, when he writes to the Romans: "I speak to you Gentiles inasmuch as I am the Apostle of the Gentiles (Romans 11:13)." Ibid.

[247] C. Rabin writes in 1957 that the phrase *al-nabī al-ummī* "has long been recognized to mean the gentile prophet derived from the Hebrew *ummôt hā-ôlām*," and he refers to Horovitz. He, however, maintains that *ummīyūn* in 2:78 is probably from ʿam hā-āreṣ. C. Rabin, *Qumran Studies* (Oxford: Oxford University Press, 1957) 123-125.

[248] Guillaume claims that his position is based on three things: 1) that among the authorities cited by Ṭabarī for the explanation of *illā amānīya* is Ibn Zayd who explained: "They lied and said: "We belong to the People of the Scripture," and they were not of them." (Ṭabarī on 2:78, vol. 1, p. 375); 2) that if one reads 2:1-78, the natural conclusion is that the *ummīyūn* are Jewish proselytes, pagan Arabs who have converted to Judaism; 3) that *amānīya* is one of the possible forms of the plurals of *āmīn* or *amīn* - a common word in Jewish, Christian and Muslim worship. Thus, he suggests that 2:78 be translated: "And some of them are gentiles who know nothing of the Scripture (i.e., the Torah) but the "Amens." They only think that they do." For a full presentation of Guillaume's view, see: A. Guillaume, "The Meaning of Amānīya in Sūra 2:78" in *The World of Islam: Studies in Honor of Philip K. Hitti*, ed. J. Kritzeck and R. Bayly Winder (London: MacMillan and Co. Ltd., 1960) 41-47.

but the most elementary words, i.e., the Amens. Guillaume arrives at this conclusion by a study of the wider context of 2:78 as well as an analysis of the term *amānīya* as used in this passage and with the help of some of the classical commentaries. The Muslim scholar K. ʿAthamina also considers *ummīyūn* in 2:78 as a group actually identified with the *ahl al-kitāb* but are to be distinguished from the general category of the *ahl al-kitāb* by virtue of their being *ummīyūn*. He provides evidences from Muslim and non-Muslim literature which show that - as Guillaume has asserted - many of the Jews of Medina and its periphery did not originate from the House of Israel. Many of them were converts to Judaism from Arab tribes. However, for him the main common denominator linking the two groups which share the same epithet *ummīyūn* is their identical religious conception, which is, that they are people who reject the Holy Scriptures.[249] At most this interpretation may be relevant only to 2:78 as the other passages do not convey the meaning of "rejection" of the Scriptures.

The position of Bell-Watt shows an acceptance of the views of Horovitz and Wensinck. He says it is "virtually certain that *ummī* means non-Jewish or gentile, and that it is derived from the Hebrew phrase *ummōt hā-ʿōlām*, 'the peoples of the world.' The use of the word by Arabs could also be influenced by the

---

249 ʿAthamina explains this by citing one of the explanations for *illā amānīya* given by Ṭabarī which is attributed to Ibn ʿAbbās, and which says that this phrase means *illā aḥādīṯ*, which he says is the plural of *uḥdūṯa* which means a tale designed to entertain, to satirize, so that 2:78 for him would be translated: "A group from among the *ahl al-kitāb* are *ummīyūn* who consider the Holy Scriptures to be merely tales and fables, nothing more nor less." This attitude, he says, was the same attitude of the opponents of Muhammad in Mecca who disputed him. This view, he says, is supported by an additional interpretation, attributed by Ṭabarī to Ibn ʿAbbās, according to which *ummīyūn* are so-called because they did not recognize the Holy Scriptures and disputed the mission of the Prophet. Cfr. K. ʿAthamina, An Inquiry Into the Meaning of a Qurʾānic Verse.... 65-66.

possibility of taking it as meaning belonging to the *umma* or community.... that is, belonging to the Arab community."[250] Likewise, Rudy Paret, in his commentary on the Qur᾿ān, prefers the positions of Horovitz and Wensinck and translates *ummī* as "Heide."[251]

In a very recent article,[252] Calder tries to revitalize the argument that *ummī* is derived from *ʿam hā-āreṣ*. Accordingly, in an early Muslim juristic literature,[253] *ummī* is used to describe a Muslim who is ignorant of Scripture, or, more precisely, a Muslim who is incapable of even that small quantity of recitation which is the minimum necessary for prayer. *Ummī* is here the functional opposite of *qāri᾿*. Thus, accordingly, while in 2:78 the reference is to Jews ignorant of Scripture, in Muslim juristic literature it refers likewise to those ignorant of Scripture among the members of the Muslim community. It is an Arabic Muslim naturalization of the Rabbinic concept of *ʿam hā-āreṣ* in its meaning of a Jew ignorant of the Scripture. The rest of the usages of *ummī* which refer to non-Jews are to be derived from one of the biblical meanings of *ʿam hā-āreṣ,* especially in the plural *(ʿamme hā-āreṣ/hā--ārasot)* i.e., non-Jews. Calder claims that "biblical usage of *ʿam hā-āreṣ* was not lost in spite of the developing semantic equation *am hā-āreṣ* = ignorant (of purity laws, of Torah)...... Rabbinic

---

250 W. M. Watt, ed. *Bell's Introduction to the Qur᾿ān* (Edinburgh: Edinburgh University Press, 1970) 34.

251 R. Paret, *Der Koran: Kommentar und Konkordanz* (Berlin: Verlag W. Kohlhammer, 1986) 22 and cfr. also R. Paret, "Ummī" in *Shorter Encyclopedia of Islam*, ed. H. A. R. Gibb and J. H. Kramers (Leiden/New York: E. J. Brill, 1991) 604.

252 N. Calder, "The *Ummī* in Early Islamic Juristic Literature" in *Der Islam* 67(1990) 111-124.

253 The text analyzed by Calder is accordingly from Muhammad b. Ḥasan al-Šaybānī, *Kitāb al-Aṣl,* vol. 1ed. A-W al-Afghānī (Hydarabad, 1386/ 1966) 185-189.

understanding of *ʿam hā-āreṣ*, in other words, included both the heathen outsiders and ignorant insiders, and, in this respect, it precisely parallels the Arabic Muslim usage of *ummī*.[254] Thus, he concludes,

> Arabic *ummī* is in all its usages (except of course the later development, *ummī* = illiterate) a reflex of Hebrew *ʿam hā-āreṣ*, meaning not only ignorant Jew (2:78), and non-Jew (+ non-Christian) but also, in its fully naturalized meaning, ignorant Muslim, ignorant, that is, of Scripture.[255]

Calder further explains that the transfer from Hebrew *ʿam* to Arabic *ummī* is to be understood not by the term "borrowing" but by the "diffusion of Rabbinic (and other) religious terminology within the increasingly Arabic-speaking 'sectarian milieu' of the 6th to 8th centuries" so that "since the transfer from Hebrew *ʿam* to Arabic *ummī* must be assumed to have taken place at a popular (colloquial?) level, the transition from a Hebrew *ʿayn* to Arabic *hamza* presents no insuperable linguistic problems."[256]

Calder's article may indeed attract further comments on the question of *ummī/ummīyūn* as the issue is by no means closed. Based on present scholarship, Calder's reference to *ʿam hā-āreṣ* in its early biblical meaning of non-Jews and the development of its usage in later times to mean a Jew ignorant of the Scripture as both in the use and in the context of the Arabic-speaking sectarian milieu of the 6th to 8th centuries, becomes difficult to accept when one considers that the nature of the "development" in the meaning was such that in the period when one was in use, the other was

---

[254] N. Calder, op. cit., 115.

[255] Ibid., 116.

[256] Ibid, for both quotations in this paragraph.

not.[257] Could they have been both in use in the context of the Arabic-speaking world of the 6th to 8th centuries? However, even if this point is conceded, the main difficulty in accepting the *ʿam hā-āreṣ* explanation would really be the question of how to satisfactorily explain the passage from *ʿayn* to *hamza*, considering the fact that *ʿayn* is a full consonant in the Semitic languages.

The position of Horovitz is still to be preferred, together with the explanations of Wensinck and Bell-Watt (as also Paret) regarding the possible connection between the two terms *ummī* and *umma*. If Guillaume's interpretation can be depended on, then it is an additional support for the use of the term in 2:78.

3.4 Conclusion

At the conclusion of this inquiry into the meaning of the qurʾānic term *ummī/ummīyūn*, we sum up the main points that we have discovered. First of all, the term does not really mean illiterate, and the Arabs as a group cannot really be described as illiterate, nor does the term properly describe Muhammad as illiterate in the contexts that we have examined. We also note that the "illiterate" interpretation started to appear only in the time of Ṭabarī, that interpretations attributed to the earliest authorities seem to concur basically with the finding of modern scholarship, that is, that *ummīyūn* means people who do not have (or do not know) the Scripture, except in the fact that modern scholarship sees a foreign derivation of the term. We also note that while it is a fact that *ummī* has been interpreted as meaning "illiterate" by traditional "orthodox" Sunnī Muslims, some Muslim scholars do not quite share the same interpretation.

The influence of the findings of modern scholarship may be

257 Cfr. "Am Ha-arez" in *Encyclopedia Judaica*, vol. 2 (Jerusalem: Keter Publishing House Ltd., 1973) 834-836.

seen in some recent translations into English of the Qur'ān by Muslims. In the 12th printing of Pickthall's English translation of the Qur'ān, *ummī* in 7:157-158 is rendered "the Prophet who can neither read nor write" but a footnote is added which says: "I give the usual rendering. Some modern criticism, while not denying the comparative illiteracy of the prophet, would prefer the rendering 'who is not of those who read the Scriptures' or 'gentile.'"[258] The English version of Mawdūdī's *Tafhīm al-Qur'ān* retains the word *ummī* and appends a note which says "reference to the Prophet in this verse as *ummī* is significant as the Israelites branded all other nations as Gentiles."[259] In the 1991 reprint of "The Qur'ān" by the Ahmadī scholar Khan, *al-nabī al-ummī* is translated as "the Prophet, the Immaculate One"[260] which is rather ambiguous.

Among the non-Muslim renderings of the term *ummī/ummī-yūn,* we find Paret's "heathen"[261] strange as this English term "is laden with images and ideas of "savages" and "pagans" and has overtones of barbarism"[262] which are not necessarily conveyed by the qur'ānic usage of *ummī.* Blachère's rendering "le prophète des Gentils,"[263] or "prophet of the Gentiles" is also inaccurate

---

[258] M. M. Pickthall, *The Meaning of the Glorious Koran* (New York: New American Library, 12th printing, 1953) 133.

[259] S. Aʿlā Mawdūdī, *Towards Understanding the Qur'ān,* vol. 3, trans. and ed. Z. I. Ansarī (Leicester: The Islamic Foundation, 1990) 86.

[260] M. Zafrulla Khan, *The Qur'ān* (Hungary: Curzon Press, 1991) 158.

[261] R. Paret, "Ummī" in *Shorter Encyclopedia of Islam*, ed. H. A. R. Gibb and J. H. Kramers (Leiden/New York: E. J. Brill, 1991) 604.

[262] F. Denny, "The Meaning of *Umma* in the Qur'ān" in *History of Religions* 15 (1975) 42. The German term *Heiden* (R. Paret, *Der Koran: Kommentar und Konkordanz* (Berlin: Verlag W. Kohlhammer, 1986) 22) means "Gentiles" and does not have the implications that the English "heathen" has. Ibid.

[263] R. Blachère, *Le Coran III* (Paris: Maisonneuve, 1950) 644.

because while it makes the point of contrast to Jews, it lacks the element that makes that contrast, namely, not having a Scripture. The same criticism would be true for Bell's "native prophet"[264] and Arberry's "prophet of the common folk."[265] Cragg prefers the translation "unlettered" but, although he explains that it is to be taken in the sense of "untutored" rather than "illiterate,"[266] it is still ambiguous if not tendentious. We prefer Izutsu's rendering "non-Scripture people"[267] or Denny's "unscriptured" because, although a clumsy term, it

> best serves as an expression which can differentiate the Arabs from the Jews and Christians, satisfy the requirements of the probable *ummōt hā-ʿōlām* etymology (which connects the term not only to *umma* proper, but also to "the nations" or "Gentiles"), and escape the harsher implications of the word "heathen," which Muhammad certainly could not have intended either as conscious irony or as description, especially when the Muslim community was taking on definite shape and character in Medina.[268]

The *ummī/ummīyūn* verses also reveal the scope of the mission of Muhammad. Based on our findings, he is then the

---

[264] R. Bell, *The Qur'ān Translated, with a Critical Rearrangement of the Sūras*, vol. 1, (Edinburgh: T. & T. Clark, 1960) 152.

[265] A. Arberry, *The Koran Interpreted* (Oxford: Oxford University Press, 1982) 162.

[266] K. Cragg, *Readings in the Qur'ān* (London: Collins Religious Publishing, 1993) 276 and, by the same author, *The Event of the Qur'ān: Islam in its Scripture* (London: George Allen & Unwin Ltd., 1971) 58.

[267] T. Izutsu, *God and Man in the Qur'ān* (Tokyo: The Keio Institute of Cultural and Linguistic Studies, 1964) 79.

[268] F. Denny, "The Meaning of *Umma* in the Qur'ān" in *History of Religions* 15 (1975) 42.

Prophet sent to all people (Arabs and others) who have not as yet received a Scripture as well as to those who only nominally belong (2:78) to any of the "scriptured" communities (Jewish, Christian, and others). Thus the mission of Muhammad covers a field wider than the Arab world, but not all of humankind. The Qurʾān recognizes some of the people of the Scripture as *umam*, as religious communities, and sees them as the ones with whom the *umma* of Muhammad will have to vie in works of goodness, so that in the end, this world will become one world, one community of communities of goodness.

4. Other Qurʾānic Terms For "Human Collectivity" or "Community."

The most important group or community term in the Qurʾān is *umma*. As used in the Qurʾān it is the kind of word that lends itself to new shades of meaning; and within a particular shade of meaning it is capable of a further subsequent development, the fullest and most important development of which is its designation of the Muslims as a special religious community. The Qurʾān also employs other terms which mean group or community and many of these terms are used in connection with *umma*. By way of ending this chapter, we devote a few pages to these terms in order to properly distinguish them from *umma*.

4.1 *Qawm*

Qawm is a pre-Islamic term occurring also in the Nabatean, Palmyrene and Ṣafaitic inscriptions in the name of the deity *Šayʿ al-Qawm*, "support of the people."[269] The first meaning of the word is men in opposition to women *(nisāʾ)*, then it came to mean men and women together, "for the *qawm* of every man is his *šīʿa* or party and his kinsfolk or tribe *(ʿašīra)*," or "the *qawm* of every prophet is of men and women."[270] "Used without the article, it has the same meaning as English "people," French "gens" and German "Leute."[271]

---

269 A. J. Wensinck, "Qawm" in *Encyclopedia of Islam*, new ed., vol. 4, ed. Gibbs and Kramers (Leiden: E. J. Brill, 1971) 780.

270 E. W. Lane, *Arabic-English Lexicon*, vol. 2 (Cambridge: The Islamic Texts Society, 1984 edition) 2996.

271 A. J. Wensinck, "Qawm" in *Encyclopedia of Islam*, new ed., vol. 4, ed. Gibbs and Kramers (Leiden: E. J. Brill, 1971) 780.

In the Qur'ān the word *qawm* appears a lot more times than *umma*. It is employed before the term *umma* begins to be put into use,[272] and continues to be used even after *umma* ceases to be mentioned.[273] In five passages *qawm* is employed in connection with *umma*: in 7:159-160 it refers to the people of Moses, in 7:164 to the Jews as a people, in 40:5 to the People of Noah and in 23:44 to unbelieving people in general. As in the foregoing, most of the usages of *qawm* are in connection with the prophets, i.e., as kinship or ethnic groups. In some of the term's early appearances before *umma*, there is a distinct religious reference: in 52:32 the Meccans who reject Muhammad are called an outrageous/ transgressing *qawm* (قَوْمٌ طاغُونَ) while in 69:7 a disobedient community destroyed by a whirlwind is described as a *qawm* thrown down (القَوْمَ فيها صَرْعَى). A rare instance of the use of *qawm* to denote people who are believers is found in a post *umma* passage[274] but there is no hint of a reference to the people as a community.

Some of the first usages of *umma* in the Qur'ān render it hardly distinguishable from *qawm*; every species of animals and birds is even said to be an *umma* (6:38).[275] However, even in such usages, the reference is not to their being a species or kinship or ethnic group but their being objects of divine judgment. Gradually, however, it becomes clear that *umma* refers to a group or community based on religion, until in the last instances it is applied almost exclusively to Muslim, Jewish and Christian comunities. On the other hand, *qawm* is used all along, and even after *umma*, to refer to kinship or ethnic groups of people.

---

[272] e.g.,38:12, 50:12, 54:9, 54:33, 53:52.

[273] e.g., 9:6, 9:13-14, 10:101.

[274] "He will heal the breasts of people who are believers." (9:14) = (يَشْفِ صُدُورَ قَومٍ مُؤْمِنِينَ)

[275] Cf. above, p. 29.

In its post-qurʾānic use, *qawm* continued to be the term which refers to a group of people having or claiming a common ancestor, or a tribe descending from a common ancestor. In modern times, in answer to the western concept of nation, *qawm* came to be the Arabic term and concept which means people with a common language, territory, ethnicity and history. Nationalism in Arabic would be *qawmiyya*. The sense of Arab nationalism or *qawmiyya* had its first stirrings as a reaction to Ottoman rule with its emerging Turkification program which emphasized Turkish ethnic and linguistic identity; but *al-qawmiyyat-l-ʿarabiyya* took shape as a reaction against European colonial rule which, among other things, carved out a number of modern nation-states out of the Arab world.

> In contrast to the traditional Islamic ideal in which political loyalty and solidarity rest in a transnational Islamic community *(umma)* based upon common belief, modern nationalism represented the notion of national communities based not upon religion but upon common language, territory, ethnic ties and history.[276]

As such, therefore, *al-qawmiyyat-l-ʿarabiyya* is secular in orientation and is seen as a bulwark against *waṭaniyya*, (not a qurʾānic term) i.e., particular nationalism or love of one's country or homeland.[277] At the same time, however, Arab nationalism and

---

[276] J. Esposito, *The Islamic Threat: Myth or Reality?* (New York/Oxford: Oxford University Press, 1992) 62.

[277] Among the more recent advocates of Arab nationalism were the Baʿath party of Syria (founded in 1943) and Gamal ʿAbd-l-Nasser of Egypt (1955). *Al-qawmiyyat-l-ʿarabiyya* was the ideology that paved the way for the union of Egypt and Syria in 1958 through the formation of the United Arab Republic, with Nasser elected as its first president. A Baʿthist coup in Iraq in 1963 seemed to signal the incorporation of these three major countries in a new Arab order. It was a shortlived promise. Ibid., 73.

the Muslim *umma* or *al-ummat-l-islamiyya* are intertwined because of linguistic, historical and religious affinity; for which reason, many Muslims (fundamentalists?) see the former only as an exigency of the present situation and a stepping-stone to the latter, i.e., the transnational Islamic community or Pan-Islamism.[278]

4.2 *Ḥizb* (pl. *aḥzāb*)

According to some lexicons, this term is, "in its primary acceptation, a party or company of men, assembling themselves on account of an event that has befallen them."[279] Thus, it means a faction, a group of supporters of a man who share his ideas and are ready to defend him. Among other meanings, it also means a part or portion, in which meaning the term may be borrowed from the Ethiopic according to Nöldeke, because it does not flow from the Arabic root which means "to happen (speaking of a

---

[278] Cfr. Abd al-Rahman al-Bazzaz, "Islam and Arab Nationalism" in *Arab Nationalism, An Anthology*, ed. S. G. Haim (Berkeley: University of California Press, 1976)172-224) 184. The Muslim Brotherhood initially supported Nasser's *qawmiyyat-l-ʿarabiyya* as a stepping-stone to Pan-Islamism. When it became clear to them that the latter did not move in that direction, Sayyid Quṭb in the name of the Muslim Brotherhood denounced Nasser's government and *al-qawmiyyat-l-ʿarabiyya* itself as alien to the divine scheme of things: "God, the Omniscient and Wise, did not set His Prophet in that direction;" moreover, he said, *qawmiyya* belongs to the *jahilīya* and, has thus "completed its role in world history" and Islam must take over the stage. Cfr. J. Piscatori, *Islam in a World of Nation-States* (Cambridge: Cambridge University Press, 1986) 109; S. Quṭb's words were quoted by the author from the *Maʿalimfī-ttariq*, p. 28.

[279] E. Lane, *Arabic-English Lexicon*, vol. 1 (Cambridge: The Islamic Texts Society, 1984 edition) 559.

misfortune); to be painful."[280]

In the Qur'ān, the term appears seventeen times in all in the singular, dual and plural, and is used chiefly to refer to groups or factions or parties within a larger group. The expression "the party of God," حِزْبَ اللهُ, is used twice (5:56,58:22). In practically all its other usages, the term is used in a bad sense: religion split into sects (30:32); the devil's party (58:19); the sects that differ (19:37); the groups that are distinguished from the true believers (33:22); a defeated host are the factions (38:11); etc. The term appears in two *umma* passages: in 40:5 to refer to the factions that denied the messengers and in 23:53 to refer to the divided groups in an *umma*. In all its usages, the word in itself does not have an intrinsic religious meaning, but when connected with another concept, like حِزْبَ اللهُ, it may be interchangeable with *umma*.

In the later extra-qur'ānic usages of this term, from the meaning of "part" or "portion" its technical use has been derived to indicate first a definite portion of the Qur'ān which a believer binds himself to recite, the division into *ḥizbs* being intended to facilitate the individual or collective recitation of the Qur'ān especially on certain occasions like during the night of the Ramaḍān. Later, religious fraternities were formed in connection with the division and recitation of the Qur'ān into *ḥizbs*. In effect, especially in Egypt, each fraternity is a *ḥizb* as well as its office which consists of the recital during the Friday service. On the other hand, dating from the beginning of the twentieth century or thereabouts, from the traditional and classical meaning of "party" or "company of men," the use of the word *ḥizb* has developed to mean a political party. Thus, among others, the *al-ḥizb al-waṭanī* (patriotic party) in Egypt in 1879 and *al-ḥizb al-dimuqrāṭī* (democratic party) in 1918.

---

[280] D. B. MacDonald, "Ḥizb" in *The Encyclopedia of Islam*, new edition, ed. by B. Lewis, V. L. Ménage, et. al. (Leiden: E. J. Brill, 1971) 513-535.

4.3 *Fawj* (pl. *afwāj*)

This term which means "a company, congregated body, party, or group, of men, or a crowd,"[281] occurs six times in the Qurʾān, one of the occurrences is in connection with *umma*. The context of all the passages (27:83, 38:59, 67:8, 78:18, 110:2) in which this term occurs is judgment day. Thus in the *umma* passage 27:83, the term *fawj* refers to the bad elements of an *umma* that will be singled out on judgment day. Like in 27:83, in all the other occurrences the term is used in a bad sense, except in 110:2 which depicts the multitudes, crowds entering the religion of God.

4.4 *Asbāṭ* and *Qabāʾil*

Asbāṭ is the plural of *sibṭ*, which means grandchild. Some lexicons emphasize that the term signifies "the particularly distinguished, and choicest, of children."[282] *Qabāʾil*, on the other hand, is the plural of *qabīla* which means a body of men from one father, but when used without the feminine ending, it means a body of men from several ancestors.[283]

Asbāṭ occurs in the Qurʾān five times (2:136, 2:140, 3:84, 4:163, 7:160 = all Medinan) and in all its occurrences it refers to the Israelite tribes. In the one passage where it is used in connection with *umma* (i.e., 7:160), it is used as another word, *badal*, for the twelve divisions (tribes).[284] On the other hand,

---

[281] E. Lane, *Arabic-English Lexicon*, vol. 2, p. 2455.

[282] E. Lane, *Arabic-English Lexicon*, vol. 1, p. 1294.

[283] E. Lane, *Arabic-English Lexicon*, vol. 2, p. 2984.

[284] The lexicons explain that here, "اسباطا is a substitute for اثنتى عشرة not a specificative, because the specificative may only be a singular; the meaning being وقطّعناهم اثنتى عشرة فرقةً , and therefore the numeral is feminine." Ibid., 1295.

qabāʾil appears once (49:13) to refer to tribes of people in general while *qabīl* occurs also once (7:27) to refer to Satan and his group. Accordingly, *Asbāṭ* is the term for tribe when talking about the Jews while *qabīla* and *qabāʾil* are used in relation to tribes in general and to the Arabs in particular.[285]

4.5 *Ahl* and *Āl*

Ahl originally means "those who occupy with one the same tent (Hebrew *ôhel),* thus family, inmates;"[286] a man's cohabitants of one dwelling place or house. When the *ahl* of a town or a country is spoken of, it denotes its inhabitants, especially those who were born there and own houses. Afterwards, it also applied to a man's fellow-members of one family or race or religion or people who share the same craft or art or the like; or, as some authorities also add, relations, whether they have followers or dependents, or not.[287] In its numerous appearances in the Qurʾān, *ahl* is often connected with other concepts, "so that it may come to mean 'sharing in a thing,' 'belonging to it,' or 'owner of the same,' etc."[288] Some such compounds of *ahl* are: *ahl al-kitāb,* "People of the Scripture;" *ahl al-injīl,* "People of the Gospel;" *ahl al-qurā, ahl al-ḏikr; ahl al-maġfira; ahluhu*; etc.

Āl originally signifies one's family, i.e., his *ʿašīra* or his relations or kinsfolk or nearest relations by descent from the

---

285 Ibid., 1294. Cfr. also, W. M. Watt, *Companion to the Qurʾān,* 93.

286 I. Goldziher, "Ahl" in *The Encyclopedia of Islam*, vol. 1, new edition, ed. by H. A. R. Gibb, J. H. Kramers, et. al. (Leiden: E. J. Brill, 1986) 257. See J. Horovitz, "Jewish Proper Names and Derivatives in the Qurʾān" in *Hebrew Union College Annual*, vol. 2 (Hildesheim: Georg Olms, 1964) 191.

287 E. Lane, *Arabic-English Lexicon,* vol. 1, p. 121.

288 I. Goldziher, "Ahl" in *The Encyclopedia of Islam,* New edition, vol. 1 (1986) 257.

same father or ancestor.[289] It refers to the clan, a genealogical group between the family *(ahl)* and the tribe *(qabīla)*. It also signifies relations with followers or dependents; sometimes is applied to followers or dependents. Thus, precisely because of its original meaning of relations, in its numerous appearances in the Qur'ān the word does not stand alone but together with the head of the relations. In most of its appearances, it is used to indicate the family or clan of the prophets: *āl Ibrāhīm, āl Mūsā, āl Lūṭ, āl Yaʿqūb, āl ʿImrān*, etc. The only use of *āl* other than to refer to the family of the prophets, is the compound *āl Firʿawn* or the Family of Pharaoh, which occurs often. As the examples show, unlike *ahl, āl* is generally used in relation to that in which there is eminence or nobility and, "is peculiarly used as a prefix to the proper names of rational beings, not to indeterminate nouns, nor to nouns of places or of times."

In its post-qur'ānic usage, the term *āl* was first of all used in connection with the Prophet Muhammad. In this case the expressions *Āl al-bayt*[290] or *ahl al-bayt* or *Āl al-Nabī* all mean the same, i.e., "the household of the Prophet." The *āl* of the Prophet are the descendants of Hāšim and al-Muṭṭalib. Then the Šīʿa restricted this concept to his nearest relatives and descendants

---

289 Cfr. E.Lane, *Arabic-English Lexicon*, vol. 1, p. 121 & 127, and A. Haffner, "Āl" in *The Encyclopedia of Islam*, vol. 1, new edition, ed. by H. A. R. Gibb, J. H. Kramers, p. 345.

290 "The origin of the phrase is to be found in the strong clan sense of the pre-Islamic Arabs, among whom the term *Āl-Bayt* was applied to or adopted by the ruling family of a tribe (by a derivation from an ancient right of guardianship of the symbol of the tribal deity, according to H. Lammens, "Le Culte des Bétyles" in *L'arabic occidentale avant l'Hégire* (Beirut: 1928, 136ff., 154ff.), and survived into later centuries in the plural form *al-buyūtāt* for the noble tribal families. In early Islamic times the term *bayt* was applied to themselves by a number of families." I. Goldziher, "Ahl" in *The Encyclopedia of Islam*, p. 257.

while the Sunnīs enlarged this to include all his followers. Later, the term came to mean the dynasty of a ruler.[291]

Other qur'ānic terms which mean human groups but, like the foregoing, have no intrinsic religious meaning are as follows: *faṣīla* (appears once, in 70:13), meaning a man's nearer relations, signifying less than a *qabīla*, thus, sub-tribe, kinsfolk; *ʿašīra* (occurs three times, in 26:214, 9:24, 58:22), meaning the smallest subdivision of a tribe, less than a *faṣīla*, and thus a synonym of *āl*; *farīq* (occurs many times), meaning a party of men apart from others; *fiʾa* (occurs once, in 18:19), meaning a band or party of men, an army;[292] and *šuʿūb* (appears once, in 49:13), meaning nations, races, peoples.

The terms *nās* and *bašar* also appear very frequently, meaning people, man, human being, or humankind, not as a group or community but as human creatures as such; they are too vague or too general terms to be considered human-group or community terms. On the other hand, there are also terms in the Qurʾān which, though they do not really mean group or community nor do they have intrinsic religious meaning, relate to or describe human groups. Among them are: *aṣḥāb* (meaning "companions", and once combined with another word may acquire a religious sense, as in 11:23 = *aṣḥāb al-janna*, "companions or inhabitants of the Garden" and in 5:29 = *aṣḥāb al-nār* or "inhabitants of the Fire"; *ʿabnāʾ*, *banū*, (meaning "sons, children," occurs often with Israel or Adam, though it is used in other connections, too); *muhājirūn*, "emigrants," and *anṣār*, "helpers."

There are also human-group terms in the Qurʾān which are

---

291 e.g., Āl Uṯmān = the Ottoman dynasty, āl Fayṣal āl Suʿūd = the official title of the Saudi Arabian dynasty. Cfr., *The Encyclopedia of Islam*, vol. 1, new edition, ed. by H. A. R. Gibb, J. H. Kramers, p. 345.

292 See F. Denny, "Some Religio-Communal Terms and Concepts in the Qurʾān" in *Numen*, vol. 24 (1977) 45.

religious because they designate actual historical traditions, i.e., they are among the historical extensions of the concept "religious community": *naṣāra* ("Christians" - 14 occurrences, all Medinan); *al-yahūd* ("the Jews" - 8 times, all Medinan); *banū Isrāʾīl* ("Children of Israel" - 41 occurrences, Meccan and Medinan); *ahl aḏ-ḏikr* ("people of the reminder/remembrance" - 16:43, 21:7); *ahl al-injīl* ("People of the Gospel" - 5:47, Medinan); *ṣābiʾūn* ("Sabeans" - 2:62, 5:69, 22:17, Medinan); *majūs* ("Magians/ Zoroastrians" - 22:17, Medinan). To these may be added terms which further describe historical religious groups: *ruhbān* ("monks" - 5:82, 9:31, 9:34, all Medinan); *rabbāniyyūn* ("rabbis" - 3:79, 5:44, 5:63, Medinan); *aḥbār* ("teachers, rabbis" - 5:44, 5:63, 9:34, Medinan).[293]

There are important and interesting aspects to many of the terms mentioned above and a full-scale examination and discussion of them will comprise another dissertation. We point them out here to show that in fact the Qurʾān employs numerous terms which either mean or describe neutral human communities or groups, but that the single word and concept which comprehends a true religious community is *umma*.[294]

---

[293] For an explanation of how *rabbānī* was derived from the Jewish *rabbān*, see J. Horovitz, "Jewish Proper Names and Derivatives in the Koran" in *Hebrew Union College Annual*, vol. 2 (Hildesheim: Georg Olms, 1964 reprint of the 1924 first edition) 200-201.

[294] It may be noted that the term *jamāʿa* is not a qurʾānic term, although, along with *ḥizb allāh*, it does have an early use as a synonym for *umma*, to designate the Islamic community.

CHAPTER TWO

UMMA IN THE CONTEXT OF THE *TAFSĪR*

This chapter deals with *umma* in the *tafsīr*.[1] We have seen in our contextual reading of the Qur'ān that in the definitive stage of its development, a true *umma* is an *umma muslima*; more importantly, that the *umma par excellence* as a reality in this world is the *umma* of Muhammad. It is this *umma* which is exclusively described in the Qur'ān as the *umma wasaṭ*, the *ḫayra umma* or

[1] *Tafsīr* (plural is *tafāsīr*), the verbal noun or *maṣdar* of *fassara*, to explain, is and has been traditionally the term used by Muslims for explanation of a text. In the age of compilation and translation in Islam, it was applied to the Greek and Arabic commentaries on works of philosophy. It has been applied also to interpretations of poetry, and in general to any kind of exposition or explanation. In the course of time, when religious knowledge had been divided into various branches, *tafsīr* became the technical term for commentary on the Qur'ān, the usage to which we will refer in this study. *Tafsīr* was originally synonymous with *ta'wīl*, both meaning exposition or explanation of a text, gradually limited specifically to the Qur'ān. Gradually *tafsīr* came to be applied more to the external philological exegesis of the Qur'ān while *ta'wīl* took over the interpretive function, i.e., the "inner" meaning, to be grasped through intuition. Later *ta'wīl* became more and more used to characterize the *tafsīr* of the Ṣūfīs and the Šī'a, hence it took on the meaning of allegorical or symbolic interpretation. Cf. Rashid Ahmad, "Qur'ānic Exegesis and Classical Tafsīr" in *The Islamic Quarterly*, Vol. XII, Nos. 1 and 2 (January-June 1968) 73f.

best community. Our own contextual reading of the Qur'ān was not without the help of the commentaries. In this chapter, however, we would like to see how the *umma* verses that refer to the Muslim community in an exclusive sense have been understood or interpreted by the Muslim commentators or *mufassirūn* throughout the centuries. The verses concerned are 2:143, 3:104 and 3:110. Of all the texts where the term *umma* occurs, these have been most extensively commented upon by the *mufassirūn*. As we shall see, the explanations given to these verses have not always been the same.

Our review will be historical in the sense that we consider representative *tafāsīr* from the different periods in Muslim qur'ānic exegesis, in order to ascertain how the above-mentioned verses have been interpreted both in relation to previous commentaries and in terms of their reflection of the peculiar historical circumstances in which each *mufassir* wrote. The method then is a description both of what the exegetes have said about the verses in question and the historical situations out of which each wrote, in an attempt to indicate whether and how change has developed in the usage and interpretations of the term. This will lead to an appreciation of the complex and truly dynamic nature of the *umma*.

The number of Muslim exegetes from whom we can choose for this study is, of course, enormous and the total volume of their *tafsīr* monumental. In order to hit the double advantage of fulfilling our aim and at the same time imposing a limit on what could be an endless number of possibilities, we will work on a somewhat similar idea to the Muslim practice of selecting a *mujaddid* for each age. In our case, we will choose three representative *tafāsīr* each from the classical, post-classical and modern periods of Muslim civilization.[2] This decision of ours needs little justification.

---

[2] The classical period is generally reckoned to have spanned about 350 years beginning at the turn of the fourth/tenth century and drawing to a close with the sacking of Baghdad by the Mongols in 656/1258.

Many of the exegetical works written during the formative period of Islam are either no longer extant or have not yet been edited, thus making a thorough study of pre-classical exegesis impracticable.[3] Since pre-classical exegesis was predominantly if not purely based on tradition, it is sufficient that we begin with the *tafsīr* of Ṭabarī, who stood on the threshold of the classical period and whose *tafsīr* brings together the entire breadth of the material of traditional exegesis extant at his time.

On the other hand, for the post-classical period of seven centuries, we again consider three representative *tafāsīr*. This is in order to avoid too much repetition of the same material since this period was one of cultural decline and its qurʾānic commentaries are compilations and repetitions of classical works. They solidify the traditionalism in qurʾānic exegesis.

Some of the *tafāsīr* that sprung up in the late nineteenth up to the twentieth century have not been repetitions of traditional ones. They, instead, show new directions in *tafsīr*. Thus we shall also consider three representatives of this group.

---

[3] "Independent source material from this first phase of exegetical activity... is virtually non-existent. All we know about the early period is from later ascriptions. Later works, from the middle of the second century AH at the earliest, claim to contain the exegesis of earlier authorities. But whether or not these claims are valid cannot be checked, because no objective criteria can be applied. Or to put it differently, original material, such as papyri from this early period... has as yet not been found." Fred Leemhuis, "Origins of the Tafsīr Tradition" in *Approaches to the History of the Interpretation of the Qurʾān*, edited by Andrew Rippin (New York: Oxford University Press, 1988) 14. For contrasting ideas regarding the historicity of *tafāsīr* whose authorship is attributed to pre-classical exegetes, see, among others, F. Sezgin, *Geschichte der arabischen Literatur* (Leiden, 1968-) 19f; and John Wansbrough, *Qurʾānic Studies: Sources and Methods of Scriptural Interpretation* (London: Oxford University Press, 1977) 119-246. A most recent summary of the pros and cons of the debate is found in F. Leemhuis, Ibid. 15f.

The principle that we used in the selection of representative *tafāsīr* is an attempt to choose those most widely-read and highly esteemed by Sunnī Muslims throughout the ages. The authors and works to be considered are listed as follows:

1. Abū Jaʿfar Muḥammad ibn Jarīr al-Ṭabarī (224/839 - 310/923), *Jāmiʿ al-bayān ʿan taʾwīl al-Qurʾān* (Collection of Explanations for the Interpretation of the Qurʾān).

2. Abū-l-Qāsim Maḥmūd ibn ʿUmar al-Zamaḫšarī (467/1075 - 538/1144), *Al-Kaššāf ʿan ḥaqāʾiqi-l-tanzīl* (The Unveiler of the Realities of the Revelation).

3. Faḫr al-Dīn al-Rāzī (543/1149 - 606/1209), *Mafātīḥ al-ġayb* (The Keys to the Unseen).

4. ʿAbd-Allāh ibn ʿUmar al-Bayḍāwī (d. ca. 685?, 691?/1286?, 1291?), *Anwār-al-tanzīl wa asrār-al-taʾwīl* (The Lights of Inspiration and the Secrets of Interpretation).

5. Ismāʿīl ibn ʿUmar abū-l-Fidāʾ ibn Kaṯīr (701/1301 - 774/1373), *Tafsīr al-Qurʾān al-ʿaẓīm* (Commentary on the Sublime Qurʾān).

6. Al-Jalālayn, i.e., Abū-l-Faḍl ʿAbd-al-Raḥmān ibn Abī-Bakr Jalāl-al-Dīn al-Suyūṭī (849/1445 - 911/1505) and Al-Maḥallī Jalāl-al-Dīn (d. 864/1459), *Tafsīr al-Qurʾān al-karīm* (Commentary on the Noble Qurʾān).

7. Šayḫ Muḥammad ʿAbduh (1849-1323/1905) and Rašīd Riḍā (1865 - 1354/1935), *Tafsīr al-Manār* (*Tafsīr al-Qurʾān al-Karīm*/Commentary on the Noble Qurʾān).

8. Sayyid Abū-l-Aʿlā Mawdūdī (1903 - 1979), *Towards Under-*

standing the Qurʾān (English version of the Urdu original "Tafhīm al-Qurʾān").

9. Sayyid Quṭb (1324/1906 - 1386/1966), *Fī ẓilāli-l-Qurʾān* (In the Shades of the Qurʾān).

Following are the three passages of the Qurʾān which refer to the Muslims in an exclusive sense. In our review of the commentaries on these verses, we will consider only those sections which elucidate the meaning and function of the Muslim *umma*.

وَكَذَٰلِكَ جَعَلْنَاكُمْ أُمَّةً وَسَطًا لِّتَكُونُوا شُهَدَاءَ عَلَى ٱلنَّاسِ
وَيَكُونَ ٱلرَّسُولُ عَلَيْكُمْ شَهِيدًا وَمَا جَعَلْنَا ٱلْقِبْلَةَ ٱلَّتِى كُنتَ
عَلَيْهَا إِلَّا لِنَعْلَمَ مَن يَتَّبِعُ ٱلرَّسُولَ مِمَّن يَنقَلِبُ عَلَىٰ عَقِبَيْهِ
وَإِن كَانَتْ لَكَبِيرَةً إِلَّا عَلَى ٱلَّذِينَ هَدَى ٱللَّهُ وَمَا كَانَ ٱللَّهُ
لِيُضِيعَ إِيمَانَكُمْ إِنَّ ٱللَّهَ بِٱلنَّاسِ لَرَءُوفٌ رَّحِيمٌ.

Thus we have established you an *umma wasaṭ*, that you may be witnesses to the people (to humankind), and the Messenger may be a witness to you. And we appointed the *qibla* which you formerly observed only that We might distinguish him who followed the Messenger from him who turned on his heels. In truth it was a hard (test) except for those whom God guided. But it was not God's purpose to destroy your faith, for God is merciful and compassionate towards mankind (2:143).

وَلْتَكُن مِّنكُمْ أُمَّةٌ يَدْعُونَ إِلَى ٱلْخَيْرِ، وَيَأْمُرُونَ بِٱلْمَعْرُوفِ
وَيَنْهَوْنَ عَنِ ٱلْمُنكَرِ وَأُولَٰئِكَ هُمُ ٱلْمُفْلِحُونَ.

That of you be [formed] an *umma* inviting to the good, ordering equity and forbidding iniquity; such are the prosperous (3:104).

كُنْتُمْ خَيْرَ أُمَّةٍ أُخْرِجَتْ لِلنَّاسِ، تَأْمُرُونَ بِٱلْمَعْرُوفِ وَتَنْهَوْنَ عَنِ ٱلْمُنْكَرِ وَتُؤْمِنُونَ بِٱللّٰهِ.

You are the best *umma* ever brought forth for humankind: you order equity, you forbid iniquity and you believe in God (3:110).

I. *Tafsīr bi-l-Maʾṯūr* and *Tafsīr bi-l-Raʾy*

Muslim scholars distinguish between *tafsīr bi-l-maʾṯūr* and *tafsīr bi-l-raʾy*. The former consists exclusively of explanations that can be traced back to the Prophet and his companions and their successors; whereas the latter makes extensive use of reasoning. In practice, as we will see, the distinction is not a hard and fast one.

Bi-l-maʾṯūr stands at the center of the earliest period of exegesis of the Qurʾān. There is the fact that Muhammad is considered to be the first exegete of the Scripture,[4] that is, after the Qurʾān itself, which is esteemed to be its own best interpreter. It is generally known, based on Muslim reports, that the prophet, by his words and deeds, elucidated many passages of the revealed text. These elucidations/explanations were testified to, recalled and passed on by his companions *(ṣaḥāba)* and their successors *(tābiʿūn)*, and stood in the center of older exegesis as religious Tradition *(ḥadīṯ)*. In the first centuries of Islam, the knowledge *(ʿilm)* required in *tafsīr* means knowledge of the *ḥadīṯ*. As long as a *tafsīr* was supported by a respectable *isnād* (chain of authority) that went back to this proper source it was acceptable, while one which was supported by personal judgment or opinion *(raʾy)* was

[4] The Qurʾān itself announces this role of Muhammad in *sura* 16:44: "We have revealed to you the message (*ḏkr*) so that you might explain to people that which has been revealed to them."

not acceptable. Muslim reports,[5] however, also indicate that already beginning with the Companions of the Prophet as well as in the next generation called Successors, could be found a modest expression of individual personal opinion *(raʾy)* in their explanation of the Qurʾān. Vis-a-vis the circumstances of revelations, pre-Islamic poetry and free discussions with Muslims of Jewish origin, they exercised reason and discernment based on, and, to a degree, controlled by, the store of religious knowledge (or knowledge of *ḥadīṯ*) called *ʿilm*. Thus while right from the beginning the dominant mode of doing *tafsīr* was *bi-l-maʾṯūr*, it was not possible to separate it from *bi-l-raʾy* in an absolute way.[6] We will see in the following consideration of the representative *tafāsīr* of the first six centuries of Islam that this period was marked by an increasing tendency toward the use of personal opinion and interpretation as well as philosophical speculation.

From the end of the second century onward, *tafsīr* material of different kinds that could be considered authoritative on the basis of a sound *isnād* was collected more and more into compilatory *tafāsīr*. Such an activity was crowned by the achievement of Muḥammad ibn Jarīr al-Ṭabarī in the third century (d. 311/923).

---

[5] Cf., among others, Jalāl al-Dīn al-Suyūṭī, *Tadrīb al-rāwī fī šarḥ taqrīb al-āwawī* (Medina: 1392/1972) 192-193 as well as his *al-Itqān fī ʿulūm al-Qurʾān* (Cairo: 1318/1900) vol. 1, pp. 121-134 and vol. II, pp. 189-190; Al-Ġazālī, *Iḥyā al-ʿUlūm* (Cairo: 1356/1937) vol. III, pp. 136-137; R. Blachère, *Introduction au Coran* (Paris: Maisonneuve, 1950) 230; R. Marston Speight, "The Function of *ḤADĪṮ* as Commentary on the Qurʾān, as Seen in the Six Authoritative Collections" in *Approaches to the History of the Interpretation of the Qurʾān*, edited by A. Rippin (Oxford: Clarendon Press, 1988) 63-81.

[6] M. M. Bravmann has thoroughly discussed the way in which *ʿilm* and *raʾy* were counterparts in the thought of early Islam. See, M.M. Bravmann, *The Spiritual Background of Early Islam* (Leiden: E. J. Brill, 1972) 177-188.

1.1 Ṭabarī [7]

1.1.1 Introduction

The purpose of this introduction is to situate Ṭabarī within the framework of the *bi-l-maʾṯūr* and *bi-l-raʾy* forms of Qurʾānic exegesis which are characteristic traits of the first six centuries of Qurʾān commentary. This is important not only because his *tafsīr* marks the high point of traditional exegesis but also because it constitutes the basic work on which the majority of the exegesis of the succeeding centuries has been based.

The fruits of Ṭabarī's studies and Traditions-collecting trips to different centers of Islamic learning were to become the determining factors in his life back in Baghdad. Having become acquainted with the Šāfiʿī *maḏhab* in Egypt, for ten years after his return to Baghdad Ṭabarī adhered closely to the teachings of this school with the determination to judge personally the sources of law as he was unwilling to accept the legal dogma prescribed by others without his own critical analysis. For this reason, later

---

[7] Ṭabarī was born at the end of 224 or the beginning of 225 AH (839 AD) in Amūl in northern Iran, in the region known then as Ṭabaristān, from which his name, al-Ṭabarī, derives. After receiving his early education in his hometown, he went to study in the religious center of Raʾy. Afterwards, in search of Traditions, he left for Baghdad and then later went to other important centers of Islamic learning like Kūfa and Baṣra in Iraq, then on to Syria and Egypt. Then he returned to Baghdad and there led a professional life of persistent scholarship, dedicated teaching (especially of *ḥadīṯ* and *fiqh)* and prolific writing. Except for two more trips to Ṭabaristān, he remained in Baghdad until his death in 310/923. For Ṭabarī's biography, see, among others, Yāqūt (1179 - 1229 AH?), *Iršād al-arīb ilā maʿrifat al-adīb*, D. S. Margoliouth, ed. (Leiden: E. J. Brill, 1325 - 1345/1907 -1926), vol. IV, pp. 423-462; R. Paret, "Al-Ṭabarī" in *E. J. Brill's First Encyclopedia of Islam*, vol. VII (Leiden and New York: E. J. Brill, 1987) 578-579.

historians credited him with being an independent *mujtahid*.[8] Later he decided to found his own legal school, the Jarīrīya - after his father's name. Soon this move earned him the severe criticism of the Ḥanbalī partisans in Baghdad, especially because in writing about the various extant legal views, he did not recognize Aḥmad b. Ḥanbal as an authority on *fiqh* (law) but as a traditionist.

Another group with whom Ṭabarī encountered difficulties because of his views was the Rāfidīya - a group of more extreme Šīʿa which had been prominent in Ṭabaristān and were attracted by Ṭabarī's early appreciation of ʿAlī. When he also praised Abū Bakr they became antagonized and Ṭabarī had to flee.[9] Ṭabarī's own school of law, which accordingly differed only slightly from that of al-Šāfiʿī, faded away soon after his death and most of his early works on *fiqh* have disappeared.

It appears that the most immediate concerns of Ṭabarī were not really law and the direct application of law, but the revelation of God. Forming a kind of two-pronged approach to this primary concern of his are his two major life works: the Qurʾān *tafsīr*[10] which is concerned with the word of God and his great world

---

[8] Muhammad Ibrahim H. I. Surty, "The Qurʾān in Islamic Scholarship: A Survey of *Tafsīr* Exegesis Literature in Arabic" in *The Muslim World Book Review*, vol. 7, no. 4 (Summer, 1987) 52.

[9] It is reported in Yāqūt, *Iršād*, vol. VI, pt. 6, 425, that "al-Ṭabarī's funeral had to be held at night for fear of the anger of the crowd at his suspected *Šīʿī* leanings."

[10] Until recently, Ṭabarī's Qurʾān commentary was considered lost. It was discovered by O. Loth and was first published in 1903. This relatively late discovery of Ṭabarī's *Tafsīr* in comparison to his "world history" may have been the reason many scholars in the West consider Ṭabarī a historian first and foremost and his Annals his most outstanding achievement. For a summary of western views in this regard, see J. J. G. Jansen, *The Interpretation of the Koran in Modern Egypt* (Leiden: E. J. Brill, 1980) 56, note 5.

history[11] which is concerned with the manifestation of God's will in time. Oral tradition, which is the main source for Ṭabarī's *Annals,* also forms the basis of his great *tafsīr.* Ṭabarī utilized *ḥadīṯ* as the basis of his commentary. The scope of Ṭabarī's collection of *ḥadīṯ* far exceeded that of his predecessor Ibn ʿAbbās.[12] More than simply a collection and compilation of the first two and a half centuries of *bi-l-maʾṯūr* exegesis,[13] it is a methodically arranged work which evinces considerable critical analysis and personal judgment on the material passed down. In other words, while the primary criterion for Ṭabarī's exegetical activity is *aḥādīṯ* transmitted by an uninterrupted chain of authority, in cases where a chain of authority is faulty, he is free to claim the authority of the consensus of the community or give his own personal judgment.

---

11 Entitled *"Taʾrīḫ al-rusul wa-l-mulūk wa-l-ḫulafāʾ/History of the Messengers, Kings and Caliphs"* or *Annals* as it is commonly referred to.

12 Ibn ʿAbbās was a cousin of the prophet, born about three years before the *hijra.* He devoted himself to collecting material about the prophet which he imparted to his students and became a frequently quoted commentator on the Qurʾān. He is known especially in the West as the "father of qurʾānic exegesis." However, serious doubts are raised regarding whether or not he himself wrote a *tafsīr* and regarding the authenticity of many of the exegetical comments attributed to him with *asānīd* going back to his own pupils. Cf. above, page 173, note 3.

13 The material which Ṭabarī quotes generally falls into two kinds. First, the Traditions from the people of *tafsīr* and *taʾwīl* which are cited with full *asānīd.* (It may be noted that although *taʾwīl* came to denote a more allegorical style of interpretation - as we noted above, page 171, note 1 - in Ṭabarī these two terms are synonyms, as the very title of his commentary indicates). Second, the opinions of grammarians, which are usually quoted anonymously as coming from "a Baṣran grammarian" or "a Kūfan grammarian." The oldest traditionists to which the *asānīd* lead are Ibn ʿAbbās and his students Muǧāhid and al-Daḥḥāk. The Baṣran and Kūfan grammarians are usually Abū ʿUbayda and al-Farrāʾ respectively.

Scholars[14] have recognized that while Ṭabarī's tendency towards comprehensiveness[15] made him incorporate even contradictory material,[16] he took care not to include the interpretations of such exegetes as were considered unreliable.[17] On the whole, he collected only what he considered to be reliably transmitted from orthodox Sunni authorities, thus excluding, for example, also Šīʿī exegesis, with its body of traditions from their Imāms, and Sūfī exegesis, with its more allegorical and mystical

---

14 Cfr. Helmut Gätje, *The Qurʾān and its Exegesis* (London and Henley: Routledge and Kegan Paul, 1971) 34f; J. Cooper, *The Commentary on the Qurʾān by Al-Ṭabarī* (Oxford: Oxford University Press, 1987) xiiff; J. I. Smith, *An Historical and Semantic Study of The Term "Islām"* (Missoula, Montana: Scholars Press, 1975) 60-61.

15 The *asānīd* in Ṭabarī's commentary have been studied by Dr. Heribert Horst (in his "Zur Überlieferung im Koran-Kommentar al-Ṭabarī," *Zeitschrift der Deutschen Morgenländischen Gesellschaft* 103 (1953) 290-307) who concluded that in addition to oral traditions, Ṭabarī did use written sources in the compilation of his material. A decade later, the Turkish Muslim scholar Dr. F. Sezgin (in his *Geschichte des Arabischen Schrifttums,* Volume I (Leiden: E. J. Brill, 1967) 19f) compared Ṭabarī's quotations with the original sources as far as available and came to the conclusion that in Ṭabarī's commentary much material lost elsewhere has been preserved *in extenso.* Cited also in J. J. G. Jansen, *The Interpretation of the Koran in Modern Egypt* (Leiden: E. J. Brill, 1980) 56, note 5.

16 As J. Cooper notes "...within this material there could sometimes be twenty or more different opinions on the interpretation of a single qurʾānic word or phrase, these differences occurring not only between authorities, but even between traditions from the same authority." J. Cooper, Ibid.

17 Thus, for instance, he does not cite the second century exegete Muqātil b. Sulaymān whose knowledge reportedly came from the people of the Scripture and whom traditionists consider as untrustworthy. Cf. Rashid Ahmad, "Qurʾānic Exegesis and Classical Tafsīr" in *The Islamic Quarterly,* vol. XII, Nos. 1-2 (January-June, 1968) 81.

approach. Ṭabarī also explains the various methods[18] which guide him in his exegetical activity, which methods are secondary only to what he feels to be the clear and obvious external *(ẓāhir)* meaning of the word or words under consideration, based on their common usage in Arabic.

Thus, to the question of where or how to place Ṭabarī especially in relation to the atmosphere of emerging *tafsīr bi-l-raʾy* tendencies, we say the following. In intent, and for the most part in deed, Ṭabarī was traditionist. He nevertheless occasionally seems to have departed from this approach. He was censured by the followers of Ibn Ḥanbal not only for what he said about their *imām* but also and especially because he was perceived as moving toward the kind of speculative dogmatics which was objectionable to the traditionists, although he himself claimed to be the opponent of such tendencies. While his *tafsīr* is the crowning point of the first centuries of traditionist commentaries, he implicitly or explicitly allowed for a certain breadth of interpretation which on occasions led to his being associated with other groups like the Muʿtazila and the Šīʿa.[19] Despite this, the basic orientation of his interpretation remains a traditionist one. He was at all times arguing against a metaphorical or figurative interpretation. His flexibility was one which was controlled by his store of *ʿilm* which put him in direct line with those who practised *tafsīr bi-l-maʾṯūr* and

---

[18] For a thorough discussion of Ṭabarī's qurʾānic hermeneutics, see Jane Dammen McAuliffe, "Qurʾānic Hermeneutics: The Views of al-Ṭabarī and Ibn Kaṯīr" in *Approaches to the History of the Interpretation of the Qurʾān*, Andrew Rippin (ed.) (Oxford: Clarendon Press, 1988) 46-62.

[19] There is an allusion by Yāqūt (*Iršād*, IV, pt. 6, 453-4) to Ṭabarī's having been called a Muʿtazilī because of certain elements in his *tafsīr*. This is also cited in J. I. Smith, *An Historical And Semantic Study of the Term "Islām"* (Missoula, Montana: Scholars Press, 1975) 60. In most of the instances where Ṭabarī's own opinion is recorded, his words are prefaced with "Abū Jaʿfar said/قال أبو جعفر

it is in this capacity that he has been cherished by centuries of Muslims[20] as an incomparable source of information for scholars of Islam.

1.1.2 *Tafsīr*

Ṭabarī comments on the whole Qur'ān in sequence dividing each *sūra* into subsections which vary in length from a single phrase to several *āyas*. He introduces each subsection with a formula that reminds the reader that it is God's word. Then he gives the text followed by his *tafsīr*. In general, his *tafsīr* follows a pattern of giving a fairly brief and clear explanation of the text based on the general Arabic usage of words, with copious references to Arabic poetry and other kinds of literature. Sometimes he follows this with other passages in the Qur'ān which help to elucidate the meaning. This then is usually followed with any number of clearly cited *aḥādīṯ* and often concludes these with his

---

[20] This is not to say that Ṭabarī is without critics, especially among western writers. In the Muslim world, this commentary enjoys a prestigious position with only high commendations heaped upon it by Arab biographers for many centuries. One of the most often quoted sayings to show the high esteem for this commentary is that of the Baghdad jurist Abū Ḥāmid al-Isfarāyīnī: "If a man were to travel to China in order to obtain the *tafsīr* of M. b. Jarīr that would not be too great an effort." (Yāqūt, *Iršād*, VI, pt. 6, 424; Ibn al-ʿImād, Abū-l-Falāḥ, *Šaḏrāt-l-ḏahab fī aḫbār man ḏahab* (Cairo: Maktabat-l-Qudsī, 1350-51/1931-32) vol. II, 260). However, a main criticism of Ṭabarī's *tafsīr* by later orthodoxy is his inclusion of so much material with faulty *asānīd*, one of the links is sometimes missing, or is alluded to without being named, or is named but is known to have been discredited. Cf. Muḥammad Ḥusayn al-Ḏahabī, *al-Tafsīr wa-l-mufassirūn* (Cairo: Dār al-Kutub al-Ḥadīṯa, 1381/1961), vol. I, 157-183. Cited also in R. Marston Speight, "The Function of *Ḥadīṯ* as Commentary on the Qur'ān, as Seen in the Six Authoritative Collections" in *Approaches to the History of the Interpretation of the Qur'ān*, Andrew Rippin, ed. (Oxford: Clarendon Press, 1988) 66-68.

own opinion of their relative merit. In cases where he stresses his own opinion without a corresponding *isnād* to support it, he nevertheless enumerates the *aḥādīṯ* on the matter without giving his opinion on their relative merit.

In his treatment of 2:143, Ṭabarī explains the part which is our concern (i.e., "Thus we have established you a middle *umma*...") saying:

> Just as we have guided you, O believers in Muhammad and in what he brought you from God, and thus have singled you out for the *qibla* and religion of Abraham; in that same way we preferred you to everybody else among the people of religions (وفضلناكم بذلك على من سواكم من أهل الملل).... by making you an *umma wasaṭ*.[21]

Here is made clear the context in which *wasaṭ* as a description of the Muslim community is to be understood. It is in relation to other communities that the Muslims are described as *wasaṭ*. Then follows Ṭabarī's explanation of *wasaṭ*. Citing a phrase from Arabic poetry, he points out that *al-wasaṭ* in common Arabic usage means "the choice" or "the best"/*ḫiyār*.[22] In the context of 2:143, Ṭabarī presents three possible ways of understanding the term *wasaṭ*. First, he gives his own interpretation which is that *wasaṭ* here means *middle in religion*. Second, he cites the opinion of those who say that *wasaṭ* means justice (*ʿadl*) because the best (*ḫiyār*) among the people are the just ones (عدول).[23] Thirdly, he cites the opinion of those who say that here *wasaṭ* means

---

[21] Ṭabarī (on 2:143) 6.

[22] In common Arabic usage, one may be spoken of as "the best of respect (most respected)" among his people - ...وسط الحسب في قومه which means that such a person is placed in the middle/center of esteem - متوسط الحسب and thus the best among his people - وسط في قومه.

[23] Ṭabarī (on 2:143) 7.

middle or mediator between the prophet and the other nations.[24] Ṭabarī does not give his judgment as to the merit of these other opinions and it is clear that he prefers his own opinion which he explains further.

Wasaṭ in this place, he says, means the middle or that part which is between two extremities. When God describes the Muslims as *wasaṭ*, it is due to their being positioned in the middle of two extremities in religion.

> They (Muslims) are not a people who exaggerate in it (religion). The Christians exaggerate in religion with their monastic life and in what they say about Jesus. Nor are they (Muslims) a people who neglect in it (religion). The Jews have neglected in religion: they changed God's Scripture, killed their prophets, lied to their Lord and don't believe in Him. But they (Muslims) are a people positioned in the middle «أهل توسط» and are moderate «اعتدال» in it (religion). Thus God describes them in that manner *(i.e., umma wasaṭ)* because the dearest of things to God are the moderate ones. [25]

Wasaṭ thus describes the position of the Muslim community, seen in relation to other communities. As such it is a position of moderation or a balanced position which is the "choice" or "best" position. Most important of all, it is a position established on the basis of their religion, i.e., the religion brought to them from God by Muhammad.

If *wasaṭ* describes *what* the Muslims are, compared to others, 3:104 in Ṭabarī expresses the *task* of the Muslims concerning others (i.e., the non-Muslims). We will see from his explanation of the verse that the Muslim community is a centrifugal community; it exists not for itself but primarily for its

---

[24] Ṭabarī (on 2:143) 8.

[25] Ṭabarī (on 2:143) 6.

task. He explains the verse as follows:

> Let there be from among you, O believers, an *umma*, i.e., a group of people *(jamāʿa)* who call to what is good, i.e., to Islam and its laws which God has laid down for His servants, and who order that which is acceptable, i.e., they order the people to follow Muhammad and his religion which he brought from God, and who forbid that which is rejectable, i.e., they forbid disbelief in God and the denial of Muhammad and that which he brought from God; [and they do this] with their utmost efforts until they (non-Muslims) submit to you in obedience.[26]

As is clear from the explanation, the task of the Muslim *umma* is centrifugal in character. The good and that which is acceptable are equated with the Islamic religion which, as we have seen in 2:143 above, has made the Muslims *wasaṭ*. The ordering of Islam together with the forbidding of what is not Islam concerns the non-Muslims with the view of making them submit in obedience to the Muslim community. Two aspects of Islam as a reality in the world is here made clear, namely: surrender to God *(islām)* and obedience to the Muslim community. (The explanation of these two aspects are further elaborated in Ṭabarī's *tafsīr* of 3:110, below). While it is clear from Ṭabarī's commentary on 3:104 that the task of inviting, ordering and forbidding is directed to non-Muslims, he does not elaborate much as regards the agents of this task except to say at the beginning of the commentary that this task belongs to a group of people *(jamāʿa)* within the Muslim community, and to cite at the end a chain of authority that goes back to Al-Ḍaḥḥāk which says that referred to here are the Companions of the Prophet, especially the transmitters/ narrators.[27] This question is further studied in his commentary on 3:110.

---

[26] Ṭabarī (on 3:104) 38.

[27] Ṭabarī (on 3;104) 38.

In his commentary on 3:110, Ṭabarī devotes himself first to the question of <u>who</u> are referred to as the "best community" and then secondly to the question of <u>why</u> it is the best community.

As regards the first question, the varying traditions provided by Ṭabarī may be divided into two general categories. The first category is composed of *aḥādīṯ* that all refer back to Ibn ʿAbbās and emphasize that, referred to as the best community/*ḫayra umma* are the faithful who migrated with the prophet from Mecca to Medina, especially those who fought for the faith with him. Accordingly, it is for this reason that while God could have said *"antum*/you" which would have referred to all Muslims past and present, God says *"kuntum*/you were/you have been."[28] In the second group of *aḥādīṯ* is the opinion of those who say that, referred to here is the Muslim community of all time as long as it fulfills in its time the conditions which God describes in this verse.[29] While Ṭabarī does not discount either of these interpretations, he does not occupy himself with giving his opinion as to their relative merit. His main concern in this verse is the *why* of the "best community," and, as we will see, his discussion of this second question also brings out in the end his answer to the first.

As regards the second question, Ṭabarī provides a variety of interpretations with supporting *aḥādīṯ* and offers his preferred opinion. In the first group are *aḥādīṯ* which stress that, compared to other communities, the Muslims are the best because they are

---

[28] Ṭabarī (on 3:110) 43.

[29] Ṭabarī (on 3:110) 44. From these two opinions may be gauged the varying notions of "being the best" prevailing in Ṭabarī's time, namely: 1) that being the best is not inherent in the nature of every historical Muslim community but is something that the community has always to earn and thus the Islamic community in its beginnings is seen as the ideal; 2) and that being the best is always the inherent character of every Muslim community.

more numerous than any other community.[30] In the second category are traditions that indicate that the Muslim community is the best simply because God brought it forth as the best for humankind.[31] The third is the opinion that the Muslims are the best because they are people of the *ṭarīqa*/right direction.[32] While not discrediting any one of these interpretations, Ṭabarī stresses the second opinion as the most important one, i.e., that God brought forth the Muslim community as the best, supporting it with sayings that go back to the prophet himself.[33] In the explanations that follow, he says that it is correct to understand *uḫrijat* in the verse as meaning "you were created/*ḫuliqtum*" or "you were found/*wujidtum*" because such an understanding corresponds to the most important reason the Muslim *umma* is the best. The Muslim *umma*, Ṭabarī emphasizes, "is the best community before God in the Preserved Tablet *(lawḥ maḥfūẓ)* and brought forth for

---

[30] Ṭabarī (on 3:110) 44.

[31] Ṭabarī (on 3:110) 44-45.

[32] Ṭabarī (on 3:110) 46. *Ṭarīqa* in its original common Arabic usage means a way, course, rule, mode, or manner of acting or conduct or the like, of a man, whether it be approved or disapproved. In its use in the Qur'ān, it means right path, right conduct, right direction. Cf. E. W. Lane, *Arabic-English Lexicon*, vol Two (Cambridge: The Islamic Texts Society, 1984 edition) 1849. Later, this word "acquired two successive technical meanings in Muslim mysticism: 1. In the 9th and 10th centuries A. D. it was a method of moral psychology for the practical guidance of individuals who had a mystic call; 2. after the 11th century, it becomes the whole system of rites for spiritual training laid down for communal life in the various Muslim religious orders which began to be founded at this time." L. Massignon, "Ṭarīqa" in *Shorter Encyclopedia of Islam*, edited by H. A. R. Gibb and J. H. Kramers (leiden: E. J. Brill, 1991)573.

[33] Ṭabarī (on 3:110) 45.

humankind,"[34] and *kuntum* then in the verse would refer to the whole Muslim community of all time.[35]

For Ṭabarī then, the meaning of the "best" of the *umam* is to be found in the meta-history realm, i.e., he situates the basis of the excellence of the Muslim *umma* in God's pre-decision before the creation of the world and he puts this in the words of the Qur᾽ān - فِي لَوْحٍ مَّحْفُوظٍ (cf. Sūra 85:22), which is understood as the Preserved Tablet which exists in heaven for eternity whereon are said to be inscribed all the divine decrees.[36] This *umma* is brought forth for humankind as the revealer and bearer of God's will and whatever is pleasing in the eyes of God.

> Precisely, obedience to God is called acceptable because it is what the people of faith (Muslims) consider as acceptable and what they do not forbid to be done. And the basis of what is rejectable is that which God has disapproved...Disobedience to God is called rejectable because the people who believe in God (Muslims) disapprove its being done.[37]

Looking at the whole of Ṭabarī's *tafsīr* on *umma* as it has been outlined here, we draw the following main points:

1. The Muslim *umma* is the "best community" before the eyes of God because it has been foreordained by God to be so before the creation of the world. Thus its character of being "best"

---

[34] Ṭabarī (on 3:110) 46.

[35] Ṭabarī (on 3:110) 45.

[36] A similar way of seeing things, it is worth noting, was already known within the Judaeo-Christian world, as may be witnessed by the concepts of the "pre-existent Torah" and Jesus as the *logos* who was with God in the beginning: "In the beginning was the Word: the Word was with God and the Word was God (John 1:1)."

[37] Ṭabarī (on 3:110) 45.

applies to every generation of Muslim *umma* in history.

2. "Middle community" *(umma wasaṭ)* is the mode of being "best" of this *umma* in so far as its stance in the world, vis-a-vis other communities, is concerned. It means the balanced, moderate position between two extremities in religion, and thus, the "best."

3. This *umma* is centrifugal or "missionary"[38] in character, which is consistent with its position of being "middle in religion." In concrete, its task is to call and order non-Muslims to "what is good," which is the religion of Islam as brought by Muhammad, and to submit to the Muslim community because the criterion of what is good and what is evil, what is acceptable and what is rejectable, is the Muslim community. It is only through the Muslim community that God's will can be known in history, or, in other words, that outside of Islam there is no salvation.

Ṭabarī lived in a historical situation marked by the height of the quick expansion of Muslim dominion. In his time, Muslim dominion had expanded to as far west as Morocco and Spain. The question then was the stand of Islam in its contact or confrontation with foreign civilizations or uncongenial cultures. His *tafsīr* then was written at a time when the Muslims needed what may be termed the Islamic theology of conquest.

-- ++ --

Ṭabarī's commentary stands at the end of the early period of *tafsīr* with its concentration on Traditional exegesis, serving at the same time as the climax of this period with its collection and summation of the traditional material available at that time. However,

---

[38] See A. A. Roest Crollius, "Mission and Morality: *Al-amr bi-l-maʿrūf* as expression of the communitarian and missionary dimensions of qurʾānic ethics" in *Studia Missionalia*, vol. 27 (Roma: Università Gregoriana Editrice, 1978), 265.

Ṭabarī's having made his own judgments on material passed down has in a way ushered in an air of rationalism which was to sweep across the face of Muslim scholarship in the next three centuries after him. Many commentators felt that the exercise of the mind was more valuable than recollections of the memory or felt that dependence on the traditions was not enough for a true understanding of the Qur'ān. These commentators then preferred to exercise what has been called *tafsīr bi-l-ra'y* or exposition by means of independent opinion. This kind of exegesis was championed by the school of theology of the Mu'tazila, whose influence was felt in the third century and which regarded reason as a fundamental source of knowledge and mere imitation an insult to human dignity. If the Mu'tazila gained influence in the third century, the fourth century belonged to another branch of Islam - i.e., the Šī'ī - whose traditionist writing really came into its own then as it was also the time when Šī'ī rulers were in power. It should be noted, however, that if in the first centuries after Ṭabarī no significant commentary on the Qur'ān was written within Sunnite Islam, this in no way implies that stagnation occurred in qur'ānic exegesis. Interpretation of the Qur'ān is not limited to the comprehensive works of the commentaries, but rather is to be found everywhere in theological, judicial and other works. In this sense, for instance, Ġazālī's theological work entitled *"Iḥyā' 'ulūm-al-dīn"* (Revival of the Religious Sciences) also contains a number of basic reflections concerning exegesis and a large number of individual interpretations. Sunnī works of *tafsīr* in the centuries after Ṭabarī were either specifically non-traditionist in their orientation or were very heavily dependent on the compilation of *ḥadīṯ* materials made by Ṭabarī.

An outstanding example of the kind of *tafsīr* that swept the air of Muslim scholarship in the first centuries after Ṭabarī is that of Zamaḫšarī, who was a Mu'tazilī and therefore not an orthodox *mufassir*, yet his *tafsīr bi-l-ra'y* on the Qur'ān is among the most-widely read and highly esteemed by Sunnī Muslims.

--++--

1.2 Zamaḫšarī

1.2.1 Introduction

The Muʿtazila school first appeared during the Abbasid period, about a century after Muhammad, but, as mentioned above, did not make its influence felt until the next century, especially during the reign of Caliph Maʾmūn (198/813 -218/833), who attempted in vain to force their theological position[39] on the majority. They were the first to introduce the Greek mode of reasoning and argumentation into Islamic religious discussions, changing the face of Muslim theology for all time as a result. By

---

[39] Muʿtazila theology is summed up under five principles *(uṣūl)* or fundamental doctrines which one must accept in their integrity to be recognized as a Muʿtazilī. They are the following: 1) *Aṣl al-tawḥīd*: the strictest profession of monotheism, against any kind of dualism (thus the idea of the createdness of the Qurʾān) and against any resemblance between God and His creatures (i.e., against anthropomorphism); 2) *Aṣl al-ʿadl:* God is just and what he does aims at what is best for his creation; human actions result from man"s free will; no predestination; 3) *Aṣl al-waʿd wa-l-waʿīd* (or *al-asmāʾ wa-l-aḥkām):* practical theology; God of his grace may forgive; he who is not a Muslim obeys God if he does something which God has commanded in the Qurʾān; 4) *Aṣl al-manzila baina ʾl-manzilatain:* "the intermediate position:" the Muslim who sins is to be regarded as neither an infidel nor a believer. A connected issue was the ranking of the first four caiphs. 5) *Aṣl al-amr bi-l-maʿrūf wa-l-nahy ʿani-l-munkar:* programme of Muʿtazila activity before the coming of the Abbasids; the faith must be spread by the tongue, the hand and the sword; later this *aṣl* was little discussed and its obligatory character denied. Cf. H. S. Nyberg, "Al-Muʿtazila" in *Shorter Encyclopedia of Islam*, edited by H. A. R. Gibb and J. H. Kramers (Leiden: E. J. Brill, 1991) 426; Cf. also, A. J. Wensinck, *The Muslim Creed: Its Genesis and Historical Development* (Cambridge: Cambridge University Press, 1932/1965) 58f; and D. Gimaret, "Muʿtazila" in *The Encyclopedia of Islam*, new edition, volume VII (1993) 783-793.

the fifth and early sixth centuries (the era of Zamaḫšarī), the Muʿtazilī school had ceased to be the influential movement it once had been since it failed to achieve an official sanction as "orthodoxy." The Muʿtazila then gradually faded into small pockets of the Islamic world, one of which was the region where Abū-l-Qāsim Maḥmūd b. ʿUmar al-Zamaḫšarī was raised.[40]

That Zamaḫšarī considered himself to be of Muʿtazila persuasion we know from his own insistence as well as through his writings. He is quoted to have said in opposition to the traditionists' attitude: "A man with proof is more honorable than a lion in its lair. An imitator is more despicable than a mangy goat.... Knowledge is a city which has two doors for entry, one reason, the other tradition."[41]

Accordingly, it was during Zamaḫšarī's second stay in Mecca that the Muʿtazilites living there persuaded him to write his famous commentary on the Qurʾān entitled *Al-Kaššāf ʿan ḥaqāʾiqi-l-tanzīl* (The Unveiler of the Realities of the Revelation). He originally began his commentary on the Qurʾān with the words: *"al-hamdu*

---

[40] It was about a century and a half after Ṭabarī's death that Zamaḫšarī was born in the small town of Zamaḫšarī in the Muʿtazila dominated province of Ḫwārizm. He studied under the leading Muʿtazilite scholar of his day Mūḍar Maḥmūd b. Jarīr al-Ḍabbī. He travelled widely, visiting Buḫāra, Ḫurāsān, Iṣfahān, Baghdad and Mecca. He was a master of a great many fields and wrote a number of highly respected works, one of which is his famous commentary on the Qurʾān. For Zamaḫšarī's biographical and bibliographical details, see, among others, Lutpi Ibrahim, "Al-Zamaḫšarī: His Life and Works" in *Islamic Studies*, XIX (1980) 95-110. Cf. also C. Brockelmann, "Al-Zamaḫšarī" in *Shorter Encyclopedia of Islam*, edited by H. A. R. Gibb and J. H. Kramers (Leiden: E. J. Brill, 1991) 656.

[41] Quoted by Rashid Ahmad (in his "Qurʾānic Exegesis and Classical Tafsīr," *Islamic Quarterly*, vol. XII, Nos. 1-2 (1968) 86-87) from Yāqūt, *Iršād*, VII, 150. From these remarks it is evident that Zamaḫšarī was not against tradition itself but was against tradition which did not allow room for reason.

liʾllāhi-llaḏī ḫalaqa-l-Qurʾān," which is an announcement of the Muʿtazilite doctrine of the createdness of the Qurʾān.[42] The circumstances surrounding Zamaḫšarī's writing of his *tafsīr* has been summarized by Lutpi Ibrahim as follows.

> In his introduction to *al-Kaššāf* (p. 3), Zamaḫšarī states that the idea of writing *al-Kaššāf* was originally motivated by the great need of the Muʿtazilites in Mecca for a qurʾānic exegesis which explained the Qurʾān in accordance with the Muʿtazilite views. Zamaḫšarī was not happy with their suggestion and begged to be excused, but they insisted that he should carry out the task, and finally he agreed. Perhaps their insistence is not the main reason for Zamaḫšarī's later decision, since he considered it afterwards as obligatory upon him to fulfill it. This, however, is due to the fact that Zamaḫšarī himself was fully aware of the real situation at that time and also of the low level of intellectual development among the Meccans...besides this, he was encouraged by Ibn Wahhās, the Amīr of Mecca who welcomed him and offered him many facilities in completing his *tafsīr*.[43]

Despite his heretical beliefs, Zamaḫšarī's *tafsīr* is extremely popular in the Muslim world. It is valued by Sunnī Muslims as one of the classical bases of *tafsīr*. In modern times and, in Cairo alone, it "was printed at least five times before 1919 and went

---

[42] However, in order to earn public approval, he changed *ḫalaqa* to *jaʿala* (to make or establish), a verb which could imply either that God was the agent (to please the orthodox) or the creator (to please the Muʿtazila), but *anzala* has been substituted by later editors. Cf. J. I. Smith, *An Historical and Semantic Study of the Term "Islām"* (Missoula, Montana: Scholars Press: 1975) 91.

[43] Lutpi Ibrahim, "Az-Zamaḫšarī: His Life and Works" in *Islamic Studies,* XIX (1980) 101-102.

through no less than three editions between 1926 and 1970."[44]

While Ṭabarī's style was, on the whole, to present various understandings of the text based on traditional interpretations, Zamaḫšarī[45] generally gives the sense of the passage as appears most obvious, followed by grammatical and philological analyses

---

[44] As it is now, al-Kaššāf is available in printed edition with orthodox glosses at the foot of the page.

[45] Among the assessments of Zamaḫšarī's al-Kaššāf are the following: Rashid Ahmad says: "This sort of *tafsīr* is not only allowed but also encouraged by the prophet, but when reason exceeds its own limitations and tries to interpret the Qur'ān on its own terms, then the Qur'ān is relegated into a secondary place and commentary becomes more or less a collection of dialectical and theological views. Zamaḫšarī sometimes appears in his commentary more as a rigid Muʿtazilī than as a commentator." See Rashid Ahmad, "Qur'ānic Exegesis and Classical Tafsīr" in *The Islamic Quarterly*, vol. XII, Nos. 1-2 (1968) 95; Muhammad Ibrahim H. I. Surty, in his survey of *tafsīr* exegesis literature in Arabic in 1987, has the following to say of al-Zamaḫšarī's al-Kaššaf: "Scholars and students of almost all schools of thought have benefited greatly from his unique contribution in *Iʿjāz* (inimitability) *al-Qur'ān* and quoted from him copiously in their works with great veneration and admiration - and done so in spite of the fact that al-Zamaḫšarī was one of the champions of the Muʿtazila school of thought...This indicates clearly the academic and intellectual tolerance practised by Muslim scholars and their love for and commitment to the acquisition of knowledge, wherever it is available... A number of *tafāsīr* have been written on al-Kaššaf in which its *iʿtizāl* is condemned but its *iʿjāz* is much admired and further elucidated." Cf. Muhammad Ibrahim H. I. Surty, "The Qur'ān in Islamic Scholarship" in *The Muslim World Book Review*, vol. 7, no. 4 (Summer 1987) 54-55. Accordingly, it was one of the *tafsīr* texts studied in the advanced courses at the Azhar University in Cairo in the eighteenth century together with the *tafāsīr* of al-Suyūṭī and al-Mahallī, al-Bayḍāwī, al-Širbīnī and Abū-l-Sūʿūd. Heyworth-Dunne, *An Introduction to the History of Education in Modern Egypt* (London: Luzac and Co., no date) 45-46.

and, based on these, draws possible interpretations. He pays only slight attention to traditions, sometimes mentioning them but almost as an afterthought, without *asānīd* and often without naming the authorities.

1.2.2 *Tafsīr*

One of the central themes of the Muᶜtazila school is the attribution to God of JUSTICE *(ᶜadl)*. It is therefore not surprising to discover that this concept forms the rationale for 2:142-143 in Zamaḫšarī's *tafsīr*, verses which he sees as a continuing thought. *Wasaṭ* (2:143) as a description of the *umma muslima* is to be understood in the context of the change of the *qibla*. The change of the *qibla* is God's guidance for the Muslims

> to a straight path «إلى صراط مستقيم» which is what the wisdom *(ḥikma)* and the good *(maṣlaḥa)* demand in directing them, at first towards Jerusalem, and now towards the *Kaᶜba*.[46]

In other words, when the wisdom and the good (which God is) direct, it is *always* to a straight path. This statement expresses the Muᶜtazilite doctrine of the absolute justice of God. It is in this same manner that God exalted the Muslim community as *wasaṭ*, as "best"/*ḫiyār*.

Then, Zamaḫšarī deals with grammatical and philological analyses to explain the meaning of *wasaṭ*. First, he explains the unusual grammatical usage of the term *wasaṭ* in the verse as well as its nature, saying that here, *wasaṭ*

> is the adjectival use of the substance which is "the middle of the thing - وسط الشيء" For that reason, in it (i.e., in this adjective) are made equal or put on the same level the

[46] Zamaḫšarī (on 2:142b) 317.

singular and the plural, the masculine and the feminine.[47]

Then he says that the best is middle because the extremities or other parts enclose it. The center or middle of a thing is thus protected and defended.[48] Being *wasaṭ* or middle is something that has to be protected or maintained, otherwise it can be lost, i.e., the middle can become the edge as Zamaḫšarī explains by quoting a line from an Arab poet which says:

> It was the protected middle but then problems accumulated from all sides until it became an extreme [i.e., a marginal reality].[49]

Zamaḫšarī concludes by citing his own experience of the use of the term *wasaṭ* among the Arabs in Mecca which shows that it means justice or well balanced "because the middle is justice *(ʿadl)* or a just distance between the extremities."[50]

The following are the main points made by Zamaḫšarī. To be described as middle *(wasaṭ)* is the same as being described as the best *(ḫiyār)* or as just or justice *(ʿadl)* because the nature of the best is being middle, i.e., equally distant from all the extremities, thus it is a situation of justice or being well balanced.

---

[47] Zamaḫšarī (on 2:143) 317.

[48] Zamaḫšarī (on 2:143) 317: للخيار وسط لأن الأطراف يتسارع إليها الخلل والأعوار والأوساط محمية محوطة In this connection, Katsh notes: "A similar explanation is found in Judah Hallevi's *Kitab Al-Khazari,* in connection with the high qualities of Israel and the Holy Land. Being situated in the midst of the world, the Holy Land enjoys the most well-balanced climate." A. I. Katsh, *Judaism in Islam* (New York: New York University Press, 1954) 112.

[49] Zamaḫšarī (on 2:143) 317 (كانت هى الوسط المحمىّ فاكتنفت بها الحوادث حتى أصبحت طرفا)

[50] Ibid. "لأن الوسط عدل بين الأطراف ليس إلى بعضها أقرب من بعض."

Furthermore, being middle or well balanced is something that has to be protected and maintained, otherwise it can find itself not being middle anymore but a periphery or edge. Consequently, the Muslim community as an *umma wasaṭ* is one which is a balanced community or a community of justice. It has to constantly maintain its being so because on the day of the resurrection Muslims are expected to witness to their being a just community so that the prophet can witness to their integrity.

If in Ṭabarī's *tafsīr wasaṭ* is the description of the Muslim community as it stands in relation to other communities, we have just seen from the foregoing that in Zamaḫšarī it is the description of the Muslim community as it should be in itself. Thus when we turn to Zamaḫšarī's *tafsīr* of 3:104 and 3:110, we see that the Muslim community is a centripetal community and the task expressed therein is one which is to be fulfilled within the Muslim community. Thus, again if in Ṭabarī the task is centrifugal in character, here in Zamaḫšarī we will see that it is centripetal, one which, when seen in the light of what he had to say about *umma wasaṭ*, is intended for the maintenance of the community's quality of being *wasaṭ*. It is due to this emphasis that Zamaḫšarī discusses in detail the various aspects of this task. He does so by first clarifying a twofold understanding of the particle *min* (from) in the phrase "That there be from among you..." (3:104). He writes:

> *Min* [is to be understood here as a] *min partitivum* » من للتبعيض « because the ordering of what is acceptable and the forbidding of what is rejectable belong to the collective duties « فروض الكفايات » since it does not apply to anyone but to him who knows what is acceptable and what is rejectable, and knows how to arrange the ordering when the need arises, and how to carry it out. An ignorant person might forbid what is acceptable and order what is rejectable; or, he might know the principles in his own religious denomination but ignorant of that of the other and thus

might forbid the latter what is not rejectable; he could be harsh in the situation where he ought to be gentle or gentle in the situation where he ought to be harsh; or he might rebuke someone whose reprehension ought to be done only in the long run or whose reprehension would be to no avail as is the case with villains, executioners and those like them.

It is also said [that it is] a *min explicativum* «من للتبيين» with the meaning of: "Be a community that orders..." the same as God's saying: "You are the best community that has been brought forth for mankind; you order.... " (3:110).[51]

Thus, putting the above-mentioned explanations together, we see that *min* here has a double function: 1) as *min explicativum*, i.e., to explain that the task mentioned in the verse belongs to the whole community for the maintenance of its distinctive quality of being "best" and 2) as *min partitivum* in regard to the execution of the task as it belongs to the collective duties[52] since the performance of this task requires certain conditions which are not necessarily shared by everyone, the principal condition being knowledge of what is acceptable and what is not, as well as the knowledge of the technique or stages in the process of ordering and forbidding. Thus it is clear from Zamaḫšarī's explanations that the task is not imposed on each individual member of the community and not centrifugal or missionary in character (i.e., for the propagation of Islam) but centripetal, i.e., for the maintenance

---

51 Zamaḫšarī (on 3:104) 207-208.

52 *Farḍ-al-kifāya* or *farḍ ʿala-l-kifāya* is the juridical term to designate those duties which are incumbent on the whole community but whose fulfilment by a sufficient number of individuals excuses the other individuals from fulfilling them; such duties, among others, are funeral prayers. A duty that is obligatory for each individual person is called *farḍ-al-ʿayn;* such duties, among others, are ritual prayer, fasting, etc.

of the Muslim community as an Islamic community. We will outline here Zamaḫšarī's systematic presentation - in a typical Muʿtazilite way of "question and answer" - of the various aspects in the actualization of this task, in order for us to gain more insight into its nature as a duty which is to be exercised within the Muslim community. He first clarifies the nature of the obligation, saying:

> The ordering of what is acceptable should concur with its content: if it (the content) is obligatory *(wājib)*, then doing it is obligatory; if it is recommendable, then doing it is only recommendatory. As regards forbidding what is rejectable, it is always obligatory.[53]
>
> To the question: how can this obligation be known? I answer: On this point the two *Šayḫs* differ: according to Abū ʿAlī it is by hearing and deduction while according to Abū Hāšim it is by hearing alone.[54]

---

[53] Zamaḫšarī (on 3:104, Book 1) 452f, also for the following series of quotations. *Wājib*/obligatory and *mandūb*/recommended belong to the *al-aḥkām al-ḫamsa/* the five qualifications of the human acts according to their accordance or non-accordance with divine law; the other juridical categories being 3) indifferent *(mubāḥ)*, to be distinguished from *jāʾiz* (allowed, unobjectionable) 4)*makrūh* (reprehensible, disapproved) and 5) *ḥarām* (forbidden; the opposite of which is *ḥalāl* - everything that is not forbidden. Cf. J. Schacht, *An Introduction to Islamic Law* (Oxford: Clarendon Press, 1991) 121.

[54] Referred to by the honorific appellation "the two *Šayḫs*" *(al-šayḫayn)* are the Muʿtazila's two most famous luminaries who are father and son, namely: Abū ʿAlī Muḥammad al-Jubbāʾi (d. 303/915) and Abū Hāšim ʿAbd-al-Salām (d. 321/933). Cf. A. A. Roest Crollius, "Mission and Morality" in *Studia Missionalia*, vol. 27 (Roma: Università Gregoriana Editrice, 1978) 267. It may be noted that *samʿ*("hearing') and *ʿaql* (literally, "intellect, understanding") are the rallying points of the traditionalists and the rationalists, respectively, in exegesis and other religious sciences. The Muʿtazila claimed to hold the ideal of reconciling both. See, A. A. Roest Crollius, Ibid, note 32.

And if you ask what are the conditions for forbidding that which is rejectable, I answer:

1) That the one who forbids knows that what he censures is wrong, otherwise he might censure what is good.
2) That what he forbids is not an accomplished fact, because it is useless to forbid what has been done; however, it should be criticized and similar acts should be forbidden.
3) That it does not get the better of his opinion that the one who is forbidden will go on in his reprehensible actions.
4) That he does not think that his forbidding will not produce any effect because he [the other] does not take it seriously.

And if you ask on what condition forbidding becomes a duty, I answer:

It has to be likely for him that a transgression is going to take place, as for instance, when he sees a drinker preparing his instruments and thus getting ready to imbibe liquor. At the same time, he should hold it most probable that if he reprehends, no great harm will befall him.

And if you ask how reprehending is to be carried out, I answer:

He should begin with the easy [way]; and if it does not work he advances to the difficult one [which he has to do] because the aim is the cessation of what is rejectable.[55]

And if you ask who must do it, I answer:

---

[55] To support this answer, Zamaḫšarī, in a typically Muʿtazilite vein, quotes the words in the Qurʾān as regards two parties of believers who fall to fighting: "Make peace between them. Then [if it does not work], fight them." Zamaḫšarī (on 3:104) 208. Cf. Sūra 49:9.

> Every Muslim who qualifies according to the conditions has the power to do it...As regards censure which is fighting, the Imām and his deputies are the main [ones to order] because they are more learned in politics and with them is its equipment [for fighting]. [56]

Thus we see the different aspects in the actualization of the centripetal task of the community in view of the maintenance of the community's being *wasaṭ*, or being a community of justice. Here is expressed the consciousness of being a community with a "mission" to itself, not to other communities, as in Ṭabarī. By way of conclusion, Zamaḫšarī[57] cites one more point to explain the manner in which the order in the verse is given.

> To the question: How come it is said "they call to what is good and they order what is acceptable"? I answer:
>
> The call to what is good is general (for everybody) in the authorization of the actions while the ordering of what is acceptable as well as the forbidding of what is rejectable is special (for some only). Thus the general is mentioned first

---

[56] Thus during the time of the Abbasids, when the Muʿtazila became influential, what used to be the office of "inspector of the market" during the time of the Umayyads was now transformed and Islamicized "by entrusting its holder with discharging the collective obligation, enjoined in the Qurʾān, to 'encourage good and discourage evil', making him responsible for enforcing Islamic morals and behavior in the community of Muslims, and giving him the Islamic title of *muḥtasib* (his office is called *ḥisba)*. In addition to his ancient powers of enforcing traffic, building, sanitary, and trading regulations and deciding disputes arising from them, it was now part of his duties to bring transgressors to justice and to impose summary punishments which came to include the flogging of the drunk and the unchaste and even the amputation of the hands of thieves caught in the act..." Cf. Joseph Schacht, *An Introduction to Islamic Law* (Oxford: Clarendon Press, 1964/1991) 52.

[57] Zamaḫšarī (on 3:104, Book 1) 453.

and the special/particular is attached to it in order to make known its importance.

Thus it is made clear what he said in many words in the beginning of his commentary on this text, i.e. that "as *partitivum*" and "as *explicativum*" do not express two contradictory (either the one or the other) interpretations of the *"min"* (from) in the text, but together form two inseparable aspects to the proper understanding of the command expressed in the text.

When we turn to Zamaḫšarī's commentary on 3:110, we see that he enumerates three ways of interpreting the phrase "You are the best nation brought forth for mankind," namely: 1) you were found to be the best nation, 2) you are in the knowledge of God the best nation, and 3) in the communities before you, you were mentioned and described to be the best community.[58] We already saw this mentioned in Ṭabarī with corresponding *asānīd*. Here in Zamaḫšarī they are mentioned without any further remarks and without corresponding *asānīd*. It is clear from the explanations of Zamaḫšarī that his main concern is the "why" or "how" of *ḫayra umma*. He cites a tradition which says that the prophet, in answer to a question asked as regards who are the best people, said:

> Those who order what is acceptable and forbid what is rejectable and who preserve their faith in God and who put [these things] in practice. Whoever orders what is acceptable and forbids what is rejectable is the vicar *(ḫalīfa)* of God in this world, and the vicar of His prophet and the vicar of His Scripture.[59]

Zamaḫšarī thus sees 3:110 as God putting into clear words that the Muslim community is the best *umma* as long as it orders what is acceptable, forbids what is rejectable and believes in God.

---

[58] Zamaḫšarī (on 3:110, Book 1) 454.

[59] Zamaḫšarī (on 3:104 & 3:110, Book 1) 452.

He concludes his commentary on these verses by emphasizing that the most important is faith in God from which everything else expected of an Islamic community will follow.

The whole of Zamaḫšarī's *tafsīr* as it has been outlined above, shows that the nature and task of the Muslim *umma* are to be derived from the understanding of the terms *wasaṭ* and *ḫiyār*. The Muslim community is marked distinctively by its being middle which means justice and thus excellent. This distinctive quality is seen as a project that has to be earned constantly. Thus the task of this community is directed upon itself, i.e., the maintenance of its being middle, just, an excellent community. In all of this, Zamaḫšarī is true to the basic tenets of the Muʿtazila.[60]

If Ṭabarī's commentary on *umma* is an answer to the historical situation in which he lived, so is that of Zamaḫšarī. If Ṭabarī wrote his commentary when the threat to the Muslim community was seen as coming from the outside, Zamaḫšarī wrote his within the heartland of Islam, where conflicting views and practices among Muslims were a threat to the oneness of the Muslim community. Zamaḫšarī wrote his *tafsīr* in Mecca itself, and emphasized the various aspects in the Muslim community's task of maintaining its being a community of justice.

---

[60] As Zamaḫšarī makes known in his preface to his commentary on 2:143 (see above), every guidance of God is always to a straight path, i.e., God acts justly. Since for the Muʿtazila there is no existence of divine attributes apart from God's essence, this means He is justice and, as we saw in our review of his commentary, He orders the Muslims to act or live in a *wasaṭ* or just manner. Thus a Muslim's act of justice is his *islām*, his submission to God. Therefore, the religious and ethical aspects of the Muslim community are concretized in the life of justice among its members. Zamaḫšarī's idea of a "centripetal community" is consistent with the Muʿtazila principle of "practical theology" which says, among other things, that "a non-Muslim obeys God if he does something which is commanded in the Qurʾān." Thus, if in Ṭabarī there is no salvation outside the Islamic religion, in Zamaḫšarī there may be salvation also outside the Islamic religion.

1.3 Rāzī

1.3.1 Introduction

In the sixth century, i.e., the century following Zamaḫšarī, *Kalām* or scholastic theology had come into its own in the lively disputation between the rationalists and the traditionalists. The outstanding figure in the "synthesis" of philosophy and theology -- Al-Ġazālī - had come and gone. In this period, Sunnī systematic exegesis reached another high point with the coming into the fore of Rāzī.[61] The variety of influences apparently at play in the development of Rāzī's thought may be summarized as follows:

> Rāzī was well-versed in the thought world of Greek philosophy - his commentary of Ibn Sīna is famous - but was

---

[61] Abū ʿAbd Allāh Muḥammad b. ʿUmar al-Rāzī was born in 543/1149 (or five years after Zamaḫšarī's death) at Rayy - where Ṭabarī begun his religious studies - in Ṭabaristān. Known most commonly as Faḫr al-Dīn, he is also called Ibn al-Ḫaṭīb (son of the preacher). His father was the city's public preacher and was also a Šāfiʿī jurist. Little is known about Rāzī's early years other than that he was trained as a Šāfiʿī and Ašʿarī scholar. One of the first endeavors of Rāzī about which we are informed is his journey from Rayy to Ḫwārizm where he attempted to combat the Muʿtazilite doctrines still prevalent there, but later on was compelled to leave the country. He was above all concerned with the integration of philosophy and religious traditions. He gained real stature in Hirāt, where he gained many disciples and even became the eponym of a *madrasa*. His life though was not without difficulties as he also had many enemies, among whom was his own brother Rukn al-Dīn, as well as the sect of Karrāmīya, who charged him with having betrayed Islam in following the philosophical directions of Aristotle, Ibn Sīna and al-Fārābī. It is reported that when he died - poisoned allegedly at the instigation of the Karrāmīyā - he had to be buried in his house for fear that his enemies might mutilate his body. See G. C. Anawati, "Fakhr al-Dīn al-Rāzī" in *Encyclopedia of Islam*. New edition. vol. II (1990) 751-755.

not bound by it. Exercising his own capacity for reason he accepted certain elements of it and rejected others. The same is true of his occupation with theology. Trained in the school of Aš^carī[62] he remained of that persuasion, but felt free to contradict those elements with which he could not agree. Like Ġazālī he was very seriously concerned with reconciling philosophy and theology, but throughout his life he continued to be far more dedicated to the former than his predecessor. While Ġazālī became increasingly involved in the mystical understanding of the divine, Rāzī devoted his attentions in the main to articulating the relationship between the qur'ānic worldview and the primary tenets of contemporary philosophical understanding. Despite this continuing devotion to the philosophical approach, however, Rāzī in so far as it was necessary to choose sides in the controversy between Sunnī orthodoxy and rationalist philosophy, aligned himself with the former.[63]

Rāzī wrote many works of which the one that concerns us here primarily is his enormous commentary on the Qur'ān[64]

---

[62] Abūl-Ḥasan-al-Aš'arī (d. 324/935) was a Mu'tazilite who emerged out of the movement to enunciate a theological position midway between the scripturalism of the traditionalists and the rationalism of the Mu'tazilites, a position which was to last as the most significant statement in Islamic theology. His method was based on extensive use of the Qur'ān and the *aḥādīṯ* in order to formulate his rational arguments.

[63] J. I. Smith, *An Historical and Semantic Study of the Term "Islām"* (Missoula, Montana: Scholars Press, 1975) 104.

[64] Rāzī's commentary was incomplete at the time of his death. It was brought to completion by his students. "His disciples Šams al-Dīn Aḥmad b. Ḫalīl-al-Ḫuwaiyī (d. 629/1242) and Najm al-Dīn Aḥmad b. Muḥammad al-Kanulī completed the work, so faithfully adopting the style and technique of al-Rāzī that the reader would believe that it was entirely al-Rāzī's work." Muhammad Ibrahim H. I. Surty, "The Qur'ān in Islamic Scholarship" in *The Muslim World Book Rview*, vol. 7, no. 4 (Summer 1987) 56.

"Mafātīḥ al-Ġayb" (The Keys to the Unseen) which is also known as *"al-Tafsīr-al-Kabīr"* (The Great Commentary). It is considered by many to be the most comprehensive and inclusive commentary on the Qurʾān ever composed.[65] As regards its content as a whole, Kramers may be voicing the evaluation by many scholars (especially Orientalists) when he claims that "this work is not only an Ašʿarīte answer to the Muʿtazilite Qurʾān exegesis which had found its exponent in the *Kaššāf* of Zamaḫšarī, but also provides him [Rāzī] with a means to expose his philosophical ideas."[66] The Muslim scholar Surty has the following to say of Rāzī's commentary:

> *Tafsīr Kabīr* makes clear, among other things, 1) the degree of intellectual progress Muslims had achieved in different disciplines during the time of Rāzī; 2) that the scholars who contributed in different Islamic disciplines were not learned in the religious sciences alone but also possessed extensive knowledge of other disciplines.... He refutes through philosophical argument the Muʿtazila doctrine so extravagantly promoted in *al-Kaššāf*.[67]

The assessment of Surty summarizes the reasons Rāzī has been to a large extent recognized in Sunnī circles as the most brilliant light in the sixth century. Rāzī's approach,

---

[65] It is called "the greatest speculative *tafsīr*... an ocean of various waters, having as ingredients reports of later sectarian developments." Daud Rahbar, "Reflections on the Tradition of Qurʾānic Exegesis" in *The Muslim World*, vol. LII, no. 4 (October 1962) 303. Daud Rahbar has since converted to Christianity.

[66] G. C. Anawati, "Fakhr al-Dīn al-Rāzī" in *Encyclopedia of Islam*. New edition. vol. II (1990) 754.

[67] Muhammad Ibrahim H. I. Surty, "The Qurʾān in Islamic Scholarship: A Survey of *Tafsīr* Exegesis Literature in Arabic" in *The Muslim World Book Review*, vol. 7, no. 4 (Summer 1987) 56.

is philosophical and analytical; he enumerates the "questions" or "problems" which are raised by each *āya* or a group of *āyas* and then tackles them one at a time, listing the various solutions which have been proposed regardless of the generation or doctrinal persuasion of the persons who proposed them. He gives the views of the Companions and Successors but in a less thorough fashion than Ṭabarī and usually without *asānid*. On the other hand he cites two early commentaries which were not used by Ṭabarī; those of al-Kalbī (d. 146/763-4) and Muqātil b. Sulaymān (d. 150/767). Of the classical commentators he occasionally mentions al-Qaffāl (d. 365/976) and Ṭabarī (d. 310/923) although he draws much more frequently on Ṭabarī's pupil al-Wāḥidī (d. 468/1075). He gives extensive references to the views of the grammarians, philologists and the founders of the legal schools. He is an important source of information about Muᶜtazilite exegesis for he cites Abū Muslim (d. 322/934) and ᶜAbd al-Jabbār (d. 415/1024) as well as drawing extensively on the commentary of Zamaḫšarī.[68]

As is clear from the foregoing, while Ṭabarī and Rāzī are both exponents of Sunnī *tafsīr*, they differ not only in the approach and method of presentation but also in their references. This only shows that while Ṭabarī's *tafsīr* was the representative Sunnī exegesis in his time, Rāzī expresses the *ijmāᶜ* of his time and thus gives us along with his philosophical interpretations a good understanding of orthodox interpretation in the sixth century A. H.

1.3.2 *Tafsīr*

Rāzī begins his discussion of 2:143 in his usual style by saying that there are several issues to be considered here. The first concerns the *ka* (thus; in the same manner) in *kaḏālika*

---

68 Neal Robinson, *Christ in Islam and Christianity* (London: Macmillan Press, 1991) 72.

*ja*ʿ*alnākum*... (In the same manner we established you...) which he says is the *kāf* of similitude *(kāf al-tašbīh)* which, like in Zamaḫšarī, gives the same rationale for both the changing of the *qibla* and the appointment of *umma wasaṭ* which is God's guidance to a straight path. It is in the explanation of this "guidance" that the two commentators differ. We have seen that Zamaḫšarī, expressing the view of the Muʿtazila, emphasizes that God's willing is always to what is good, to a straight path, because He is just.

Rāzī, expressing the orthodox view, points out in his systematic discussion of the implications of the *kāf* that, as God's is the east and the west (i.e., to Him belongs everything) - He who can give honor *(i*ʿ*zāz)* or humiliation *(iḏlāl)*, has guided the Muslims to the *qibla* which is better than the previous one; in the same manner He made them *umma wasaṭ*.[69] Here we see Rāzī making two specific points - which are repeated in other areas of his *tafsīr* - to taunt the Muʿtazila who proposed a different view. One is that guidance or misguidance is God's will *(al-hidāya wal-iḏlāl min Allāh ta*ʿ*ālā)*; and the other, which is a consequence, is that *wasaṭ* as a distinctive character of the Muslim community, is not something which is deserved nor is it the community's choice. It is God's creation.

It is in consideration of the second issue that we come to Rāzī's interpretation of *umma wasaṭ*. As he proceeds step by step, he begins with an admission of the difficulty in deciphering or explaining the grammatical form of the word *wasaṭ* in this verse saying it is neither a noun nor an adverb.[70] Then he proceeds with the explanation of the meaning of the term. Emphasizing that the foremost concern is that the *wasaṭ* is the ʿ*adl* (the middle is the just), he says that its proof or evidence can be shown by the following: a verse *(āya)* from the Qurʾān, a citation from tradition/

---

[69] See Rāzī (on 2:143) 96-97.

[70] Rāzī (on 2:143) 97.

report *(ḫabar)*, a line from poetry *(šiʿr)*, an explanation from a translation [dictionary] *(naql)* and from the sense or meaning *(maʿnā)*.

> As regards the verse, it is God's saying "The best of them said - قَالَ أَوْسَطُهُمْ " (68:28), i.e., the most just of them - أعدلهم. As regards the report (الخبر). we have it from al-Qaffāl that ....the prophet said "middle community means justice - أمة وسطا قال عدلا". and of it the prophet said "the best of matters is its middle - خير الأمور أوسطها," i.e., the most just of it - أعدلها. And it is said: "The prophet was the best of the Qurayš as a family - كان النبى أوسط قريش نسبا" and about it the prophet said: "You are in this manner to be the middle - عليكم بالنمط الأوسط ." As regards poetry (الشعر) , it is the saying of the poet Zuhayr: "They are middle who satisfy humankind with their administration of justice - هم وسط يرضى الأنام بحكمهم ... As regards the translation (النقل) , al-Jūharī in the [dictionary] *al-ṣiḥāḥ* says "In the same manner we have appointed you a middle nation - وكذالك جعلناكم أمة وسطاً ," i.e., just - عدلا , and it is the same thing said by [the language authorities] al-Aḫfaš, al-Ḫalīl and Quṭrub.[71]

As regards the meaning, Rāzī mentions four aspects in which it may be viewed. First is that the middle is the essence *(ḥaqīqa)* in the distance between the two extremities and as such it is superior *(fāḍil)* and balanced *(muʿtadal)* compared to the two extremities *(ṭarafayn)* which are excessive. Second is that justice *(ʿadl)* is exalted as middle because it does not lean towards one of the extremities. Third, it is necessary that *wasaṭ* in 2:143 mean

---

[71] Rāzī (on 2:143) 97.

justice because to be described as *wasaṭ* with the meaning of best as witness belongs properly to the Messenger. Fourth is "that the best or the most just of the spots of a thing is its middle spot because its judgment in relation to all its parts must be on the strength of equality and moderation - أن أعدل بقاع الشيء وسطه لأن حكمه مع سائر أطرافه على سواه وعلى اعتدال."[72]

After his elaboration of the meaning of "the *wasaṭ* is the just or justice," Rāzī returns to the quotations or sayings from tradition/ report, verse from the Qur'ān, poetry and translation in order to consider their relative merit. First of all, he says, the reported saying of the prophet that the middle of every thing is its best is the primary or basic explanation. He gives two reasons for this: 1) citing the example given by Zamaḫšarī in the *"Kaššāf"* regarding the use of the word among the Meccan Arabs, Rāzī concludes that while in the ordinary Meccan usage *wasaṭ* means best as a description of inanimate objects, the Qur'ān uses it not for inanimate objects but for people to mean justice (عدالة) ; 2) that this saying of the prophet conforms to the verse "You are the best *umma* that has been brought forth for humankind" (3:110). Secondly, he cites the opinion of those who say that the meaning of *wasaṭ* is to be found in the report which says "someone is in the middle of us in terms of family or origin" because the meaning is that such a one is the greatest or most privileged among them, like the middle of a necklace or like the head (leader) who is in the middle and around whom the followers gather. Thirdly, in reference to the fourth saying, i.e., that the prophet said: "In this manner you (Muslims) are to be middle," Rāzī writes:

> In sum, they (Muslims) are middle in the sense that they are positioned in the middle in religion, between excesses and between laxity and fanaticism, because they don't exaggerate like the Christians exaggerate by making a son

---

[72] Rāzī (on 2:143) 97.

and a God; and they are not lax as the Jews are lax in the killing of the prophets and the altering of the Scripture, and, also in shortening its content.[73]

Then, in conclusion, he says that all these sayings are interrelated and do not contradict each other, and he adds *"Allah aʿlam"* - a phrase recurrent in his *tafsīr* - to indicate the limit of the human activity of *tafsīr*, which cannot be more than an approximation of sense of the revealed text.

Looking at Rāzī's *tafsīr* of 2:143 as it has been outlined here, we draw the following main points. First of all, *wasaṭ* means just or justice because it is the essence in the distance between two extremities, without leaning or tending to either side, and because its judgment in relation to its own parts or members is on the basis of temperance or moderation. Secondly, *wasaṭ* as justice is what the Muslim community is in itself, i.e., it is a community where justice reigns among its members. Thirdly, when this Muslim community is seen in relation to other comunities, it is *wasaṭ* or middle in the sense of "middle or moderate in religion."

After his discussion of the meaning of *wasaṭ* as a characterization of the Muslim community, Rāzī tackles a third issue which concerns the nature of this characterization and a fourth issue which concerns the implication of such a nature on the *umma* as a historical reality. It begins with the question of how to interpret *jaʿl* (from the phrase "We established you" *(jaʿalnākum)*. Here he presents his view (orthodox view) and at the same time refutes the Muʿtazilite view. For the Muʿtazilites: "The purpose of this creation *(jaʿl)* is to effect the graces *(alṭāf)* which God knows that when He does it for this *umma*, they will

[73] Rāzī (on 2:143) 98. «يجوز أن يكونوا وسطاً على معنى أنهم متوسطون في الدين بين المفرط والمفرط والغالي والمقصر في الأشياء لأنهم لم يغلوا كما غلت النصارى فجعلوا ابناً وإلهاً ولا قصروا كتقصير اليهود في قتل الأنبياء وتبديل الكتب وغير ذلك مما قصروا فيه.»

then choose that which is proper in words and deeds,"[74] which means then that the actualization of *wasaṭ* is by man's free will.[75] Then what follows is Rāzī's long discussion on the nature of this characterizing note of the Muslim *umma* which we can summarize as follows: the being "middle" of this *umma* is not because of their choice but of God's;[76] this *umma* is already in the middle of God's work right from the beginning (this point will be taken up again in Rāzī's commentary on 3:110); and as this *umma* bursts forth in history, it actualizes this characterizing note, in a manner which may be described as the will or action of the Muslim community by God's creation; moreover, even if in some members this note may not be visible, the community as a Muslim community does not lose this characterizing note; consequently, the consensus of this community as a community is a valid authority.[77]

Furthermore, being "middle" applies to every generation of Muslim *umma* throughout the centuries. Every generation of Muslim *umma* is just - from the first to the last - because the Muslim *umma* is to witness from the time of its establishment in this world until Judgment Day. Thus "God said *umma wasaṭ*, hence designating them with the formulation of the indefinite noun and there is no doubt that this includes people (Muslims) of all time
تعالى قال (أمة وسطاً) فعبر عنهم بلفظ النكرة ولا شك أن -
هذا يتناول أهل كل عصر ."[78] Finally, Rāzī emphasizes also that God has already "made" the Muslims "middle" in this world, that they be witnesses already at every period in this world so that

[74] Rāzī (on 2:143)98.

[75] It is a project that has to be constantly earned or realized. Cf. *tafsīr* of Zamaḫšarī, above.

[76] Rāzī (on 2:143)98.

[77] Rāzī (on 2:143) 98-99.

[78] Rāzī (on 2:143) 100.

they can be witnesses also in the next.[79]

Rāzī's understanding of *umma wasaṭ* forms the basis and is a preview of how he will deal with verses 3:104 and 3:110. We will see that 3:104 corresponds to the meaning of *wasaṭ* as referring to the Muslim community in itself, while 3:110 corresponds to the meaning of *wasaṭ* as referring to the Muslim community in relation to other communities.

Rāzī's treatment of 3:104 begins with a preface which gives the context in which this verse is clearly to be understood as mentioning a task that is to be fulfilled within the Muslim community. He refers to the preceding verses in which God accuses the People of the Scripture of unbelief and of making unbelievers of others, and tells the believers (Muslims) not to follow the people of the Scripture but to hold fast together to the cord (حَبْل) of God and not to separate (3:103). In view of this, God said, "Let there be from among you an *umma*..." (3:104). The object of the order being understood, Rāzī's main concern now is the question of who has to do the ordering and forbidding. In answering this question, he classifies the various opinions according to the two ways of understanding the particle *min* (from):

> As regards God's saying *minkum* (from among you), there are two opinions. First opinion: *Min* here is not a *min partitivum* (i.e., it does not mean "some") for two reasons: 1) God has made it a duty for the whole community to order what is acceptable and to forbid what is rejectable in His saying "You are the best *umma* ever brought forth for humankind; you order what is acceptable and you forbid what is rejectable" (3:110). 2) Everyone who is subject to the law has also the duty to order what is acceptable and to forbid what is rejectable - with his hand, tongue or heart, and it is the duty of everyone to drive away from the soul any certain damage. Thus the meaning of the verse is: Be a community that calls to what is good, that orders what is

---

[79] Rāzī (on 2:143) 102.

acceptable and that forbids what is rejectable. As regards the preposition *min*, here it is explicative, not partitive.[80]

Rāzī then explains that this duty belongs to the category of the *farḍ-al-kifāya*, i.e., when sufficiently taken care of by some members of the community, it no longer obliges the others.[81]

The second opinion is that *min* here is partitive, i.e., it obliges only some members of the community. Accordingly, there are those who say that excluded from carrying out this obligation are the women, the sick and the aged; on the other hand, there are also those who say that the verse concerns only those who are learned in religious matters, i.e., the *ᶜūlamā*ʾ.[82]

Rāzī does not make a judgment regarding the relative merit of these opinions although one can discern from his explanation a preference for the first opinion.[83] Instead, he closes the discussion with his standard "Allāh aᶜlam."[84] From the following discussion it becomes clear that what is more important is that the task is fulfilled within the Muslim community. Here he cites the three things to be done as mentioned in the verse, emphasizing that the best of them is the first one, i.e., "the calling to the good": what is important is that the person must not be a sinner *(fāsiq)* but must be a good person so that he can with integrity call to

---

80 Rāzī (on 3:104) 166.

81 Rāzī (on 3:104) 167.

82 Rāzī (on 3:104) 167.

83 A. A. Roest Crollius, "Mission and Morality" in *Studia Missionalia*, vol. 27 (Roma: Università Gregoriana Editrice, 1978) 272.

84 After his *"Allāh aᶜlam,"* Rāzī cites the opinion of al-Ḍaḥḥāk who says that the verse refers to the Companions of the Prophet, "since they were instructed by the holy Messenger and taught the people." Rāzī (on 3:104) 167. (Al-Ḍaḥḥāk was a disciple of Saᶜid b. Jubayr, who was in turn a disciple of Ibn ᶜAbbās and known to be a trustworthy authority).

what is good.[85]

When we now turn to Rāzī's commentary on 3:110, we will see that the emphasis is consistent with the second aspect of the meaning of *wasaṭ*, i.e. middle in religion. Here in 3:110, Rāzī views the Muslim community in relation to other communities like the Jewish and Christian communities.

First, he emphasizes what he had mentioned in his commentary on 2:143, i.e., that the being *wasaṭ* of the Muslim *umma* belongs to Muslims of all generations because, when God says "You are the best nation," it means "You (Muslims) in the Preserved Tablet are the best of the *umam*."[86] Thus, like Ṭabarī, Rāzī views the Muslim community as one preordained by God to be the best *umma*. Accordingly, *kuntum* would then refer to its having been "best" in the past (i.e., since the beginning) but it does not mean that it has stopped; or *kuntum* may be understood as *ṣirtum* (you became) to stress the moment the Muslims became a historical community.[87] Then he asks: Why is the Muslim community the best of all when the ordering of *maʿrūf*, the forbidding of *munkar*, and faith in God also exist in other communities *(umam)*?[88] He answers that it is because the order of the *jihād* is stronger in the law of Islam than it is in other laws in the sense that Muslims are willing to sacrifice themselves by fighting (قتال) if a non-believer cannot be won over to the true faith (i.e., Islam) by heart (بالقلب) by tongue (باللسان) or by hand (باليد).[89] الجهاد is thus seen as the reason for the excellence of

---

[85] See Rāzī (on 3:104) 167-8.

[86] Rāzī (on 3:110) 177.

[87] See Rāzī (on 3:110) 177ff.

[88] Rāzī (on 3:110) 180.

[89] See Rāzī on (3:110) 180.

the Muslim community in relation to other communities.[90] For this explanation, Rāzī cites the authority of Al-Qaffāl whom he further reports as saying, in addition:

> The righteous man does not disapprove of fighting for the sake of religion since most people love their religion because of habit and custom and do not consider the arguments that are brought against them. For fear of being killed, one will enter the [Muslim] religion. Then slowly he will see the truth in it and thus his love for the false religion will become weak and his love for the true religion will grow strong in his heart until he fully follows the right path to God and forgets the wrong one and thus deserves eternal reward instead of eternal punishment.[91]

In Rāzī, therefore, the duty to order and forbid which concerns the internal life of the Muslim community - which is the

---

90 *Jihād* is the verbal noun of the verb *jāhada* which means to strive, to endeavor. *Jihād* thus literally means "striving or the expending of effort," and one who performs it is called *mujāhid*. Technically, *jihād* is any endeavor that is made to further the cause of God, whether the endeavor is positive (i.e., promoting good) or negative (i.e., eradicating evil) in character, takes the form of social action or private effort, involves monetary expenditure or physical struggle, or is made against the enemy without or the enemy within (i.e., against the bidding self). The comprehensive nature of *jihād* is evidenced by such verses as 29:69: "Those who strive in Us [Our Way], We guide them to Our ways." The same word occurs in the Qurʾān a number of times in the military sense of making war against the unbelievers (8:74,75; 9:44). When *jihād* takes the form of war, it is known as *qitāl* (fighting). Mustansir Mir, *Dictionary of Qurʾānic Terms and Concepts* (New York and London: Garland Publshing, Inc., 1987) 112.

91 Rāzī (on 3:110) 180. Abū Bakr Muḥammad b. Ismaʿīl al-Qaffāl al-Šāšī (365/976) is known principally as a jurist who introduced the šāfiʿī *maḏhab* in Transoxania. Cf. A. A. Roest Crollius, "Mission and Morality" in *Missionalia*, vol. 27 (Roma: Università Gregoriana Editrice, 1978) 272-273.

emphasis in Zamaḫšarī's *tafsīr* - and the duty to order and forbid which is a task of the Muslim community directed to non-Muslims - which is the emphasis in Ṭabarī's *tafsīr* - are, so to say, two sides of the same coin. In Rāzī, the task of the Muslim community is both centripetal and centrifugal in character. It is a task that goes with their being middle or *wasaṭ* which means "justice" when applied to the Muslim community in itself and thus, in the concrete, one which is concerned with how the legal prescriptions are to be applied to and by the community members; and which means "middle or best in religion" when applied to the Muslim community in relation to other communities and thus, in the concrete, one which is concerned with making non-Muslims embrace the true religion which is Islam.

By way of concluding this section, we recapitulate what we have seen in our study of the three commentaries representing the first six centuries of qurʾānic exegesis. Ṭabarī lived in a historical situation marked by the height of the quick expansion of the Muslim dominion. The problem consisted in the contact with foreign civilizations on the one hand, and the fact that explanations for the faith and commentaries on the Qurʾān based on *ḥadīṯ* were scattered in various places in the wide Muslim empire with no one place possessing a complete copy or knowledge of all of them. Thus Ṭabarī's *tafsīr* comes out to be, first of all, a collection, compilation and methodical arrangement of the first two and a half centuries of *bi-l-maʾṯūr* exegesis. Ṭabarī's mark would be seen in his considerable critical analysis and personal judgment on the material passed down. The emphasis of his *tafsīr* is on a clear definition of the Muslim *umma* in relation to non-Muslims: the nature of the *umma* is centrifugal; in concrete, the task of the Muslim community is to call non-Muslims to what is good, i.e., Islam.

Zamaḫšarī wrote his *tafsīr* in Mecca - the heartland of Islam. The threat to the oneness of the Muslim community was posed by internal squabbles and conflicting sectarian views. The emphasis of his *tafsīr* is on a clear definition of the internal life of the Muslim community as the best community: the nature of the *umma* is centripetal; in concrete, the task of the Muslim community is to arrange its internal life in such a way that it maintains its being a community of justice. His *tafsīr* is based on reason and only very slightly are traditions cited.

Rāzī's preoccupation was how to reconcile Islamic tradition with Hellenistic thought that was influencing the Muslim intellectual world at his time. His *tafsīr* thus evinces a combination of what is good in tradition and what is good in philosophy. His emphasis was to re-state or re-interpret traditional views - many of which are found also in Ṭabarī and Zamaḫšarī - in a way that was faithful to tradition as well as to the imperative of his time.

2. The Solidification of Traditionalism

The first six centuries of qurʾānic exegesis was one which exhibited major variations on the theme of traditionalism. The dominant form of exegesis was of course *bi-l-maʾṯūr* - as exemplified by Ṭabarī - an approach which considers the Qurʾān text primarily in terms of the dominant *ijmāʿ* (consensus) of the community expressed in *aḥadīṯ* and sayings, but which did not preclude a considerable amount of personal opinion and conclusions on the part of the writer. The other approach was *bi-l-raʾy* - as exemplified by the *tafāsīr* of Zamaḫšarī and Rāzī - one in which personal opinions, speculations and conclusions of their writers played a major role in addition to *aḥādīṯ* and sayings.

When the period of *ijtihād* or individual interpretation ended in the seventh century, its reflection in the Qurʾān commentary resulted in an era, lasting some seven centuries, in which repetition was considered more valid than initiative. Scholars have noted that commentators in this period would generally take, in many cases verbatim, material from previous commentaries and incorporate it into their own works without acknowledgment.

Thus, since the nature of the *tafāsīr* in this period was to a great extent repetitious of what had been established in the first six centuries of Islam, or, is a solidification of material already judged by the community to be acceptable, we don't have to consider a representative *tafsīr* for each of the seven centuries that follow. Instead, we will consider as representatives three *tafāsīr* of this era which are among the most-widely read and highly esteemed by Muslims. These are the *tafāsīr* of Bayḍāwī, Ibn Kaṯīr and al-Jalālayn. Their great popularity among Sunnī Muslims makes their works representatives of the *ijmāʿ* of the Sunnī community in this period.

2.1 Bayḍāwī

2.1.1 Introduction

Abd Allāh b. ᶜUmar al-Bayḍāwī was born in the small town of al-Bayḍāʾ, situated in the province of Fārs, north of its capital called Šīrāz.[92] The population of Fārs were Sunnites of the Šāfiᶜite rite although there were also Šīᶜites. Bayḍāwī grew up to be a staunch Šāfiᶜite in jurisprudence and Ašᶜarite in theology and was, not surprisingly, a bitter opponent of Šīᶜites and Muᶜtazilites. He studied under his father who was then the Chief Justice of Fārs. Bayḍāwī himself later became a judge *(qāḍī)* in Šīrāz, then later on at Tabrīz where he died sometime between 685 and 710.[93]

Bayḍāwī produced many works on various topics, of which the one that became most famous was his great commentary on the Qurʾān called "Anwār al-tanzīl wa asrār al-taʾwīl" (The Lights of Inspiration and the Secrets of Interpretation), which was written during his stay in Tabrīz. Bayḍāwī's *tafsīr* follows closely the

---

[92] The details of Bayḍāwī's biography are assembled by Lutpi Ibrahim in his article "Al-Bayḍāwī's Life and Works" in *Islamic Studies* XVIII (1979) 311-321. Sources do not tell us the year of Bayḍāwī's birth. However, L. Ibrahim writes: "Judging from the fact that in 674 A. H. he had completed a book called *"Niẓām al-Tawāriḫ"*, and about the same year that he had held the office of Chief Justice of Fārs, it can be presumed that he was born during the reign of the Atabak Abū Bakr b. Saʾd I (628/1231 - 658/1260)." Lutpi Ibrahim, Ibid., 311. Bayḍāwī's biographical sketch may also be found summarized in J. Robson, "Al-Bayḍāwī" in *Encyclopedia of Islam*, new edition, vol. 1 (1960) 1129.

[93] The sources are divided and give a variety of possibilities for his death date. Lutpi Ibrahim enumerates them all and seems to give more credence to Ibn Zarkūb (in Šīrāz Nāmah, p. 136), who maintains that al-Bayḍāwī died in Tabrīz in 708 A. H. and was buried at a place called Jurundab. L. Ibrahim, Ibid., 315.

Kaššāf of Zamaḫšarī but eliminates all its traces of Muʿtazilism. It has been assessed by many Muslim scholars as a *tafsīr* aimed at moderation and a combination of the most relevant and cogent elements of Zamaḫšarī's *Kaššāf* and Rāzī's *Tafsīr al-Kabīr*,[94] presented in a nutshell, and for which reasons it has been very popular among non-Muslim students of the Qurʾān and indeed the most widely-read in the Muslim world. It has been used as the basis of many succeeding commentaries.[95]

2.1.2 *Tafsīr*

Bayḍāwī's explanation of 2:143 is a typical example of one of the main characteristics of his *tafsīr* that we mentioned [in the introduction] above, that it is a presentation in a nutshell of the main points in the commentaries of Zamaḫšarī and of Rāzī which were more detailed in their explanations.

He begins by explaining the word "Thus" *(kaḏālika)* in terms that clearly show that it is God who is the author or creator of the Muslim community's being *wasaṭ*, saying:

> Thus refers to the preceding verse and it means "just as we have made you a people guided to the straight path" or "just as we have made your *qibla* more excellent than the previous one," we have made you a middle community i.e.,

---

[94] Cf. Muhammad H. I. Ibrahim Surty, "The Qurʾān in Islamic Scholarship" in *The Mission World Book Review*, vol. 7, no. 4 (Summer 1987) 57; Cf. also Ḥājjī Ḫalīfa Muṣṭafā b. ʿAbd Allāh, *Kašf al-ẓunūn ʿan asāmī-l-kutub wa-l-funūn*, vol. 1, ed. by Gustaf Flügel (Leipzig: Oriental Translation fund, 1251/1835) 471.

[95] Lutpi Ibrahim notes that this commentary has received more careful study by later Muslim scholars than has that of any other commentator and that there have been more than eighty different books by Muslim commentators based on that of al-Bayḍāwī. L. Ibrahim, Ibid., 316.

excellent *(ḫiyār)* and just *(ʿudūl)*, pure in knowledge and action.[96]

Then follows his explanation of the term *wasaṭ* which is a description of the thing in itself and thus, consequently, of the Muslim community in itself as in Zamaḫšarī and in Rāzī. He says:

> It *(wasaṭ)* was originally a designation for a place where the area on the sides are equal. Then it came to refer to praiseworthy attributes of character because they take place between the extremes of excess and exaggeration on both sides. Thus being generous is what lies between being wasteful and being stingy, courage is what lies between hastiness and cowardice. Now it is also a designation for the one characterized by them (attributes) and in it (in such characterization) are put on the same level the one and the many, the masculine and the feminine...[97]

Thus it is clear that "middle" or *wasaṭ* is a description of the internal life of the Muslim community, which is one of justice. In this brief but clear explanation, the justification for the unusual form of the word *wasaṭ* as a description of the term *umma* is also mentioned.

Bayḍāwī then draws a conclusion saying that "consensus *(ijmāʿ)* is a valid authority *(ḥujja)* because if that upon which they [the Muslims] agree were a falsehood, then their integrity *(ʿadāla)* would have a fissure,"[98] which means they would not be "middle" anymore which is a contradiction to God's creation.

What follows is Bayḍāwī's commentary on the succeeding

---

[96] Bayḍāwī (on 2:143) 34 = «وكذلك» اشارة الى مفهوم الآية المتقدمة أى كما جعلناكم مهديين الى الصراط المستقيم أو جعلنا قبلتكم أفضل القبل «جعلناكم أمة وسطا» أى خيارا أو عدولا مزكين بالعلم والعمل.

[97] Ibid.

[98] Ibid.

phrase, i.e., "that you may be witness to the people..." It is God's motive for making the Muslims a community in the "middle," and it is on the day of the resurrection that they have to witness against the people before God to their having lived God's justice in this world.[99]

Consistent with this view of *umma wasaṭ*, it is not surprising that in his commentary on 3:104, the duty to order and forbid is seen as one to be fulfilled within the Muslim community, for the maintenance of their being "middle." His explanation of the verse so closely parallels Zamaḫšarī's - although it is an abridgment of it - that we are almost tempted to skip it and to refer the reader to the discussion above on Zamaḫšarī's commentary on 3:104. However, we present it here not only because we want to be consistent with our aforementioned aim of viewing the repetitious trend of qur'ānic commentary after the sixth century but also because it manifests the brilliance of the commentator in presenting briefly and clearly what had been explained in so many words previously and it gives us greater insight into what was considered more important by Sunnī Muslims especially at his time. On 3:104, Bayḍāwī comments:

> *Min* is partitive because the ordering of *maʿrūf* and the forbidding of *munkar* are *furūḍ al-kifāya*, and because not everyone is fit for it [the task] since for its accomplishment are conditions - in which the whole *umma* does not take part - like the knowledge of the laws, the steps to be considered, the manner of its performance, the capability for its execution. He [God] addresses the whole community but demands the action of some of them to show that it is binding upon all so that if they entirely neglect it, they would all be guilty, but the action of some of them is sufficient. This is true for every duty which is *farḍ al-kifāya*.
>
> Or *Min* may be explicative with the meaning of "Be a community that calls" like God's saying "You are the best

---

[99] Ibid.

> *umma* brought forth for humankind, you order...." The call to what is good comprises the call to that in which [there] is spiritual or temporal goodness. The adjoining of the ordering of what is acceptable *(maʿrūf)* and forbidding of what is rejectable *(munkar)* means the adjoining of the special to the general in order to confirm its importance.[100]

When we turn to Bayḍāwī's commentary on 3:110, we see that the focus is also centripetal, i.e., a look at the *umma* as it is in itself. First he stresses the permanence of "the best" *(ḫayr)* as a characterizing note of the *umma*:

> "<u>You were the best *umma*</u>" shows their being best in the past but it does not imply that a discontinuance occurred,[101] just like God's saying "And God was forgiving, merciful" (4:23). And it is said that *kuntum* (You were) means "in the knowledge of God" or "in the Tablet" or "in what is between the earlier *umam* [among past *umam*]."[102]

Thus Bayḍawī sees the origin of the excellence of the Muslim *umma* in meta-historic time, an idea that we already saw in Ṭabarī and in Rāzī but presented here in a nutshell, so to say. What

---

[100] Bayḍāwī (on 3:104) 169.

[101] This is the "perfectum praesens" in Arabic, i.e., an act which, at the moment of speaking, has already been completed and remains in a state of completion. "A Semitic Perfect or Imperfect has, in and of itself, no reference to the temporal relations of the speaker (thinker or writer) and of other actions which are brought into juxtaposition with it. It is precisely these relations which determine in what sphere of time (past, present, or future) a Semitic Perfect or Imperfect lies, and by which of our tenses it is to be expressed - whether by our Past, Perfect, Pluperfect, or Future-perfect; by our Present, Imperfect, or Future." W. Wright, *A Grammar of the Arabic Language* (Cambridge: Cambridge University Press, 1991) 51.

[102] Bayḍāwī (on 3:110) 170, also for the following quotation.

follows is a description still of this *umma* as seen in itself but this time in the context of its being a historical reality. Bayḍāwī writes:

> "... brought forth for humankind," that is, shown to them (humankind); "you order what is acceptable and you forbid what is rejectable" is a fresh start to explain their being the best *umma*, or, a second predicate to *kuntum* (you are), "and believed in God" includes the belief in everything that is to be believed.... this (the phrase "believed in God") is put at the end instead of at the beginning because He (God) intends, by stating it, that they (Muslims) ordered that which is acceptable *(maʿrūf)* and forbade that which is rejectable *(munkar)* as the indication of their faith in God and as approval and disclosure of His religion.

Thus if in the conceptual order the "being best" of this *umma* is to be found in the divine decree before creation, in the real (historical) order it is demonstrated by the Muslim community's faith in God which is manifested in their ordering and forbidding. Bayḍāwī concludes his commentary on *ḫayra umma* with the deduction that the *ijmāʿ* (consensus) of the Muslim community is then a valid authority *(ḥujja)* -like he said in 2:143 - because the verse "makes it necessary that they ordered everything acceptable and forbade everything rejectable, the collective community being referred to."

Looking at the whole of Bayḍāwī's *tafsīr* as it is outlined here, it can be observed that most, if not all, of the interpretations he has given have already been presented by the earlier commentators that we have considered. However, like we have mentioned above, his special asset is to be seen in the brilliance of his presentation of previous conclusions in brief and in a manner which makes us see the points more easily and clearly, which then lets us understand why his *Anwār at-Tanzīl* has been the most widely-read Muslim commentary of all time.

On the whole, Bayḍāwī's *tafsīr* follows closely the *Kaššāf* of Zamaḫšarī. Both Bayḍāwī and Zamaḫšarī wrote their respective commentaries under similar conditions, that is, marked by the existence of sectarian antagonism. In the fifth century, upon the prodding of the Muʿtazilites in Mecca, Zamaḫšarī wrote his *tafsīr*. Despite its Muʿtazilite slant, this *tafsīr* in time attracted Sunnī readers. About two centuries later, Bayḍāwī, living in a situation marked by sectarian hostilities, wrote his *Anwār at-Tanzīl* which followed closely the *Kaššāf* of Zamaḫšarī but eliminated its traces of Muʿtazilism.

2.2 Ibn Kaṯīr[103]

2.2.1 Introduction

Unlike the four commentators that we have considered thus far, ʿImād al-Dīn Ismāʿīl did not come from Persia but from Syria. He was born in 701 (1301) in the citadel town of Baṣrā but, orphaned at the age of six, he moved to Damascus as the ward of his brother. There he had the opportunity of studying under some of the best Sunnī teachers of his time where he was an oustanding student of *ḥadīṯ* and jurisprudence, and later became an eminent professor of tradition and preacher in his own right. Although a Šāfiʿite, he was deeply influenced by the renowned Ḥanbalite theologian Ibn Taymīya (d. 728/1328) near whose tomb

---

[103] I have not found any secondary literature on Ibn Kaṯīr in any European languages except a recent one by J. D. McAuliffe, entitled "Qurʾānic Hermeneutics: The Views of al-Ṭabarī and Ibn Kaṯīr" in *Approaches to the History of the Interpretation of the Qurʾān*, edited by Andrew Rippin (Oxford: Clarendon Press, 1988), 46-62. There is no treatment of Ibn Kaṯīr in the *Shorter Encyclopedia of Islam* (1991 edition) and he gets very scant treatment (hardly more than a few lines) in *Encyclopedia of Islam*, volume III (1987).

he was buried after his death in 774 (1373).[104]

A celebrated historian and commentator on the Qur'ān, Ibn Kaṯīr's best known works are his universal history entitled *Al-bidāya wa-l-nihāya*, as well as his *Tafsīr al-Qur'ān al-ʿaẓīm*. The latter is the one with which we are primarily concerned here.

True to his reputed prominence in the science of *ḥadīṯ*, Ibn Kaṯīr's *Tafsīr* al-Qur'ān al-ʿAẓīm is firmly in the class of *tafsīr bi-l-ma'ṯūr* and is a radically revised version of the work of Ṭabarī. Although his work is only slowly attracting attention in the West, it has been extremely popular among Muslim scholars and

---

[104] Ibn Taymīya has been regarded as the epitome of traditionalism especially at the time in which the more middle-of-the-road Ašʿarī compromise between *kalām* and traditionalism had won the day as orthodoxy. He was a conservative Ḥanbalī and he opposed innovations, allegorical interpretation of the Qur'ān, *kalām*, and all the sects which in any way advocated these. As the most powerful thinker of his time, Ibn Taymīya influenced a broad spectrum of Muslim thought in his century, giving rise to what some scholars have called "the Fourteenth Century renaissance of Islamic thought." Just how was Ibn Kaṯīr, a Šāfiʿī, influenced by Ibn Taymīya, a Ḥanbalī, is explained by George Makdisi (in his *Ašʿarī and the Ašʿarites* (Paris: G. - P. Maisonneuve, 1962) as follows: "... one could be a Šāfiʿī strongly advocating the use of *kalām* or a Šāfiʿī who was absolutely opposed to such usage. The Ašʿarī advocates of *kalām* really failed in their efforts to infiltrate the schools of law, particularly the Šāfiʿī school, and the vast majority of Muslims always had been and continued through and past the fifth, sixth and seventh centuries predominantly traditionalist in approach.... While professors of law necessarily instructed those in the same school of law, a student from one legal persuasion interested in traditions could study under a professor of traditions from another school of law. In this way, Ḥanbalite traditionalism was able to bolster and strengthen Šāfiʿite traditionalism against the common enemy: rationalism." Thus, he says, the Ḥanbalī traditionalist Ibn Taymīya influenced a long line of Šāfiʿīya, including Ibn Kaṯīr. As cited in J.I. Smith, *An Historical and Semantic Study of the Term "Islām"* (Missoula, Montana: Scholars Press, 129-130.

students.[105]

Ibn Kaṯīr's commentary includes a long, scholarly introduction in which he spells out the different steps in doing *tafsīr*. He mentions three main and sound sources for his qurʾānic commentary:[106] the first and best procedure is to let the Qurʾān interpret itself, because what is said concisely in one place is usually treated in detail in another place; the second step is to examine the prophetic tradition - the words and deeds of the prophet - because it is an elucidation of the Qurʾān; the third step - which is to be resorted to if the first two sources don't provide adequate resources - is to resort to the transmitted sayings of the Companions of Muhammad because they were eyewitnesses, especially the first four caliphs as well as Ibn Masʿūd and Ibn ʿAbbās. In regard to the application of the third step/source, one has to distinguish between the sayings that the Companions received from the prophet of Islam and those which they received from the people of the Scripture (known technically as *isrāʾīliyāt)*. Accordingly, the *isrāʾīliyāt* should be assessed as follows: 1) those which are true because they are attested to in the Qurʾān, 2) those which are false because they are in conflict with what is in the Qurʾān, and 3) those which fall into neither category. Ibn

[105] See Muhammad Ibrahim H. I. Surty, "The Qurʾān in Islamic Scholaship: A Survey of *Tafsīr* Exegesis Literature in Arabic" in *The Muslim World Book Review*, vo. 7, no. 4 (Summer 1987), 57; J. I. Smith cites (in her *An Historical and Semantic Study of the Term "Islam"* (Missoula, Montana: Scholars Press, 1975, 130) the 13th/19th century al-Šawkānī, for whom traditionalism is the *sine qua non* of Qurʾān commentary, praises Ibn Kaṯīr's work as one of the best of the *tafāsīr*, of which there is none better; J. D. McAuliffe (op. cit., 56) cites that according to the contemporary scholar ʿAbd Allāh Maḥmūd Šihāta, Ibn Kaṯīr's *tafsīr* is "one of the soundest of *tafāsīr bi-l-maʾṯūr* if not absolutely the soundest."

[106] This is discussed in ʾImād al-Dīn Abū-l-Fidāʾ Ismāʿīl ibn Kaṯīr, *Tafsīr al-Qurʾān al-ʿaẓīm* (Beirut, 1385/1966) i, 7-8.

Kaṯīr adds that to resort to the interpretations of the pupils of the Companions - referred to as the Successors or Followers *(al-tābiʿūn)* - while being followed by many exegetes, is not really obligatory in qurʾānic exegesis.

Thus, while in his commentary Ibn Kaṯīr follows Ṭabarī closely, the former's commentary becomes a radically revised version of the latter's because in applying the above-mentioned principles, Ibn Kaṯīr, among other things, discards many of the interpretations which Ṭabarī traced back to the Companions by faulty *asānīd* and reduced to the barest minimum the amount of material derived from the *tābiʿūn*. These characteristic traits of Ibn Kaṯīr's *tafsīr* form the objective basis for the high esteem given to it by Muslim scholars as well as for the growing attention accorded it by non-Muslim ones.

2.2.2 *Tafsīr*

Like many others before him, Ibn Kaṯīr sees verse 2:143 in the same context of God's guidance as expressed in the preceding verse. Thus he praphrases 2:143 as follows:

> God says: We have guided you to the *qibla* of Ibrahim and have chosen it for you in order to make you the best/choice of the *umam* (خيار الأمم) in order that on the day of the resurrection you be witnesses against the *umam* because all acknowledge that you are the favored (لأن الجميع معترفون لكم بالفضل).[107]

The focus is on God's being the author or creator of the being *wasaṭ* or being "best" of the Muslims. Two points in the above paraphrase which Ibn Kaṯīr elaborates on are 1) the meaning of being *wasaṭ* and 2) the meaning of being "witnesses." First he explains the meaning of *wasaṭ*, saying,

---

107 Ibn Kaṯīr (on 2:143) 190, also for the following two quotations.

The *wasaṭ* here means the choice and the excellent or the "best" (والوسطُ ههنا: الخيار والأجود) just as it is said "the Qurayš are the best Arabs in terms of descent and as a house, i.e., its best (قريش أوسط العرب نسباً وداراً أي خيرها). And the Prophet was the middle among his people (وسطاً في قومه), i.e., the most honored of them in descent (أشرفهم نسباً).

Secondly, continuing with his discussion, Ibn Kaṯir now explains the meaning of *wasaṭ* as a description of the Muslim community.

> When God made this *umma wasaṭ*, He characterized it with the most perfect of laws, the most straight of ways, and the most clear religious creeds (خصّها بأكمل الشرائع، وأقوم المناهج وأوضح المذاهب), as God says, "He has chosen you (اجتباكم) and has not placed upon you in religion any difficulty, [it being] the religion of your father Abraham. He has named you Muslims before and in this [Scripture], that the Messenger may be a witness against you and that you may be witnesses against humankind (22:78)."

The Muslim community as a community in itself is *wasaṭ* or "best" because it is God's choice and thus is bestowed the necessary distinguishing elements to become *umma wasaṭ*.

As he continues his discussion, Ibn Kaṯir explains *wasaṭ* in view of the task of the Muslims to be witnesses against the *umam*. First, he reports a series of traditions that are traced back to Muhammad by unbroken chains of authorities, and which relate how on the day of the resurrection the Muslim community will witness against the *umam* and how Muhammad will be a witness on the witness of the Muslim community. Here, the being *wasaṭ* of the Muslim community means "justice" (*ʿadl*).[108] Second, Ibn Kaṯīr then gives examples from the internal life of the Muslim community during the time of Muhammad, in which the Prophet, noting the ability of the Muslims to distinguish the good and the bad by "praising" or by "censuring," is quoted as having told the Muslims: "You are God's witnesses in the world."[109]

Thus, the Muslim community as *umma wasaṭ* means that the Muslims are a community "chosen" by God and thus endowed with the elements that make a community the "best" before the eyes of God. In so far as *wasaṭ* refers to the Muslim community being a witness against humankind, it means "just" or "justice," i.e., their being a community of justice is a witness against humankind. From the examples given, it is clear that the witness of this community against humankind on the day of the resurrection is seen as the climax of a witnessing that has already been done or has already started in this world. This easily leads to Ibn Kaṯīr's *tafsīr* of 3:104 and 3:110, in which, as we will see, unlike in Ṭabarī and in Rāzī, Ibn Kaṯīr does not see in this witnessing a consequent action (missionary action) of ordering non-Muslims to embrace Islam, but a consistent centripetal view, i.e., a persistent action or life of justice within the Muslim community which will "conscientize" the non-Muslims.

In Ibn Kaṯīr's commentary on 3:104, it is understood that the task is to be directed to the internal life of the Muslim community and his main concern is the necessity of fulfilling such a duty. As a preface to his interpretation he first of all cites al-Ḍaḥḥāk for whom the verse speaks especially of "the educated ones among the companions [of the prophet], the educated ones among the

108 Ibn Kaṯīr (on 2:143) 190.

109 Ibn Kaṯīr (on 2:143) 191. قال "بالثناء الحسن والثناء السيء أنتم شهداء الله في الأرض"

transmitters [of *aḥādīṯ*) and the *ʿulamāʾ*."[110] Secondly, he cites a tradition referring to the Prophet who, in connection with this verse, said: "The good is following the Qurʾān and my *sunna*."[111] Then he gives his explanation:

> The meaning of this verse is that a group *(firqa)* of this *umma* be set apart for this matter, even though it is a duty for each single individual of the *umma* as what has been established in the *ṣaḥīḥ* of Muslim[112] who cites Abū Hurayra [who] said that the Messenger of God said: "who from among you sees a renegade *(munkir)* should change him with his hand (fighting him); and if he cannot [at least] with his tongue (with his words); and if he cannot then at least in his heart - which is the minimum of faith, and thus [is said] in the tradition "beyond that is not even a mustard seed of faith."[113]

Thus Ibn Kaṯīr's concern is not so much regarding who exactly must do it but 1) that it should be done since Muhammad himself stressed its importance and 2) that, like Zamaḫšarī, Rāzī and Bayḍāwī before him, this duty is *farḍ al-kifāya*. What follows is Ibn Kaṯīr's further explanation which connects this verse to the succeeding one in which God's punishment upon renegade

---

110 Ibn Kaṯīr (on 3:104) 390: (قال الضحاك: هم خاصة الصحابة وخاصة الرواة يعني المجاهدين والعلماء)

111 Ibid.: (الخير اتباع القرآن وسنتي)

112 Ṣaḥīḥ of Muslim is one of the six collections of traditions *(aḥādīṯ)* that the Muslims have elevated to canonical rank, the whole being known as "The Six Books" *(al-kutubu-l-sitta)* or "The Six Authentic Collections" *(Ṣaḥāḥ sitta)*. The other five books are: *Ṣaḥīḥ* of Al-Buḫārī which is considered the first and most important of the six, *Sunan* of Abū Dāūd, *Jāmiʿ* of al-Tirmiḏī, *Sunan* of Ibn Māja and the *Sunan* of al-Nasāʾī.

113 Ibn Kaṯīr (on 3:104) 390.

members of the Muslim community is talked about.[114] He is thus consistent with his interpretation of *umma wasaṭ* and sees this verse as especially referring to the life of the Muslim community in itself.

When we turn to Ibn Kaṯīr's commentary on 3:110, we shall see that the interpretation of "best community" *(ḫayra umma)* is also centripetal. Ibn Kaṯīr first narrates the various opinions on this and then gives his own interpretation. In regard to the various opinions: 1) For those who stress the "missionary" character of the *umma*, a tradition based on the authority of Buḫārī is traced back to Abū Hurayra who is quoted as having said that the Muslims are the best because "they bring others (non-Muslims) in chains around their necks that they may enter Islam;"[115] 2) There are also those who consider the internal life of the Islamic community in its beginnings as the only genuine one, one that has not been equalled thus far, and thus refer to the opinion of Ibn ʿAbbās who is quoted as having said that meant here are "the faithful who migrated with the prophet from Mecca to Medina;" accordingly, "they are the best of the *umam* and the most profitable people for others, and thus for them is said, "you order what is acceptable, you forbid what is rejectable and you believe in God;" 3) Finally, there are those who prefer to stress the "what" instead of the "who" of the best people and cite a tradition - on the authority of Imām Aḥmad: "The best for people [consists in] reading for them the Qurʾān and bringing them to trust in God and ordering them what is acceptable and forbidding them what is rejectable and leading them to mercy." After these varying interpretations, Ibn Kaṯīr now gives his own interpretation. He says:

> The correct interpretation is that this verse concerns in a general way every *umma* of every generation [considered in

---

114 Ibid.

115 Ibn Kaṯīr (on 3:110) 391, also for the following quotations.

itself], and the best of their generations are those among whom the Messenger of God [Muhammad] has been sent; then those who follow them, etc. - والصحيح أن هذه الآية عامة في جميع الأمة كل قرن بحسبه ، وخير قرونهم الذين بعث فيهم رسول الله ثم الذين يلونهم ثم الذين يلونهم ، as the Qur'ān says [in 2:143] "And thus we have made you *umma wasaṭ*," i.e., the best , in order that you witness against humankind.

Here we see Ibn Kaṯīr following Ṭabarī's style of allowing space for every traditional opinion but his own stamp may be seen in his not judging such opinions as well as in giving his own interpretation in such a way that no traditional opinion is rejected outright but may even find its place in his synthesis. Consistent with his understanding of *umma wasaṭ*, *ḫayra umma* is seen in the context of the best among the different generations of Muslim communities as well as in the context of every generation of Muslim community in relation to other communities: among the generations of Muslim communities the best was the one which existed at the time of Muhammad while at the same time every generation of Muslim community is the best in comparison to non-Muslim communities; which latter is because, as Ibn Kaṯīr reiterates his explanation in 2:143, every Muslim community by its nature follows the perfect way of Muhammad given by God and which God never gave to any one of the prophets before Muhammad.[116] He concludes by saying that it follows that observing even a little of the law of Muhammad is better than observing even a large part of any other law.

It may be observed that in many ways Ibn Katīr's commentary closely follows the *bi-l-ma'tūr* way of Ṭabarī as well

[116] See Ibn Kaṯīr (on 3:110) 391: وبعثه الله بشرع كامل عظيم لم يعطه نبي قبله

as some basic ideas of Rāzī. However, unlike these latter two, his view of the Muslim *umma* does not include a "missionary" trait but is consistent in being centripetal. The reason may be found in the fact that, from the little that we know about the historical situation out of which he wrote, Ibn Kaṯīr's situation was not marked by a threat from other religious communities or by sectarian polemics within the Muslim community. His main concern was to deepen the knowledge and spirituality of Muslims.

2.3 Al-Jalālayn

2.3.1 Introduction

As the name suggests, the next commentary that we will consider is the work of two authors, namely: Jalāl al-Dīn al-Maḥallī (d. 864/1459) who began it, and his pupil, the great scholar Jalāl al-Dīn al-Suyūṭī (d. 911/1505), who completed it. Accordingly, al-Maḥallī started the commentary from *Sūra al-Kahf* and carried it to *Sūra al-Nās*; then just as he was about to start again from *Sūra al-Fātiḥa* to complete the whole, he met his death.[117] Jalāl al-Dīn al-Suyūṭī, who completed the work, was then the one who did the commentary on the verses that concern us here.

Persian by descent,[118] Abū-l-Faḍl ʿAbd-al-Raḥmān b. Abī Bakr Jalāl-al-Dīn al-Suyūṭī was born in 849/1445 in the famous city

[117] Cf. Muhammad Ibrahim H. I. Surty, "The Qurʾān in Islamic Scholarship: A Survey of *Tafsīr* Exegesis Literature in Arabic" in *The Muslim World Book Review*, vol. 7, no. 4 (Summer 1987) 58.

[118] The details of al-Suyūṭī's life from various Arabic sources have been summarized in F. Wustenfeld, *Die Geschichtschreiber der Araber* (Göttingen: Dieterichsche Verlags- Buchhandlung, 1882).

of Suyūṭ in Upper Egypt.[119] He studied in practically all centers of learning in his homeland and under the most renowned teachers. His concentration on law, grammar and tradition resulted in his becoming thoroughly familiar with nearly all of the dominant branches of learning. He was known for his excellent knowledge of the Qur'ān and the *aḥādīṯ*. The completion of his studies was followed by a pilgrimage to Mecca. Afterwards, Jalāl al-Dīn settled down in Cairo to a life of teaching and writing. Later, he retired to the island of Rawḍa on the Nile - where he remained until his death - after having been accused of shady financial dealings in the management of the school in which he taught.[120]

The period of qur'ānic exegesis in which "repetition" became the name of the game started in the seventh century - the time of Bayḍawī - and reached its peak in the span of time starting from the ninth century - the time of Jalāl al-Dīn - until the thirteenth/ nineteenth century. Thus Jalāl al-Dīn lived at a time in which there was very little creative effort in the realm of theology and in which the dominant mode of Qur'ān commentary was a renewed emphasis on the traditionalism of the early centuries. It was a period which non-Muslim scholars usually refer to as the real dark ages of Islam or, as von Grünebaum puts it, the time "when Muslim science had been gripped by *rigor mortis*."[121] This was then the situation in which Jalāl al-Dīn professed to write on all the areas of Islamic science, and, his writings - numbered at somewhere over 500, despite harsh criticisms especially by non-

---

119 Instead of Suyūṭ, some author gives al-Asyūṭ.

120 J. Cooper, *The commentary on the Qur'ān by Al-Ṭabarī, Volume I*, edited by W. F. Madelung and A. Jones (Oxford: Oxford University Press, 1987) xxvi.

121 Gustave E. Von Grunebaum, *Medieval Islam*, second edition (Chicago: University of Chicago Press, 1962) 246.

Muslim scholars and some Muslim writers as well,[122] - remain as impressive compilations of Islamic knowledge at his time. There is no question of the great respect and reverence accorded him by the majority of the people from his own time up to the present. Perhaps the two most popular of Jalāl al-Dīn's works are the *Al-Itqān fī ʿulūm al-Qurʾān* and the so-called *Tafsīr al-Jalālayn*. The former has been considered the definitive Medieval Muslim work on qurʾānic sciences since it is a summary compilation of all the subjects having to do with *tafsīr* with which, in Jalāl al-Dīn's opinion, a commentator of his time ought to be conversant. The latter, i.e., *Tafsīr* al-Jalālayn, is the main concern of our study here.

Al-Jalālayn is a *tafsīr* which surpasses that of Bayḍawī in brevity. In the words of I. Surty, "it contains about the same number of words as the Qurʾān and yet it is a commentary... it became extremely popular and has since been included in the curriculum of many religious institutions,"[123] and "saw at least seven editions between 1926 and 1940 in Cairo"[124] alone. Its extreme popularity is to be seen not only on account of its brevity

---

[122] For instance, Muḥammad b. ʿAbd al-Hayy al-Kattānī (in his *Fihris al-fahāris* (Fās: al-Maṭbaʿa al-Jadīda, 1346-47/1928-29) vol. II, 309) dismisses many of Jalāl al-Dīn's works as extremely brief, really just pamphlets; or Goldziher, noting especially Jalāl al-Dīn's remarks in the latter's autobiography which says "I am now the most learned among all of God's creatures, both in what concerns the pen and in what concerns the mouth," concludes that a good deal of Jalāl al-Dīn's work was designed to advertise the writer.

[123] Muhammad Ibrahim H. I. Surty, "The Qurʾān in Islamic Scholarship: A Survey of *Tafsīr* Exegesis Literature in Arabic" in *The Muslim World Book Review*, vol. 7, no. 4 (Summer 1987) 57.

[124] As cited by J. J. G. Jansen (from A. I. Nussayr, *Arabic Books 1926-1940*, nr. 187/2-190/2 and 192/2-193/2, p. 26) in his *The Interpretation of the Koran in Modern Egypt* (Leiden: E. J. Brill, 1980) 10.

but especially on account of its giving the gist of the accepted views in the briefest possible form.[125] It is thus very important as it gives only the relevant aspects of past *tafāsīr* and thus gives us the accepted views during his time and a summary of the preceding voluminous *tafāsīr* in a clear way.

2.3.2 *Tafsīr*

In his *tafsīr* of 2:143, Jalāl al-Dīn explains *umma wasaṭ* in a brief way which brings out very clearly the main elements in its meaning. He writes:

> Likewise, just as we have guided you to it *[qibla]* we made you O *umma* of Muhammad *umma wasaṭ*, as "best" *(ḫiyār)* and "just" *(ʿudūl)* that you may be witnesses against humankind on the day of the resurrection, that their messengers are [witnesses] in their language and the Messenger [Muhammad] will be a witness against you that he had communicated to you.[126]

Here, the meaning and purpose of *wasaṭ* which we already saw in earlier commentaries, are presented briefly. The Muslim community as *wasaṭ* is God's "choice" and thus the "best" and, as a community is a "just" one (which is a synopsis of Rāzī's view of *wasaṭ*). This is because they are to be witnesses on the day of the resurrection. Here also is shown the ranking of the categories of witnesses: at the top or the best of witnesses is Muhammad who will witness against all others including the Muslim community; the Muslim community comes next as it witnesses to the witnesses of the prophets against their respective *umam*; then, finally, the other messengers who will witness against their

---

125 W. Montgomery Watt, *Bell's Introduction to the Qurʾān* (Edinburgh: University Press, 1970/177) 170.

126 Al-Jalālayn (on 2:143) 29.

respective communities. Thus we see here once more a presentation in a nutshell of the *tafsīr* of Rāzī which says that *wasaṭ* means "best" in so far as it refers to the Muslim community in itself compared to other communities in themselves because the former is the "choice" *(ḫiyār)* while *wasaṭ* means "just" *(ʿadl)* in so far as it refers to the community being a witness, for as a witness they cannot be the best because the Messenger [Muhammad] is. The statement that the witness of the Muslim community is second only to Muhammad's may also be the gist of Ibn Kaṯīr's explanations in which he concludes that observing even just a little of the law of Muhammad is better than keeping the whole of the law brought by any other prophet.

In the same manner, the commentaries of al-Jalālayn on 3:104 and 3:110 bring out the gist of the explanations found in Ṭabarī, Zamaḫšarī and Rāzī as he saw it. We translate them here as they are - like Bayḍāwī's - a presentation in a nutshell of the conclusions of earlier commentaries accepted at his time and done in such a way as to make the passages in question clear and comprehensible to the reader wishing a quick reference rather than a comprehensive analysis. Thus, he writes,

> That there be from among you an *umma* that calls to what is good - i.e., "the Islamic religion;" and that orders what is acceptable and forbids that which is rejectable. Those - i.e., "the callers, the orderers and the forbidders," are the successul - i.e., "the victorious." And *min* [here] is partitive because it [the duty] is that which is called *farḍ kifāya,* which is not obligatory for the whole community and is not appropriate for everyone like the ignorant.[127]

And on 3:110, he comments as follows:

> You are, "O *umma* of Muhammad, in the knowledge of God" the best *umma* brought forth, i.e., "manifested;" you

---

[127] Al-Jalālayn (on 3:104) 81.

order that which is acceptable, you forbid that which is rejectable and you believe in God.[128]

Thus, there is really nothing much to say about the commentary just quoted except to reiterate that, however brief, it presents a kind of synopsis of the ideas we have seen in the classical works of *tafsīr*.

The second period of *tafsīr* writing, represented by Bayḍāwī, Ibn Kaṯīr and al-Jalālayn, served as a solidification of traditionalism. If the repetition of traditional material is already shown in the *tafāsīr* of these three commentators, other popular commentaries of this period not only use traditional material but they actually borrow whole passages of *tafsīr* from earlier commentaries, often regardless of their coming from different backgrounds and representing divergent persuasions, and often without changing so much as a word.[129] We thus end here our consideration of the second period of *tafsīr* writing, a period in which *ijtihād* was considered reprehensible and repetition a virtue.

---

[128] Al-Jalālayn (on 3:110) 81.

[129] For example, J. I. Smith (op. cit., 142) cites two commentaries from the tenth and eleventh centuries: "the *Iršād al-ʿAql* of Abū-l-Suʿūd and the *al-Ṣāfī* of al-Kāšāmī both borrow very heavily from al-Bayḍāwī's *Anwār al-tanzīl* of the seventh century....one of these writers was a Sunnī *Šayḫ al-islām*, the other a Šīʿī mystic." Or J. J. G. Jansen *(The Interpretation of the Koran in Modern Egypt....* p. 9), writing about the interpretation of the Qurʾān in modern Egypt, says: "... it is not only ideas which the Egyptian exegetes take over from each other. Every now and then it turns out that whole pages of their works are identical. For instance what Sheikh Higāzī writes about polygamy (in his *Al-Tafsīr al-Wāḍiḥ*, iv, 71) is identical with the passage on polygamy printed in the commentary (*Al-Tafsīr al-Farīd*, 502) by Muhammad ʿAbd al-Munʿim Gamāl."

3. New Directions in *Tafsīr*

Traditional commentaries continue to capture the interest of Muslims up to the present. This is shown by the fact that commentaries of *mufassirūn* like Zamaḫšarī and al-Jalālayn continue to be reprinted as well as taught in many religious institutions *(madāris)* in the Muslim world. On the other hand, however, many *tafāsīr* written in the late 19th century and the present century show new directions in *tafsīr* characterized by a discussion of the modern situation. Unlike the kind of *tafsīr* which was standard until the 19th century, in these *tafāsīr* we usually are reading the ideas of the *mufassirūn* themselves rather than those of centuries of their predecessors.

The *mufassirūn* in a discussion of modernity may be seen as the contemporary counterpart of the classical commentators in dialogue with the historical situation they lived in. We have seen that the classical commentators wrote in historical situations marked by a threat or problem to Islam and the Muslim empire. Most notable was the threat posed by the following: first, the foreign civilizations or uncongenial non-Muslim cultures that Islam was exposed to through the quick expansion of Muslim dominion; secondly, the impact of Greek philosophy upon the Muslim intellectual world; and thirdly, the sectarian differences within Islam. These problems were respectively addressed by the classical commentators whose commentaries then formed the basis of the classical works of the theology and philosophy of Islam. In the next seven centuries that followed, the Muslim empire was a closed community, secure in itself. The main challenge to Islamic identity was generally seen as coming from within, and the solution was to close the gate of *ijtihād*. Consequently, qurʾānic exegesis in the period, as we have seen, consisted in repetition or recasting of previous works.

Since the late 19th century, the impact of western influence was felt as a challenge and a real threat to Islamic identity, unprecedented in Islamic history, which challenge elicited various Muslim responses. In the field of qurʾānic exegesis, these responses have represented new directions, characterized especially by the use of reason over legend. The main theme is the Qurʾān vis-a-vis modern civilization. In terms of form or technique, commentators who address the problem of modernity on the whole also depart from the traditional way. We have seen that, until the 19th century, standard *tafsīr* - as exemplified by the representatives we have outlined in the above sections - undertook a passage-by-passage or interlinear explanation or interpretation of the Qurʾān. The new directions in *tafsīr* are characterized more by being commentaries of single verses or groups of verses or topical commentaries.

We will now consider, as representatives of the "new directions in *tafsīr*," the *tafsīr al-Manār* of Muhammad ʿAbduh and Rašīd Riḍā, as well as the respective commentaries of Abū al-Aʿlā Mawdūdī and Sayyid Quṭb.

3.1 *Tafsīr al-Manār* (of Muhammad ʿAbduh and Rašīd Riḍā)

3.1.1 Introduction

The *tafsīr* which has come to be commonly called *al-Manār* is the work of Muḥammad ʿAbduh and Rašīd Riḍā. The details of ʿAbduh's life, particularly his relationship with Jamāl al-Dīn al-Afġānī, are generally well known.[130] Al-Afġānī (1838-1897) epitomized the concerns and program of Islamic modernism which aimed at accommodating and assimilating the sources of

---

130 See, among others, Muḥammad Rašīd Riḍā, *Taʾrīḫ al-ustaḏ al-imām al-šayḫ Muḥammad ʿAbduh* (Cairo: Maṭbaʿat-al-Manār, 1324-1350/1906-1931) 3 vols. in 2; C. C. Adams, *Islam and Modernism in Egypt* (London: Oxford University Press, 1933) 1-103; J. Schacht, "Muhammad ʿAbduh" in *The Encyclopedia of Islam*. New Edition. Volume VII (1993) 418 - 420.

the West's strength in the reform of Islam. Whereas Afġānī was primarily a political activist, his protegè Muḥammad ᶜAbduh was the developer of the intellectual and social reformist dimensions of Islamic modernism. ᶜAbduh - who was trained as a religious scholar and a member of the *ᶜūlamā*ᵓ - founded the movement *al-Salafīya* - so named because for him the renewal of Islam in the modern age could only take place by following the example of the elders *(al-salafī)*[131] of the early Muslim community, those who followed the example of the Prophet.

Muhammad ᶜAbduh was born in 1849 in the countryside of lower Egypt. At an early age, he began his theological studies at a mosque school in Ṭanṭā. His great enthusiasm for religious studies, however, came to the fore when he was exposed to the mystical approach, and, in 1865 he entered the Azhar Mosque where he devoted himself to mysticism and the practice of asceticism. Then in 1872 he came into contact with al-Afġānī who made him see traditional learning in a new light, introduced him to the European outlook and attracted his interest to the Egyptian and Muslim problems of the day.[132] In 1877 he completed his studies at the Azhar and the influence of al-Afġānī gradually made him become actually involved in pragmatic concerns, prompting him to practice journalism alongside his teaching stint at the *Dār al-ᶜulūm*.

He ran into political disfavor for a short period. For this reason he was sent back to his native village. During the same time al-Afġānī was also banished from Egypt. After a brief period ᶜAbduh was recalled and was appointed chief editor of the official newspaper *al-Waqāᵓiᶜ al-Miṣrīya* - which paper became the

---

[131] The period of the *Salaf* is considered as closed approximately at the death of Ibn Ḥanbal (241/855). Cf. E. Chaumont, "Salaf" in *Encyclopedia of Islam*, New edition, vol. VIII, 900.

[132] J. Schacht, "Muḥammad Abduh" in *Encyclopedia of Islam*, New edition, vol. VII (1993) 418-420.

mouthpiece of liberal ideas. Because of an alleged involvement in a revolt in 1882 he was condemned to years of exile which he spent in Beirut, Syria, Paris and elsewhere. In 1884 he met al-Afġānī in Paris and together the two founded a society called *al-ʿurwa al-wuṯqā* which supported a short-lived publication of the same name for the propagation of Muslim nationalism. However,

> In spite of a common ultimate goal: the liberation of the Muslim peoples and a renaissance of Islam by its own strength, there was an essential difference between Muhammad ʿAbduh's programme and that of Jamal al-Dīn: the latter was a revolutionary who aimed at a forcible upheaval; Muhammad Abduh on the oher hand, held that no political revolution could take the place of a gradual transformation of mentality.[133]

For this reason ʿAbduh left al-Afġānī and devoted himself entirely to his interest in theological reform which made him the founder of the modernist school in Islam. In 1889 he was pardoned, returned to Egypt, and two years later was appointed judge and member of the legislative council. He was also allowed to resume his interest in education. In 1894 he became a member of the governing body of the Azhar, which had been constituted at his suggestion and in this capacity not only acquired great renown by his reforms in the university but himself took an active part in the teaching. In 1899 he attained the highest religious post in Egypt, that of state *muftī* - an office he held until his death in 1905 - through which post he was able to introduce reforms in the religious courts. It was in this last period of his life that he published some of his most important works, like his principal theological work *Risālat al-tawḥīd* (1315/1897) and a defense of Islam against Christianity entitled *al-islām wa-l-naṣrānīya maʿa-l-ʿilm wa l-madanīya* (1320/1902). It was also at this time that he entered into close association with his disciple and friend Rašīd

---

133 Ibid., 418.

Riḍā who was the editor of the monthly publication *al-Manār* which became the principal organ of his views.

Rašīd Riḍā (1282/1865 - 1354/1935) was born in the Syrian village of al-Qalamūn about three miles from the city of Tripoli (now in Lebanon). Our interest in him lies in his association with Muḥammad ʿAbduh in the composition of the Qurʾān commentary called *al-Manār.*[134] It was through the ideas projected in the publication *al-ʿurwa al-wuṯqā* that Riḍā came to admire his twin idols Afġānī and ʿAbduh. In 1897 he met Afġānī in Istanbul and decided to widen his knowledge on pan-Islamism under the latter's tutelage. The death of al-Afġānī later that year, together with the suspicious circumstances that surrounded it, made Riḍā decide to leave the Ottoman Empire and go to Egypt. There he joined the second man whom he admired, the Islamic reformer - Muḥammad ʿAbduh, who, thereafter, became his spiritual teacher. In March 1898, Riḍā began publishing a paper, *al-Manār* - first as a weekly of eight pages, and, a year later, as a monthly periodical which was to last until his death in 1935 - which became the vehicle of the dissemination of reformist ideas especially of ʿAbduh and himself. It was through the pages of *al-Manār* that ʿAbduh's Qurʾān commentary came into view.

Muḥammad ʿAbduh presented his qurʾānic exegesis in the form of lectures at the al-Azhar. From notes on these lectures Riḍā compiled the *tafsīr*, approved and revised by ʿAbduh, first published in *al-Manār* in 1900 and attributed to Muḥammad ʿAbduh. The work thus created, Ṭafsīr al-Qurʾān al-Ḥakīm, now goes by the title of *tafsīr* al-Manār. ʿAbduh was never able to complete past *sūra* 4:125 and Riḍā himself continued it in what he

---

[134] For a discussion of the views of Riḍā, see, among others: Malcolm Kerr, *Islamic Reform* (Berkeley: University of California Press, 1966) chapter five; Eliezer Tauber, "Rašīd Riḍā as Pan-Arabist Before World War I" in *The Muslim World* vol.LXXIX, no. 2 (April1989) 102-112 and Emad Eldin Shahin, "Muḥammad Rašīd Riḍā's Perspectives on the West as Reflected in *Al-Manār*" in *The Muslim World*, vol. LXXIX, no. 2 (April 1989) 113-132.

intended to be a style and content with which his teacher would have been in full agreement. Riḍā himself added his own interpretations, distinguishing them by the introduction *aqūlu* ("I say") from the passages beginning with *qāla al-ustāḏ al-imām* ("the Master said"). Published later in book form,[135] the whole work itself deals only with the first 12 *sūras* of the Qurʾān. The commentary on the verses that we are concerned about here - namely 2:143, 3:104 and 3:110 - are among those that were approved and revised by ʿAbduh. However, as *tafsīr al-Manār* in its final form was compiled and written by Riḍā, in our discussion we will ascribe authorship to him while indicating clearly those passages coming directly from ʿAbduh and those that are Riḍā's own interpretation.

On principle ʿAbduh objected to the interpretation of the Qurʾān seen as mainly an academic affair, with commentaries written by scholars for other scholars, so that it took an enormous amount of intellectual energy to profit from the knowledge stored up in such commentaries. ʿAbduh intended to explain the Qurʾān in a practical manner to a public wider than merely the professional theologians. He wanted it to be understood by every present-day man as a guidance for his life and actions. Thus, with this practical approach, *al-Manār* (in so far as this was completed), unlike most other modern *tafāsīr*, comments on all the verses of the Qurʾān in the same manner as the interlinear exegesis which was standard until the 19th century. However, it also shares many of the qualities of contemporary commentaries and apologetic writings. It is thus traditional in form but modern in content as it also relates the Qurʾān to the issues and problems of contemporary life in such a way which the early *tafāsīr* did not.

While *tafsīr al-Manār* is traditional at least in its form as interlinear *tafsīr*, it is not heavily reliant on the traditional material of

---

[135] Rašīd Riḍā, *Tafsīr-al-Qurʾān al-ḥakīm al-šahīr bi-Tafsīr-al-Manār*, 12 vols. (Cairo, 1346-1353 (1927-1934). We quote here from the edition Cairo 1972.

exegesis that we have seen in the previous works. For Muḥammad ʿAbduh there is no contradiction between the insights of the intellect and the revelation of the Qurʾān. Here, traditions based on Ṭabarī's commentary are sometimes cited and discussions on the commentaries of Zamaḫšarī, Rāzī and others are frequent, and yet we are reading the ideas of ʿAbduh and Riḍā instead of those of their predecessors. A real difference in approach from the earlier commentaries - despite the similarity in form - is to be seen in the fact that while in those of previous centuries the lines of the Qurʾān were taken quite clearly as the points of departure, sometimes at the expense of clear continuity from one passage of exegesis to the next, in *tafsīr al-Manār* the *āyas* seem to be used as a proof for the point(s) ʿAbduh and Riḍā are making.[136]

Criticisms have been hurled at ʿAbduh's Qurʾān interpretation - one which aims to ensure both a progressing and conserving Islam - not only by non-Muslim scholars but by Muslims as well.[137] They, however, don't overshadow the appreciation accorded it by many Muslims and westerners alike, the reason for

[136] Ibid., 194.

[137] Muhammad Ibrahim H. I. Surty writes: " ʿAbduh's vigorous campaign of seeking guidance from the Qurʾān is commendable but his reduction of the immense contributions of past commentators is disappointing. Those Muslim intellectuals who applied their excellence in their specialized disciplines yet did so in order to understand the message of the Qurʾān - their efforts reveal the extent and profundity of the Qurʾān which it cannot be right to either ignore or minimize. Muhammad Ibrahim H. I. Surty, "The Qurʾān in Islamic Scholarship: A Survey of *Tafsīr* Exegesis Literature in Arabic" in *The Muslim World Book Review*, vol. 7, no. 4 (summer 1987) 59. Malcolm Kerr, on the other hand, indicates that precisely where ʿAbdu and Riḍā fell short was in their not having gone all the way in discarding the classical doctrines which they claimed were not adequate for the modern era. Cf. Malcolm Kerr, *Islamic Reform* (Berkeley: University of California Press, 1966) 15.

which is to be seen not only in ʿAbduh's having given modern Islamic thought a center of gravity,[138] but especially for his "practical approach, which does not grow weary of admonishing the Muslims to put into action the doctrine of the Qurʾān."[139]

3.1.2 *Tafsīr* of 2:143

3.1.2.1 The Term *Wasaṭ*: "Best" and "Just"

Riḍā begins the commentary on 2:143 by pointing out its connection to the preceding phrase.

> Thus we made you a middle *umma* and this [phrase] is an explication (تصريح) of that which is contained in God's saying "God guides whom He will" (in 2:142b; 2:213; etc.), i.e., in this manner of guidance we have established you a middle *umma*.[140]

This guidance to a straight path, as explained in the preceding verse, "is the way of moderation (الاعتدال) in thinking (الأفكار) in moral principles (الأخلاق) and actions (الأعمال). As we

---

[138] Cf. Kenneth Cragg, *Counsels in Contemporary Islam* (Edinburgh: University Press, 1965) 41.

[139] Arij Roest Crollius, "Mission And Morality" in *Studia Missionalia*, vol. 27 (Roma: Università Gregoriana Editrice, 1978) 275. Roest Crollius adds, "And precisely in this respect, the commentary has, at times, a certain freshness and originality, through the straightforwardness with which the Islamic ideal is exposed and the strength of conviction with which the principles for action are put forward." Ibid. Cf. also, J. M. S. Baljon, *Modern Muslim Koran Interpretation* (Leiden: E. J. Brill, 1968) 5.

[140] *Tafsīr-al-Manār* (on 2:143) 4, also for the following two quotations.

have already seen in the earlier commentaries, especially in Zamaḫšarī and Rāzī, also in *al-Manār* the "middle" is the just (العدل) and the best (الخيار) which means

> that the excess of the desires in things is immoderation while the deficiency of these is negligence and laxity. Everything of excess and negligence is a turning away from the straight middle of the road and it is evil and thus is objectionable, while the best is the middle between the two extremes of excess and neglect, i.e., it is that which stands between the two of them.

What follows is ʿAbduh's explanation of his preference for the term "middle" *(wasaṭ)* in a manner suggested in Zamaḫšarī and Rāzī but put more straightforwardly here. The term "middle" or *wasaṭ*, specifies the meaning of "best" and "just."

> The Master said....: Why is the term "middle" *(wasaṭ)* preferred to the term "best" *(ḫiyār)* when the latter is what is meant here? The answer has two aspects. First, because the purpose of the preference is to introduce the following explanation, that the witness has definite certainty that he is cognizant of it [the best position], and whoever is standing in the middle between two things sees one of them on one side and the other on the other side; and he who is in one of the two extremes does not know the reality of the position of the other extreme nor the position of the middle. Second, because in the term "middle" is the information of causality, as though it is an indication on itself, i.e., that the Muslims are the best and the just because they are middle. They are not among those characterized by exaggeration in religion nor among those characterized by negligence. They are in that manner also in the doctrines, moral principles and actions.

3.1.2.2 "Middle" or *Wasaṭ* in Religion: Reality and Ideal of the Muslim *Umma*

What follows is an elucidation of what it means to be, in religion, in either extreme and in the middle. Belonging to one extreme are those who take upon themselves "an uncritical faith in pure materialism «المادية المحضة» especially its bodily or corporal aspects, like the Jews and those who associate partners with God;" and belonging to the other extreme are those who take upon themselves "an uncritical faith in pure spiritualism «الروحانية الخالصة» and renounce the world and that which is in it of bodily pleasure, like the Christians, the Ṣābians and a group of idolaters in India."[141] It may be noted that the idea of division or differing among people outside of or before the coming of Islam has been expressed by earlier *mufassirūn*, but ʿAbduh and Riḍā, writing from the perspective of the 14th/20th century, offer a new description of this division, i.e., "pure materialism" and "pure spiritualism." As regards the "middle" which is the Islamic *umma*, it is the one for whom God brought together the truth about the spirit and about the body, which truth is "corporal and spiritual."

> He [God] gave it [Islamic *umma*] all the truths of humanity because man is body and spirit, animal and angel, as God said: We appointed you a middle *umma* knowledgeable of the two truths and worthy of the two perfections "that you may be witnesses" with the truth "against the people" who are materialistic in that which they neglect in regard to religion and spiritualistic because they go too far. They are of the extremists... You surpass all the *umam* by your moderation *(iʿtidāl)* and by your being positioned in the middle in all things. That is because that which you are guided to is human perfection in which after it there is no [other] perfection.

---

141 *Tafsīr al-Manār* (on 2:143) 5, for all the quotations on this page.

Here is expressed the universal character of Islam. As "middle" religion, it is the perfection of whatever truth is found in other religions. It is the true religion and the community [i.e., the Muslim community] that bears it is the only authentic religious community. The idea of "perfection" of the Muslim community or society and not just of the individual could be read as well in the earlier commentaries, but its newness lies in its being developed much more fully here in the sense of being explicitly stated. The Muslim *umma* is endowed with the knowledge and worthiness of achieving this perfection. They are *umma wasaṭ* only if they maintain this perfection and only when they are in that state that they can be witnesses against the *umam*. Just what is the way to that perfection is spelled out in the following explanation.

> The Messenger [Muhammad] will be a witness against you, i.e., that the Messenger is the perfect example of *wasaṭ*. However, this *umma* is *wasaṭ* only by its conformity to him in his way of acting and his law.... if you [Muslims] want the characterization *wasaṭ* to be true to you, then you maintain the course of action with the guidance of the Messenger and stand right on his *sunna*. And if you turn away from this course then the Messenger by himself and his religion and his deeds will be the authority against you because [in that case] you are not of his *umma* which God describes in His Scripture by this verse and in His saying "You are the best *umma* ever brought for humankind, you order what is acceptable and you forbid what is rejectable " (3:110), etc. Rather, you go out by inventing something other than the *wasaṭ* and you become one of the two extremes/edges like it is said in the poetry quoted by al-Zamaḫšarī in his *tafsīr* of this verse; "It was the protected middle but then problems accumulated from all sides until it became an extreme/a marginal reality."[142]

[142] *Tafsīr al-Manār* (on 2:143) 5-6.

The reality of being "middle" of the Muslim *umma* is something that has to be maintained, otherwise it can be lost. The only way to do it is to live the doctrine of the Qurʾān according to the guidance of the Messenger and his *sunna*. The presentation of the reality of the Muslim *umma* is here substantially different from what we have seen before. Formerly when speaking of division or disintegration in religion, Jews and Christians and others outside the Muslim *umma* were referred to. Here, Riḍā, writing from a 20th century point of view, refers not only to Jews and Christians and others but also explicitly to the Muslim *umma* as subject to the forces of disintegration. This idea was of course already suggested in the *tafsīr* of Zamaḫšārī (as also quoted by Riḍā) but is straightforwardly put here as also referring to the reality of the Muslim *umma*. This is followed by ʿAbduh's discourse on being "middle" as a great blessing from God and how this became a reality in the beginning of Islam, the crucial point of which was the event of the change of the *qibla*, the purpose for which change was the "getting together of the people of religion in one direction and one characterization in [their] turning to God;"[143] in other words, to see who were the true followers of the Messenger.

Thus to summarize what *al-Manār* 2:143 says about *umma wasaṭ*: 1) *Wasaṭ* is middle and it means just and best. 2) The Muslim *umma* is the middle and being so as a historical reality has two aspects: a) that such a characterization can be lost and thus has to be constantly maintained by following the Messenger and his *sunna* and, b) that in such a characterization they are to witness against other *umam*. The elaboration of this twofold aspect - centripetal and centrifugal - of the Muslim *umma* is to be found in *al-Manār* 3:104 and 3:110.

---

143 *Tafsīr al-Manār* (on 2:143) 6.

3.1.3 *Tafsīr* of 3:104

Verse 3:104 (as also 3:110)[144] is seen in the context of the preceding phrase in which God commands the Muslims to "hold fast together to the cord *(ḥabl)* of God and not be divided" (3:103).[145] Holding fast to the cord of God or commitment to God, ʿAbduh says, "is the base *(qāʿida)* to refer to in order to overcome the danger of division or differences in opinion." It is with this as context that the *tafsīr* provides explanations for 3:104 (and 3:110), which, as we shall see, are done by way of a critique of some earlier opinions and may be seen as the formulations in the order of reality of the twofold movement of the "middle *umma*" which we have described as centripetal and centrifugal.

3.1.3.1 The general sense of the command.

The commentary on 3:104 begins by refuting those exegetes who take *min* (مِن) here in the partitive sense - like Zamaḫšarī and al-Jalālayn (who are expressly mentioned) who claim that the recommendation in this verse is given only to those Muslims who are knowledgeable of the religion and its prescriptions.

The first argument is from the point of view of language, i.e., that from the formulation itself of the command in this verse one can draw the conclusion that it is meant for everybody.

> The Master said: it is clear that the manner of expression is the same as "Let there be a friend to me from you" and thus <u>the command is general</u> and addresses everybody,

---

[144] An analysis of *Tafsīr al-Manār* on 3:104 and 3:110 has been done by Arij Roest Crollius, "Mission and Morality" in *Studia Missionalia*, vol. 27 (Roma: Università Gregoriana Editrice, 1978) 273-282, which work has been a great help in our own analysis of these verses.

[145] *Tafsīr al-Manār* (on 3:104) 22.

> like God's saying: "By the declining day perdition shall be the lot of man, except those who believe and do good works, who exhort one another to truth and endurance." (103:1-3).[146]

The second argument is from the point of view of the nature of the addressees, i.e., the Muslims. It is necessary that a Muslim

> is not ignorant of that which is obligatory upon him, which obligation is to the knowledge and the distinction between that which is acceptable and that which is rejectable; and what is acceptable is that which is viewed as such by sound minds and characters, and what is rejectable is the opposite of it.[147]

That which leads to this knowledge is the knowledge of the Qurʾān and the *sunna* of the Prophet and "no Muslim is a Muslim without it." Therefore,

> those who deny the general sense of the ordering of what is acceptable and the forbidding of what is rejectable admit that there can exist a Muslim [so] ignorant as not to know good from evil and not to distinguish between what is acceptable and what is rejectable - and this does not befit a religion.

3.1.3.2 The two degrees of the command.

What follows is a distinction of two degrees in the task of calling to the good and the ordering and forbidding. The first degree, which is more extensively treated, is centrifugal, i.e., the calling of all non-Muslims to the good which is the Islamic

---

146 *Tafsīr al-Manār* (on 3:104) 23.

147 *Tafsīr al-Manār* (on 3:104) 23, also for the following quotation.

religion.[148] This is the consequent task of the Muslim *umma*'s being "the middle community" (2:143) and being "the best community ever brought forth for humankind" (3:110).[149] The second degree is the calling to what is good and the ordering and forbidding within the Muslim community.

As regards the second degree of the command, two ways of its execution are also to be distinguished. The first way is the guidance of the community of believers in "the ways to apply the law of God in their conditions," which is a special responsibility of the leading personalities of the community, who have a profound knowledge of the religion and its laws.[150] The second way is the admonition and fraternal correction which should take place among all the members of the community in their relationship to one another and in which each one contributes according to his capacity.[151]

---

[148] The good which is Islam is that which is accepted by sound minds and characters. "It is the religion of God proclaimed by all the prophets to all the nations," and thus a universal religion. *Tafsīr al-Manār* (on 3:104) 23.

[149] *Tafsīr al-Manār* (on 3:104) 23, also for the following quotation.

[150] *Tafsīr al-Manār* (on 3:104) 24. To support this, the *tafsīr* quotes a verse of the Qur'ān as referring to such a special group of people with special responsibility as a participation in the general command expressed in 3:104. The text quoted says: "It is impossible for the believers to go forth all together [in order to obtain religious instruction]. But why should not a party from every group of them go forth, to become instructed in religion, and to warn the people when they return to them - perhaps they will give heed?" (9:122). Translation adopted from Arij Roest Crollius, "Mission and Morality" in *Studia Missionalia*, vol. 27 (Roma: Università Gregoriana Editrice, 1978) 276, footnote 58.

[151] The "bad conditions" which the Muslims are in now, the *tafsīr* emphasizes, is due to negligence in following the Qur'ān and the *sunna* of Muhammad; and thus the need to return to the sources. Cf. *Tafsīr al-Manār* (on 3:104) 24.

As regards the first degree of the order, i.e., the duty of the Muslim community to call non-Muslims to Islam, the *tafsīr* makes it clear that this task is a *farḍ al-ʿayn,* i.e., it is a task that every individual Muslim must do; however, it is not expected that each individual Muslim perform this obligation in the same manner.

> The Master said: Indeed, the [duty of] the community to call the other communities to the good that is its own, does not demand from each individual the duty to undertake action, since not everyone can do it. However, it is an obligation for each individual to keep this before his eyes, till the occasion presents itself to him to reach one of the members of those communities with his call. It is not that he should give all his time to this, and travel for this sake. That is the task of a group *(ṭāʾifa)* [of people] who are especially prepared for it. The other members of the community fullfil this task when they can. It is like the duty of the pilgrimage which is a *farḍ ʿayn* but applies to him who can do it. The duty of ordering what is acceptable and forbidding what is rejectable is even more rigorous than the duty of pilgrimage: its being possible does not depend on [special] conditions since it is always possible.... and ignorance is not an excuse because every Muslim must be knowledgeable [of his religion]. [152]

To demonstrate further the *farḍ ʿayn* sense of this twofold duty, the *tafsīr* cites other passages of the Qurʾān as well as examples from the first ages of Islam. Thus, the *tafsīr* recapitulates, the two degrees in the order, i.e., the calling of non-Muslims to Islam and the ordering of what is acceptable and the forbidding of what is rejectable within the Muslim community, are imposed on every Muslim. Only if these two degrees are in simultaneous function that Muslims can call themselves an *umma,*

---

[152] *Tafsīr al-Manār* (on 3:104) 29.

that which the verse describes as "successful - مُفْلِحُونَ."[153]

3.1.3.3 The Partitive Sense of the Command: A Society for the *Daʿwa*.

After having thus explained the general sense and the twofold degree of the command in 3:104, the *tafsīr* points out that, within this general sense of the command, is also to be understood a partitive sense. The verse may be paraphrased thus: "Let there be from you [Muslims] a special group *(ṭāʾifa)* which carries out the call *(daʿwa)*, the ordering of what is acceptable and the forbidding of what is rejectable."[154] There are two duties which are involved in this understanding: 1) the duty of the Muslim community to choose this special group, and 2) the duty that is incumbent upon the chosen group to do the *Daʿwa*.[155] The term *umma* is applied to this special group in order to emphasize that this special group has force and unity - which are among the qualities of the *umma* - which will therefore make the members of this special group act as one person although with different jobs and careers.[156]

---

153 *Tafsīr al-Manār* (on 3:104) 29-30.

154 *Tafsīr all-Manār* (on 3:104) 30.

155 The word *Daʿwa* could be rendered with the English terms "propaganda" or "mission." However, as Arij Roest Crollius points out, it "is better not translated, in order to bring out its being different from Christian Mission and also from other kinds of propaganda. This was also the way chosen by the participants in the Chambéry Conference on "Christian Mission and Islamic *Daʿwa*," June 26-30, 1976.... Likewise, we do not translate the Arabic term for the workers in the *Daʿwa: duʿāh* (plural of *dāʿin*)." Arij Roest Crollius, "Mission and Morality".....p. 278, note 62.

156 Cf. *Tafsīr al-Manār* (on3:104) 30-31.

As regards the duty of the Muslim community to form this special group,[157] the *tafsīr* points out that it is not a collective obligation but is the duty of each individual person, i.e., it is a *farḍ ʿayn.*

> If every individual Muslim is obligated to call to what is good, to order that which is acceptable and to forbid that which is rejectable according to the first aspect of the explanation of the verse, according to this second aspect of the explanation, they are to choose a society from among them to carry out this task, so that it can take care of it and is capable of doing it, if this [task] does not exist spontaneously as in the time of the Companions. The forming of this special society is a *farḍ ʿayn.* It is the obligation of everyone who is subject to the law to participate in it [the formation of this society] together with the others.[158]

The *tafsīr* then explains that in the "time of the Companions" there was no need of this special group because its function coincided with what the whole community was doing - it was an ideal situation - and it was the whole community that was the special group because

> the Companions of the Prophet followed him and continued what he had started, maintained their unity and each one of them felt the same urgency of spreading and

---

157 In this chapter of *Al-Manār*, this *umma* within the larger *umma* is also expressed with the words *ṭāifa* and *jamʿīya* - words which mean "association" or "community." This is especially made clear towards the end of this chapter of *Al-Manār* where, instead of *umma*, the word *jamʿīya* is used (p. 35: *jamʿīya li–l-daʿwa)* and the *tafsīr* explains that what is meant with the *umma* which the *umma* forms for the *daʿwa* is expressed in present-day manner by *jamʿīya* (p. 37).

158 *Tafsīr al-Manār* (on 3:104) 31.

guarding Islam and fighting everything that could harm any of its doctrines, morality, laws or the interest of its people.[159]

The *tafsīr* recognizes that this ideal situation is no longer true, and thus calls for the establishment of a special society for the *Daʿwa*. What follows in this place of the *tafsīr* is an entire program of studies for an institute for training *duʿah*, which we shall report on in detail here since it is a showcase of what may be called the "modernity and orthodoxy at the same time" of this *tafsīr*.[160]

1. In the first place, the *duʿah* should have a perfect knowledge of the content of their message. This means: they should know the Qurʾān, the *Sunna*, the life of the Prophet, of the "Well-guided caliphs" and of the *Salaf*. They should also have a sufficient knowledge of the legal prescriptions.
2. Moreover, they should know the social conditions of those to whom they direct their *Daʿwa*: their character, temperament and customs. An example is given from the beginnings of Islam: the first Companions agreed on Abū Bakr as Caliph because of his knowledge of the character and customs of the Arabs.
3. A basic knowledge of universal history is necessary "in order to know the corruption in religious doctrines, in morality and customs, so that they establish their *Daʿwa* on a sound basis, and know how an argumentation is pertinent and the discourse can be most effective. Thus they know how those to whom the *Daʿwa* is directed can be brought to another state of life. For this reason, the Qurʾān is filled with lessons from history."
4. Also for the study of geography, the first Companions

---

159 *Tafsīr al-Manār* (on3:104) 32.

160 *Tafsīr al-Manār* (on3:104) 32-36. We quote here the summary in English made by Arij Roest Crollius in "Mission and Morality," *Studia Missionalia*, vol. 27 (Roma: Università Gregoriana Editrice, 1978) 279-280. Emphasis through underlining is mine.

are mentioned as an example: "Those who have an aversion against history and geography [------] have severed the link between them and the good example of the *Salaf*."

5. Psychology is needed in order to understand others and to know how to deal with them. The *Salaf* had this insight without study, from the words and the example of the Prophet.

6. Moral Science has to be studied in order to know the virtues and vices, and to be able to promote the first and to eradicate the latter. Qur'ān and Tradition are the main sources of this science.

7. Sociology was not mentioned by the Master. Rašīd Riḍā describes it as the science that deals with the conditions of the various human societies, their way of life - nomadic or sedentary - the causes of their weakness and strength, their decadence and progress. This knowledge, so it is said, can be deduced from history and moral science. Not everyone, however, is capable of drawing these conclusions. The *tafsīr*, therefore, urges the study of sociology and the writing of books on it, making use of what has been produced along this line in the West.

8. Political Science is also a new discipline, which did not exist in the times of the Salaf. Today it is necessary for the accomplishment of the *Daʿwa*.

9. The need of studying languages is exposed at some length. Also here is an example from the beginnings of Islam: the Prophet ordered some Companions to study Hebrew in view of a better contact and understanding among them and their Jewish neighbours, even though the latter knew Arabic. The Society for the *Daʿwa* cannot manage with non-Muslim interpreters, but should follow the example of the Christian missionary Societies: "They have people who learn the languages of all peoples." This point had not been explained by the Master in his course at the Azhar, because his enemies would have protested, saying "that he wanted to destroy religion at the Azhar by encouraging the students to study foreign languages."

10. The knowledge of the arts and sciences of the various nations and (11) of their various religious trends and sects is necessary in order to be able to convince others of the falseness of their doctrines. Ignorance in these matters is

harmful to religion. This experience was made by the Christians, who for this reason give a great attention to these profane studies.[161]

Thus the Islamic "missionary programme" as proposed by the *Tafsīr al-Manār*, aims both "at a faithful imitation of the *Salaf* and at an adaptation to present-day conditions following the example of western men of science and of Christian missionaries."[162] Or, in the words of Kenneth Cragg, it is a program which aims "to ensure both a progressing and conserving Islam."[163] Thus, to sum up in practical terms the general and the partitive senses of the command in 3:104: every individual Muslim must participate in the *Daʿwa* itself as well as in the establishment of a special society for the *Daʿwa*.

3.1.4 *Tafsīr* of 3:110

As with verse 3:104, verse 3:110 is to be seen in the context of God's order for the believers to preserve their loyalty and unity of hearts and the brotherhood of Islam. It is for the purpose of giving them a point of reference in the preservation of their faith in God and brotherhood in Islam that God describes them with the words "You are the best *umma*---" (3:110).[164]

3.1.4.1 The BEST Muslim Community in History.

The *tafsīr* stresses the three characteristics of the "best community" as mentioned in the verse, namely: "ordering what is

---

161 A. Roest Crollius, Ibid.

162 Arij Roest Crollius, Ibid, 280.

163 Kenneth Cragg, *Counsels in Contemporary Islam* (Edinburgh: University Press, 1965) 41.

164 *Tafsīr al-Manār* (on 3:110) 47.

acceptable, forbidding what is rejectable and believing in God," then begins the explanation of the verse by dealing with the proper understanding of "*kuntum*/you were" in a manner which is a critique or evaluation of the three traditional interpretations of the word.

> The first is complete and the meaning is "you were found/ *wujidtum*" as the best *umma*, as though God is saying "You are the best *umma* in existence now because all the [other] *umam* are dominated by corruption, right conduct is not known in them and what is rejectable is not forbidden and they don't follow the right religion; while you order what is acceptable and forbid what is rejectable and believe in God with the right faith which is manifested in good deeds. The second is incomplete and the meaning then is "You were in the knowledge of God, or you were, among the previous *umam* as it is in their missionary Scriptures, the best *umma*, etc..... The third one is that "*kāna*/was" here means "*ṣāra*/ became," i.e., you became the best *umma* - and this is the weakest interpretation.[165]

Then the *tafsīr* says that this verse is really "a testimony from God for His Prophet and those from among the true believers who followed him, until the time of its (the community of Muhammad's) proclamation as the best *umma* ever raised up for mankind with those three characteristics."[166] We already have seen this identification of the best community in the earlier commentaries as well as in our study of *al-Manār* thus far. In this place of the *tafsīr*, however, this best community is outlined and specified as clearly as possible, important as this community is as the model for the Islamic reform. Thus the *tafsīr* makes clear those who are excluded from this description.

---

165 *Tafsīr al-Manār* (on 3:110) 47-48.

166 *Tafsīr al-Manār* (on 3:110) 48.

> This "being the best" is not merited by those who do not have anything to do with Islam; and those who follow the Prophet only by pretense and make the religion their identification, and even those who pray and pay the alms tax, fast at Ramaḍān, make the pilgrimage to the *Ka*ʿ*ba*, and stick to that which is lawful and avoid that which is unlawful with the sincerity which is the soul of Islam - [all these] do not deserve "being the best" until after the execution of the command to order that which is acceptable and forbid that which is rejectable and to hold fast to the cord of God together with the avoidance of division and deviation in the religion.[167]

After the enumeration of those who do not merit the description of "best," the Master is cited to have said something to the effect that this characterization "holds true of those who were first addressed by it, i.e., the Prophet and his Companions who were with him."[168] Riḍā then further identifies this best community, saying that with the words "his Companions who were with him," the Master "wants to say that these lofty descriptions and perfect virtues of that perfect faith are not [applicable] to all those that the narrators of *aḥādīṯ* designate as the Companions of the Prophet."[169] With the support of some verses of the Qurʾān as well as *aḥādīṯ*, Riḍā says that the ones referred to here are those who struggled and migrated with the Prophet to Medina. The further clarifications that Riḍā makes give a clear picture of the Muslim community that is to be the model to be followed.

> If it is said that some of the genuine Companions from the emigrants and the helpers separated and disagreed during the sedition which was triggered by Muʿāwiya against the Prince of the believers, does that mean that the *umma* was

167 *Tafsīr al-Manār* (on 3:110) 48.

168 *Tafsīr al-Manār* (on 3:110) 48.

169 *Tafsīr al-Manār* (on 3:110) 48.

> then deprived of being the best *umma* brought forth for mankind? The answer has three aspects: 1.) the disagreement and separation was not in religion but in worldly affair in which the belief of both groups did not change... 2.) Muʿāwiya who caused that separation was not one of the emigrants because he became a Muslim the year the Muslims took over Mecca, at which time the *hijra* had stopped. 3.) those who are aware of history know that the Companions did enjoin right conduct and forbid indecency the way they could, and that all this became weaker after most of them had died.[170]

In conclusion, Riḍā says:

> The truth I say: that this *umma* did not cease being the best *umma* brought forth for humankind until it abandoned ordering what is acceptable and forbidding what is rejectable not because it wanted to nor because it was not afraid of God but because of disgust at the high-handedness of the kings and princes.[171]

Thus, the best community in the eyes of God is the one which is characterized by an internal life of ordering of what is acceptable, forbidding of what is rejectable and the right faith in God. This community has been singled out by God as the Muslim community. However, the Muslim community that genuinely lived these characterizations was the one which consisted of Muhammad and his Companions, i.e., those who struggled with him in the *hijra*. It is in this original Muslim community that the Islamic religion in its pristine form is to be found and to its return

---

[170] *Tafsīr al-Manār* (on 3:110) 49.

[171] *Tafsīr al-Manār* (on 3:110) 50. (الملوك والأمراء). Accordingly, this tyrannical rule started with the Banū Umayya and those who came after them while the first ruler who showed corruption publicly was ʿAbd Mālik b. Marwān. Ibid.

every Muslim is called.[172] It is thus in the centripetal dimension of the Muslim *umma* that its being "best" is to have its basis.

3.1.4.2 The False Idealization of the *jihād*.

With its understanding of the "best community" that we have just outlined, it is not surprising that the *tafsīr* takes exception to criticize another explanation of 3:110, the one of al-Qaffāl as reported by Rāzī (cf. above, section "Rāzī"), which purports that the reason for the being best of the Muslim community is that its members propagate Islam in a dangerous but most powerful way, i.e., by fighting. In such a view, "the *jihād* in religion is done with the infliction of great harm for the [final] purpose of making the other attain the great benefits [i.e., the true religion] and of liberating him from the great danger [i.e., of remaining an unbeliever], and thus *jihād* is the greatest observance of the faith (الجهاد أعظم العبادات) ."[173] Riḍā rejects this interpretation for several reasons.[174]

> 1. The supposition of al-Qaffāl and Rāzī that the other *umam* did not have violent religious war and no compulsion in religion is due to their ignorance of [other] religions and of history; and the truth is that the people of the Scripture were more intense than the Muslims in their religious wars, and it is told that their compulsion in religion is such that nothing like it is found among the Muslims.

---

172 J. Schacht says: "This primitive Islam of Muḥammad ʿAbduh is however not the historical Islam but a very much idealized one." J. Schchat, op. cit., 420.

173 *Tafsīr al-Manār* (on 3:110) 50.

174 *Tafsīr al-Manār* (on 3:110) 51.

2. compulsion in religion is rejected in Islam by the text of the Qur'ān.....[175]

3. This interpretation makes ordering right conduct and forbidding indecency a form of the call *(da'wa)* to Islam and the coercion to it. But the preceding verse "Let there be from you----" (3:104) requires that the ordering and forbidding be different from that call and different from coercion by the friendly acceptance of it which is an action, not guidance and instruction [which is for the calling of non-Muslims].

In other words, neither is compulsion employed in the ordering of the right conduct and the forbidding of indecency within the Muslim community, an order a member accepts because of one's edifying action; nor is compulsion employed in calling non-Muslims to Islam, a calling that is to be done by guidance and instruction. Furthermore, Riḍā rejects as not true neither during the time of al-Qaffāl nor today, an assertion of the latter that most people love their religion because of habit and tradition with the implication that "Muslims are the only ones who stick to the proofs and don't accept in religion anything without proof, and thus have the right to compel others..."[176] Finally, Riḍā rejects the validity of the question itself, formulated by Rāzī and confirmed with the statement from al-Qaffāl because it supposes that the three qualities that make up the "best community," i.e., ordering of right conduct, forbidding of indecency and believing in God, also exist in the other communities. The verse shows the command as something unparalleled in the earlier Scriptures and no other community than the Muslim *umma* accomplishes this duty in such

---

175 Here the *tafsīr* quotes two famous texts of the Qur'ān: "Will you then force people to become believers?" (10:99) and "There shall be no compulsion in religion" (2:256).

176 *Tafsīr al-Manār* (on 3:110) 51.

a manner.[177] "In the same way, the faith of these other communities is not considered by the Qur'ān as an authentic faith. Hence the verse continues: 'Had the people of the Scripture believed, it would be good for them' (3:110b)."[178] Thus, once more, it is in the centripetal dimension of the Muslim *umma* that its "being best" has its basis.

Looking at the whole of the *tafsīr* of *umma* in *al-Manār* as it has been outlined here, we draw the following main points:

1. The term *wasaṭ* specifies the attributes of "just" and "best" because both are situated in the middle. The Muslim *umma* is *wasaṭ* because it is a community characterized by justice or moderation in thoughts, in moral principles and in actions. This community characterized as such is the "best" in relation to other communities. It follows that this community can lose its being "best" if it ceases to be a community of justice. The formula for maintaining it is by constantly following the Messenger and his *sunna*.

2. The twofold task of ordering of what is acceptable and forbidding of what is rejectable among Muslims is a task that every member shares according to his capacity. This includes fraternal admonition and correction among the individual members, and special responsibilities for leading personalities and leaders of the community.

3. The task of the Muslim community to call non-Muslims to Islam is an obligation of every individual Muslim. It is a *farḍ-al-ʿayn*. What is important is that every Muslim must be conscious of this obligation, although not every Muslim has to respond to this in the same manner. This task was spontaneously done by the whole Muslim community during the time of the Prophet and

177 Cf. *Tafsīr al-Manār* (on 3:110) 52.

178 Arij Roest Crollius, "Mission and Morality" in *Studia Missionalia*, vol. 27 (Roma: Università Gregoriana Editrice, 1978) 281-282.

maintained during the time of the *Salaf*. This ideal situation is no longer true nowadays. Thus, while every individual Muslim does the calling according to his capacity, a specialized group must also be formed by the community for this purpose. This special group is an *umma* wihin the larger *umma* in the sense that it is the expression of the force, unity and character of the whole large *umma* and, at the same time, it acts as one body although its members have different jobs and careers or specializations, all for the calling of non-Muslims to Islam. The training of this group must, on the whole, consist in a faithful imitation of the ideal of the *Salaf* and an adaptation to present-day conditions, following the example of western men of science and of Christian missionaries.

4. The main characterizations that make the Muslims the best are: their faith in God that maintains their unity, and their being a community of justice, i.e., they order what is good and forbid what is evil. In history, these characterizations were fully realized during the time of the Prophet and the *Salaf*. Deterioration came about when ordering what is good and forbidding what is evil were abandoned by the community because of disgust at the high-handedness of succeeding Muslim leaders. Nevertheless, no other community than the Muslim *umma* possesses this faith and accomplishes the consequent duty. The idealization of the *jihād* in al-Qaffāl and Rāzī is false. The calling of non-Muslims to Islam is done not by compulsion but by guidance and instruction.

Tafsīr al-Manār is indeed a departure from traditional exegesis. It is an attempt at modernizing Islam, i.e., it takes into consideration the modern situation in its interpretation of the Qur'ān. On the whole, its approach may be summed up as one based on the twin principles that the Qur'ān and the *sunna* of the Prophet are the sole determinants of Islam and that the existence of the *umma* in the present situation must be defined through *ijtihād* based on those principles. The modernity of *tafsīr al-Manār* is to be seen especially in its trying to establish positive links between the Qur'ān and the *sunna* and modern thought and practices.

-------*******-------

Islamic modernism which began with ʿAbduh in the late 19th century took a significant ideological turn after some decades in the twentieth century with the creation of two modern Islamic organizations: the *Iḫwān al-Muslimīn* of Egypt (founded in 1928 by Ḥasan al-Bannāʾ) and the *Jamāʿat Islāmī* in the Indian subcontinent (founded in 1941 by al-Mawdūdī). If ʿAbduh and Riḍā saw the need to apply the Islamic ideal to present-day conditions by learning from the example of the West and thus by aiming at bridging the gap between Western and Islamic cultures, these two organizations see Western innovations as having totally eclipsed Islam and thus aim at a reform of Islam that should come solely from within itself. Thus if ʿAbduh's movement was reformist, these two organizations are radical, rejecting the modernism of their predecessors as a westernization of Islam. The desire of the leaders of these two organizations to transform society invariably led to their involvement in politics and, at times, confrontations with their national governments which, in some cases, led to imprisonments and condemnations to death of some of their members.

The importance of these two organizations extended far beyond their national homelands and in time took on transnational significance. The *Jamāʿat* developed sister organizations in India, Pakistan, Bangladesh, Afghanistan, Kashmir and Sri Lanka. The Brotherhood inspired the establishment of similar organizations in the Sudan, Syria, Jordan, the Gulf and Africa. The writings of the leaders of these organizations in time became widely disseminated throughout much of the Islamic world. Their vision of Islam and the example of their organizations and activities provided a model for the future generations of Muslims. As such, they constituted a link between the traditional religious heritage and the realities of modern life for many.

One exegete from each of these two organizations, stands out as among if not the most widely-read in the present century: Mawlāna Sayyid Abū-l-Aʿlā Mawdūdī and Sayyid Quṭb - authors of the last two commentaries that we will consider in this study.

3.2 Abū al-Aʿlā Mawdūdī[179]

3.2.1 Introduction

Sayyid Mawdūdī has been credited with being one of the chief architects of contemporary Islamic resurgence. *Jāhilīya* and 'nationalism' are among the notable modern Islamic concepts which are associated with Mawdūdī'. Mawdūdī branded with the stigma of *jāhilīya* modern political ideologies along with certain intellectuals and politicians in the Islamic world. As an Islamic radicalist concept, *jāhilīya* was first articulated by Indian Muslim

---

[179] Sayyid Abū-l-Aʿlā Mawdūdī was born on Rajab 3, 1321/September 25, 1903 in Aurangabad, a well-known town in the former princely state of Hyderabad, presently known as Andhra Pradesh, India. His ancestry, on the paternal side, is traced back to the Prophet. He received an early traditional religious education which was supplemented by his self-taught knowledge of western thought. He pursued a career in journalism. In 1933 he assumed editorship of *Tarjuman al-Qurʾān* (Exegesis of the Qurʾān), which throughout the years served as a vehicle of his thought. In 1941 he established the *Jamāʿat-i-Islāmī*, a well-organized association committed to the reestablishment of an Islamic world order. Although originally against any form of nationalism and thus opposed to the establishment of Pakistan, Mawdūdī nevertheless migrated to Pakistan, after the partitioning, where the *Jamāʿat-i-Islāmī* has been very active in politics and where he lived until his death in 1979. For more details of Mawlānā Mawdūdī's life, see, among other works, the following: "Mawlānā Mawdūdī's Autobiography," translated with an introduction by Seyyed Vali Reza Nasr in *The Muslim World*, vol. LXXXV, nos. 1-2 (January-April, 1995) 49-62; Allahbukhsh K. Brohi, "Mawlānā Abū-l-Aʿlā Mawdūdī, The Man, The Scholar, The Reformer" in *Islamic Perspectives: Studies in Honor of Mawlānā Sayyid Abū-l-Aʿlā Mawdūdī*, edited by K. Ahmad and Z. I. Ansari (Leicester/Jeddah: The Islamic Foundation/ Saudi Publishing House, 1979) 289-311; and F. C. R. Robinson, "Mawdūdī" in *The Encyclopedia of Islam*, new edition, volume VI (1991) 872-874.

writers and political leaders in the 1930's and 1940's[180] one of whom was Mawdūdī. For Mawdūdī, Muslims in general were still worthy of carrying the name of their religion once its principles were explained to them.[181]

Like his Egyptian counterpart Sayyid Quṭb, al-Mawdūdī was fiercely opposed especially to the west-introduced concept of nationalism which he perceived as a direct threat to the establishment of Muslim norms of loyalty and conduct, and which, as a movement, was sweeping the Indian subcontinent in the 1930's. Al-Mawdūdī had witnessed the collapse of the Ottoman empire and the failure of the Caliphate Movement to save that empire from being divided into different nations based on the western concept of nationalism. For Mawdūdī, "the whole conceptual system of nationalism was an irrational approach which destroyed the deep bonds between human beings; it divided mankind into racial groups, set up barriers and demarcated artificial territorial boundaries."[182] Thus Mawdūdī rallied for his new concept of nationalism, one which pertained to the spiritual and intrinsic nature of man in which the materialistic and incidental differences were disregarded. He sees humanity as divided into two nationalisms which are irreconciliable, namely: Islam and belief vs. misguidance and unbelief. The loyalty of a "nationalist Muslim" was to a certain spiritual and political system, rather than territory, race and language. Thus was founded the *Jamāʿat-i-Islāmī*.

Mawdūdī's radical ideas were spread through his numerous writings. He authored more than 150 books and treatises on dif-

---

180 It was initially applied to the Hindus, whose religion represented according to Muslim criteria a form of paganism. It was then generalized to include all non-Islamic philosophies.

181 Cf. Andrew Lane, "What is Radical Islam? One Answer" in *Encounter*, no. 216 (June-July, 1995) 12. See also Youssef Choueiri, *Islamic fundamentalism* (London: Printer Publishers, 1990) 93-119.

182 Ibid.

ferent aspects of Islam, ranging from *Al-Jihād Fi-l-Islām* to the Manifesto of the *Jamāʿat-i-Islāmī*. His opus magnum, however, is the *Tafhīm al-Qurʾān*[183] which is an interpretative translation and *tafsīr* of the Qurʾān. It will be the subject of our study here. It was when the *Jamāʿat-i-Islāmī* was formally launched on August 26, 1941[184] that "he devoted most of his energies to writing the *Tafhīm al-Qurʾān* so that this movement would imbibe the message of the Qurʾān and engage in its struggle to establish the world order that the Qurʾān wants to establish."[185] The first volume which contains the verses that are of interest to us appeared in 1950, when Mawdūdī was in prison; the last one appeared in 1973.

3.2.2 *Tafsīr* : Muslim *Umma*, For the Leadership of Mankind.

A point which Mawdūdī claims as very important for the proper understanding of the message of the verses of the Qurʾān is the situational background. "Every *sūra* is so vitally linked with its situational background and its circumstantial setting that any-

---

[183] The original was written in Urdu. For our study, we use the English version entitled *Towards Understanding The Qurʾān*, translated and edited by Zafar Ishaq Ansari (Leicester: The Islamic Foundation, 1988).

[184] Initially formed in India, the *Jamāʿat-i-Islāmī*, following the partition of India in 1947, was divided into three independent branches, namely: *Jamāʿat-i-Islāmī's* of India, Pakistan and Jammu and Kashmir. Although the three followed Mawdūdī's teachings, organizationally they were separate and independent. In 1947 Mawdūdī became the *Amīr* (President) of the *Jamāʿat-i-Islāmī* of Pakistan. In later years additional independent *Jamāʿat-i-Islāmī's* were established in other countries. A long list of bibliography on these organizations is found in "Mawlānā Mawdūdī's Autobiography," trans. by Seyyed Vali Reza Nasr in *The Muslim World*, vol. LXXXV, No. 1-2 (January-April, 1995) 49, note 2.

[185] *Towards Understanding the Qurʾān*, vol. 1, xiii (editor's preface).

one reading a mere verbal translation, divorced from its context, would fail to appreciate many of the points made."[186] Thus at the beginning of each *sūra* he gives the historical background of its revelation. In the case of *sūra* 2 where *umma wasaṭ* belongs, he provides a long exposition of what he considers as the historical background of its revelation which he says must be grasped in order to better understand the contents of *sūra* 2 as well as the contents of *sūra* 3 since the latter is "so intimately related to *sūra* 2 that it can be considered a logical supplement to it."[187] The following is an outline of the elements in this background information which in itself is a summary of the message of the whole *sūra* and which shall help elucidate Mawdūdī's explanation of the verses that concern us.[188]

1. "Until the time of migration *(hijra)*, the message of Islam was confined to Mecca and was addressed to the polytheists of Arabia, for whom it was altogether new and foreign. After his migration to Medina, however, the Prophet found the Jews living in nearby settlements...In principle, their religion was the same as that being preached by Muhammad. Over many centuries, however, they had passed through a process of degeneration which had left them far removed from their true religion...When the Prophet arrived in Medina, God instructed him to recall the Jews to their true and original faith. This call is embodied roughly in the first sixteen sections of the *sūra* (i.e., from the opening verse up to verse 141). In these verses both the past of the Jews and their present moral and religious conditions are subjected to severe criticism. Moreover, the principles of the true faith are elucidated in contrast with the corrupted forms of religion and morality."

2. "With the arrival of the Prophet in Medina, the Islamic

---

186 *Towards Understanding the Qur'ān,* vol. 1, 3 (Author's Preface).

187 *Towards Understanding the Qur'ān,* vol. 1, 230.

188 *Towards Understanding the Qur'ān,* vol. 1, 40-43, for the following summary and quotations.

movement entered a new stage." Whereas in Mecca the Prophet devoted himself almost exclusively to expounding the basic principles of the true faith and to the moral training of his followers, in Medina the group of Muslims began to lay the foundations of a small Islamic state and so God began to issue directives explaining how a new order of life could be established on the basis of Islam. Verse 141 up to the end of the *sūra* contains these directives for the *umma*, of which *sūra* 3 is a logical supplement as it continues to speak about the Jews and Christians on the one hand, and the Muslims on the other. The first group, i.e., Jews and Christians, are "censured for their doctrinal errors and moral corruption, and are told that the Prophet and the Qurʾān invite them to the same true religion preached by the Prophets from the earliest times." On the other hand, "further directives, similar to those found in *sūra* 2, are addressed to the second group of people (the Muslims), since they are proclaimed to be the "best nation."[189]

A second background information which Mawdūdī says must be borne in mind is the history of the Abrahamic religion, in order to understand the message of the section which includes the verses that concern us.[190]

1. "After Noah, Abraham was the first Prophet appointed by God to spread the universal message of Islam. At the outset, he journeyed for many years from Iraq to Egypt, and from Syria and Palestine to various parts of Arabia inviting people to serve and obey God. Later he appointed deputies in various regions to carry on his mission. He sent his nephew Lot to Transjordan, his son Isaac to Syria and Palestine, and his eldest son Ishmael to Arabia.

---

[189] *Towards Understanding the Qurʾān*, vol. 1, 229-230.

[190] *Towards Understanding the Qurʾān*, vol. 1, 107-110, for the following summary and quotations.

Then he built, in Mecca, the shrine called the *Kaʿba* which subsequently, and under God's own command, was made the centre of the prophetic mission."

2. "Abraham's progeny descended in two main branches. One of these, the children of Ishmael, lived in Arabia. The Qurayš and other Arabian tribes belonged to this branch of Abraham's line.... The other branch consisted of the children of Isaac. In this branch there arose a great number of Prophets, for example Jacob, Joseph, Moses, David, Solomon, John and Jesus. Since Jacob was called Israel, his offspring came to be known as the children of Israel. Other peoples who accepted their faith as a result of preaching, either lost their former identity and became assimilated with them, or remained separate from them but identified with them religiously. At the time when decadence flourished, this branch of the Abrahamic family gave birth first to Judaism, and subsequently to Christianity."

3. After Abraham's death, the task of guiding the world was entrusted to the branch which had issued from Isaac and Jacob and which came to be known as the children of Israel. It was "this branch which was given the knowlege of the Straight Way, and was designated to lead all the nations of the world along that Way.... In the time of Solomon this branch took Jerusalem as the center of its mission. Jerusalem maintained its central position for all devotees of God and remained the *qibla* (direction) in which all worshippers of God were required to turn in their Prayer."

4. "It is also intimated that the religious leadership of all mankind is not an exclusive privilege of Abrahamic blood, but rather the fruit of Abraham's sincere obedience and service to God, to which he had wholly consecrated himself. Only those who follow the way of Abraham, and guide the world along that way, are therefore entitled to the position of guidance and leadership. And since the Jews had abandoned it and become incapable of carrying out the mission of Abraham they were being removed from that position."

5. "At the same time it is hinted that the non-Israelite peoples

who identified themselves with Abraham through Moses and Jesus had also veered from the way of Abraham. The same was true of the polytheists of Arabia, who felt proud of belonging to Abraham and Ishmael and based this pride on lineage alone.... They did not deserve, therefore, to be entrusted with the religious leadership of the world."

6. "It is also made clear that by God's will a Prophet, for whose advent Abraham and Ishmael had once prayed, was born in the other branch of the Abrahamic family, i.e., the Ishmaelites. The way propounded by this Prophet is exactly the same as that by Abraham, Isaac, Ishmael, Jacob and in fact all the Messengers. His followers also confirm the truth of all those designated in the past to serve as God's Messengers, and call mankind to the same message those Messengers preached earlier. Thus leadership now naturally devolves on those who follow this Prophet."

7. "This proclamation of a transfer of leadership naturally called for the proclamation of a change in the direction of Prayer. As long as the Israelites held the reins of the world's religious leadership, Jerusalem remained the centre of the mission of Islam and the *qibla* of truth-loving people. The Arabian Prophet as well as his followers had accepted Jerusalem as the *qibla* until God duly proclaimed the removal of the Jews from their position of leadership. With this proclamation Jerusalem ceased to enjoy its central position. So it was proclaimed that from then on the centre of God's true religion would be the place from which the message of the Prophet Muhammad had radiated... in the past it had been the center of the mission of Abraham."

With this background, 2:143 (as also 3:110), is considered as constituting the proclamation appointing the Muslim community to religious guidance and leadership of the world.

> "And it is thus," which precedes this proclamation, contains two allusions. It alludes, in the first place, to that Divine Guidance which enabled the followers of Muhammad to

> know the Straight Way so that they could attain progress to the point of being proclaimed "the community of the middle way." In the second place there is an allusion to the change in the direction of Prayer from Jerusalem to the *Kaʿba*.[191]

The change in the direction of Prayer from Jerusalem to the *Kaʿba*, the *tafsīr* continues, "amounted to the removal of the children of Israel from their position of world leadership and their replacement by the *umma* of Muhammad."[192]

Like we have already seen in the earlier commentaries, the "being middle" *(wasaṭ)* of the Muslim community is due to Divine Guidance or God's will. However, what is new here is the idea of "leadership," i.e., that to be made "middle" is to be appointed to the position of "leadership." Furthermore, the presentation of the connection between the change of the *qibla* and the "being middle" of the community is different from what we have seen in earlier commentaries. Whereas, the earlier commentaries point to their common origin or causality (i.e., Divine guidance), Mawdūdī sees them as two inseparable sides of the same coin, i.e., a change in leadership necessarily means a change in the *qibla* of prayer. As regards the meaning of the term "middle" *(wasaṭ)*, al-Mawdūdī says,

> It signifies that distinguished group of people which follows the path of justice and equity, of balance and moderation, a group which occupies a central position among the nations of the world so that its friendship with all is based on righteousness and justice and none receives its support in wrong and injustice.[193]

Thus the meaning of the term is the same as we have seen in

---

191 *Towards Understanding the Qurʾān*, vol. 1, 120-121.

192 *Towards Understanding the Qurʾān*, vol. 1, 121.

193 *Towards Understanding the Qurʾān*, vol. 1, 121.

earlier commentaries. However, the Mawdūdī stamp lies in its elaboration which easily points to a conclusion that its role is one of "leadership." This is stressed all the more clearly in his explanation of the succeeding phrase "that you may be witnesses before all mankind," which Mawdūdī explains thus: "The position of standing witness before all mankind on behalf of God, which has been conferred on this community, amounts to its being invested with the leadership of all mankind,"[194] which is

> . . . at once a great honor and a heavy responsibility. For what it actually means is that just as the Prophet served as a living example of godliness and moral rectitude, of equity and fair play before the Muslim community, so is the Muslim community required to stand vis-a-vis the whole world.... to make known, both by word and deed, the meaning of godliness and righteousness, of equity and fair play. Furthermore, just as the Prophet had been entrusted with the heavy responsibility of conveying to the Muslims the guidance which he had received, in a like manner a heavy responsibility has been laid on the Muslims to communicate this guidance to all mankind. If the Muslims fail to establish before God that they did their duty in conveying to mankind the guidance they had received through the Prophet, they will be taken to task seriously and their honorable position as the leaders of the whole world, far from being of any help to them, will spell their disaster.[195]

Here we see basically an adaptation of Zamahšarī's interpretation of the "middle community" as something that has to be protected and maintained, otherwise it loses "being middle" and becomes a marginal reality. We already saw an adaptation of this basic idea in ʿAbduh's *tafsīr*, and here in Mawdūdī we see another modernization of the Zamahšarian concept. On the whole, Mawdūdī's concept of "middle community as witnesses unto man-

---

194 *Towards Understanding the Qurʾān*, vol. 1, 121.

195 *Towards Understanding the Qurʾān*, vol. 1, 121.

kind which means leadership" is a modern presentation of the centripetal view of Zamaḫšarī together with the centrifugal view of Ṭabarī.

Under the umbrella of the overall theme of "leadership," Mawdūdī explains verse 3:110 ("You are the best community---") as the same declaration as the one in 2:143 but that 3:110 is a declaration which emphasizes the "competence" of the Muslim community.

> They were the best people in terms of character and morals and had developed in theory and in practice the qualities essential for truly righteous leadership, namely the spirit and practical commitment to promoting good and suppressing evil and the acknowledgment of the One True God as their Lord and Master. [196]

Looking now at the whole of Mawdūdī's *tafsīr* as it has been outlined here, we say that it is indeed an example of a new direction in *tafsīr* both in form and in content. As far as form is concerned, it is a departure from the traditional one which was a line by line explanation of the Qur'ān, sometimes at the expense of clear continuity from one passage of exegesis to the next. Mawdūdī's *tafsīr* may be classified as thematic or topical. A very important role is played by background information based on some tradition which contains at the same time his interpretative summary of the contents of a whole *sūra* or a large section of a *sūra*. Consequently, he does not see any need to explain every single verse but only the ones which need particular elaborations. As far as content is concerned, its newness is to be seen in the fact that, although we detect some reliance on traditional material of exegesis which we have seen in previous works, yet we are reading Mawdūdī's ideas instead of those of his predecessors. The overriding theme in his *tafsīr* of *umma* is "leadership."

---

[196] *Towards Understanding the Qur'ān*, vol. 1, 278.

3.3 Sayyid Quṭb[197]

3.3.1 Introduction

Born in 1324/1906 in Asyūṭ, Egypt, Sayyid Quṭb was the eldest of five children of a landowner who hailed from the Arabian peninsula. After receiving a traditional education, Sayyid Quṭb completed college studies in the Dār al-ʿUlūm in Cairo where in 1933 he obtained a licentiate in Arabic language and literature. After a brief tenure as a lecturer at the same institution and afterwards as inspector of schools for the Ministry of Education, he visited the U.S.A. for two years. At about this time in his career as a public servant, he was reportedly offered the position of head of the Ministry of Education. He refused it on grounds that education in Egypt was not truly Islamic. On his return to Egypt in 1945, he joined the *Iḫwān al-Muslimīn* (The Brotherhood of Muslims or Muslim Brotherhood) of Egypt, which at that time was extremely popular, boasting of over two and a half million members.

While the movement started by ʿAbduh and Riḍā continued to have its influence through the formal processes of education, the *Iḫwān* was intended to be a movement of the common people. It eventually became a revolutionary party which was banned consequently by the Egyptian government. Ḥasan al-Bannāʾ - the founder of the Iḫwān, was assassinated in 1948 and by 1952 Sayyid Quṭb became one of the leaders of the *Iḫwān* until his

---

197 For general biographical information on S. Quṭb, see: Yvonne Haddad, "Sayyid Quṭb: Ideologue of Islamic Revival" in *Voices of Resurgent Islam*, ed. by J. Esposito (New York/Oxford: Oxford University Press, 1983) 67-98; Ahmed Salah al-Moussalli, *Radical Islamic Fundamentalism: The Ideological and Political Discourse of Sayyid Quṭb* (Beirut, 1992); Sayyid Quṭb, *Ṭifl min al-Qarya* (Cairo, 1946) - S. Quṭb's autobiographical novel; and J. J. G. Jansen, "Sayyid Quṭb" in *The Encyclopedia of Islam*, new edition, volume IX (1997) 117-118.

death by execution in 1386/1966.[198] As a journalist and author of a wide repute, he became the editor of the magazine of the *Iḫwān*. Sayyid Quṭb was implicated in the conspiracy to assassinate Jamāl ʿAbd al-Nāṣir in November of 1954. From then on he spent the rest of his life in and out of prison. What led to his last imprisonment and consequent execution along with six other members of the *Iḫwān*, was the publication of his book *Maʿālim al-ṭarīq* which was particularly critical of the current regime. Many of Sayyid Quṭb's writings are widely accepted. Through these writings he has posthumously continued to serve as a popular Islamic spiritual and intellectual guide throughout the Muslim world, particularly in Egypt and the Arab countries. Quṭb's antipathy to those who do not govern 'according to what God has revealed' has influenced the thinking in many political movements carrying the Islamic banner.[199] For this reason, the *Iḫwān* which he most outstandingly and dynamically led during his lifetime, remains until now a most popular movement in the Islamic world.[200] Of the many writings of Sayyid Quṭb, our concern here is his *tafsīr* called *Fī Ẓilāl-l-Qurʾān*.

Sayyid Quṭb explains his understanding of the Qurʾān - *sūra* by *sūra* and verse by verse - in order to build a theory of, and a

---

[198] "The supreme frustration of the Iḫwān has been the failure to have its program -- which it considers the embodiment of the ideal Islamic life -- accepted by the political authority. This has forced it, ironically, into a position of opposition, when its basic premise is the unity of all Muslims." J. I. Smith, *An Historical and Semantic Study of the Term "Islām"* (Missoula, Montana: Scholars Press, 1975) 204.

[199] See Ronald Nettler, "A Modern Islamic Confession of Faith And the Conception of Religion" in *British Journal of Middle Eastern Studies*, vol. 21, no. 1 (1994) 102.

[200] Muhammad Ibrahim H. I. Surty, "The Qurʾān in Islamic Scholarship: A Survey of *Tafsīr* Exegesis literature in Arabic" in *The Muslim World Book Review*, vol. 7, no. 4 (Summer 1987) 59.

practical program for, modern Islam. As such, it is largely independent from traditional textual exegesis because his epistemological and spiritual base is his "having tasted God's favor of life in the shade of the Qur'ān" about which he informs us in the introduction *(Muqaddima)* to his *tafsīr*. *Fī Ẓilāl al-Qur'ān* would then be putting into words his immediate experience of the Qur'ān arrived at through a period of withdrawal in contemplation which, based on his own account, has a quasi-revelational tone.

> Life in the shade of the Qur'ān is a (divine) favor which only those who have tasted it know. It is a favor which elevates, blesses and purifies life. Glory be to God who has bestowed upon me during a period of time, life in the shade of the Qur'ān. [201]

For this reason, some scholars question the *"tafsīr-ness"* of *Fī Ẓilāl al-Qur'ān*. The Muslim scholar Muhammad Ibrahim H. I. Surty says,

> In the strict sense of the word, *Fī Ẓilāl al-Qur'ān* cannot be reckoned as *tafsīr*. It is a comprehensive guide, a message, a polemic about how to practise the Faith in the unprecedented circumstances and challenges of modern life which has been plunging ever deeper into not one but many man-made ideologies.[202]

---

[201] Sayyid Quṭb, *Fī Ẓilāl al-Qur'ān* (Beirut: Dār al-Šurūq, 1982) 11. Ronald Nettler says that this "spiritual retreat" of Sayyid Quṭb is reminiscent of that seen in accounts of the Prophet Muhammad's life as well as in that of traditional Islamic pietistic and mystical withdrawals. "Muhammad's period "in retreat" was inspirational and experiential. The resulting knowledge was claimed as a direct revelation from God." Quṭb's retreat for him also produced the most profound unmediated understanding of the Qur'ān. See: Ronald Nettler, "A Modern Islamic Confession of Faith and Conception of Religion" in *British Journal of Middle Eastern Studies*, vol. 21, no. 1 (1994) 105.

[202] Muhammad Ibrahim H. I. Surty, op. cit., 59.

Or, in the words of the Dutch scholar J. J. Jansen, the *Fī Ẓilāl al-Qurʾān* of Sayyid Quṭb "is hardly a commentary on the Koran in the strict sense of the word, but rather an enormous collection of sermons."[203] However, as K. Cragg says, "Sayyid Quṭb's mind about his Qurʾān and his life story belong together.... His whole biography can be seen as a reading of the Qurʾān, a commentary given in a personality."[204] Thus, indeed, Sayyid Quṭb's commentary of the Qurʾān is not strictly speaking a *tafsīr* if we go by the rules of the traditional form of exegesis; however, scholars, including the ones we have just quoted, agree that it is *tafsīr* nonetheless, i.e., of the modern type.

3.3.2 *Tafsīr* of 2:143

Sayyid Quṭb's *tafsīr* groups the verses into pericopes with each pericope having one main lesson. Verse 2:143 belongs to the pericope comprising verses 2:142 to 152 inclusive. This pericope is about the "occurrence of the change of the *qibla* (direction of prayer) for the Muslims from Jerusalem to the *Kaʿba* and the relations surrounding it, as well as the criticisms by the Jews and the sayings which repudiate such criticisms."[205] The point of departure in all the discussions here is the "change of the *qibla*" whose meaning then will have to be understood first in order to understand the meaning of *umma wasaṭ*.

3.3.2.1 The *Qibla*: visible expression of the *fiṭra* of man

Sayyid Quṭb sees a profound connection between the *qibla* and the *fiṭra* and explains it in the following way. If the *qibla* is

---

[203] J. J. G. Jansen, *The Interpretation of the Koran..* 79, note 15.

[204] Kenneth Cragg, *The Pen and The Faith* (London: George Allen and Unwin, 1985) 69-70.

[205] *Fī Ẓilāl* (on2:143) 125.

observed purely as an external appearance, then it is nothing but pure fanaticism. However, the *qibla* as such has a material function for the human being. It reveals the most profound character of creation *(fiṭra)* which is

> the human spirit (النفس الإنسانية) as a natural disposition (ميلاً فطرياً) -- emanating from the creation of man as a being of a visible body and an invisible soul -- for the taking of visible forms for the expression of the inner feelings.[206]

In other words, to have a *qibla* is part of human nature. It is the proof that man is religious by nature or that man is naturally predisposed to find God, and the *qibla* is the external expression of his religiosity. Thus the human spirit finds rest only when the innate disposition for God attains externalization.

3.3.2.2 The Islamic Religion: the final and definitive constitution of the *fiṭra* in human history.

It is on the basis of this natural predisposition of human beings which is pure Islam, that the Islamic religion brings into being all of its religious rites and worship with a twofold aspect: 1) the spiritual direction and 2) the visible form of this spiritual direction as an existence and a direction to the *qibla* and all the other Muslim religious rites and cultic practices,

> in order to put together its external and interior identity and to put an order in its powers and to respond to the *fiṭra* completely in a manner that is in harmony with its special idea (تتفق مع تصوره الخاص).[207]

---

206 *Fī Ẓilāl* (on 2:143) 127.

207 *Fī Ẓilāl* (on 2:143) 128.

Thus the differentiation and the specification of the place which the Muslim turns his face towards in prayer, in worship and particular devotion, are necessary in order to show that the Islamic religion is set apart and distinguished by its ideal, its way and its orientation as independent from others.[208] Consequently, "the imitating of whatever is not of the Muslims in their characteristics"[209] and "the experiencing of other than from God and His special way which this *umma* came to bring to reality in the world,"[210] are forbidden.

The dialectic of "interior (spiritual direction) and exterior (visible form)" in Sayyid Quṭb is reminiscent of ʿAbduh's dialectic of "spiritual and corporal." However, while the ramifications of this idea in *al-Manār* leads to an Islamic reform that shows willingness to learn from the West, Sayyid Quṭb sees in it the basis for historical Islam's being absolutely independent from others.

3.3.2.3 The Mission of Leadership

After outlining the elements of the Islamic religion which is based on man's *fiṭra*, Sayyid Quṭb discusses the role of the community which is the bearer of this religion, i.e., the Muslim community. "The Muslim community rises in order to be in the place of leadership for mankind (والجماعة المسلمة قامت لتكون في مكان القيادة للبشرية)."[211] For this role "it has to draw for itself traditions (تقاليد) and doctrines (عقيدة) from the source [God] that

---

[208] *Fī Ẓilāl* (on 2:143) 128.

[209] *Fī Ẓilāl* (on 2:143) 128 (التشبه بمن دون المسلمين في خصائصهم)

[210] *Fī Ẓilāl* (on 2:143) 128 (التلقي من غير الله ومنهجه الخاص الذي جاءت هذه الأمة لتحققه في الأرض)

[211] *Fī Ẓilāl* (on 2:143) 129, also for the other quotations within this paragraph.

chose it for this leadership." In this role "the Muslims are most elevated, and are *umma wasaṭ* and best community." And as they draw their being, their traditions, ideas and system from God, Islam becomes the safeguard for humankind "as the peak of the horizon in being and as a most straight way in life." Accordingly, this role of leadership is characterized 1) by the duty to call humankind to return to its original unity on the basis of the religion of the Muslims and 2) by the Muslims' constant consciousness of the meaning of their *qibla*.

We encountered the idea of "leadership" for the first time in Mawdūdī, as the overriding theme of his *tafsīr*. As also in Mawdūdī, we see in Sayyid Quṭb's two characterizations of the role of leadership his own version of the centrifugal *umma* in Ṭabarī and the centripetal *umma* in Zamaḫšarī. The *tafsīr* concludes this part with a view of the present reality,

> The Muslim community today is in the midst of various pagan *(jāhilīya)* concerns which occupy the relations among the entire people, and in the midst of the various pagan designs which aim at the whole world, pagan ideas which swarm the entire world, and in the midst of pagan banners which lift entire nations. [212]

and an admonition.

> The Muslim community today is in need of being distinguished by a special, particular way of life which does not get involved in the prevailing pagan ways of life; and distinguished by a special ideal for the presence and the life that don't get involved in the prevailing paganism; and distinguished by designs and concerns in harmony with that way of life and the special ideal; and distinguished by a special banner which takes the name of God alone. And characterized by all this is the *umma wasaṭ* which God brought forth for humankind.

---

212 *Fī Ẓilāl*, (on 2:143) 129, also for the following quotation.

Al-jāhilīya, as is clear in the foregoing as elsewhere in Sayyid Quṭb's *tafsīr,* is no longer just the pagan culture of ancient Arabia before Islam, but rather the universal principle of anti-Islam, exemplified at its worst now in secular, relativistic modernity. Like the idea of "leadership," it was from al-Mawdūdī that Sayyid Quṭb borrowed the concept although developed and used by the latter in his own way. Only by being true to its own distinctive characterizations which it receives from the giver of its being who is God and not from any other that the Muslim *umma* will be able to assume the place of leadership for humankind today.

3.3.2.4 *Umma Wasaṭ*

After the excursus on the occasion of the change of the *qibla,* the *tafsīr* now deals with the particular qurʾānic texts involved, one of which is our main concern here, namely, 2:143. The purpose of this verse, the *tafsīr* says, is to tell this *umma* about the truth of its reality in this world "that it may recognize itself and feel its greatness and have the power to do its duty and be prepared for it."[213] Accordingly, *wasaṭ* or "middle" is to be understood in all the senses in which it has been interpreted by earlier *mufassirīn.*

> This *umma* is *wasaṭ* in all the senses of the term *wasaṭ* like the "middle" with the meaning of excellence or superiority; or the "middle" with the meaning of balanced or right intention; or the "middle" in its material sense.

What follows is an elucidation of each of the senses of the term *wasaṭ* in a manner which at the same time addresses the situation of Islam in the modern world.[214] We outline them here as they showcase the unity of spirituality and politics in Sayyid Quṭb.

---

213 *Fī Ẓilāl* (on 2:143) 131, also for the following quotation.

214 See *Fī Ẓilāl* (on 2:143) 131.

1. *Umma wasaṭ* ...... in the idea and firm belief (في التصور والاعتقاد , which means that the Muslims should not exaggerate in spiritual freedom (التجرد الروحي) nor in material degeneration (الارتكاس المادي) . Rather, they should follow the representative natural predisposition, a spirit clothed in a body or a body that clothes itself with the spirit. This *umma* has to promote this life and safeguard its growth and be active in the world of desires, inclinations and intentions, not in excess but in harmony and moderation.

2. *Umma wasaṭ*..... in thinking and in knowledge (في التفكير والشعور , which means that Muslims should not grow weary of acquiring knowledge and experiences the results of which have always to be seen in the light of their own ideals, ways and foundations.

3. *Umma wasaṭ*......... in organization and systematization (في التنظيم والتنسيق) , which means that it should lift up the conscience of men by guidance and education... and should not make the people exhausted by the scourge of power nor by too much life of emotions... it should make the two blend.

4. *Umma wasaṭ*................... in commitments and relations (في الارتباطات والعلاقات) , which means it should not nullify the individuality of a person in the plurality of the community nor leave him to be greedy. Rather it should support those incentives and the capability of the individual for the service of the community.

5. *Umma wasaṭ*.... in the place (في المكان)... in the center of the world (في سرة الأرض) ... and in its most middle spot (وفي أوسط بقاعها) ....which means it is the *umma* that is situated in the middle of the land from which position it sees all the people and witnesses against them and gives that which it has to all the people of the land.

6. *Umma wasaṭ* ... .in time (في الزمان) ... which means it holds back the era of the childhood of the people before them and nurtures the era of maturity of reason. And it stands in the middle in order to shake off from the human race the errors and superstitions from its childhood era.

To summarize what Sayyid Quṭb says about the *umma muslima* thus far: 1) it is *wasaṭ* which comprises all the different shades in the interpretation of the term, 2) God is the source of the being of this *umma*, and, therefore, 3) this *umma* must draw whatever it should have of traditions, etc. only from its being which is from God, 4) any taking of something from outside this *umma* will lead to its non-being the "middle" and 5) the purpose of this *umma* is for leadership of humankind.

Sayyid Quṭb concludes by citing that the task of the *umma* is not an easy one; that the actual big hindrance to the *umma*'s taking the place for which God has created it is following roads other than the one God laid down for it.

3.3.3 *Tafsīr* of 3:104 and 3:110

Sayyid Quṭb sees these two verses as belonging to the pericope that comprises 3:93-120 which is about the relation between the Muslim *umma* and the People of the Scripture, especially the Jews. Accordingly, this lesson provides the high point of the discussion about these two groups. In such a context God also makes clear to the Muslims the reality of their role in the life of humanity. What concerns us here are those parts of the lesson that speak about the Muslim *umma*. The main idea from which will flow Sayyid Quṭb's comments in connection with verses 3:104 and 3:110 has been seen in his *tafsīr* of 2:143 regarding the source of the being of the Muslim *umma* and its mission of leadership. Sayyid Quṭb emphasizes this once more, saying that

> the existence of this *umma* comes from God... This *umma* exists for the leadership (قيادة) of humanity. How then should it take guidance from the non-Muslims (الجاهلية) whom it came to replace in order to unite them with God and to lead them by the way of God? And if it abandons the task of leadership, then what is the authorization for its existence? In such a case, there is no purpose to its existence.[215]

It is against the nature or origin of the existence of the Muslim *umma* to learn from any society, least of all the People of the Scripture. In the same manner, it is against the purpose of its existence, which is leadership, to receive ordinances other than its own way which is God's way.

3.3.3.1 Realization of God's Way Through Faith and Brotherhood

The commentary then points out Faith and Brotherhood as the two basic principles by which God's way, i.e., the Islamic religion, is realized in the world. Through faith in God (الإيمان بالله), the Muslim community receives correct guidance for the realization of its being in this world. It is the kind of faith that "trusts in God and pays attention to His presence in every moment of life."[216] Through brotherhood (الأخوة في الله) the "Muslim society becomes a living, strong and compact building, as the Qurān says: 'And remember God's favor given to you: how you were enemies and He made friendship between your hearts so that you became as brothers by His grace (3:103b)'." The pages of the *tafsīr* that describe this "brotherhood" emphasize that it is based

---

[215] *Fī ẓilāl*, vol. 1: 438.

[216] *Fī Ẓilāl*, vol. 1:441, also for the following quotation.

on the observance of religion.

These two principles make the existence of the Muslim *umma* real and make it capable of fulfilling its great role in human life, i.e., the role of ordering what is acceptable and forbidding what is rejectable, and grounding its own life on the same basis. With this as background, Sayyid Quṭb now comments on the particular verses involved in the pericope, among which are the verses of our concern, i.e., 3:104 and 3:110.

3.3.3.2 The Necessity of "Power/Authority."

Sayyid Quṭb's commentary on 3:104 is also a departure from the traditional view. He does not make a detailed description of the agent or of the nature of the command other than emphasizing that there are three tasks involved. Instead, he sees another aspect which for him is clearly conveyed by the verse, and that is, the necessity of "power." He writes:

> It is necessary that there be a society[217] *(jamāʿa)* that calls to what is good and orders that which is acceptable and forbids that which is rejectable. It is necessary that there is an authority/power (سلطة) on earth which calls to what is good, orders what is acceptable and forbids what is rejectable. And that which establishes the necessity for such a power is the clear text of the Qurʾān itself.[218]

Thus, according to this *tafsīr*, the text itself clearly means that there must be power or authority on the group or society that

---

[217] It may be noted that in Sayyid Quṭb's *tafsīr*, the general expression he uses for the Muslim *umma* is "Islamic Society" *(mujtamaʿ islāmī)* or "Muslim Community" *(jamāʿat muslima)*. When *jamāʿa* is used alone, as in the case of 3;104, it means a group.

[218] *Fī Ẓilāl*, vol. 1: 444, also for the following quotation.

does the threefold task of calling, ordering and forbidding, because "while someone who has no power may be able to perform the calling, the ordering and forbidding cannot be fulfilled unless someone has power." The Muslim ideal with regard to the performance of the command is then the possession of power, according to this *tafsīr*. This is a new concept, we did not encounter it in the commentaries of the earlier centuries, neither do we find it in *al-Manār* or in Mawdūdī.

As mentioned in the *tafsīr*, "power" makes the Muslim community fulfill the "calling, ordering and forbidding and unites the individuals and binds them together in the two pillars, i.e., God's cord or faith in God and the cord of Brotherhood in God." God's way can be known only if the "ordering and forbidding" is obeyed and this can be done only if there is an authority or power, "and God says of those who perform this: 'They are those who are successful (3:104b)'."[219]

What Sayyid Quṭb then is saying in all this is that the Way of God on earth 1) is known through the Islamic faith, 2) is manifested or proven in the brotherhood among Muslims and their faith in God, and 3) is brought to others through the calling, ordering and forbidding which is to be done with "power." The *tafsīr* does not point out the exact nature of this power or authority. However, a hint may be given in Sayyid Quṭb's saying that all the relations in Islam - whether social, economic, political, etc. - are inseparable and have the same moral basis.[220]

3.3.3.3 The Best *Umma*

Sayyid Quṭb's *tafsīr* of 3:110 begins by emphasizing the mysterious or divine origin of the Muslim *umma*. The employment here of the verb in its passive form *"uḫrijat"* (brought forth), and

---

219 *Fī Ẓilāl*, vol. 1: 444.

220 *Fx Ẓilāl*, vol. 1: 440.

thus without mention of an agent, is to show that this *umma* appeared from all eternity, i.e., from the secret of God.[221] This verse, revealed in the context of the argumentation with the Jews, is meant

> to make the Muslim *umma* understand itself, that it may know its reality and its value; and that it may know that it has come into existence in order to be a vanguard and in order that to it be leadership. Since it exists, it is the best *umma*.[222]

As in the case of God's declaration of the Muslim *umma* as "middle *umma*," the reason for God's declaration here is, on the whole, the same, i.e., to make the Muslim *umma* recognize itself. While *wasaṭ* describes the *umma* as a being first and foremost in-itself, "best" describes the *umma* as a being first and foremost in relation to others. Being "best," translated into action, means leadership

> . . . in order to preserve human life from what is rejectable, and to establish it upon the basis of what is recommended, together with faith which defines what is recommended and what is rejected.[223]..... and their [Muslims] provision is faith, and their equipment is faith, and their support is God.[224]

Accordingly, it is only the ordering and forbidding by the Muslim *umma* that can result in the preservation of human life. In 3:104 God orders the Muslims that there be a group to do the task of calling, ordering and forbidding. In 3:110 God makes these

---

221 *Fī Ẓilāl*, vol. 1: 447.

222 *Fi Ẓilāl*, vol. 1: 447.

223 *Fī Ẓilāl*, vol. 1: 447.

224 *Fī Ẓilāl*, vol. 1: 448.

tasks the distinctive note of the *umma*.[225] Quṭb says that this is to point out that the Muslim community

> does not find a true existence unless there be in it an abundance of this basic note, by which it is known in the human society. And if it performs the duty to call to what is good, to order what is acceptable *(maʿrūf)* and to forbid what is rejectable *(munkar)*, together with faith in God, then it really exists and it is really Muslim. And if it does not perform anything of this, then it does not exist, and the characterizing note of Islam is not realized in it.[226]

We now recapitulate Sayyid Quṭb's *tafsīr* of *umma* as it has been outlined here.

1. The Muslim *umma* is the realization in history of the human response to the *fiṭra*. God is the source of its being and everything that it possesses of religious doctrine and worship, ideals, social order, morality, knowledge, science, etc. As such, this *umma* is in itself *wasaṭ*, i.e., in all the senses that this term has been understood by the early *mufassirūn*. In relation to other communities, this *umma* is the best.

2. This *umma* finds true existence as *wasaṭ* and best only if it brings into reality what God has given it, summed up as calling to what is good, ordering what is acceptable, forbidding what is evil, and faith in God. The way to the realization of this *umma*'s existence is to be found in its own being, through Faith and

---

[225] And here Sayyid Quṭb criticizes the People of the Scripture. For him their style is superficial and really far from God's way: "not with flattery or doing nice and not just perchance or at random -- God is far beyond all this, and neither by distributing charities and gifts as the people of the Scripture say: We are God's children and His beloved ones." *Fī Ẓilāl*, vol. 1: 447.

[226] *Fī Ẓilāl*, vol. 1: 448.

Brotherhood.

3. As the bearer or realization of the pure religion in the world, the mission of this *umma* is guidance or leadership for humankind. Thus this *umma* is not to receive orders from others, least of all from the people of the Scripture, but to give to them what it has received from God, i.e., to call others to the Islamic religion.

4. While the leadership for humankind is expressed in the moral guidelines of *maʿrūf* and *munkar*, all other relationships in society - whether political, economic or social - are founded on and cannot be separated from, the moral guidelines.

5. Finally, in order for this *umma* to be able to fulfill its task of guidance and leadership for humankind through ordering and forbidding, it is necessary that it should have authority and power.

Looking at the three *tafāsīr* that we have considered in this section, we note the following. First of all, the approach to exegesis exhibited by ʿAbduh/Riḍā, Mawdūdī and Sayyid Quṭb is indeed a departure from the traditional one which was standard until the 19th century. Some scholars have classified these three, among others, as "modern' commentators. Here, the adjective 'modern' has to be qualified.[227] It may be used, for lack of a better

---

[227] Considering "modern" as a category of time, Muslim and non-Muslim scholars usually classify as modern commentaries those written within the period starting from mid 13th/19th century up to the present. Practically all lists of modern Qurʾān commentaries that I have encountered, whether by Muslim or non-Muslim scholars, have as first entry for modern commentaries, the commentary of Sayyid Maḥmūd al-Ālūsī (1217/1802 - 1270/1854), followed by several others, which are all traditional ones. Cf., among others, Muhammad Ibrahim H. I. Surty, "The Qurʾān in Islamic Scholarship: A Survey of *Tafsīr* Exegesis Literature in Arabic" in *The Muslim World Book Review*, vol. 7, no. 4 (Summer 1987) 64; Harris Birkeland, "The Lord Guideth: Studies on Primitive Islam" in *Skrifter* [of the Oslo Academy], Part II (1956) 1-140; Regis Blachère, *Introduction au Coran* (Paris: Editions Besson and Chantemerle, 1952) 222.

term, to distinguish this approach - found in modern time - from the previous, traditional one. However, this qualification can be misleading since many *tafāsīr* written in modern time, are very traditional. This approach may be classified as modern in the sense that it is characterized by the fact that it addresses the modern situation. On the other hand, if the term modern is to be applied to the ideas in the *tafāsīr* of these commentators, there is again the need to qualify the description. ʿAbduh and Riḍā may be classified as modernist or modern in a "reconciliatory" sense as they try to stick to the ideal of the *Salaf* and at the same time learn from the example of the West, i.e., they try to reconcile the Islamic ideal and the modern situation. Mawdūdī and Sayyid Quṭb (but especially the latter) may be classified as non-modern or modern but in a reactionary sense, for they want a totalitarian view of Islam. Modernity is addressed in order to be rejected. It is in order to avoid ambiguities and equivocations that we have entitled this section as "New Directions in Tafsīr."

Finally, in a few words, the views of the three representatives of this section may be distinguished as follows: ʿAbduh/Riḍā reconciles the ideal of the Islamic *umma* with what is good in modernity; Mawdūdī emphasizes the leadership role of the Muslim *umma* and sees a stigma of *jāhilīya* in modern political ideologies; Sayyid Quṭb also emphasizes the leadership role of the Muslim *umma* but is more sweeping in his view that whatever is non-Muslim is *jāhilīya*.

4. Summary and Conclusion

A general picture of the commentaries on the *umma* that we have studied may be captured by the saying - attributed to Muhammad - that *al-islām* began as a stem, then doubles, then quadruples, then is made sixfold, then splits into many branches.[228] The *umma muslima* as the true religious community is the common stem that remains as the point of departure from which various levels of interpretations and differences in meaning have sprung up, and in which they all continue to share. We will now briefly review the main points in the various *tafāsīr* and then point out the various changes and developments in the concept from one *tafsīr* to another as well as from one age to another. Afterwards, we shall end with a remark in light of what we have seen in our study of *umma* in the context of the Qur'ān as well as of what some Muslim scholars of today have said.

Ṭabarī: The Muslim *umma* is the best community because it has been pre-ordained by God before the creation of the world. Being "best" thus describes every generation of Muslim *umma*. "Middle community" (*umma wasaṭ*) is the mode of being "best" of this *umma* in so far as its stance in the world, vis-a-vis other communities, is concerned. It means the balanced, moderate position between two extremities in religion, and thus, the "best." The good is identical with the Islamic faith of this community. This community is thus the revealer and bearer of God's will in history, and thus the criterion of what is good and what is evil, of what is acceptable and what is rejectable. The mission of this *umma* then is to call non-Muslims to Islam because, outside of Islam there is no salvation.

---

228 Aḥmad b. Muḥammad Ibn Ḥanbal, *Musnad,* vol. III (Egypt: al-Maṭbaʿa al-Maymanīya, 1313 [1895] 363.

Zamaḫšarī: The Muslim *umma* is marked distinctively by its being middle, *wasaṭ,* which means justice, and thus the best. The Muslim *umma* is the best because it is a community of justice. God has guided this community to being *wasaṭ,* being a community of justice, because of its faith. The task of this community, therefore, is directed upon itself, i.e., the maintenance of its being middle, being a community of justice. Otherwise, this distinctive character can be lost. The life of this community must thus be marked by the ordering of what is just and the forbidding of what is unjust among the community members. At the base of this must be faith in God, from which everything else expected of a community of justice will follow. This is because God who is absolute justice, will guide a community because of its faith; and when God guides, it is always to the straight path, the path of justice.

Rāzī: *Wasaṭ* or "middle" is a term that expresses the two inseparable notes of the Muslim *umma,* namely, "just" and "best." The Muslim community in itself is a community of justice; in relation to other communities, it is the best community. The task of the Muslim community is both centripetal and centrifugal in character. It is a task that goes with its being *wasaṭ*. *Wasaṭ* means "justice" when applied to the Muslim community in itself and thus, in the concrete, one which is concerned with how the legal prescriptions are to be applied to and by the community members. *Wasaṭ,* on the other hand, means "middle or best in religion" when applied to the Muslim community in relation to other communities and thus, in the concrete, one which is concerned with making non-Muslims embrace the true religion which is Islam. The being best of every generation of Muslims has been decreed by God before the creation of the world. As a historical reality, the Muslims have demonstrated their being best by their willingness to fight, if a non-Muslim cannot be won over to Islam through other means.

Bayḍāwī: The Muslim *umma* is *wasaṭ,* is best, as decreed by God before the creation of the world. *Wasaṭ* is a description of the internal life of the Muslim community, which is one of justice, i.e. consisting in the ordering of what is good, forbidding of what is evil, and faith in God. The Muslims have been described as the best to emphasize the permanence of their being a community of justice and faith. On Judgment Day they will witness against other communities before God to their having lived God's justice in this world.

Ibn Kaṯīr: The Muslim community in itself is *wasaṭ* because it is God's choice, and thus is bestowed with the most perfect of laws, the most straight of ways and the most clear religious creeds, which make it the best before the eyes of God. In relation to the rest of humankind, the Muslim community is *wasaṭ* in the sense of "just" or "justice." The Muslims' being a community of justice is a witness against humankind, i.e., they become the conscience of the world, and the climax of such a witnessing will be on the Day of Judgment. The Muslim *umma*, therefore, has to maintain its being a community of justice, following the example of the Prophet. For the best among the generations of Muslim *umma* has been the one that obtained during the time of the Prophet, followed by the generation after him.

Al-Jalālayn: The Muslim community is *wasaṭ*, which means it is God's choice and thus the best, and, as a community, is one of justice. It is the best community in the knowledge of God; it calls to what is good, it orders what is acceptable, and forbids what is evil.

Al-Manār: The Muslim *umma* is *wasaṭ* because it is a community characterized by justice or moderation in thoughts, in moral principles and in actions. This community characterized as such is the "best" in relation to other communities. It follows that this community can lose its being "best" if it ceases to be a community of justice, which consists in the twofold task of ordering what is acceptable and ordering what is rejectable among Muslims. It is the task of the Muslim community to call non-Muslims to Islam, not by compulsion or fighting but by guidance and instruction. The ideal existence of the *umma* today consists in a faithful imitation of the *Salaf* and an adaptation to present-day conditions. In the context of today, a special group of Muslims, an *umma* within the larger *umma*, must be formed for the *Daʿwa*, i.e., the calling of non-Muslims to Islam.

Mawdūdī: *Umma wasaṭ* signifies that distinguished group of people which follows the path of justice and equity, of balance and moderation, a group which occupies a central position among the nations of the world. To be *wasaṭ*, therefore, is to be appointed as guide and leader of humankind. Such is the vocation of the Muslim community. The change of the *qibla* goes with being *wasaṭ*. It means that the Muslims have to turn their backs on the leadership of others and must assume the role of leadership. To be *wasaṭ* is a project they constantly have to become; otherwise, disaster will fall on them like it did on their predecessors, i.e., God will replace them with another. Thus, following the example of the Prophet, the Muslims must live the guidance they have received from God through the Prophet, and must convey to the rest of humankind the guidance received and lived.

Sayyid Quṭb: The Muslim *umma* is *wasaṭ* because it is the realization in history of the human response to the *fiṭra*. Its being is from God and it rises in this world for the leadership of humankind. In relation to other communities, therefore, this *umma* is the best. This *umma* finds true existence as *wasaṭ* and best only by bringing into reality what God has given it. It must never learn from others because outside of the Muslim *umma* there is only paganism. Instead, it must live its own being through Faith and Brotherhood among Muslims. Thus this *umma* is not to receive orders from others but to give to them what it has received from God, i.e., to call others to the Islamic religion, to order what is good and to forbid what is evil. All other relationships in society -

whether political, economic or social - are founded on and cannot be separated from, these moral guidelines. In order for this *umma* to be able to fulfill its task of guidance and leadership, it is necessary that it should have power.

What then is the Muslim *umma* according to these commentators? Based on our study of the commentaries, the main points of which we have just outlined, the basic answer that will comprehend all the various ideas presented by the *mufassirīn* is that the Muslim *umma* is the religious community that God has established as WASAṬ. The being *wasaṭ* of the Muslim *umma* is the common stem, the point of departure from which the various levels of interpretation and the differences in meaning have sprung, and in which they all continue to share. The pluri-dynamism of the term *wasaṭ* has permitted the various interpretations of the nature and task of the Muslim *umma*.

We note that Ṭabarī sees *wasaṭ* as meaning "middle" in religion when applied to the Muslim community. This understanding emphasizes the centrifugal character of the Muslim *umma*. Its task thus concerns immediately the non-Muslims, i.e., to bring them to Islam. This is also present in Rāzī in which is added the virtue of fighting in order to convert people to Islam. The same understanding is emphasized in *Tafsīr al-Manār* in which fighting is condemned, and in which the proper ways to be followed are guidance and instruction as well as adaptation to present-day conditions which includes learning from the examples of other communities. Mawdūdī and Quṭb both express the centrifugal or missionary dimension in terms of the Muslim community's role of guidance and leadership for humankind. For Quṭb, in particular, power is necessary to accomplish this task, and non-Muslims are called pagans.

Zamaḫšarī sees *wasaṭ* as meaning justice when applied to the Muslim *umma*. This understanding emphasizes the centripetal character of the *umma*. Its task thus immediately concerns the Muslims, i.e., the maintenance of its being a community of justice.

This idea is also present in the other commentaries after Zamaḫšarī, especially in Bayḍāwī who, like Zamaḫšarī, does not mention a missionary dimension. Ibn Kaṯīr also emphasizes the same idea which includes a missionary dimension that may be considered as his original version, i.e., that the Muslim *umma* as a community of justice will serve as the conscience of the world. This idea is also seen in Mawdūdī's *tafsīr* but presented in such a manner that we are reading Mawdūdī's idea and not Kaṯīr's.

It may also be noted that the representatives of the first two periods in qur'ānic exegesis have each a synthesizer of ideas. Of the three representatives of the classical period, Rāzī stands out as the one in whom, in addition to his original ideas, ideas found in Ṭabarī but not in Zamaḫšarī and vice versa, are synthesized; thus "middle in religion" and "community of justice" are seen in Rāzī as two sides of the same coin. For the post-classical period, which we have described as the "solidification of traditionalism," *Tafsīr al-Jalālayn* provides a synthesis in the sense that its very brief explanations can comprehend the various emphases found in the other *tafāsīr*.

For a fuller understanding of the various levels of interpretations or differences of emphasis in the meaning of *umma wasaṭ*, we will now review them in relation to the historical contexts out of which the commentators wrote.

Ṭabarī lived in a historical situation marked by the victory of the Muslims over other peoples. It may be said that he wrote his *tafsīr* to give a qur'ānic basis to an Islamic theology of conquest. He made use of traditions but also applied personal judgment in order to define the *umma* in the historical context he was in. Zamaḫšarī wrote his *tafsīr* in Mecca - the heartland of Islam- and addressed the Muslim situation marked by internal squabbles and sectarian differences. He made much use of the Greek mode of reasoning and argumentation in doing his *tafsīr*. Rāzī lived in a historical situation in which the atmosphere was a combination of those of the times of Ṭabarī and Zamaḫšarī. He wrote his *tafsīr* in which he tried to reconcile tradition and Greek philosophy which was influencing the Muslim intellectual world, especially the Muʿtazilite exegesis of Zamaḫšarī. Two things may be said regarding classical commentaries as represented by the foregoing. First, they all addressed the historical situations they were in, not by escapism but by adaptation. Thus Ṭabarī's view expressed an adaptation of the *umma* concept to a situation in which the mentality prevailing everywhere was such that it was not a virtue to consider other peoples or communities as equal. Rāzī's and Zamaḫšarī's showed, among other things, an adaptation to a foreign philosophy that was influencing the intellectual world. Secondly, the classical period then shows that the *umma* concept, interpreted in light of the prevailing historical conditions, has allowed the expression of its meaning in a variety of ways, which also reveals its richness.

The next seven centuries were basically an extension of the conditions obtaining in the classical period. Basically, exclusivism was the prevailing mentality among the various communities and civilizations everywhere in the world. The Muslim community was secure in itself, with Islam embracing every aspect of the life of the believers. The geographical extension of the *umma* concept was defined, self-sufficient with its superstructure. Because of this, in the eyes of Muslim theologians, the world was physically divisible into the abode of Islam or *dār al-islām,* and the rest of the world as the abode of war or *dār al-ḥarb*. Non-Muslim communities had to fit, as well as they could, if they were to be allowed to exist within the boundaries of the *umma*. The main challenge to Islamic identity and unity was generally seen as coming from within, and the solution was to close the gate of *ijtihād* (independent judgment or interpretation). Consequently, qurʾānic exegesis in the period, as we have seen, consisted in repetition or recasting of previous works.

The modern situation, faced by the last three commentaries that we studied, is a far different situation, unprecedented in Islamic history, marked by the disintegration of the geographical boundaries of the *umma* and by modern secular views brought on by Western colonizers. ʿAbduh/Riḍā tried to establish positive links between the Qurʾān and the *sunna* and modern ideas. Mawdūdī and Quṭb together see the existence of the *umma* as one for the leadership and guidance of humankind, i.e., to call humankind to unity on the basis of the religion of the Muslims. For Quṭb, particularly, to achieve this, it is necessary that the *umma* must have power. Mawdūdī branded modern ideologies with the stigma of paganism. Quṭb branded anything non-Muslim as paganism. Thus they address modernity by turning their backs on it, advocating a brotherhood of Muslims that would continue the powerful *umma* in times past, in order to lead, to exercise power and authority over all of humankind. This view, therefore, denies historical change any positive value.

Would the traditional commentators have disagreed with the interpretations put forward by the modern commentators? Based on our study of the commentaries, it seems safe to presume that modern commentators made explicit certain things that earlier were so naturally understood as to have been taken simply as a matter of course. The concept of *umma* in a special sense - which is the *umma muslima* - that we have seen in our study of the Qurʾān, is hardly mirrored by the *umma muslima* that the commentators talk about in their commentaries. Among other things, I cannot read in the commentaries the *ḥanīf* attitude which is the essential thing that makes the *umma muslima* the *umma* in a special sense. The strong feeling that I receive from reviewing the commentaries representing the various periods in qurʾānic exegesis is that the Muslim *umma* verses are commented on in terms of the particular Muslim community existing at the time of the commentator, in such a way that either the particular historical *umma* existing in his time is idealized, or an ideal *umma* is conceived as a reaction to the historical situation of the commentator, but an ideal which hardly coincides with the qurʾānic concept of *umma*. These feelings of mine may find corroboration in the remarks of not a few modern Muslim scholars. For instance, Mushir-ul-Haq of the Algerian Muslim University says that one must consult first of all the Qur'ān instead of what Muslims have done and viewed in the past, emphasizing that "this is necessary because the practices of a religious community are not always consistent with its religion's scriptural injunctions."[229] The Pakistani scholar Fazlur Rahman also remarked that Islamic decadence is to be traced all the way back to the original institutionalization of Islam, particularly in law, theology and exegesis which all had as their primary concern the preservation of the Muslim empire, rather than the preservation of the principles on which it was founded.[230]

Aside from these feelings and remarks, our study of the commentaries has given us a deeper realization of the fact that the study of Islam becomes a study of the Muslim faith as it is lived by the Muslims themselves. It has thus afforded us an appreciation of how the Qur'ān has fired the imagination, inspired the minds, and nurtured the piety of Muslims throughout the different centuries. We have thus seen the historical flow of the Muslim understanding of the *umma*, involving both movement and continuity, that takes us from what *umma* "meant" to what it "has meant" and what it "means." Our study of the commentaries has thus shown us that *umma* is dynamic both in the understandings of the individual *mufassirūn* and as expressed by the historical development of the concept from one age to another.

---

[229] Mushir-ul-Haq, "Inter-Religious Understanding" in *Christian-Muslim Dialogue, Broumana 12-18 July 1972* (Geneva: WCC, 1973) 32.

[230] See Fazlur Rahman, *Islam and Modernity: Transformation of an Intellectual Tradition* (Chicago and London: The University of Chicago Press, 1984) 26.

CHAPTER THREE

UMMA IN THE CONTEXT OF THE PHILIPPINES

This chapter is hermeneutical in nature, i.e., it explains or describes how the concept of *umma* has been translated or understood in Islam as it is found in the Philippines. This will be done in two main articulations. The first is a reading of the coming of Islam to the Philippines. In this part, we will analyze the materials available regarding the coming of Islam to the Philippines in order to discover how it was received, and, consequently, in order to see how the concept of the *umma* was expressed in the form that Islam was received. This will then give us a picture of the *umma* in the pre-colonial period. The second main part is a reading of the *umma* in the Philippines, i.e., the *umma* vis-a-vis foreign dominion. As will be made clearer below, the Muslim *umma* was already established in some of the islands that were otherwise independent of one another, but would later be appropriated and grouped together by the western colonizers and would be given the name "The Philippines." Thus, since the birth of the Philippines the *umma* would always be defined or understood in terms of the Muslim struggle against foreign dominion. In this part, therefore, we will outline the phases of the evolution of the *umma* since the beginning of the colonial period until the present. With these two main articulations, we shall have the necessary elements for assessing the way *umma* was understood in the context of the Philippines.

1. The Coming of Islam to the Philippines

The modern Philippine nation state is an archipelago of 7,109 tropical islands with a total land area of 115,600 square miles or 29,629,000 hectares, making it only slightly smaller than Japan or Italy and slightly bigger than the British isles. As such, the Philippine islands form part of the still greater archipelago of the Malay world (including the Malay Peninsula) which encompasses the modern nation-states of, other than the Philippines: Malaysia, Singapore, Brunei and Indonesia. Southeast Asia has one of the heaviest concentrations of Muslim peoples in the world.[1] In Malaysia, Indonesia and Brunei, Islam has an imposing position and, Indonesia lays claim to being numerically the world's largest Muslim nation - some ninety percent of its total population. In the Philippines, on the other hand, the Muslims are a cultural minority and, historically, they constitute about five percent of the total national population. Translated into the official Philippine census of 1990, their number comes to 2.8 million out of the sixty-five million people in the country.

Before the birth of the Philippine state and before the coming of Islam or Christianity to the Philippines, the inhabitants of the islands used to be scattered into small chiefdoms independent of and not necessarily at peace with, one another.[2] The groups or tribes that inhabited the inland or highland areas were engaged in hunting or planting, while those that inhabited the plain or flat coastlines or big river banks had for their means of livelihood

---

[1] A recent study of Islam in Southeast Asia, which includes statistical information, may be found in Thomas Michel, S. J., *Islam in Asia* (Estella, Spain: Editorial Verbo Divino, 1991).

[2] See, among others, J. L. Phelan, *The Hispanization of the Phlippines: Spanish Aims and Filipino Responses, 1565-1700* (Madison: University of Wisconsin Press, 1959) 15-18; Renato Constantino, *The Philippines: A Past Revisited,* vol. 1 (Manila: Renato Constantino, 1993) 26-41.

fishing and trade with people from other islands; it is to the latter division that the Philippine Muslim groups would mostly belong.

Philippine Muslims are found principally in the southern Philippine island of Mindanao, the southernmost tip of Palawan and the Sulu archipelago. In this region as a whole, again according to the official Philippine census of 1990, the Muslims number about 2.6 million or over 90 percent of the total Philippine Muslim population and about twenty-four percent of the close to eleven million inhabitants of the whole region. Thirteen linguistic groups have been identified as Muslim,[3] of which the three largest groups - which make up seventy-five percent of the total Philippine Muslim population - are the Maranao, the Tausug and the Maguindanao. These main groups have always been concentrated respectively in the provinces of Lanao (mostly in the Lake Lanao region), in the Cotabato area and in the Sulu archipelago, that is to say, the southern Philippine areas which are nearest to the rest of Southeast Asia - particularly Malacca, northern Sumatra, Borneo and Celebes. It is with the peoples of these neighboring Southeast Asian countries that Philippine Muslims have more contact - especially through trade and inter-migrations[4] which antedate the advent of Islam - and with whom they thus have come to share many more cultural features than with the rest of

---

[3] For. details about the various Muslim Filipino groups, see, among others, C. A. Majul, *The Contemporary Muslim Movement in the Philippines* (Berkeley: Mizan Press, 1985) 9-14; P. G. Gowing, *Muslim Filipinos - Heritage And Horizon* (Quezon City: New Day Publishers, 1979) 1-10 and *Mandate in Moroland* (Quezon City: New Day Publishers, 1983) 1-19.

[4] See, among others, A. Spoehr, "An Archaeological Approach to Ethnic Diversity in Zamboanga and Sulu" in *Sulu Studies* No. 2, ed. by G. Rixhon (Quezon City: Bustamante Press, 1973; A. Cutshall, *The Philippines: Nation of Islands* (Princeton: Van Nostrand Searchlight Books, 1964; R. L. P. Moore, *Women and Warriors: Defending Islam in the Southern Philippines* (San Diego, California: University Microfilms International, 1986).

the peoples of the Philippines. One main feature shared by these peoples is the religion of Islam. In fact, the Islamization of this section of present-day Philippines was a function of the general spread of Islam throughout Southeast Asia.[5] This perspective on Muslim Filipino history is important especially for our understanding of the *umma* in the Philippines. Cesar Adib Majul - regarded by many as the most eminent scholar on Filipino Muslim history - has underscored the importance of this perspective, saying that

> This is crucial; not to see this is to relegate the inquiry into Islam in the Philippines to a relatively unintelligible isolated phenomenon. In the absence of much needed or desirable historical data in the Philippines, it is precisely from a knowledge of when and how Islam became entrenched in other parts of Malaysia [i.e., the countries that we have collectively referred to, above, as Southeast Asia] that vital additional insights into Islam's coming to the Philippines can be gained.[6]

This first section then will proceed as follows. First, we will consider the coming of Islam to Southeast Asia (Greater Malaysia) in general. This will be followed by our particular inquiry into the coming of Islam to the Philippines. This twofold inquiry will

---

[5] It has been noted by some scholars that, unlike non-Muslim accounts of the original inhabitants of the present southern Philippine Muslim areas, the Philippine Muslim indigenous histories or *tarsilas* (see below) that speak about the inhabitants of the area in the pre-Islamic period contain no suggestion that any of the original inhabitants came from the now-Christianized islands of the Philippines. See R. L. P. Moore, *Women and Warriors*, p. 39. See also N. M. Saleeby, *The History of Sulu* (Manila: Filipiniana Book Guild, Inc., 1963) 38f.

[6] C. A. Majul, *Muslims in the Philippines* (Quezon City: University of the Philippines Press, 1973) 35.

tell us about the first stage of the arrival of Islam which was the arrival of Muslims as can be judged from epigraphical evidences, accounts of foreigners as well as indigenous accounts which refer to the beginnings of Islam in the region. We call these first two inquiries "the arrival of Muslims" to distinguish them from our third inquiry which marks the arrival of Islam in terms of literature and which we will call the "arrival or the penetration of Islamic thought." With these three inquiries, we shall be able to understand how the *umma* concept was expressed as Islam was accepted in the Philippines.

1.1 The Arrival of Muslims in Southeast Asia

The first contacts of the Southeast Asians with Islam came over the trade routes. Even before the rise of Islam and centuries before the Christian era, the Yemeni Arab traders were already dominating the Indian ocean, bringing their goods to "the land of gold, *suvarna bhumi,* the term by which Southeast Asia was referred to in some Sanskrit texts."[7] With the rise of Islam, Arab lands became an important commercial center for the products of India, China and Southeast Asia. The Arabs became the intermediaries between European and Asian traders. Chinese sources mention the establishment of an Arab trader colony on the west coast of Sumatra as early as 674 A.D.[8] Thus, the possibility of a Muslim presence at any point in Southeast Asia could date back to as early as the end of the seventh century. As Johns reason-

---

[7] A. H. Johns, "Islam in Southeast Asia" in *The Religious Traditions of Asia,* ed. Joseph M. Kitagawa (New York: Macmillan Publishing Company, 1989) 167.

[8] As cited in, among others, S. M. N. Al-Attas, "Indonesia" in *The Encyclopedia of Islam,* New Edition, vol. 3, 1218, and T. W. Arnold, *The Preaching of Islam* (Lahore: Ashraf Publication, 1979) 368.

ably hypothesized, "as soon as there were Muslim sailors aboard ships sailing under whatever flag in the Indian ocean trading system and disembarking goods or individuals at points in Southeast Asia, there was a possibility of a Muslim presence at those points."[9] However, there is hardly any documented evidence of the Southeast Asian presence of Muslims in the first century of Islam.

Reports by Chinese merchants and Muslim historians cite Muslim presence in Southeast Asia starting in the 9th century. According to the famous Muslim historian Abu-l-Ḥasan al-Masʿūdī (d. 345/956), in the aftermath of the Huang Ch'ao rebellion and massacre of western traders in south China in 878, surviving Muslim traders fled to the Southeast Asian archipelago and settled in Kalah on the west coast of the Malay peninsula as well as in Palembang in Sumatra. Trade was reopened half a century later. It was in connection with China's reopening of its doors to traders that an island of what is today "The Philippines" was first mentioned. Malaysian trade with China had then discovered a second route: while the first one was via the coast of Champa in Indo-China, the alternative route was from Borneo and the Philippines going directly to South China without passing along the Champa coast. Regarding these two routes, Professor Otley Beyer wrote:

> From the late 10th century onward the Arab ships pursued both routes and the first actual recorded mention of the Philippines, in Chinese written history (as so far available), is the arrival of an Arab ship at Canton with a load of native goods from Mindoro (Ma-i), in the year 982 A.D.[10]

Other early Muslim settlements mentioned were to be found in Champa in 1039; in Leran (Eastern Java) in 1082.

The earliest evidence that substantiates not simply the pres-

---

[9] A. H. Johns, "Islam in Southeast Asia" in *The Religious* ... 168.

[10] As quoted in Majul, *Muslims in the Philippines* .... 39.

ence of Muslims in the region but also the existence of sultanates dates from the thirteenth century. Accounts of travelers indicate Muslim presences in the region: Marco Polo was in the area in 1292 and describes the people of Perlak (a realm on the eastern coast of Pasai region of north Sumatra) as Muslim with a Muslim ruler; the great Moroccan traveler Ibn Baṭṭūta was in the same area in 1345 and describes Pase/Pasai as a Muslim sultanate. Another source of information "comes from Tomé Pires whose *Suma Oriental*, completed in 1515, described Pase as a cosmopolitan city with an important Muslim population among whom Bengalis were especially prominent."[11]

The evidence, from the area itself, of earliest signs of Muslim presence is supplied by some archaeological findings as well as by indigenous histories.[12] The archaeological remains are mostly gravestones containing early dates and Muslim names, of which three have been discovered in the Pase district of North Sumatra, dated in the first half of the fifteenth century, another at Gresik in east Java of 1419. Two further gravestones from Léran in Java dated 1102 and 1391 are also known although, according to recent scholars, there is considerable uncertainty about the first date. In the Philippines, a gravestone in a tempat (sacred grove) on Bud Dato, a few miles from the coastal town of Jolo, has also been considered to date back to 1310 A. D. In Trengganu, an east-coast state on the Malay Peninsula, a fragment of a stone pillar has been considered as dating from between 1321 and 1380. It contains an inscription - in the Malay language but using

---

[11] See M. B. Hooker, *Islam in Southeast Asia* (Leiden: E. J. Brill, 1983) 4.

[12] For a full account, see C. A. Majul, *Muslims in the Philippines*, 37-46; G. W. J. Drewes, "New Light on the Coming of Islam to Indonesia?" in *Bijdragen tot de Taal-, Land- en Volkenkunde*, vol. 124 (1968) 433-459; M. B. Hooker, *Islam in Southeast Asia* (Leiden: E. J. Brill, 1983) 3-4; and A. H. Johns, "Islam in Southeast Asia" in *The Encyclopedia of Religion*, vol. 7.

the Arabic script - which suggests the existence of a Muslim community under a local Muslim ruler.

The final body of evidence are the indigenous histories or traditions which relate the beginnings of Islam, although in a manner in which historical and mythological elements are mixed. These traditional accounts are found in practically all sultanates in Southeast Asia. The oldest in the region are the *Hikayat Raja Raja Pasai* (genealogy of Pasai rulers) and the *Sejarah Melayu* (Malayan history). They actually belong to the literature from late 15th century onwards (which will be considered in a later section) but are also considered here for their accounts which point to the beginnings of Islam. On the whole, these accounts of the beginning of Islam are posited on the position of the ruler or prince and assume a definite religious function for him.

The data supplied by the above-outlined evidence had been analyzed by scholars and may be summarized as follows. The first principality to become a Muslim sultanate was Pasai in the second half of the 13th century. Malacca became a sultanate in 1414 when its ruler converted to Islam following a marriage alliance with a Muslim princess from Pasai. Malacca became the center for the spread of Islam carried out especially by Sufī missionaries, and the consequent establishment of sultanates in other islands, particularly, Java. The ruler of Brunei embraced Islam after the founding of Malacca and sometime afterwards, Sulu sultanate was also established. Ternate, in the Moluccas, became Islamized around the time of the fall of the Madjapahit Empire[13] in 1478. On the other hand, the Trengganu inscription suggests a Muslim principality in the early 14th century on the

[13] Founded as a little kingdom in Madjapahit, Java in 1293 by Raden Widjaya, a celebrated Malay conqueror, the empire extended its sovereignty over the Malay Archipelago and other territories such as Taiwan, Thailand, Cambodia, Indo-China, southern Burma and New Guinea. It was overthrown in 1478 by the Muslim Malays under Rajah Bonang of Champa. See, among others, R. O. Winstedt, *A History of Malaya* (Singapore, 1935) 26-36.

eastern side of the Malay peninsula. This principality belongs to another line of Islam's expansion, parallel with the western one with Pasai in northern Sumatra as starting point. Professor Fatimi[14] calls this the eastern line which runs through all the eastern coasts facing the China Sea: Phan-rang, Patane, Trengganu, Pahang and Leran (Java). The community at Phan-rang was known to have been descendants of Šīʿī refugees who had fled and settled in Hainan, China, before fleeing again and settling in Phan-rang after the 878 Chinese rebellion. They used to live and govern themselves apart from their neighboring Muslim communities. Professor Fatemi's theory of two movements then may represent the Sunnī and Šīʿī movements in the Malay world and their eventual fusion. Johns adds that "although today the region is Sunnī, there are some remnants of Šīʿī influence from the past.[15]

Based on the foregoing outline of the coming of Islam to Southeast Asia, we make the following notes and interpretations. First of all, the coming and spread of Islam in the Malay world did not go off with a bang. Rather, it was hesitant, modest and discreet: as early as the end of the 7th century there were Muslims in foreign trader colonies scattered along the trade routes and this increased in number in the 9th and 10th centuries in Malaysia; by the end of the 13th century, continuing to the next century, local Islamic sultanates were established; this was followed by expansion in the other parts of the region in the 15th and 16th centuries.

Secondly, as regards the provenance of Southeast Asian

---

[14] As cited in C. A. Majul, *Muslims in the Philippines*... 43. Majul adds: Further investigation on the matter might possibly demonstrate how these two lines, two separate but related tides, one eastern and another western, eventually met and fused in Java and Borneo." Ibid.

[15] A. H. Johns, "Islam in Southeast Asia" in *The Religious* ... 178.

Islam, there has been no consensus among the various scholars' interpretations of the evidence. We don't have to discuss the various theses that have been put forward.[16] The following words of Johns should suffice:

> Given the diversities and discontinuities of the region, the provenance of Southeast Asian Islam is not a practical topic for discussion, although hypotheses have located it anywhere from Egypt to Bengal. One thing is certain: all movement of ideas and peoples from West and South Asia to Southeast Asia is related to the maritime history of the Indian Ocean (although it is still possible that communities made part of the journey by land across the Indian subcontinent, or even the "great circle" route via the Silk Road through Central Asia, and then by sea from Canton to the islands).[17]

Finally, we are now in a position to point out the factors in the initial accommodation of Islam in the area, i.e., how it was received. This refers to the period from the end of the 13th century to the early 15th century. First of all, evidence tells us that the "arrival or reception area" of Islam in this initial stage was characteristically the "court of the ruler"; it was here that the local rulers

---

16 Three places of origin have actually been put forward by earlier scholars: that Islam derived directly from the Arabs of the Hadramaut (by Niemann and de Hollander in 1861); that it is of Indian origin (by Snouck in 1894); that it is of Bengali origin (by S. Q. Fatimi in 1963). M. B. Hooker (op. cit., 4-7) has demonstrated that the interpretation of the evidence is not conclusive as to origins. See also A. H. Johns, "Islam in Southeast Asia" in *The Encyclopedia of Religion*, vol. 7, p. 407. All we can say is that we do not know the place of origin. The more important issue for us is *what* came, so that an undue emphasis on provenance especially since the evidence is meager, is both inhibiting to an understanding of and damaging to any proper definition of Islam in the area.

17 A. H. Johns, "Islam in Southeast Asia" in *The Religious* ... 168.

became involved with the religion. It can thus be consequently said that rule/ruler was the primary referent of Islam for the people. While the accounts of foreign travelers emphasize this point, Hooker points out that this interpretation is confirmed especially by the lone epigraphical material - the Trengganu inscription[18] - which provides more information than just Muslim names and dates. The inscription is written in Malay (in Arabic script) and contains a short list of ten rules, the breach of which was punished. We note some points of importance: 1) the content of the rules is not Islamic but local Malay/Javanese; and substantially the same provisions can be found in the Malacca and Malacca-derived law texts of the seventeenth century and later; 2) the "Islamic" element in the inscription is confined to the preamble which defines the bearers of authority as "expounders on earth of the doctrines of God's Apostle [Muhammad].... such exposition being incumbent on all Muslim Raja Mandalikas..." In other words, the inscription is not Islam-derived in either substance or technical terminology; the Islamic reference is solely confined to validating the rules which are local in content by reference to God's will. Thus, the initial Islamic experience in the formative period is to be seen in the change in the definition and pattern of authority under the impulse of the Islamic ethic, as it manifested itself in the relations between the sovereign and the foreigner. By embracing Islam the ruler becomes not only a political but a religious leader at the same time: he becomes the connecting link to the wider *umma* for his followers; his rule or kingdom becomes an extension of the one Islamic *umma*. It is also to be noted that "Middle Eastern" formalism was not necessarily a constituent part of the initial Islamic experience. This is corroborated by the interpretation of scholars that the *makhdums* that came in this stage of Islam's coming were Sufi

---

18 For a full description, see M. B. Hooker, "The Trengganu Inscription in Malayan Legal History" in *Journal of the Royal Asiatic Society - Malaysian Branch* 49/2 (1976) 127-131.

missionaries. Sufism is not a cultural form but is basically the concern with religion as an experience of God and thus easily adapts to local cultural forms or traditions.

1.2 The Arrival of Muslims in the Philippines

Islam in the Philippines first obtained a foothold in Sulu. However, due to lack of archaeological data and contemporary accounts of the period before the advent of Europeans in the area, our main and indispensable source for a knowledge of how Islam was received is the Sulu Genealogy or *tarsila*,[19] supplemented by traditions. Like the genealogies of the other sultanates in Southeast Asia, the *tarsilas* contain mythological elements (the significance of which will be considered in the following section). In addition, neither the *tarsilas* nor the traditions contain dates. Despite these handicaps, the *tarsilas* follow a well-ordered pattern in presenting the sequence of events regarding the beginnings of Islam. Scholars like Saleeby and Majul have done studies on the *tarsilas* and have dated many of the events mentioned with the help of materials from other sultanates in Southeast Asia. As we will see, Sulu presents in miniature what had generally happened in Malaysia as a whole regarding Islamization. The following main sequence of events regarding the beginnings of Islam in the Philippines can be deduced from the principal Sulu *tarsila*,[20]

---

[19] The term is derived from the Arabic *silsila*, meaning link or chain. It is the local term to refer to genealogical narrations.

[20] It has been considered the principal genealogy because it was the one in the possession of the prime minister of the Sultan of Sulu who gave it to Saleeby for translation into English. For a full account, see N. M. Saleeby, *The History of Sulu* (Manila: Filipiniana Book Guild, 1963 reprint of the 1908 edition), 30-37.

written in Malay with an introduction in a Sulu language.[21]

First is narrated the arrival of a foreigner who bore the title Tuan Mashaika.[22] He came to Jolo at the head of a fleet of Muslim traders a long time ago.[23] "The people were ignorant and simple-minded in those days and were not Mohammedans [sic] of the Sunni sect. Some of them worshipped tombs, and some worshipped stones of various kinds." The *tarsilas* don't attribute anything to Tuan[24] Mashaʾika other than his marriage to the daughter of the local chieftain Raja Sipad the Younger and the raising of his children as Muslims. The *tarsilas* mention that some time after the arrival of Tuan Mashaʾika, the Tagimahas also arrived, followed

---

[21] Cesar Majul discovered other *tarsilas* which he used as support materials to the Saleeby-translated main *tarsila* for his reconstruction of the history of Islam in Sulu. The same is true as regards the Maguindanao. Majul uses as principal source a Saleeby-translated one, supported by other *tarsilas* found by Majul. See the following works, among others, by C. A. Majul: *Muslims in the Philippines* (Quezon City: University of the Philippines Press for the Asian Center, 1973) esp. 51-67 and "The Genealogy of Sulu" in *Readings on Islam in Southeast Asia,* compiled by A. Ibrahim et. al. (Singapore: Institute of Southeast Asian Studies, 1985) 48-57.

[22] *Mashaʾika* is derived from one of the plural forms of the Arabic term *šayḫ,* a term of respect for elder men or heads of certain religious institutions to distinguish them from the "sayyids" or "sharīfs" who are descendants of the Prophet of Islam. C. A. Majul, "The Genealogy of Sulu," 51.

[23] Regarding the origin of Mashaʾika, there are at least two explanations. The original genealogy says "He was a prophet who was not descended from Adam. He was born out of a bamboo and was esteemed and respected by all the people." N. Saleeby, *The History of Sulu,* 32. In the "historical notes" which were added later to supplement the original genealogy, it is mentioned that "Tuan Mashaʾika was the son of Jamiyun Kulisa and Indiriga Suga, who came to Sulu with Alexander the Great." Ibid., 35 and 38. This will be explained in the next section, which deals with Islamic literature.

[24] The title "Tuan" in Sulu has been generally associated with Muslims.

after some time by the Badjaos (Samals) from Johore. Then the Genealogy continues:

> Some time after that there came Karimul Makdum. He crossed the sea in a vase or pot of iron and was called Sarip.[25] He settled at Bwansa, the place where the Tagimaha nobles lived. There the people floc,'ed to him in all directions, and he built a house for religious worship.

Later in the genealogy the Karim ul-Makhdum[26] is called Tuan Sharif Aulia. As Majul has noted, the title *Sharīf* suggests that the Karim ul-makhdum was considered by the people as a descendant of the Prophet of Islam while the title *awliyā*[27] implies that he was a pious man or a missionary preacher "since the term

---

[25] The title *šarīf (sarip or salip* in Moroland) usually implies descent from Muhammad through his daughter Fatima and her husband the Caliph Ali. The title *sayyid* literally means "lord" and is more loosely applied but can also indicate descent either from Muhammad or from his clan, the Qurayš. The terms are sometimes used interchangeably in Southeast Asia. See P. Gowing, *Muslim Filipinos - Heritage and Horizon* (Quezon City: New Day Publishers, 1979) 49.

[26] "The term *"makhdūm,"* which in Arab lands usually meant "master" in the sense of "one who is served," was later on used in India and Malaysia in the sense of teacher or learned man." C. A. Majul, *Muslims in the Philippines,* 55.

[27] *Awliyā"* is the Arabic plural for *"walīy"* and in Malaysia it is used for "saint" or for departed saintly men who were members of *tariqats*. Possibly the makhdum Karim was a Sufī." Citing other Sulu *tarsilas* that narrate how the Makhdum came walking over the water, Majul says that this suggests that the Makhdum was a member of a mystical (Sūfī) brotherhood *(ṭarīqa)* of the Qādirīya order as its founder ʿAbdul Qādir Al-Jīlānī (470 - 561/1077 - 1166) is believed to have been given by God the power to walk over the waters of rivers and seas. C. A. Majul, *Muslims in the Philippines,* 53. See note immediately following.

"awliyā" sometimes carried this connotation in Malaysia." With information from traditions as well as from other Sulu genealogies, Majul concludes that there were several *makhdūms*[28] or at least one more that came to Sulu perhaps in the late 14th or early 15th century. Accordingly, these *makhdūms*, like the *makhdūms* that came to Java, Borneo and Malacca in the same period, were Sufi missionaries[29] who came to consolidate or reinforce Islam among the Muslims in Bwansa and, according to tradition, to make some conversions. The Genealogy then continues:

> Ten years later Raja Baguinda came from Menangkabaw to Sambuwangan. From there he moved to Basilan and later to Sulu. When he arrived at Sulu the chiefs of Bwansa tried to sink his boat and drown him in the sea. He therefore resisted and fought them. During the fight he inquired as to the reason why they wanted to sink his boats and drown him. He told them that he had committed no crime against them and that he was not driven there by the tempest, but that he was simply traveling, and came to Sulu to live

---

[28] Gravestones that are traditionally claimed by Filipino Muslims as tombs of *maḫdūmīn* are found in different places in the Sulu archipelago, such as Tandu Banak in Sibutu Island, Bud Agad in Jolo, and Lugus Island in Tapul. See C. A. Majul, "Muslims in the Philippines: An Historical Perspective" in *The Muslim Filipinos*, ed. P. G. Gowing and R. D. McAmis (Manila: Solidaridad Publishing House, 1974) 3 and Osman Bin Bakar, "Sufism in the Malay-Indonesian World" in *Islamic Spirituality*, vol. 2, ed. Seyyed Hossein Nasr (London: SCM Press, 1991) 264.

[29] O. Bin Bakar says that the terms *faqīrs* (dervishes), *walīs* (saints) and *shaykhs* (masters) used for the early propagators of Islam in various parts of the Southeast Asian archipelago during the 13th to 15th centuries are "all technical terms belonging to the vocabulary of Sufism, which even after their adoption into the Malay language and in popular usage continue to retain the specific technical meanings in which they are understood in Sufism, thus suggesting very strongly that these propagators were Sufis." O. B. Bakr, op. cit., 262 and 271.

among them because they were Mohammedans [sic]. When they learned that he was a Mohammedan [sic], they respected him and received him hospitably.

The Tagimaha chiefs of Bwansa, as enumerated in the Genealogy, all had the title of *Šayḫ*. They were thus presumably Muslims. The other chiefs mentioned in the Genealogy were all entitled "Tuan" and had Muslim names. Accordingly, they were the grandchildren of Tuan Mashaʾika. The Genealogy does not mention the proper name of Rajah Baguinda.[30] His arrival took place roughly about 50 years after Tuan Mashaʾika's arrival, (i.e., late in the 14th or early in the 15th century). He was accompanied by ministers and came to Bwansa to stay and rule. "His coming was an ordinary kind of invasion, which proved successful." He consequently married a Sulu woman. The Genealogy then continues:

> After that time there came Sayid Abu Bakr from Palembang, to Bruney and from there to Sulu. When he arrived near the latter place he met some people and asked them: "Where is your town and where is your place of worship?" They said, "At Bwansa." He then came to Bwansa and lived with Raja Baginda. The people respected him, and he established a religion for Sulu. They accepted the new religion and declared their faith in it. After that Sayid Abu Bakr married Paramisuli, the daughter of Raja Baginda, and he received the title of Sultan Sharif. He begot children, and his descendants are living to the present day. He lived about thirty years in Bwansa.

This is followed by an enumeration of the descendants of Abu

---

[30] Accordingly, "*Baguinda* is a Menangkabaw honorific for prince. In Sulu, it was used in the sense of ruler. Whether he had the title when he arrived or assumed it after his arrival is not known." C. A. Majul, *Muslims in the Philippines*, 56.

Bakr, especially those who succeeded him as sultan.[31] Here, the establishment of a religion attributed to Abu Bakr is to be understood as his introduction of Islamic political institutions, especially the sultanate. This means the Bwansa chiefs (and their followers) had been Islamized to the extent that they accepted the Islamic political institution. Accordingly, Abu Bakr succeeded Baginda after the latter's death and, consequently, established a sultanate. All *tarsilas* agree that the first sultan's title was Sharif ul-Hashim and a descendant of the prophet of Islam, but not all state that his proper name was Abu Bakr. Another *tarsila*, which Majul claims is "quite a credible one," says that prior to Borneo and Bwansa in Sulu, the would-be first sultan had travelled from Arabia through Baghdad to Palembang, and then to Borneo.[32]

Based on the above-outlined data, the stages in the early part of the Islamization of Sulu may be put forward, as follows:[33] 1) The existence of a Muslim settlement or community in Sulu, consisting probably of foreign traders, who perhaps married members of ruling families. Tuan Mashaʾika belongs to this stage which occurred as early as the last quarter of the 13th century. 2) The rise to social and political prominence of the descendants of some such personages, as in the case of the descendants of Tuan Mashaʾika. This is the stage of the *makhdūms*, who came for the Islamic education of the Muslim descendants as well as to effect conversions to Islam among the native population. This has been estimated to have taken place about the second half of the 14th century. 3.) The coming of Muslim Malays from Sumatra at the beginning of the 15th century with political implications. This is the

---

31 Judging from the last name in this list of sultans, this enumeration of sultans was completed around 1808 since ʿAzīm ud-Dīn III (Alimud Din III), no. 17 and last in the list, ruled and died in this same year. See C. A. Majul, *The Genealogy of Sulu,* 50.

32 C. A. Majul, *Muslims in the Philippines,* 57.

33 Cf. Ibid., 63.

stage represented by Rajah Baginda. It is not clear whether he was the chief only of the expatriate Muslim community in Sulu or of one of the principalities in Sulu. In ny case, his rule was characterized by contacts with other principalities and sultanates in other parts of Southeast Asia and a deepening of Islamic consciousness among the people. It was the last stage before the institution of the sultanate in Sulu. 4) The establishment of political institutions, especially the sultanate under the Sharif ul-Hashim by the middle of the 15th century. At this time Islam spread throughout the coastal and mountain areas through the conversion of the local chiefs to Islam. Sultanate code of laws were made and promulgated.[34]

As can be seen, the early stages of the Islamization of Sulu followed a pattern similar to those elsewhere in the Malay world, which we have described in a general way earlier in this section: initial existence of foreign Muslim trader colonies; members of such colonies exercising some political power or the ruler of the principality becoming Muslim; the coming of missionaries to strengthen Islam; institution of the sultanate and contacts with other sultanates and principalities. As it were, Sulu presents in miniature what had generally happened in Malaysia as a whole regarding Islamization.

The same pattern can be seen in the early stages of the Islamization of Maguindanao, which occurred years after Sulu had become a sultanate. We do not have to go into its details anymore. It is enough to point out the main stages:[35] 1) In mid 15th century, Muslims who were Arabs or of Arab descent came from Malaysia and were reinforced in Sulu on their way to Maguin-

---

[34] N. Saleeby, *The History of Sulu,* 46-48.

[35] The main sources are the Maguindanao *tarsilas* and traditions. For a full account, see C. A. Majul, *Muslims in the Philippines,* 64-71 and Najeeb Saleeby, "Studies in Moro History, Law, and Religion" in *The Notre Dame Journal* 6/1 (April 1975) 1-38.

danao. While some of them left the country, the others remained, raised families, and settled in the area of the Pulangi Basin. To this stage belongs the Sharif Awliya and the Sharif Maraja. 2) The immigration of Islamic peoples, followed by the arrival - in the first quarter of the 16th century of the Sharif Muhammad Kabungsuwan, who consequently founded the Maguindanao sultanate by a combination of proselytizing and military conquests. According to the Maguindanao *tarsilas*, Kabungsuwan was the son of a Malaccan princess and an Arab from Mecca who allegedly descended from Muhammad. He is said to have come from Johore (in early 16th century) with a group of Samal people to the mouth of the Pulangi River in Cotabato. He is also credited with the consequent spread of Islam among the Maranaos and some southern areas of Davao.

To recapitulate, the period from the end of the 13th century to the end of 14th century marked the first century of the presence of Islam in Southeast Asia. Available evidence of the period would point to the presence of Muslims in the area. The Islam that came was mysticism which explains why Middle Eastern formalism was not a constituent part of this stage of the formative period of Islam (and which may also explain the consequent "syncretic" character of Philippine Islam, as will be discussed below). With the help from the indigenous histories or genealogies, we may describe those who came as: first,[36] the *makhdūms* or mystics, then the Rajahs or noblemen, then the noblemen who would trace their ascendancies to the Prophet of Islam and who would consequently found the sultanates. The place of "reception," as it were, of Islam was the royal court; the local ruler became a political and

[36] There is the question of whether the earliest gravestones would belong to the *makhdūms* or to Muslim traders who came earlier than the *makhdūms* or whether the earliest *makhdūms* were traders at the same time. There are several theories on the earliest Muslims to come and introduce Islam. These are discussed in C. A. Majul, *Muslims in the Philippines,* 46-50.

religious leader at the same time while his subjects became political and religious subjects at the same time. Thus, they became part of the historical extension of the *umma* of Muhammad by means of the sultan who was seen as a descendant, and thus a caliph of, the prophet of islam. Here we see the concept of *umma* in its Southeast Asian translation.

In the particular context of the Philippines, the *umma* concept was at work as the Islamization of the existing structure which was the *barangay* type of society. The pre-Islamic structure was retained, except that the supreme datu or overlord of the *barangay* confederation was now called the sultan, in whose veins ran the blood of the prophet of Islam. Consequently, the *barangay*[37] confederation was now called a sultanate, and became an integral part of the commonwealth of sultanates as the expression in Southeast Asia of the world-encompassing Islamic *umma*.

---

[37] *Barangay* is derived from the Malay term *balangay,* meaning a boat. The Malays (so named after their word *Malaya,* meaning "free") who had come to settle in various parts of the Philippines, formed small communities of one boat-load of people each. The barangays were generally small. For mutual protection against common enemies, various barangays would form a confederation with the wisest datu or the strongest (being the datu of the largest barangay) recognized as the overlord or supreme datu of the confederation. Before the arrival of the Muslims, large confederations of barangays had been formed in Madya-as (Panay), established in the middle of the 13th century A.D. and known to be the oldest. Other large ones were to be found in Sugbu (Cebu) and Maynila (Manila). Among other sources, see, especially for an analytical presentation, Renato Constantino, *The Philippines: A Past Revisited,* vol. 1, esp. Chapter 3. Mednick and Gowing have pointed out that Islam did not introduce a totally alien type of social and political organization in southern Philippines but only produced an "Islamic variant" of the *barangay* type of society. M. Mednick, *Encampment of the Lake: The Social Organizationof a Moslem-Philippine (Moro) People,* Research Series No. 5 (Chicago: Philippine Studies Program, University of Chicago, 1965) 13-14 and P. Gowing, *Muslim Filipinos - Heritage and Horizon* , 45.

1.3 The Penetration of Islamic Thought

In order to complete our understanding of how the concept of *umma* was at work as Islam came to the Philippines, we also have to complete our understanding of the arrival of Islam. Thus far we have described the arrival of Islam as a religion brought by Muslims from elsewhere. But we have also to describe the arrival of Islamic thought as reflected in the extant manuscripts on literature and law in the region itself. It is from the late 15th century onwards that these extant manuscripts date. Here we are concerned with the forms through which the values of Islam and the structure of its thought were communicated and received. In this regard, Muslim Filipino literature cannot be understood properly as a transmitter of Islamic values if not seen in the Southeast Asian context. In particular, we have to see it in the context of the Islamic intellectual capital of Southeast Asia in the 17th century, namely, the North Sumatran state of Aceh. The intellectual prominence of Aceh has been explained by the fact that it was in political contact with the Ottoman Empire in the 16th century and attracted a constant stream of Islamic scholars from the Indian sub-continent and Western Asia, as well as being the gateway out of Southeast Asia for Muslim intellectuals traveling to the great centers of Islamic learning in the Middle East. From the late 15th century to the 17th century, Islam was firmly enjoying a vigorous intellectual life. The holders of power, the rulers, were Muslim. Other than Arabic, Malay (and, to a certain measure, also Javanese) became an Islamic language. The Arabic script was widely used in the Southeast Asian Islamic archipelago. In the 17th century, it was from the North Sumatran state of Aceh that outstanding religious writing would originate and would be diffused in the rest of the Malay world. In Sulu, indigenous as well as copied Islamic manuscripts were in the Malay language and written in Arabic script, with later additions in Tausug language. The same situation also existed among the Maranaos and the Maguindanaos.

> . . . . the Arab alphabet was applied to the Mindanao tongue, and old Arabic and Malay books on religion and law were translated into the native Magindanao and Ranao dialects. The Moros of Magindanao have translations of the Qur'ān, *Ḥadīṯ*, some books on law, some commentaries of the Qur'ān, some magic, and other varied literature. [38]

Thus we see that especially in the area of Islamic thought, the Philippines is a fringe area, compared to Malaysia or Indonesia. Moreover, among the sub-regions or fringe areas, the Philippines derives much of its Islamic outlook from what came to it from the northern Sumatran-Malaccan center. Hence, our inquiry into what came of Islamic thought and how it was received in Philippine Islam will have to be done in the context of the Southeast Asian intellectual capital of the 17th century.

In the general context of Southeast Asia, two modes of transmission and reception of Islamic thought may be distinguished, namely: 1) literature and philosophy which may be ascertained through the extant general non-legalistic works on religious history and religion; 2) Jurisprudence, i.e., the presence of standard texts of Islamic legal scholasticism of Middle Eastern origin coupled with the presence of local Legal Digests which contain rules of local origin together with elements of *fiqh* in various combinations.

1.3.1 Literature and Philosophy

The spreading of Islamic thought in Southeast Asia may be seen first of all in general works on religion and religious history. These works were written in northern Sumatra but were diffused all over the Southeast Asian archipelago and thus shaped the way Islamic thought and values were received especially in fringe

---

[38] N. Saleeby, *Studies in Moro History, law and Religion* (Manila: Bureau of Public Printing, 1905) 63.

areas like the Philippines. In the context of northern Sumatra, the question of what was transmitted and what was received cannot be easily distinguished because "transmission merges into translation."[39] These works were either in Arabic (mostly representing important works from the lands further west) or re-worked or translated into Malay, which was the *lingua franca* of the whole area, or other regional languages such as Javanese.[40] What we will do here is, first of all, give a summary of the different genres of these works as well as the findings of scholars who have analyzed these works. Afterwards will follow our own analysis of indigenous Filipino Islamic literature as this latter serves as a particular example of some of the areas of the penetration of Islamic thought in Southeast Asia.

The first of these is the genre of theological works, the so-called *kitāb* literature, works which undoubtedly were read by only a small minority of the archipelago populations: the religious teachers and the educated. These works cover all aspects of Islam from commentaries on the Qurʾān and *ḥadīṯ* to numerous works on mystical knowledge *(ʿilm Ṣūfī, ʿilm taṣawwuf)*, the Ṣūfī orders, treatises on recitations *(ḏikr)*, collections of litanies *(rawātib)*, prayers *(duʿāʾ)*, and charms *(jimat)*. The main exam-

---

[39] M. B. Hooker, *Islam in Southeast Asia* (Leiden: E. J. Brill, 1983) 11.

[40] For an outline of the whole of the literature, see *Encyclopedia of Islam*, seond ed. (1971) 3: 1230 ff. The material indicated in this source is in the Malay language which was the medium by which Islam was spread in the archipelago. "Malay literature, unlike, e.g., Javanese literature, is in fact an Islamic literature." Ibid., 1231. See also M. B. Hooker, *Islamic Law in Southeast Asia* (Singapore: Oxford University Press, 1984) 5-8. Malay became the *lingua franca* in the whole archipelago as a result of Malacca's long dominance in the trading world. See *Encyclopedia of Islam*, second edition (1971) 6: 235. See also Osman Bin Bakar, "Sufism in the Malay-Indonesian World," 283-287.

ples of this genre are the works of the so-called great Sumatran quartet of mystic authors in the 17th century, who, though Malay was not their mother tongue, re-worked in or translated into Malay, important religious tracts on Ṣūfī mysticism, in order to be comprehensible in the whole Southeast Asian or Malay archipelago. At that time, there flourished in Aceh a heterodox mysticism known under the name of *wujūdiyya*. It may be noted that the 6th/12th century scholar Ibn ʿArabī's theory of *waḥdat al-wujūd* (the oneness of existence) was then already for centuries heatedly discussed in Arab, Persian and Indian societies. Ibn ʿArabī's theory perceives all creation as nothing but a series of manifestations of the sole existing reality, that is, God. In India, the 16th century scholar Ahmad Sirhindi proposed, as an alternative to the theory of *waḥdat al-wujūd*, the theory of *waḥdat aš-šuhūd* (the oneness of perception).[41] The so-called great Sumatran quartet of mystic authors continued or translated in Southeast Asia the controversy between these two schools of Sufī thought, namely: *waḥdat al-wujūd* and *waḥdat aš-šuhūd*.

The earliest of the Sumatran quartet of mystic authors and regarded as the greatest was Ḥamza Fanṣūrī (d. 1600) of Barus (in Sumatra), regarded as the principal proponent in Southeast Asia of *wujūdiyya* mysticism with its central doctrine of *waḥdat al-wujūd* (the oneness of existence) as well as *al-insān al-kāmil* (the Perfect Man). Ḥamza enjoyed the protection and patronage of the sultan ʿAlāʾ al-Dīn Riʿāyat Šāh in carrying out his intellectual activities in the face of strong opposition from the exoteric *ʿulamāʾ*. He is famous for his *šaʿir* (a genre of Malay poetry) and for being a mystical thinker of the first rank. In his *Šarāb al-ʿĀshiqīn* (Drink for those athirst with Love), he discusses the four stages of the mystical path: *Šarīʿa*, the law of Islam; the path of renunciation or *ṭarīqa*; the self-knowledge and awareness of being or *ḥaqīqa*; and *maʿrifa*, gnosis of ultimate reality and union with God. This is

---

41 See Thomas Michel, S. J., *Islam in Asia*, 14f.

followed by a discussion of the nature of God and of His relation with the world, the latter being defined as a series of manifestations of the sole existing reality, that is, God. The last section deals with mystical love: the man who is drunk with love of God can say only "I am God." Ḥamza's second prose work, *Asrār al-ʿĀrifīn fī bayān ʿilm al-sulū wal-tawḥīd*, is an exposition of the nature of God, where he emphasizes that the immanence of God is the definition of His perfection. In developing his exposition, Ḥamza quotes the earlier mystic writer Ibn ʿArabī. Ḥamza's treatment of the doctrine of the transcendent unity of being has been regarded as an admirably rendered Malay reproduction and exposition of the teachings of Ibn ʿArabī.

The next to emerge of the Sumatran quartet was Šayẖ Šams al-Dīn - also known as al-Sumatrānī (d. 1630) of Pasai. He enjoyed the patronage of Aceh's greatest ruler, Makota ʿAlam/ Sultan Iskandar Muda (A.D. 1607-1636). He was known as the guide and teacher of the sultan as well as writer of commentaries on Ḥamza's work. Šams al-Dīn's complete work that has survived is the *Mirʾāt al-muʾmin* (1601) which is a work on dogma in the form of a catechism about the attributes of God, the Prophets, revelations and resurrection. On the other hand, only fragments have survived of his speculative work *Mirʾāt al-Muḥaqqiqīn*, which is about admonitions and recitations of the name of God.

The next great writer that emerged was Šayẖ Nūr al-Dīn al-Rānīrī (died A.D. 1658), in whose work is found a reaction to the type of theological discussion found in the abovementioned writers. He is the principal proponent in Southeast Asia of the position of *waḥdat aš-šuhūd* (the oneness of perception) as a reaction to the *waḥdat al-wujūd* of Ḥamza Fanṣūrī. Al-Rānīrī was born in India but resided in Aceh from A.D. 1637 to A.D. 1644. In this brief space of time he wrote a number of important works in both Arabic and Malay.

> Before he actually reached Aceh he had compiled a still popular work on the Pillars of Islam, called *Ṣirāṭ al-Mustaqīm*,

which deals with topics such as the correct dress for Muslims, ablutions and the cleansing of the body, burial, alms, fasting, and so on. The book is a compilation from Arabic sources but also includes a set of condemnations on the reading of non-Muslim works, such as the *Hikayat Seri Rama* .... This author also translated Arabic texts, most notably the *Šarḥ al-ʿaqāʾid al-Nasafiya* of Saʿd al-Dīn Masʿūd al-Taftazānī (compiled in A.D. 1367), under the Malay title *Durrat al-Farāʾiḍ bišarḥ al-ʿaqāʾid*. In A.D. 1638 al-Rānīrī began his most important work, the *Bustān al-Salāṭīn*, or 'The Garden of Kings,' in seven books. It describes the Muslim story of the creation of heaven and earth, the lives of the Prophets from Adam to Muhammad, the Persian, Byzantine, Umayyad, Abbasid rulers, and the rulers of Delhi, Pahang, Malacca and Aceh. The text goes on to describe wise and just rulers, the lives of pious persons and generous and noble men, the heroes of the battle and, finally, the nature of intelligence *(ʿaql)* and the sciences. The work is a compendium of Islamic knowledge.[42]

Al-Rānīrī attacked the positions of al-Fanṣūrī and Šams al-Dīn whose wrtitings he considers to be replete with "pantheistic" tendencies. In his book *Tibyān fī maʿrifat al-adyān* of A.D. 1664 he condemns the identification of Man and the world with God, comparing Ḥamza's "pantheism" with the nihilism of the (Hindu) Vedantas.

The last great Malay intellectual figure of the 17th century was ʿAbd al-Raʾūf of Singkel - also known as the Tengku di-Kuala (d. 1693), who has survived in popular esteem as a saint. He is credited with the first complete Malay translation of the Qurʾān, as well as translation into Malay of the *tafsīrs* of Bayḍāwī and the Jalālayn. He is especially known for his book on practical mysticism (entitled *ʿUmdat al-muḥtājīn*) which gives details of the methods of *ḏikr* and contains litanies *(rawātib)*, instructions on

---

[42] M. B. Hooker, *Islamic Law in Southeast Asia*, 7.

how to control breathing and the explanation of mystical truths.

In addition to the class of theological works is popular literature which transmits Islamic values and explicates philosophical concepts though in a non-theological, non-scholastic way. The subject matter is derived from Arab countries but reached the archipelago through Persian versions in most cases. The majority of these literary products, whether in the Malay language or in any of the regional languages, is anonymous, i.e., generally names of authors and editors are not known and the date when they were written cannot be established with any degree of certainty. Therefore, the best that can be done is to divide them into different genres.[43]

The first genre of this is the series of popular tales about prophets and other persons mentioned in the Qurʾān. Among such tales are the *Ḥikayat Anbia*, *Ḥikayat Jusuf*, and others, the aim of which is to explain incidents referred to in the Qurʾān and as such they serve as a commentary on the Qurʾān, not primarily in the theological sense of the word but rather with a view to adding to historical and general knowledge. Their subject matter agrees with Arabic tradition found in such works as that of Bayḍāwī or that of al-Jalālayn and in the *Kitāb Qiṣaṣ al-anbiyā of al-Kisāʾī*.[44] The effect of this work is to describe a historical hagiography in Islamic terms, particularly in the stressing of distinctions between Muslim and non-Muslim, a stress which occurs also in other genres.

---

[43] For a full account, see *Encyclopedia of Islam*, 2nd edition (1971) 3: 1231f.

[44] Versions of the standard Arabic texts are also known in the other languages of the Southeast Asian archipelago. See *Encyclopedia of Islam* (1971) 3: 1235 for reference.

The other class of literature contains tales about the prophet Muhammad himself, including accounts of his birth, life and the miracles attributed to him; a closely related genre consists of accounts of persons who lived during the time of Muhammad. An example of the former is the *Ḥikāyat Nūr Muḥammad*, known from a Batavian manuscript of A.D. 1688 copied for the then Sultan of Aceh. This and other *ḥikāyāt* stress the principles of religion as derived from the example of the prophet of Islam, and his instructions to named persons. On the other hand, examples of tales about persons who lived at the time of Muhammad are the *Ḥikāyat Muhammad Hanafiah* and the *Ḥikāyat Nabi Mengajar Ali*, tales in which a didactic element is more obvious.

Finally, there is a group of tales that deal with the heroes of Islam, among which are the following: the *Ḥikayat Iskandar Dhu'l-Karnain*, the tale of Alexander the Great. The Malay tale is probably a translation of a harmonized Arabic-Persian version; and the *Ḥikayat Saif Dhu'l-Jasan*, on the half-legendary, half-historical pre-Islamic ruler of South Arabia, translated from Arabic.[45]

We must also add here indigenous historical writing.[46] Indigenous histories were court chronicles. Considered one of the

---

[45] Ibid., 1232. "The tradition of writing on mystical subjects has persisted through the 18th century and into the 19th century and later. In addition, a great mass of literature on theology continues to be translated from the Arabic, but not to the extent that it does away with the archipelago fondness for the mystical and magical. The *ṭarīqa* (stories of miraculous deeds) continue to circulate, such as the *Ḥikayat Muhammad Samman*, and so too do the *risalat*, the book of apocalyptic literature." M. B. Hooker, *Islamic Law in Southeast Asia*, 8f.

[46] "Southeast Asian historical activity of the 17th and 18th and later centuries was a creative literary form in which Islamic values were transmitted and interpreted." M. B. Hooker, *Islam in Southeast Asia*, 11.

oldest in the whole region is the *Sejarah Melayu* (known in English as "The Malay Annals") which means a genealogy of the Malays, who are in this case the Malay rulers of Malacca.

With this brief outline of the archipelago-influencing Islamic non-legalistic literature, we will now make our observations and some assessment. As pointed out by scholars[47] who have analyzed the contents of the above-outlined literature, and as can be judged from a look at them as outlined above, the body of literature on the whole describes the history of religion, inculcates its principles by example, and provides a basic hagiography. They had the effect of transmitting general values rather than a specific scheme of normatives. In the transmission of Islamic values, they accomplished a twofold function. First, in respect of philosophy, the mystical emphasis defines the outer permissible limits of doctrine and belief.

> There is a very real sense in which Ḥamza and ʿAbd al-Raʾūf pushed the rationalization of the mystic mode to its furthest conclusions. Many were not prepared to follow this train (e.g., al-Rānīrī), even to a limited extent. . . the impact of this thought penetrated into the mass of Southeast Asian Muslims for whom the mode became "natural." Its effect was non- or indeed anti-legastic.... [48]

The result of the mystic emphasis was a multi-faceted explanation of belief in a manner that could justify any cultural form and especially the particular needs of the archipelago. The non-legalistic mode of mystic transmission of ideas like union with God, the Perfect Man, God's relation with the world, etc., can easily adapt to local forms or traditions. It may be said that since

---

[47] M. B. Hooker, *Islam in Southeast Asia*, 11f, and *Islamic Law in Southeast Asia* , 8.

[48] M. B.Hooker, *Islam in Southeast Asia,* 11.

the proponents of this mode of transmission were under the patronage of the rulers, the non-legalistic mode was the framework within which ideas of power and rule were formulated.

Secondly, in respect of literature and histories: the function was to provide a set or series of basic referents from which indigenous thought could radiate in an "Islamic" way.

> The stories about the Prophet, the accounts of the deeds of his Companions, the basic theological issues in the form of Persian speculation and rationalization all contributed to a body of historical verities. Indigenous accounts *(Sejarah, Ḥikāyat)* tell a story with reference to these outside sources. The fact of reference is itself the important point because it both gives a context to and validates the local events. The transmitted heritage, in other words, is completely functional, serving as it does to provide cosmological and historical certainty. [49]

With the above-outlined analysis of the Southeast Asian context, we can now understand the Philippine context in particular. Indigenous Muslim Filipino literature may be summarized as the Filipino Muslim way of informing or expressing the basic tenet of Islam which encompasses everything: "There is no God but God and Muhammad is the Messenger of God," i.e., something is real only if it goes back to God via Muhammad. The way this is expressed in indigenous Filipino Muslim literature shows how the mystical way of transmission has been received.

The *tarsilas* are the foremost examples of how a transmitted form and concept are received by Filipino Muslims. The extant *tarsilas* are written down usually in Arabic script, the older portions being in Arabic or Malay language, the newer portions being in the local languages. The *tarsilas* bring home the general message that nothing is real unless it can go back to God via

---

[49] Ibid., 12.

Muhammad; and, in particular, no one can claim to rule unless it is as a continuation of the rule of Muhammad.[50] The form or style ultimately goes back to the Biography of the Messenger of Allah (written by Ibn Ishaq in the first century A. H.), used by northern Sumatran rulers as a model and consequently brought to the Philippines and adopted by Filipino Muslim rulers.[51] We have already demonstrated the genealogical accounts which bring home the message that descent from Muhammad is what gives validity to anybody's claim to rule. The *tarsilas* also contain accounts of what scholars have noted as mythological elements and pre-Islamic local legends which have been infused with Islamic elements.[52] However, they are precisely a Muslim Filipino expression of the worldview that nothing is real, is valid, unless it is connected to God through Muhammad, i.e., unless it is put within the scope of what we have conveniently described as "There is no God but God and Muhammad is the Messenger of God." An example of this is the following text from a Sulu *tarsila*:

> The first person who lived on the island of Sulu was Jamiyun Kulisa. His wife was Indira Suga. They were sent here by Alexander the Great [in another version:They came

---

[50] *Tarsilas* are carefully guarded by the Moro aristocracy as they serve to validate their titles and status.

[51] C. A. Majul, "An Analysis of the Genealogy of Sulu," 48. Majul notes: "The preference for a descendant of Muhammad to serve as a sultan among the Sulus and Maguindanaos rather than someone else, is ultimately traceable to a Sunni doctrine that the *khalif* (successor of the Prophet) or the *imām* (religious leader) of the Islamic community must belong to the Qurayš, i.e., the family of the prophet of Islam."

[52] See, among others, Gerard Rixhon, "Tausug Literature: An Overview" in *Sulu Studies* 3 (Jolo: NotreDame College, 1974) 1-86 and Juan R. Francisco, "Islamic Literature in the Philippines" in *Mindanao Journal*, XIV/1-4 (July 1987 - June 1988) 225.

here with Alexander the Great]. Jamiyun Kulisa begot Tuan Masha'ika. Masha'ika begot Mawmin. Mawmin's descendants multiplied greatly. They were the original inhabitants of Sulu and chief ancestors of the present generation.[53]

The Alexander the Great[54] legend figures prominently in the *Sejarah Melayu* (Malay History) as well as in the Malay translation of the Arabic-Persian version of the saga of Alexander the Great, mentioned earlier. Another example is the following excerpt from a Maguindanao *tarsila:*

> This book speaks of the origin of the rulers of Maguindanao. The first known rulers were Tabunaway and his brother Mamalu. One day they were cutting bamboo to build a fish corral. Mamalu cut down all the trees except one small stalk that was left standing alone. Tabunaway then called to Mamalu, "Finish it up, because it omens ill for our fish corral." Mamalu therefore cut it and found in it a girl whose little finger was slightly cut by a slip of the bolo. He carried the girl to Tabunaway. But Tabunaway told him to keep her and adopt her as his child. This girl was named by Tabunaway Putri Tunina.
>
> On the other hand there came out from Mecca Sharif Ali Zayna-ul-Abidin, who proceeded to Bawangin (Malaysia)

---

[53] N. M. Saleeby, *The History of Sulu,* 35. See also Haji Buto, "Traditions, Customs and Commerce of the Sulu Moros," *The Mindanao Herald* (February 3, 1909) 21.

[54] *Ḏu'l-qarnayn* appears in the Qur'ān (18:93). Muslim and non-Muslim scholars are agreed that it is to be identified with Alexander the Great, whose attribution of two horns goes back "upon the Egyptian elements of the Alexander Book, which, in its earliest form, dated from the 2nd century B. C." For a thorough discussion on the Alexander the Great figure, see A. A. Roest Crollius, "The Source of Life at the Meeting of the Two Oceans: Reflections on the *Majmaʿ-al-baḥrayn* of Dara Shukoh." *Islam in India*, vol. 1, p. 47, note 16.

> and settled at Juhur. Here he married the daughter of Sultan Iskandar Thul-Qarnayn of Juhur, whose name was Jusul Asiqin, and begot Sharif Kabungsuwan. Sharif Kabungsuwan came to Maguindanao to the mouth of the Tinundan. There he met Tabunaway who accompanied him to the town of Maguindanao. This is Sharif Kabungsuwan, who converted to Islam all the people of Maguindanao, Silangan, Matampay, Lusud, Katittwan and Simway, and who was followed by all those who accepted Islam in the land of Maguindanao. And it came to pass that Tabunaway married Kabungsuwan to the girl that was found inside the bamboo stalk, whose name was Putri Tunina......[55]

As the tarsila validates the pre-Islamic story, it also stresses the continuity of the Moro Sultans with the pre-Islamic past in the Philippines, thus establishing the legitimacy of dynastic claim to territory.

To summarize, the mystical mode of transmitting Islamic ideas and values was not concerned with stating a system of prescriptions, except for those which are part of an immediately required religious practice. Islamic principles were inculcated by examples, especially the life of the Prophet of Islam as well as stories about the lives of the heroes and saints of Islam. The venue as it were of transmission and reception was the court of the ruler, and the agents of transmission were under the patronage of the ruler. Thus, via Malaysia, the transmission reached the Philippines. The *tarsilas* are the foremost examples of how it was accommodated locally. The *tarsilas* first of all show the connection between rule and religion. Secondly, they translated the Islamic principles received by a method of accommo-

---

[55] N. Saleeby, *Studies in Moro History, Law and Religion* (Manila: Bureau of Public Printing, 1905) 37.

dation: local pre-Islamic revered beliefs and *adat*[56] are Islamized and at the same time Islam is indigenized. Thus, since the arrival of Islam, Moro folk literature - legends, myths, epics and folktales - have become Islamic literature.[57] Islamic influences insinuated themselves into its various genres, serving to make the pre-Islamic heroes, heroes of Islam, and the values transmitted, Islamic.[58] This was how Philippine Islam received and communicated the Muslim ethos.

1.3.2 Jurisprudence *(Fiqh)*

When it comes to jurisprudence, Southeast Asia is Shafi'ite. The standard works of the Šāfiᶜī school circulated, as they still do, either in the form of translations into the local languages or in their Arabic original with a paraphrase. "From the evidence of the surviving manuscripts such books are known to have been read and studied in the archipelago from at least the middle of the 16th

---

[56] *Adat* (Arabic: *ᶜĀda*), custom or customary. It can refer to customary or traditional practices in general. Sometimes it is used as an adjective to describe anything traditional. When used as a noun, its meaning is to be seen in the context. Thus, in the context of law, *"adat"* or *"adat law"* may be used, to mean the same thing.

[57] J. R. Francisco has noted: "From the early years that Islam began to exert pressure upon the cultures of these peoples [Moros], there had been attempts to Islamize their literature through the convenient changes in the names and titles of heroes, setting of such literary pieces like the long narratives of the Maranao, the Tausug and the Maguindanao." J. R. Franciso, op.cit., 225.

[58] See Ibid., 226; M. Saber, "Darangen: the Epic of the Maranao" in *The Journal of History* X/3 (September 1962) 327; and P. Gowing, *Muslim Filipinos - Heritage and Horizon*, 103-119.

century and probably a good deal earlier than that."[59] They were, in other words, contemporaneous with the general religious books that we have just described. Among such standard works, as are especially used in the Philippines, are the following. First, the *Mirʾat al-Ṭullāb* (not only in Malay but also in Achenese and Patani versions) compiled by ʿAbd al-Raʾūf at the request of the ruler of Aceh from A.D. 1641 to 1675. It is a standard text of Šāfiʿī jurisprudence based on Šayḫ al-Zakariyā al-Anṣārī's *Fatḥ al-Wahhāb*, setting out all aspects of social, political and religious life. Another one is the *Fatḥ al-Qarīb* of Ibn Qāsim al-Ġazzī - known especially in Maguindanao, Malaya and Sumatra.

While the standard works of the Ṣāfiʿī school - whether in their Arabic original or in Malay translations - are diffused in Southeast Asian sultanates, it cannot be assumed that local reception of the *fiqh* form of transmission meant a simple application of principles of *fiqh* to the day to day life of the Southeast Asian Muslims. This is because as diffused as the translations of the standard works of the Ṣāfiʿī school are the so-called "Legal Digests" which contain rules of local origin together with elements of *fiqh* in various combinations. There are, in Muslim southern Philippines, examples of two quite different textual traditions in Legal Digests.[60] They are the Maguindanao *Luwaran* and the Sulu Codes.

The *Luwaran*

The term *Luwaran*, which Mindanao Muslims apply to their code of law, means "selections" or "selected." Accordingly, they

---

[59] See M. B. Hooker, *Islam in Southeast Asia*, 9. For a list of the Islamic law books commonly used in Malaysia, Indonesia and the Philippines, see M. B. Hooker, *Islamic Law in Southeast Asia*, 279 f.

[60] For a discussion of the various Legal Digests in different parts of the Malay archipelago, see M. B. Hooker, *Islamic Law in Southeast Asia*, 8-30.

were selections from Arabic texts and paraphrased or translated into the local dialect for the guidance of those who did not understand Arabic. The chief texts cited from which passages can be more or less identified in the *Luwaran*[61] are the *Mirʾat al-Ṭullab* and the *Fatḥ al-Qarib,* among others. The *Luwaran* is undated but is known to have existed in the 19th century (1886), but there is some doubt as to whether the law text tradition predates the middle of the 18th century.[62] Written in Arabic script, the *Luwaran* begins with a preamble which invokes God's blessing upon Muhammad and all his followers, followed by eighty-five articles plus an appendix of twenty more articles dealing with wounds - all these are in the Maguindanao language. Each article ends with the phrase *Allahu Aʿlam* and is annotated in the margin with a quotation in the Arabic language supposedly authorizing or confirming the main textual provision. On the whole, the *Luwaran* deals with the following subjects: slavery, oath, debt and loan, compensation and blood money, inheritance, miscellaneous offenses, miscellaneous property transactions, and dower, marriage and divorce. Is the *Luwaran* an "Islamic text"? Scholars have studied this Legal Digest vis-a-vis especially the standard law books of the Šāfiʿī school. In his comparative study of the various Southeast Asian Legal Digests, Hooker has pointed out that, as regards the *Luwaran,*

> it lacks the direct treatment of religion characteristic of the Malay and other Indonesian texts. There is no discussion as to the nature and source of law, nor of legal concepts such as sovereignty, fault, etc. Its provisions are rudimentary except on the subject of slaves and oaths. Most important, there is no evidence of a textual continuity. The function of

---

[61] An English translation of the original is found in Najeeb Saleeby, "Studies in Moro History, Law and Religion" in *Notre Dame Journal,* vol. 6, no. 1 (April 1975) 40-63.

[62] Ibid., 40.

> the *Luwaran* must be looked for outside its provisions; the isolated reference to a 'judge' in the text combined with its emphasis upon (a) a society divided on class lines, and (b) the emphasis upon oath-taking and compensation for wounding, take us to Maguindanao political structure. It is only within the ambit of this structure that we can make sense of the *Luwaran.* [63]

The Arab-American scholar Saleeby, who did research in his extensive travels in the Muslim regions in the southern Philippines in the late 19th and early 20th century, and who was the first non-Muslim to analyze the *Luwaran,* to translate it into English and consequently to have it published, observed that, as regards the making of the *Luwaran,*

> the Mindanao judges selected such laws as in their judgment suited the conditions and the requirements of order in Mindanao. They used the Arabic texts as a basis, but constructed their articles in a concrete form, embodying genuine examples and incidents of common occurrence in Mindanao. In some places they modified the Arabic so much as to make it agree with the prevailing local customs. In a few instances they made new articles which do not exist in Arabic but which conform to the local customs and practices. The authority of the *Luwaran* is universally accepted in Mindanao and is held sacred next to that of the Qurʾān.[64]

The Sulu Codes

Two Sulu Codes (in Malay/Sulu language, written in Arabic script) were translated into English and published by Saleeby in 1905. The first, known as the 'Principal Sulu Code,' was promul-

---

[63] M. B. Hooker, *Islamic Law in Southeast Asia*, 23.

[64] N. M. Saleeby, "Studies in Moro History, Law and Religion" in *Notre Dame Journal*, vol. 6, no. 1 (April 1975) 41.

gated in A.D. 1877, under the auspices of Sultan Jamāl ul-Aʿlam who ruled from A.D. 1862 until his death in April, 1881. Based on the introduction to the Principal Sulu Code, Legal codes in Sulu[65] changed frequently with the change of rulers, although the variation in content was slight and the structure remained the same. The Principal Sulu Code is said to differ considerably from the former one (used by Jamāl ul-Aʿlam's father and predecessor - Sultan Pulalun - who ruled from 1842 to 1862) "which was more in conformity with the letter of the Qurʾān, much more severe in its sentences; hence the change was welcomed."[66] Accordingly, the present Code was also used by Jamāl ul-Aʿlam's successor, Sultan Harun ar-Rashid (from 1886 until his abdication in 1894). The Code begins with a preamble which invokes God's blessing and announces that "it is concurred in by all, and is promulgated with the consent of all the *datus* [the local rulers], the *panglimas* [personal representatives of the Sultan], and subordinate officers of state." In other words it derives its authority from the consensus of the leaders. This is followed by seven long articles which are strictly practical in nature and deal with regulations for fines for such offenses as abduction, marriage by abduction, theft, adultery, killing and use of force without permission of the local official. The penalty for such offenses was a fine expressed as so many rolls or pieces *(gajahilaw)* of calico *(siddip)* or its value.[67] The penalties are calculated depending upon the status of the offended party, i.e., the higher the status, the higher the fine. The Code also sets out the ranking of offices and status which are, in descending order: Sultan, datus with official title, datus without official title, *panglima* (personal representative of the sultan) and

[65] See N. M. Saleeby, Studies in Moro History, Law and Religion (Manila: Bureau of Public Printing, 1905) 89-100, for a copy of the original texts as well as their English translations.

[66] Ibid., 89.

[67] Ibid., 90.

pandita (learned man), and children of subordinate rulers or chiefs. If the offender was a slave, the master also became involved and was required to swear on the Qurʾān as to his knowledge and consent in the affair. The Code ends with the following exhortation which shows the dynamics involved in the carrying out of the Law:

> All the *tuku-pipul* [all officers subordinate to *panglima*][68] are hereby requested to exercise all care in administering justice to all who come to them for judgment and decision. They should all adhere to the seven articles of the Muhammadan law and be deliberate in their just application.
>
> In case any complainant appeals to one of you from the decision of another authority, do not accept the appellant's statement and render your decision unless you inquire well about the case from the previous authority who judged it. In case you find the decision of that authority wrong do not be ready and quick to blame him and criticize him, but try to act in conformity and union. In case you find his decision right, notwithstanding the appellant's complaints, bring both the appellant and the appellee to the *panglima*. If the *panglima* cannot render a solution, he should bring them to the sultan, together with the authority from whose decision the appeal was made and the authority to whom the appeal was made.
>
> If the governor or the authority to whom they appeal does not investigate or inquire about the case from the governor from whom they have appealed, his decision shall be null

---

[68] The island of Sulu used to be divided into five *(lima)* main divisions for administrative purposes, each of which used to have one *panglima* entrusted with its rule. All officers subordinate to the *panglima* are called *tuku-pipul*. *Tuku* literally means the small and large poles or pillars that support the house; *pipul* is "people" in English. *Tuku-pipul* or 'support of the people' is the term used to refer to all officers lower in rank than the *panglima*.

and void.

> Any person who exercises the right to judge without authority from the sultan shall be fined one male slave.
>
> All governors and their subjects ought to abide by and aid in carrying out all the articles of this code. Any person who does not fulfill this duty will have all the curses and the calamities of this world and the world to come that befall the man who swears falsely by the thirty parts of the Qurʾān.[69]

On the other hand, the New Sulu Code[70] was compiled in 1902 by Hajji Būtu Abdul Bāqi, the prime minister or adviser of the Sultan Jamāl ul-Kirām II.[71] The 'New Sulu Code' was issued in the latter part of 1902, but never came into force, because of strong objections on the part of many datus and chiefs.

> This code greatly increases the fines exacted from the people, creates a treasury under the control of Hajji Būtu, and entitles the sultan to a share of the fines collected by the various datus and chiefs. The chiefs and the people look upon it as another form of unjust taxation. The opposition to its adoption is so strong and so bitter that nothing except the force of arms can enforce its use. This is beyond the power of the present sultan.[72]

The New Code is a rearrangement of the Principal Law Code that we have just described, with some changes and modifications, such as: offences are more elaborately set out, trade is

---

[69] N. M. Saleeby, Studies in Moro History, Law and Religion (Manila: Bureau of Public Printing, 1905) 93-94.

[70] Ibid., 94-100.

[71] Sultan Jamāl ul-Kirām II was the last Sultan of Sulu, reigning from 1884 until his death in 1936.

[72] N. M. Saleeby, op. cit., 94.

forbidden without the consent of higher officials, fines are expressed in money terms (pesos and dollars). Like the Principal Sulu Code, it exhorts officers to exercise all care and justice in their judgments and to adhere with all devotion to the seven articles of Muhammadan law. (I have not found anywhere a listing of these seven articles). Like the Principal Sulu Code, it also ends with a reminder that those who do not abide by the provisions of the Code will experience the same curse and calamities that befall a man who swears falsely by the thirty parts of the Qur'ān.

We now attempt an assessment of the law texts outlined above. To begin with, as far as the texts are concerned, it is apparent that they reflect Islam to only a minimal degree; however, they do mirror a Muslim social and political organization. The important features they show include the offices of Ruler (Sultan) and subordinate officers and their respective rights and duties, the classification of the people into upper and lower classes, the importance of slavery as an expression of political power, etc. In fact, the texts are documents concerned with the distribution and regulation of power. This is basic to both the *Luwaran* and the Sulu Codes.

A major feature of the Sulu Codes is the pattern of authority which was hierarchical in structure with the Sultan at the top and a variable number of subordinate officers. We have seen in our analysis of the *tarsilas* that the most important proof of legitimacy to succeed to the office of Sultan was descent in a 'royal *datu*' line, which should be ultimately traceable to the prophet of Islam or to his family. The Sultan was seen as the religious leader of the community and thus as its Imām, and thus assimilates a claim to both temporal and spiritual powers. Consequently, many Sulu Sultans claimed the title *Amir-ul-Muslimin*.[73] On the other hand, the

---

[73] C. E. Majul, "Succession in the Old Sulu Sultanate" in *The Muslim Filipinos*, ed. Gowing and McAmis (Manila: Solidaridad Publishing House, 1974) 62.

structure of subordinate officers owes little to direct Islamic influence. It is this aspect of the hierarchical structure which is a matter of local adoption as are the functions attached to each.[74]

At any rate, the system of authority was thus Muslim in the sense that the Sulu Sultan drew his authority from the prophet of Islam and/or by assuming the title *Amir-ul-Muslimin*, from the Turkish model, traditionally the caliph of Islam. In the words of Majul,

> The first rule of legitimacy is interesting and is not devoid of certain aspects of Islamic jurisprudence. Since the Sultan was also the religious head of the realm and therefore the *imām* of the community, it was desirable that he be a descendant of the Prophet Muhammad or his family in accordance with an Islamic tradition that the *imām* of the Muslim community should belong to the family of the Quraysh. With the expansion of *dar-ul-Islam* and then the gradual weakening of the universal caliphate, the rise of many sultanates witnessed the claim of the sultan to both temporal and spiritual powers. The assumption of various Sulu sultans of the title *Amir-ul-muslimin* only meant that they had considered themselves the 'caliphs' in their realm.[75]

The Sulu Codes are silent on many matters of substantive law, like the system of inheritance or marriage (except for the mention of fine for marriage by abduction). On the whole, the Sulu Codes consist of *adat* and locally-made regulations "Islamized" by the authority of the Sultan and the mention "at the last moment" of the Qur'ān (swearing by the thirty parts of the Qur'ān) and

---

[74] "The subordinate office system is on the pattern of other Southeast Asian lands and the various titles themselves are found in various permutations in Borneo, and the Indonesian and Malay lands." M. B. Hooker, *Islamic Law in Southeast Asia*, 26.

[75] C. E. Majul, op. cit., 62.

Muhammadan Law (seven articles of Muhammadan law). In both Codes these are mentioned only once. In no other place in either Code are they mentioned again or elaborated on or explained. Based on what we have learned thus far of Islam as it was received in the Philippines, their function may be seen as an assurance that there is nothing in the Code that is offensive to Islam. The Code did not exist in a vacuum; it existed together with the Qurʾān which was under the care of the *Imām* and *Qāḍī*. The Code and the Qurʾān, the Sultan and the *qāḍī*, and their accompanying officials constituted the Islamizing dynamism in the Sulu sultanate.

If the Sulu Codes existed together with the Qurʾān, the Luwaran existed together with selected passages from Arabic law books which find their *raison d'être* only in an Islamic context. It can be said to be an "Islamic code" in this sense. It would be taking things a little far to say that it is based explicitly on the Qurʾān.[76] The accompanying quotations, and not so much the text, are taken from Šāfiʿī material representing several centuries of jurisprudential scholarship. The two Codes are basically the same in their being reflections of the realities of the Muslim Philippine social system. Both texts deal with slavery and class distinctions - the main structural principles of Philippine Muslim society - with the differences being a function of local conditions or

---

[76] Mednick points out that "Islam is exceedingly syncretistic, and elsewhere in Malaysia has had little difficulty in accommodating Hindu, Buddhist, and pagan elements. Since each present Muslim group had its own particular belief system before conversion, it must be assumed that the pattern of combination with Islam differed from group to group. In some cases, such as the Maranao and Maguindanao, the differences may be small both because the earlier belief systems were closely related and because pressures toward orthodoxy and standardization were strong." See M. Mednick, "Some Problems of Moro History and Political Organization" in *The Muslim Filipinos*, ed. Peter G. Gowing and Robert D. McAmis (Manila: Solidaridad Publishing House, 1974) 15-16.

customs *(adat)*.[77]

Thus, looking now at the above-outlined data, we see that the scholastic texts not only co-existed with the Legal Digests but could also be partly incorporated into them. This is to be explained by the fact that the heritage of *fiqh* as a form of Islamic transmission in Southeast Asia in general and in Muslim Philippines in particular is derived from the Šāfiᶜī school. The *Luwaran* and Sulu Codes are examples of local accommodation of the major legacies of the Šāfiᶜī school, namely: the combination of tradition and the consensus of the community together with the broad recourse to reasoning by analogy. Given the cultural realities of South-East Asia, the Islam posited in these textbooks [i.e., of the Šāfiᶜī school] was not, apart from a few obvious provisions (e.g., in family law), a set of prescriptions. It was instead a mode or method for defining the search for the essence of religion. The Sulu Codes and the *Luwaran* are expressions of the ingenuity of the Philippine Muslims in translating inherited modes into their culture.

1.4 Conclusions

1.4.1 A Philippine Dimension for Islam

The data that we have outlined above show that Islam as it came to be practised among Filipino Muslims consisted in a mingling or accommodation between local practices/customs and those derived from the Middle East or other Muslim lands west of the Southeast Asian archipelago. This is corroborated by the reports of such scholars as Majul, Bruno and Kiefer as regards the process involved in the adoption of Islam by Sulu Sultans.

---

77 The relationship between *adat* and Islam in Muslim Southeast Asia is thoroughly discussed by Roy F. Ellen in his essay "Social Theory, Ethnography and the Understanding of Practical Islam in Southeast Asia" in *Islam in Southeast Asia*, ed. M. B. Hooker (Leiden: E. J. Brill, 1983) 64-70.

They have been summarized by Gowing as follows:

> In his capacity as head of the Islamic religion in Sulu, the Sultan was advised by a *kali (qādī)*, who was assumed to be one of the most learned men in the realm, well versed in the Qur'ān and the *Šarī'a*, and presumably acquainted with the work of the Muslim legist Šāfi'ī. In formulating laws for his subjects, the Sultan was obliged to consult his *kali* whose job it was to see that nothing offensive to Islam was contained in those laws [emphasis mine]. The *kali* himself consulted the *panditas ('ulamā')*. The *panditas* ministered to the religious and spiritual needs of the Muslim community, serving as jurisconsults to the *datus*, teaching the rudiments of Islamic doctrine and ritual to the children, and often acting as *imām* in the local mosques. The *kali* was the chief *pandita* of the sultanate and theoretically all *panditas* performing official functions recognized his preeminence.[78]

It should be noted, however, that this dynamic in the "becoming" of Islam was not a hard and fast one in Muslim Philippines. Stewart has pointed out that especially among the Maguindanao where the organization was not as rigidly centralized as that of Sulu, groups of *panditas* would otherwise

---

[78] P. Gowing, *Muslim Filipinos - Heritage and Horizon*, 51-52; Emphasis added. Cf. C. A. Majul, *Political and Historical Notes on the Old Sulu Sultanate*, Paper No. 30, International Conference on Asian History, University of Hongkong, 1964 (16 mimeographed pages), p. 4; J. Bruno, *The Social World of the Tausug: A Study in Culture and Education* (Manila: Centro Escolar University Research and Development Center, 1973) 140-142; and T. Kiefer, *The Tausug: Violence and Law in a Philippine Muslim Society* (New York: Holt, Rinehart and Winton, 1972) 106-111. The sultanates among the Maguindanao were organized along similar lines to that of Sulu, though in a somewhat less centralized manner, while simpler still was the manner in which the Maranao sultanates were organized.

prefer to be what Geertz[79] has termed "scripturalist," i.e., those who interpret orthodoxy in terms of paying close attention to prescriptive detail handed down by scholasticism and avoiding practices held as inconsistent with received doctrine.[80] However, as shown by the data outlined above and as we will further point out below, on the whole, the local concept of what was orthodox was determined by identification with local rule/ruler.

The presence of "Islamic" and local practices/beliefs in Islam as it came to be embraced by Muslim Filipinos, has been explained by various scholars in a number of ways. Those who see Islam as culturally alien to Philippine or Southeast Asian societies consider it as but an overlay on local tradition - a "thin veneer." Others try to reconcile the two aspects by the cultural-anthropological concept of "Little and Great" complimentary traditions.[81] Mednick[82] prefers to see the synthesis of "Islamic" and non-Islamic beliefs as symbolic of indigenous resilience to foreign influences without which the natives would be unable to comprehend reality. Another view, represented by Arlo Nimmo, explains the dichotomy in terms of the 'ideal," (i.e., orthodox Islam) and its

---

79 Cf. C. Geertz, *Islam Observed* (Chicago and London: The University of Chicago Press, 1975) 62.

80 J. C. Stewart, "Maguindanao" in *Muslim Peoples: A World Ethnographic Survey*, ed. R. V. Weekes (Westport, Connecticut: Greenwood Press, 1984) 465.

81 Cf. P. G. Gowing, *Muslim Filipinos*, 59-60 and D. Rothermond, (ed) *Islam in Southern Asia* (Wiesbaden: Franz Steiner Verlag, 1975) 6. Bauzon has pointed out that this classification is apparently adapted from Robert Redfield's *Peasant Society and Culture* (Chicago: University of Chicago Press, 1956), although no reference is made in either of the two above-cited books. K. Bauzon, *Liberalism and the Quest for Islamic Identity in the Philippines* (Manila: Ateneo de Manila University Press, 1990) 175, note 12.

82 M. Mednick, *Encapment of the Lake: The Social Organization of a Muslim Philippine (Moro) People* (Chicago: University of Chicago, 1965) 12.

"actual" approximation.[83] Proponents of this explanation assert that its value lies in its ability to explain the rather undisruptive transition from the preferred to the actual behavior in view of the acceptance by the community which, in effect, sanctions and legitimizes such a shift.

However these or other explanations may be regarded, the fact remains that traditional "Islamic" and local elements continue to be an integral part of Muslim Filipino practice; and to dichotomize these two elements may be missing the real picture. In many cases, these two elements have been reassembled into new categories which cut across simple distinctions between what is local and what is introduced. In addition to the data outlined above, another example is the fact that

> ... the Tausug [of Sulu] distinguish between *sara kuraan* (immutable qurʾānic doctrine on religious practice), *sara agama* (rules relating to a variety of offenses, theoretically changeable) and *sara adat* (customary practices). No one category is purely Islamic or local.[84]

Majul[85] has argued that Philippine Islam was never syncretic, but his explanation begs the question. The Muslim Filipinos, he explains, only misunderstood as part of Islam certain pre-Islamic Filipino beliefs and customs that came to be associated with the former. Our position is that Islam as adopted in Philippine Muslim

---

[83] H. Arlo Nimmo, *The Sea People of Sulu: A Study of Social Change in the Philippines* (San Francisco: Chandler Publishing Co., 1972) 91-96.

[84] R. F. Ellen, "Practical Islam in Southeast Asia" in *Islam in Southeast Asia*, ed. M. B. Hooker (Leiden: E. J. Brill, 1983) 68, note 75. Cf. also T. M. Kiefer, *The Tausug: Violence and Law in a Philippine Muslim Society* (New York: Holt, Rinehart and Winston, 1972) 88-90.

[85] C. A. Majul, "Islamic and Arab Influences in the South of the Philippines" in *Journal of Southeast Asian History* 7/2 (September 1966) 61-73.

societies may better not be dichotomized or seen as a "distortion" of "pure Islam." I prefer to emphasize here the ingenuity in the translation or interpretation of Islam into the local culture which thus represents a Philippine dimension for Islam. Finally, despite the coexistence of introduced and local elements in their laws and other practices, the local sultanates or Philippine "Muslim states" see their Islam as orthodox because of their basic adherence to and identification with the one *umma* of the Prophet of Islam, contained in the combination of indigenous and received ideas about rule and authority.

1.4.2 Identification with the ruler and the Belonging to the *Umma*

The relative facility with which Islam was accepted by Filipino Muslims points to the fact that many indigenous ideas were essentially compatible with Islam, foremost of which was the idea about rule and authority. Indigenous society was kinship-based, hierarchical, and essentially compatible with the prescriptions of Islam on matters of authority and obedience. As the data mentioned above shows, the winning-over of the local ruler means the winning-over of the whole empire or "state," i.e., what was an acceptable action or practice was the one identified with the ruler or kingship. Reinforcing and redefining this indigenous ideal of "divine ruler" was the legacy bequeathed by the medieval Islamic tradition originating in lands to the west of the Malay island world. One point of this was the ideology of authority, perhaps originally Persian, which expressed itself in an elaborate title system reinforcing and redefining indigenous conceptions of kingship. This is exemplified by the *tarsilas* which established a putative connection between the local sultan and Muslim heroes or rulers of the Middle East and ultimately with the prophet of Islam. It is not too far-fetched to say that this legacy is coupled with the Sufī or mystic idea of "Perfect Man" *(al-insān al-kāmil)*.[86] These legacies are intertwined with the indigenous idea of kingship and became the reference to things "Muslim" though not necessarily to definitions founded in Šarī'a. Thus the Sultan became the connecting link of the sultanate with the rest of the Muslim community *(umma)* of Muhammad. In the early period of Islamization, therefore, the *umma* concept was at work or was embodied in the ideology of ruler/rule: a true Muslim community or "state" was one in which the ruler was a descendant of the prophet of Islam; such a ruler therefore was the political and religious leader at the same time; consequently, the laws made to govern all the aspects of the life of the community were orthodox only if identified with the Sultan. The centrality of the *umma* concept, at work in this ideology of ruler/rule, also explains the fact that the "Legal Digests" could be the accepted law codes or "syncretic" practices could be the accepted norm, for what was most important was its identification with the Sultan or ruler, who was the reference to the wider or universal Muslim *umma*. The Muslims thus viewed themselves or their sultanate as one nation *(bangsa)* identified with the universal *Umma*. As we shall see, it

---

[86] Although this doctrine is not mentioned in the surviving Philippine Muslim manuscripts, it is very much present in neighboring Southeast Asian lands which exercised influence on Philippine Islam. Milner ("Islam and the Muslim State" in *Islam in Southeast Asia*, ed. M. B. Hooker (Leiden: E. J. Brill, 1983) 39-42), has pointed out indications of the influence of the "Perfect Man" ideal in Pasai and Malacca kingship. He, for instance, cites the findings of Professor Brakel ("State and Statecraft in 17th Century Aceh" in *Pre-Colonial State Systems in Southeast Asia*, ed. A. J. S. Reid et al. (Kuala Lumpur: Monographs of the Malaysian Branch of the Royal Asiatic Society VI, 56-66) which show that the Aceh Sultan Ala'u'din-Din was referred to in the sources as Sayyidī al-Mukammil. Milner contends, however, that fuller research is yet to be done to see the extent to which this Sufī ideal contributed to kingship elsewhere in Muslim Southeast Asia. Cf. A. C. Milner, op. cit., 42.

was in the later period of Islamization, marked by the influence of successive contacts with the Middle East, that the doctrines of the Šarīʿa took root as a "purificationary" development, which then removed the "Muslim" reference from ruler to *umma*; thus, also a shift from the concern to be governed by religious laws not offensive to the Šarīʿa, to a growing concern to adhere strictly to the Šarīʿa as the body of laws governing the *umma*. In other words, even before the term *umma* came to be used by Muslim Filipinos, the concept was already at work in the reinforced or redefined ideology of ruler/rule. It was not just a concept but was at the same time a living community and a geographical entity with defined boundaries, which was an Islamic transformation of the pre-Islamic socio-political institution called the confederation of *barangays* in southern Philippines.

The principality or *barangay* was relatively autonomous. When the sultanate was established, first in Sulu and later in Mindanao, the numerous principalities comprising the sultanate retained their own political and social structures, but which were Islamized. The supreme *datu* or overlord of the pre-Islamic confederation was now called the Sultan. If in the pre-Islamic confederation, a *datu* could become the supreme *datu* by showing exceptional wisdom or strength (i.e., by being the *datu* of the largest *barangay*), now the first rule was a *datu*'s being able to show that he descended from Muhammad. In this way, he would be recognized as God's representative and "the one who replaced the prophet" *(halip tul rasul)*. He was not a tyrant or dictator but he ruled with an assembly of leaders loosely composed of the *datus* belonging to the sultanate along with the lawyers and religious leaders. The unifying factor of the various *barangays* that constituted the sultanate was no longer just the need for mutual protection against common enemies, but their "Muslimness" or being "brothers" within the *umma*. As a confederation of various barangays with defined geographical boundaries, the sultanate may not have approximated the size of other large confederations of *barangays* like the ones in Sugbu

(Cebu) or Maynila (Manila). However, while the influence, relations and connections of the other confederations did not go beyond the confines of the confederation itself, the sultanate saw itself as an integral part of the world-encompassing Islamic *umma*. The Philippine and Southeast Asian sultanates saw themselves as expressions in the region of the worldwide *umma*. They considered themselves as "brothers in the faith" and thus counted on one another's support in time of need. The *umma* concept that found actualization in the Philippines and in Southeast Asia in general, was of course the *umma* as it was understood and actualized especially as a socio-politial reality in the lands of the Muslims who brought it to the Southeast Asian region.

The relative facility with which Islam came to be accepted by Filipino Muslims may be explained in part also by the non-dualistic world view of the Filipinos and, for that matter, of most Asians. For the Filipino, the ideal is harmony. "This spirit of harmony is similar to the Chinese *Yin-Yang* philosophy which recognizes the antinomy between the *Yin* and the *Yang* principles and yet tries to harmonize both."[87] Diversities and differences are seen not as oppositions to be oppressed but as complementary elements to be integrated. In practice, this holistic view finds its realization in an "attitude of tolerance and compassion, in a search for consensus, in attempts of persuasion rather than imposition, in the pursuit of peace and harmony."[88] Thus we may say, the manner of entrance of Islam in the Philippines, suited the indigenous Filipino mind's manner of reception.

---

87 Leonardo Mercado: *Elements of Filipino Philosophy* (Manila: Arnolus Press, 1974) 191, and *The Filipino Mind* (Manila: Divine Word Publications, 1994) 13f.

88 Fernando R. Capalla, "The Role of Religious Groups in Modern Pluralistic Societies - Ideals and Realities; Traditions of Harmony in Southeast Asia as a Basis for Christian-Muslim Dialogue" in *Notre Dame Journal* vol. XXIV (October 1994) 28.

2. The *Umma* in the Philippines: A Brief Survey

Strictly speaking, "Philippine" history began in the 16th century with the coming of the Spaniards to the Philippines, which resulted in their claiming of whole archipelago for the King of Spain, from whose name (Felipe II) *"Las Islas Filipinas"* as a designation for the islands was derived. By that time, among the southern Philippine Muslims, consciousness of being a nation *(umma)* belonging to a universal community *(umma)* was already evolving. While the other barangays with their traditional beliefs as well as the Muslim groups that had not yet developed into sultanates (i.e., in Manila and Batangas) were conquered and converted to Christianity, southern Philippine Muslims could not be conquered. It is in this sense that, on the whole, since the Spanish period up to the present, many Filipino Muslims see their relationship to the rest of the Philippines in terms of the *umma* vis-a-vis foreign rule or dominion.

In this section, therefore, we will briefly outline and analyze the different phases in the evolution of the *umma* in Philippine history.

2.1 The Spanish Period (late 16th - late 19th c.): Age of Faith: Cross vs. Crescent

As is well known, one of the curiosities of history is that it was the Spaniards who set the limit to the westward expansion of Islam with their defeat of the "Moors" at Granada in the late 15th century, and, less than seventy-five years later, it was also the Spaniards who managed to sail halfway around the globe and set the limits of Islam's eastward expansion with the former's arrival in the Philippines in the 16th century. In their three-and-a-third centuries of colonial rule the Spaniards were able to block the further spread of Islam from Borneo and the southern Philippines toward Luzon and the Visayan islands. From then on, Islam would be confined to the Sulu Archipelago, western Mindanao and the southernmost tip of present-day Palawan.

In addition to mercantilist and imperialist expansionism, the Spanish policy toward the Muslim Filipinos might best be understood as "an adjunct to the centuries-old crusade of European Christians against Muslims. More particularly, it was an importation. . . of the long centuries of Iberian warfare against the Moors,"[89] for which reason the Spaniards called the Filipino Muslims "Moros."[90] This attitude towards the Moros is reflected in the directions given by the Spanish governor to the commander of the first expedition against Sulu and Mindanao in 1578:

> You shall order them not to admit any more preachers of the doctrine of Mahoma, since it is evil and false, and that of the Christians alone is good. . . And you shall burn or destroy the house where that accursed doctrine has been

---

[89] The term "Moors" or "Moros" refers to the inhabitants of ancient Mauritania. It was the term used by the Spaniards to refer in general to the Muslim North African natives. "De uso en todas las épocas. . . En España *moro* se aplicó además a todos los mahometanos [sic], y de ahí pasó a significar 'gentil, pagano, no bautizado'; todavía es popular en la actualidad decir de un niño, cuando todavía no ha sido bautizado, que es *moro*, y así Berceo lo aplicaba ya a los romanos de la Antigüedad, en oposición a los judíos." Joan Corominas y José Pascual, *Diccionario Crítico Etimológico Castellano e Hispánico* (Madrid: Editorial Gredos, 1985)151.

[90] The Spanish and Christian Filipinos gave the term a pejorative connotation. In the 1950's, imbued with the postwar resurgence of Islam, many Muslims became sensitive to being called "Moros" and insisted on being called "Muslims" or "Muslim Filipinos." In the 1970s Muslim nationalists revived the term and have adopted it as a term of identity overriding the old group designations of "Tausug," "Maranao," "Maguindanao" and other cultural-linguistic groups - - the gallant; unconquered people. P. G. Gowing, *Muslim Filipinos- Heritage and Horizon*, viii-x.

preached, and you shall order that it be not rebuilt.[91]

In less than twenty years after their arrival in 1565, the Spaniards had established supremacy over the Filipino and Bornean Muslim forces in the Visayas, Mindoro and the Manila bay area. They had also dispatched the first of a series of military expeditions against the Moros in Mindanao and Sulu. Seeing the Spanish attempt at conquering and converting them as a threat not only to their physical survival but also and especially to their Islamic way of life, the disparate Moro principalities united and responded by declaring *jihād* against the Spaniards and their native collaborators. Thus for the next three hundred and twenty years, there existed - between the Spaniards together with the Christianized Filipinos on the one side and the Moros on the other - an almost continuous state of war which may be described as one between "the Cross and the Crescent." These wars served to strengthen the Moros' consciousness of the *umma*. This awareness evoked the unity and meaningful participation in the *jihād* not only of the Muslim sultanates in the southern Philippines but also of the greater Southeast Asian *umma*, with help coming from the Muslims of Ternate, Borneo and Makassar.[92] Mutual help among the Southeast Asian sultanates could not last long, however. Soon each had to grapple with their respective problems of western colonial presences. The western powers in the region by then had clear definitions of their respective colonial territories. The Mindanao and Sulu sultanates belonged to the group of islands that western colonizers had regarded as belonging to Spain. However, the Spaniards never really achieved effective sovereignty over the Moros despite a number of military suc-

---

91 Emma Blair and James Robertson, eds. *The Philippine Islands,* 1493-1898, vol. 4 (Cleveland, Ohio: A. H. Clark Company, 1903-09) 178.

92 For a full account, see, among others, C. A. Majul, *Muslims in the Philippines*, 107-248.

cesses. Their success may be seen in their having contained Islam in the southern islands and in establishing Christian missions in Moroland. The constant threat posed by the Spaniards marked by short term peace accords served to deepen the consciousness of the Muslims of their being a separate people or nation, an *umma*. At the same time, sustained by the liberal-Christian influences from Europe, the Christianized natives were developing a separate nationhood within the colonial framework. A contributing factor to the psychological, cultural and political divisions between the Christianized natives and the "Islamized" ones was the fact that when the Spaniards began to regard the inhabitants of the Philippines as Filipinos, the reference was to the Christian ones while the Muslim ones continued to be referred to as Moros.[93] In short, these wars strengthened the Muslim Filipino consciousness of being an *umma* as well as "helped to define [the

---

[93] Ibid.*"Indio"* was the original term used by the Spaniards to refer to the native inhabitants of the Philippine Islands. Later it came to refer only to the non-Muslim ones as the Muslims came to be referred to as Moros. On the other hand, the term *Filipino* was originally used to refer exclusively to full-blooded Spaniards born in the islands. As in Latin America, they were also generally known as *creoles*. Later the term included the *mestizos* - those born of Spanish-Indio parents. Much later, i.e., in the 19th century, when educational reforms allowed sons of wealthy Christian natives to enter schools run by Spanish friars, many *Indios* became highly educated and could even leave for Spain for further studies; among them was Jose Rizal, the Philippines' national hero. Exposed to liberal ideas current in Europe, these *indio* students began to conceive of themselves also as *Filipino*. Together with some Filipino expatriates, they formed a movement called the *La Liga Filipina* to press for reforms in the affairs of government back in the colony. With this common goal, the term cut across racial barriers between Spaniards, *creoles* and *indios* and gained prominence as a liberating concept; and when more radical elements back home founded a secret society, *Katipunan*, with a program of separation and independence from Spain, the term became a symbol of national identity.

Muslim Filipinos'] attitudes and relations to all non-Muslim foreigners as well as to non-Muslim Filipinos."[94]

2.2 The American Period (1899 - 1946): Age of Politics vs. Age of Faith

The Spanish-American War of 1898 resulted in Spain's cession of the Philippines to the United States. Resistance to Spanish rule did not prevent the Muslim areas from being included in the cession. The basic American policy in the Philippines was laid down by President McKinley who declared to the US Congress that "the Philippines are not ours to exploit, but to develop, to civilize, to educate, to train in the science of self-government,"[95] i.e., to transform the Philippines into a modern, democratic and eventually independent nation. In many ways, the Americans showed religious tolerance and made some attempt to accommodate Muslim Filipino customs and Islamic law.[96] The Moros, however, were no more ready to acknowledge American rule than they had been to acknowledge Spanish rule. They offered armed resistance to which the Americans responded with military operations some of which resulted in outright massacre.

---

[94] C. A. Majul, "The Muslims in the Philippines: An Historical Perspective" in Peter Gowing and Robert McAmis, eds., *The Muslim Filipinos* (Manila: Solidaridad Publishing House, 1974) 7.

[95] Quoted in, among others, the following: F. B. Harrison, *The Cornerstone of Philippine Independence* (New York: The Century Co., 1922) 36 and P. Gowing, *Mandate in Moroland: The American Government of Muslim Filipinos, 1899-1920* (Quezon City: New Day Publishers, 1983) 15f.

[96] "In their desire to raise the literacy level of the Moros, some American officers supported a few qurʾānic schools. C. A. Majul, op. cit., 314.

When Muslim armed resistance was finally crushed in 1913,[97] the Americans started the program of integrating the Muslims into the larger society. One of the means employed to promote integration was the encouragement of migration to Mindanao, a move which was seen by the Americans and the consequent Commonwealth administration as one which would not only ease overcrowding in the Visayas and the northern islands but would also serve the following ends: it would allow the natives of Mindanao to benefit from the example of the more industrious and technologically advanced rural immigrants; it would tie Mindanao more closely to Manila, and; economic development and Christian settlement among the Muslims would reduce the problem of Muslim dissidence. On the whole, however, the Americans could not solicit cooperation from the Moros despite the former's pursued "policy of attraction."[98]

The underlying reason for Moro resistance to the Americans is to be understood first and foremost in light of the concept of

---

[97] The attitude with which Gen. Leonard Wood dealt the Sultan of Sulu was typical of the American conquerors' towards the Moros during the militay pacification of Mindanao and Sulu: "I am going to be frank with you. At present, your rights as a nation are nothing. . .I believe we are here forever, unless some greater country comes and drives us away; we do not know any such country." General Leonard Wood to Sultan of Sulu, 1904, cited in P. Gowing, *Mandate in Moroland,* 107.

[98] For instance, under this policy, the American government spent substantially on roads, shools, hospitals and other services in Muslim areas; education became compulsory, scholarships were provided for Muslims to study in Manila and the USA, and Muslim participation in the emerging political system expanded, although, inevitably, in the gradual transfer of authority in the country from the Americans to qualified Filipinos as part of the preparation of the Philippines for eventual independence, many Christians dominated positions of authority in all parts of the country including the Moroland. Cf. P. Gowing, *Muslim Filipinos - Heritage and Horizon,* 37.

umma at work in the Filipino Muslim ideology of authority. The American policy of direct rule and attempts to incorporate the Muslims into the larger (Christian) society struck at the authority of the Moro *datu* or sultan. The other aspect of this is that under the American rule and the envisioned modern, independent Philippine state, the formal position of the Islamic religion would decline to the status of a mere religion among others and would no longer encompass the social and political aspects of life. Such a state would not be an Islamic state or a Philippine *umma* for it would not be embodying the ideology of "Islamic" rule embodied in the sultanate.

In view of the programmed eventual independence, many Moro leaders addressed numerous appeals to American authorities demanding, in effect, safeguards for their religion, institutions and the geographical boundaries of the Philippine *umma*. These appeals may be classified into two kinds. The first, and the ideal one, is an appeal for a separate independence for the Moros - an appeal for the preservation of the *umma* in its heretofore ideal Philippine form, i.e., the sultanate. The second one, which speaks of the alternative some Moros could accept should they emerge powerless to insist on the ideal one, is an appeal to the Americans to retain Moroland under US rule. While these appeals at bottom are understood in light of the *umma* concept, they nevertheless clearly manifest the colonial legacy of antipathy and distrust between Christian and Muslim Filipinos. Of these numerous appeals may be cited the one sent in 1924 to the US Congress by a group of Moro leaders claiming to represent nearly half-a-million Moros of Mindanao and Sulu. In 1926 the US Congress placed this appeal on record under "Declaration of Rights and Purposes." The appeal read in part,

> In the event that the United States grants independence to the Philippine Islands without provision for our retention under the American flag, it is our firm intention and resolve to declare ourselves an independent constitutional sultan-

ate to be known to the world as the Moro Nation.[99]

In response to the appeal of the Moros, in 1926 Congressman Robert Bacon[100] filed in the US Congress a Bill which sought to grant separate independence for the Moro country if the Filipinos of Luzon and Visayas were to be given independence. The US Congress did not pass the Bill. When in 1935 the Philippine Commonwealth was formed which was to be the last step towards independence, one hundred twenty Moro *datus* called their own "Congress" at Dansalan (present-day Marawi City) to demonstrate their opposition to the incorporation of Moroland as part of Philippine territory and sovereignty. They came out with a declaration which was sent to USA President Franklin Roosevelt in March 1935 which read in part:

> With regard to the forthcoming independence, we foresee what condition we and our children who shall come after us will be in. This condition will be characterized by unrest, suffering, and misery.... We would like then to pray that the American people should not release us until we are educated and become powerful because we are like a calf who, once abandoned by its mother would be devoured by a merciless lion. . . Once our religion is no more, our lives are no more.[101]

---

[99] Quoted in P. Gowing, *Muslim Filipinos - Heritage and Horizon*, 169.

[100] Robert Bacon, "The Moro Problem in the Philippine Islands," a speech in the US House of Representatives in *Congressional Record-House* (May 6, 1926) 8830-8835. Cited in Abdurasad Asani "The Bangsamoro People: A Nation in Travail" in *Journal Institute of Muslim Minority Affairs* 6/2 (1985) 301.

[101] Hadji Bogabong et al., *Letter to President Franklin D. Roosevelt*, March 18, 1935, Signed by 120 datus, 12 typed and written pages in English and Maranao (Arabic), including signature and thumbprints. Cited also in P. Gowing, *Muslim Filipinos - Heritage and Horizon*, 169-170.

On the other hand, pro "One Philippines" Moro leaders, led by Datu Facundo Mandi, also came out with a declaration which read in part:

> That in a clear and unequivocal way it may be made known that the Mohammedans [sic], like their brethren the Christian Filipinos, want the absolute, complete, and immediate independence of the Philippines and that they protest against any intent to divide and disintegrate them.[102]

Consequently, of the two lobbying groups of Muslim *datus*, those who pushed for a separate Moro nation did not succeed and thus the Moros found themselves part of the Commonwealth.[103] When the Japanese invaded the Philippines in 1941 and subsequently established their presence in Moroland, Moros and Christians fought side by side, together forming a united front under American leadership against the "yellow peril." Many Muslims joined the USAFFE (US Armed Forces in the Far East) and other anti-Japanese organizations until the enemy was ousted in 1945. After the war, the Muslims eventually became part of the Philippine Republic that was proclaimed on July 4, 1946. A contemporary Muslim scholar reads the events as follows:

> First America and then the Philippines usurped Moro sovereignty. When the Japanese came, they merely interrupted developments and muted Moro protests. The Moros fought "side by side" with the Filipinos and as

---

[102] *Proceedings of the First Independence Congress* (Manila: Sugar News Press, 1930) 281, as quoted in P. Gowing, *Muslim Filipinos - Heritage and Horizon*, 172. Among these pro "One Philippines" leaders were Hadji Butu and Hadji Gulamu Rasul of Sulu, Datu Facundo Mandi of Zamboanga and Sultan Alaoya Alonto of Ramain in Lanao. Ibid., 172.

[103] See C. A. Majul, *The Contemporary Muslim Movement in the Philippines* (Berkeley: Mizan Press, 1985) 25.

"friends" of the Americans not so much due to the myth that the Moros had become "Filipinos" but rather because Japan was one more foreign invader. If the Filipinos exhibited exemplary courage in defense of the Philippines against the Japanese, it cannot be said less of the Moros with respect to Moro country. Finally, Japan was defeated. Amid the war debris, the Philippine republic was proclaimed on July 4, 1946, effectively putting Moroland under Philippine colonial rule.[104]

2.3 From 1946 up to the Present: *Umma* vis-a-vis Philippine Nation State

By way of introduction, it may be noted that national identity (nationalism) and independence were two interrelated worldwide issues which dominated the period between the two world wars. However, it is ironical that while on the one hand nationalism was a reaction to Western imperialism, to European colonial rule, on the other hand it was also the product of a century of Westernizing reform. As many of those who led nationalist and independence movements owed their training to the West, they were influenced especially by modern Western political values and institutions such as democracy, constitutional government, parliamentary rule, individual rights, and nationalism. Consequently, the modern "nation states" that came about would be also Western or Europe-derived and, in effect, represent the notion of national communities based not upon religion but upon common language, territory, ethnic ties, and history. Independent Philippines is one such a modern nation state. The Western notion of "modern nation state" is thus in contrast to the traditional Islamic ideal in which political loyalty and solidarity rest in a transnational Islamic community (*umma*) based upon common religion. In an Islamic

---

[104] A. Asani, "The Bangsamoro People: A Nation in Travail," in *Journal Institute of Muslim Minority Affairs* 6/2 (1985) 303. Emphasis added.

perspective, therefore, the independent Philippine state was simply a successor to the colonial rules of Spain and the USA. In order to understand better the evolution of the Philippine *umma* since the declaration of Philippine independence until the present, we will treat this section under the following facets of the *umma* in the Philippines of this period: the decline of the Philippine *umma* as expressed by the sultanates; the resurgence of Islam and a growing *umma* consciousness; the struggle for the liberation of Moroland; the various perspectives of the *umma* vis-a-vis the Philippine nation state.

2.3.1 Decline of the *Umma* (Sultanate)

The Philippine Republic with its democratic form of government which aimed at the progress, development and the fulfillment of national aspirations, gave rise to two interrelated realities which together brought about the decline of the political institution and geographical entity of the sultanate as embodying the *umma*. The first of these was the influx of Christian settlers and multinational corporations in Moroland. While this was encouraged under the American regime as well as the Commonwealth government, it was accelerated after the birth of the Republic as part of the process of national integration. Very soon the Christians became a majority in many traditional Muslim areas. Consequently, political and business control in these areas went mostly to non-Moros. Having lost their temporal power, sultans and datus sought to retain their positions of influence and privilege by participating within the established framework, in the process many of them came into conflict with each other, resulting in the weaker ones being dispossessed of their territories. But the *coup de grace* in the decline of the *umma* was the subversion of the Filipino Muslim traditional leadership.

> The sultans and the datus clothed by Allah - given privileges and rights, appropriated unto themselves the

community's patrimony, i.e., the ancestral lands. The Moro ruling elite accumulated big tracts of lands by applying for title or patent of ownership over the community's patrimony and/or through the practice of usury. The datus who became owners of the lands disposed of them either by selling the lands to Christians or by using them as their counterparts in their partnership with the Indio and/or foreign capitalists' economic ventures in Mindanao. The Moro masses and the other minority nationalities who were ignorant of the intricacies of the laws and the complicated processes of land registration soon discovered themselves landless and dispossessed of the community's patrimony which from time immemorial they believed to be Allah's gift to his people. The tragedy in this sad affair was that the Moro ruling elite's betrayal of the community's patrimony and trust were made possible by the Moro masses' religious subservience and loyalties to their datus.[105]

The second reality was the "patronage politics" which was a characteristic to be found practically all over the country. As Bauzon wrote:

> Contrary, however, to the ideals of a representative democracy in which leadership is conceived as a trust symbolizing the harmony of interests between the leaders and the led, the ensuing political process was a curious blend of elite and mass participation whose outcome was determined by the extent to which the former could satisfy the particularistic *desiderata* of the latter. Scholars have referred to this as clientilist politics or patronage. In any event, the system allowed the elite to retain its privileged position. But while it satisfied specific needs of the lower class, it did not significantly alter the fundamental structure that had caused their impoverished conditions.[106]

---

[105] E. Mercado, "The Moros of the Philippines" in *MIDEO*, no. 16 (1983) 285.

[106] K. Bauzon, *Liberation and the Quest for Islamic Identity*, 70.

The more influential of the Moro leaders joined political parties of the established system. The state of affairs of Philippine politics worked in their advantage especially as the Muslim masses had been conditioned by their traditional view of authority, i.e., political decisions were left to their *datus* or sultans who were the Muslim *umma* referents. Thus, through the support of their traditional followers, Muslim traditional leaders were elected mayors and congressmen and one or two even made it to the Senate. However, as de los Santos has noted: "The tragedy about the whole thing was that Muslim leaders used the electoral process not for democratic ends, nor for national ends, but to perpetuate themselves in power."[107] In effect, from 1946 to 1972, politics in the Muslim areas was limited to less than ten powerful sultans and *datus* who were also the major beneficiaries of that tragic state of affairs. As elected leaders in the Republic, they represented not principalities or sultanates but towns or provinces created by the Philippine government.

Since the birth of the Philippine Republic (in 1946) until the declaration of Martial Law (in 1972), pockets of Moro rebellion and secessionist agitations occurred sporadically. They would be diluted and neutralized by government political concessions to the leaders concerned. In 1951, Kamlon led an uprising in Sulu which lasted for four years. The exact cause of the uprising has not been established. Economic factors were frequently blamed although conflict among local leaders also contributed to it.[108] The uprising failed to bring results beyond benefits to Hadji Kamlon and his immediate kin.[109] In 1961, with the aim of drawing national

---

[107] J. Jalal-ud-din de los Santos, "Towards a Solution of the Moro Problem" in *Dansalan Quarterly*, 1/4 (July 1980) 221.

[108] A. Asani, "The Bangsamoro People: A Nation in Travail" in *Journal Institute of Muslim Minority Affairs* 6/2 (1985) 305.

[109] S. K. Tan, *Internationalization of the Bangsamoro Struggle* (Quezon City: UP Center for Integrative and Development Studies, 1993) 33.

attention to the economic problems of the people of Sulu, Ombra Amilbangsa, a Sulu Congressman and himself one of three claimants to the Sulu sultanate, filed a bill in Congress providing for the independence of Sulu. The bill did not become a law, neither did it lead to the implementation of economic programs for the people of Sulu.[110] On 1 May 1968, Datu Udtog Matalam, one of the most prominent and powerful *datus* of Cotabato, issued a manifesto launching the Muslim Independence Movement (MIM) aimed at an independent Islamic Republic of Sulu and Mindanao. It called on all Muslims to wage a *jihād* or holy war to change Moroland into *Darul Islam*. "Although it was probably no more than a desperate attempt to bring the plight of Muslims to national attention, the announcement divided the Muslim and Christian communities even as it raised the expectations of the Muslims."[111] Thus, to allay the fears of Christian settlers as well as to solicit the support of Christians who had no love for the government and who resented the presence of capitalists from the northern provinces, the *datu* changed the name of his movement to the Mindanao Independence Movement (MIM). However, he consequently succumbed to the persuasion of the government to reconsider, following some political concessions.[112] Such a state of affairs of the *umma* has been described by the Muslim scholar Dr. Israr Ahmad as,

---

[110] C. A. Majul, "The Moro Struggle in the Philippines" in *Third World Quarterly*, 10/2 (April 1988) 900-901.

[111] C. A. Majul, "Muslims and Christians in the Philippines" in *The Vatican, Islam and the Middle East*, 319-320.

[112] "The MIM succumbed to Marcos' policy of attraction. Marcos simply appointed the leader of the movement as Presidential Adviser on Muslim Affairs. Datu Matalam changed his original goal of an Islamic republic, saying that all he had in mind was a statehood under a federal system." From "The Moro People: Is Destiny Finally in their Hands?" in *Mindev*, a bi-annual journal of the Managing Alternatives Group, Inc. (1995) 18 and C. A. Majul, "The Moro Struggle in the Philippines," 903.

> . . . like flotsam and jetsam on the surface of the flood-water, having no value or substance. Our practice of Islam and fidelity and adherence to the Qurʾān has reached the state predicted by the Holy Prophet (peace be upon him), in the following *Hadiṯ*: "There will come a time when nothing will remain in Islam except its name, and nothing will remain of reverence to the Qurʾān except its style of writing."[113]

Nevertheless, since the birth of the Philippine Republic, the independence movement initiated by Datu Matalam was the first to be launched along religious lines as an organized Muslim platform as well as the first to have as scope the whole of Moroland. As it came just two months after the massacre of thirty young Muslim soldiers[114] on Corregidor island - an incident which generated strong feelings among Muslims and galvanized their fears that their lives were of little value in Philippine society - Matalam's independence movement was seen by the Moros as the only answer to their aspirations. Datu Matalam's MIM served as a curtain-raiser to the Moroland-wide movement for the reform of the *umma* in the Philippines which would be led by the new breed of *ʿulamāʾ* together with young Muslim students and professionals.

2.3.2 The Emergence of a New *Umma* Consciousness

The 1950s and the 1960s were marked by the emergence of a heightened consciousness of Islam and the *umma*, especially

---

113 I. Ahmad, *The Rise and Decline of the Muslim Umma* (London: Ta-Ha Publishers Ltd., 1992) 22.

114 They formed part of a group of about 180 Muslims secretly recruited by the military authorities in a secret operation called "Jabidah" for training in jungle warfare, sabotage and guerilla tactics. The recruits believed that the purpose of their mission was to infiltrate Sabah. They were executed following an alleged mutiny.

among Muslim students and young professionals.[115] This was partly associated with the post-World War II general resurgence of Islam throughout the Muslim world, notably in relation to nationalism in the Arab countries, Pakistan and Indonesia. One aspect of the new sense of freedom after the declaration of Philippine independence was that many Muslim Filipinos began to travel to other parts of the Islamic world in increasing numbers to study, to attend meetings of pan-Islamic organizations and to perform the *hajj* in Mecca. Contacts with other parts of the Muslim world drew the latter's support for activities geared at deepening Islamic consciousness in Muslim Philippines. Soon the number of mosques in Moroland increased, *madrasas* (Islamic schools) increased in number and Muslim teachers and visitors from Egypt, Arabia, Pakistan, Malaysia and Indonesia came to help deepen the Muslim Filipinos' consciousness of Islam. Many Filipino Muslim youths availed themselves of scholarships offered by the Nasser regime to study in Egypt, principally in the celebrated Al-Azhar University of Cairo. The effect of all this in Muslim Philippines would be a growing Islamic consciousness and a shift of the view of Muslim reference from "ruler" to *umma*. Many of these youths would become part of a generation of new and younger *ʿulamāʾ* with a deeper understanding of Islam and exposure to religious reformist tendencies in the Muslim world.

> Upon their return, they began to correct local practices that they believed contradicted religious law and, in their own way, tried to abolish superstitions that many of the older generation believed constituted part of the faith. Many of these Muslims educated abroad began to teach in *madrasas*; others worked for Muslim politicians and the traditional leaders. Thus, in effect, many of them would form

---

[115] For a fuller account, see, among others, N. Madale, "The Resurgence of Islam and Nationalism in the Philippines" in *Islam and Society in Southeast Asia* (Singapore: Institute of Southeast Asian Studies, 1986) 282-314.

the core of a new *ʿulamāʾ*.[116]

On the other hand, thousands of Muslims studied in Philippine universities, especially in Manila, mostly under scholarships provided by the government through the Commission on National Integration for the acceleration of the progress of Muslms politically, economically and socially. From this would rise the Muslim professional class - mostly lawyers - in the late 1950s and early 1960s. As college students and later as young professionals, many of these young Muslims would belong to ideological organizations or associations that aimed at promoting social and political reform in the country. A few associations of Muslim students were also formed, some of which were founded along ethnic lines, others under Islamic principles.[117] Some Muslims from this group would adopt an ideology which later analysts would describe as a synthesis of Islamic and Marxist elements for the liberation of the Moros from their tragic situation.[118]

Thus the young *ʿulamāʾ* along with the Muslim professionals and university students would together form the new voices of Filipino Muslim aspirations. It was with the coming of these new Muslim voices that the term *umma* began to be used explicitly in

---

[116] C. A. Majul, *Contemporary Muslim Movement*, 33-34. See also M. Mastura, *Muslim Filipino Experiece, A Collection of Essays* (Manila: Ministry Of Muslim Affairs, 1984) 129-141.

[117] For a fuller account with examples, see, among others, P. Gowing, *Muslim Filipinos - Heritage and Horizon*, 70 and C. A. Majul, "The Moro Struggle in the Philippines," 901.

[118] Cf. S. K. Tan, *Internationalization of the Bangsamoro Struggle*, 34f. Nur Misuari, who was to become the famous leader of the MNLF, was a student and later a professor of Political Science at the University of the Philippines and considered by some Muslim scholars as an excellent example of a Marxism influenced Muslim professional. Cf. also C. A. Majul, *The Contemporary Muslim Movement in the Philippines*, 86.

reference to the Muslim community. On the whole, this new breed of Muslims shared in the view that the traditional authority of the sultan or *datu* had lost its Islamic reference, i.e., as point of reference for the territorial, political and religious integrity of the *umma*, as well as in the view that the Muslim *umma* in the Philippines must be reformed.[119] As we will see, it is in the answer to the question "how" that they differ in many ways.

2.3.3 The Uniting Objective: Re-emergence of the *Umma*

The Jabidah Massacre on Corregidor island triggered protest rallies in Manila and promoted unity and cooperation among Manila and Cairo trained Muslim students and professionals that otherwise belonged to various organizations. Picking up guidance and inspiration from the given-up MIM manifesto of Datu Matalam, "they clandestinely planned an organized resistance."[120] Organizational meetings started in the later part of 1968. In 1969 groups of young Muslims went to Malaysia for military training. In 1970 an organization was formalized. Nur Misuari - a political science instructor from Sulu at the University of the Philippines - was named chairman of the organization that came to be called the Moro National Liberation Front (MNLF) with its military arm, the Bangsa Moro Army (BMA).

On 18 March 1974, the MNLF issued its manifesto on the

---

[119] Confer, among others, Rita Baltazar, "Islam and Secession" in *Solidarity* 6/9 (April 1971) 68-69; F. V. Magdalena, *Ethnicity, Identity and Conflict: The Case of the Philippine Moros* (Singapore: Institute of Southeast Asian Studies, 1996) 40f; C. A. Majul, *The Contemporry Muslim Movement*, 86-87; and N. Madale, op. cit., 287.

[120] Abhoud Syed Mansur Lingga, "Salamat Hashim's Concept of Bangsamoro State and Government" in *Dansalan Quarterly* 15/3-4 (July-December 1995) 50.

establishment of the Bangsamoro Republik. Speaking for "the oppressed Bangsamoro people, wishing to free ourselves from the terror, oppression and tyranny of Filipino colonialism which has caused us untold suffering and misery by criminally usurping our land, by threatening Islam through destruction of its places of worship and its Holy Book, and murdering our innocent brothers, sisters and old folks in a genocidal campaign of terrifying magnitude," the MNLF declared the establishment of the free and independent Bangsa Moro Republik in Mindanao, Basilan, Sulu and Palawan. The republic would have a democratic system of government that tolerated neither exploitation nor oppression, an ideology and a legal system based on Islam, an economic system based on foreign investment, and a foreign policy committed to world peace and the principle of national self-determination. Filipinos wishing to remain in the "Bangsa Moro national homeland" even after independence would be welcome and given equal rights and protection, including property rights and the free exercise of their political, cultural and religious rights - if they renounced their Filipino citizenship and wholeheartedly accepted Bangsa Moro citizenship. The Bangsamoro people are committed to the preservation and growth of Islamic culture without prejudice to the development and growth of other religious and indigenous cultures in the Bangsamoro homeland.[121]

For several years, the Bangsa Moro Army and the Philippine military were engaged in armed encounters. With the help of some Muslim countries and Islamic organizations, talks and negotiations between the two protagonists were held, until the MNLF chairman Nur Misuari and the Philippine government signed an agreement in Tripoli, Libya in 1976 providing for the creation of an autonomous Muslim government in the southern Philippines, comprising thirteen Muslim provinces. However, only a few months after the signing, the process leading to its implementation bogged down

---

[121] For the complete text, see, among others, C. A. Majul, *The Contemporary Muslim Movement*, 117-119.

due to lack of consensus within the mixed committee on the interpretation of the various agreements reached in principle in Tripoli, Libya. Both parties accused each other of bad faith and gross violations of the Tripoli agreement. In the aftermath of the failed peace talks, the MNLF's central committee itself fell apart when its members realized that they had differing views regarding the establishment or preservation of the *umma* in the Philippines.

Thus in 1977 several factions emerged: The original MNLF headed by Nur Misuari, the Moro Islamic Liberation Front (MILF) established by Misuari's erstwhile vice-chairman Hashim Salamat, the MNLF-Reformist Group (MNLF-RG) under Dimas Pundato, and the Bangsa Moro Liberation Organization (BMLO) headed, among others, by Sultan Rashid Lucman, Sultan Salipada Pendatun and Macapanton Abbas.

2.3.4 Various Perspectives of the *Umma* in the Philippines

All the varying Muslim organizations or movements are one in advocating a reform of the situation the *umma* in the Philippines is presently in. However, while they are all reformist organizations or movements, they represent different visions of the *umma* vis-a-vis the Philippine nation state. The main trends discernible in these are what I prefer to describe as fundamentalist and modernist. It is important to remember that these are two labels which can be applied to a wide variety of ideologies which may even overlap in their content, and thus can be easily misused or misunderstood if taken out of the particular contexts in which they are used.[122] Our use of these two labels in the context of the Philippine Muslim situation is based on the premise that fundamentalism hinges on a commitment to implement "eternal Islamic truths" on the contemporary situation while modernism hinges on a commitment

[122] A good discussion of fundamentalism (in Islam) and its ramifications may be found in Youssef Choueiri, *Islamic Fundamentalism* (London: Printer Publishers, 1990).

to fashion a historical Islam to suit modern needs.

2.3.4.1 The Fundamentalist View

Within the fundamentalist trend, two groups are discernible depending on the interpretation of the "Islamic truths:" the first group may be identified as revivalist fundamentalist while the second may be identified as radical fundamentalist.

The revivalist fundamentalist trend envisions an *umma* in which there is close adherence to the Šariʿa as the supreme law together with a revival of the structure of the *umma* before colonial rule, i. e., the era of the *datus* and sultans who provided leadership and inspiration for the *umma* in the face of external danger. This vision is most manifest among traditional leaders who have felt displaced in the modern Philippine state and have gained strength by a greater knowledge of the Šariʿa through contact with other Islamic countries. Revivalist fundamentalism, then, represents an effort to find solace in the texts of the Šariʿa and in the memory of a glorious past. Revivalist fundamentalism may be best represented by the BMLO, organized and headed by several *datus* and sultans of Mindanao. According to this organization, under the leadership of the *datus* the *umma* in the Philippines is to be realized as a Bangsa Moro state on the ancestral lands of the Moros, to be governed under an Islamic form of government, where the basis of all actions and policies is Islam and with the Šariʿa as the supreme law of the land. This vision is to be realized through "armed, parliamentary, or diplomatic methods depending on the dictates of the situation" and "cooperation with all forces sympathetic to the Moro struggle."[123] Other than its immediate followers, the BMLO has not really gained Moroland-wide following. "As many of its leaders have come from traditional leadership ranks, they have been easily coopted into the establishment.

---

[123] Supreme Executive Council, *The Bangsa Moro Liberation Organization*, a policy statement (n.p., May 1978) 22 pp.

Some maintain that the BMLO was a creation of the Marcos government intent on sowing division and dissension within Moro ranks."[124]

The radical fundamentalist, on the other hand, repudiates traditional Filipino Muslim leadership (the *datu* system), goes back to the "authentic roots" of Islam and envisions Moroland as a purely Islamic state, to be founded on the doctrine of the sovereignty of God. This view is represented by the MILF and expounded by its chairman and main spokesman, Hashim Salamat.[125] After breaking away from the Nur Misuari-led MNLF in the late seventies, Salamat and his companions decided to adopt the name MILF or Moro Islamic Liberation Front. "The word "national" was permanently dropped in favor of the word "Islamic" to emphasize the Islamic ideological line which Salamat originally

---

[124] K. Bauzon, *Liberalism and the Quest for Islamic Identity*, 82.

[125] Salamat Hashim was born on 7 July 1947, in Pagalungan, Maguindanao. He comes from a religious family. In 1958, after finishing his high school studies, he joined the pilgrimage to Mecca where he remained for one year to study at the *Madrasatu As-Sulatiyah ad-Diniyah*. In 1959 he proceeded to Cairo where he remained for ten years to do theological studies at the Al-Azhar University. There he earned his bachelor's degree in Theology in 1963 and his Master's degree in 1969. He was pursuing doctoral studies in the same university when he had to return to the Phiippines to organize the Moro revolutionary movement. As a student in Cairo, he was an active member of various Islamic organizations. In particular, he was president of the Philippine Muslim Student Association of Cairo and was secretary-general of the Organization of Asian Students in Cairo. Accordingly, while in Cairo he planned the Bangsamoro revolution together with a core group of Filipino Muslim students there. In the late 1960s, he "was the one responsible for covertly arranging the military training of the first batch of *cadres* (Batch of 90) that was to become the military core group of the Moro National Liberation Front." See A. M. Lingga, "Salamat Hashim's Concept of Bangsamoro State and Government" in *Dansalan Quarterly*, 15/3-4 (1995) 51-52.

and invariably espoused during the founding years of the revolution."[126] In an interview at his jungle base in 1994, Salamat referred to the founding of the MILF as follows:

> After the signing of the Tripoli Agreement in 1976 between the MNLF [i.e., by Misuari] and the Philippine government, our longtime intention to launch an Islamic *jihād* materialized. Some prominent Bangsamoro revolutionary leaders supported the idea of launching *jihād* instead of waging a secular struggle to achieve independence or autonomy. Thus, the Moro Islamic Liberation Front (MILF) emerged.[127]

While both the MNLF and MILF have the same ultimate goal of self-determination for the Bangsamoro people, events following the failed peace talks about the Tripoli agreement made Salamat realize that,

> The two Fronts differ in ideology and objectives. The MILF strictly follows the Islamic line and its objective in waging *jihad fi sabillillah* to make supreme the word of Allah and to establish an Islamic government. The MNLF is more inclined to secularism and its objective is to gain autonomy within the framework of the secular Philippine nation state, a puppet of the west, especially the USA.[128]

While the MNLF-Philippine government agreement signed in Tripoli provided for the creation of an autonomous region in Moroland, the MILF maintains that "any solution less than full

---

[126] Ibid., 50.

[127] "Leader of the Moro Islamic Front Outlines his Vision for the Future from his Jungle Base," An interview of Salamat Hashim published in *Crescent* (August 16-31, 1994) 1-3.

[128] Ibid., 1.

independence of the Bangsamoro Muslims will not work"[129] because only under an Islamic government can be realized the qurānic injunction of worship of Allah and the enjoining of right conduct and forbidding of indecency (cf. Qurān 3:104, 110).[130] Consequently, only under an Islamic government can the *umma* exist.

> *ibadah* [i.e., the act of serving God] is not limited to the performance of prayer, fasting, *hajj* or giving of *zaka*, although these are basic requirements of Islam, but includes the political affairs of man, his business transactions, social relations, education, culture and all other aspects of life. All these have to be pursued in accordance with the system provided by Allah. . . a Muslim may be able to perfectly perform his prayer, observe the rules of fasting and *hajj*, but if the political authority to whom he owes obedience and allegiance does not recognize the supremacy of the law of God, he has not perfected his worship to God.[131]

Salamat sees the Bangsamoro struggle as part of the worldwide struggle of the Muslim *umma* against foreign domination. However, he makes an important distinction. The struggle in many Muslim countries formed from the remnants of the collapse of the Ottoman caliphate is one against the colonial mentality of the Muslim rulers, i.e., "west-educated elites who know little about Islam."[132] The Bangsamoro struggle, on the other hand, has "no intention to crush or overthrow the Philippine government" but to reclaim the Bangsamoro homelands which were unjustly annexed

---

[129] Ibid., 2.

[130] Abhoud Syed Mansur Lingga, *The Political Thought of Salamat Hashim* (M. A. thesis, University of the Philippines, 1995) vii.

[131] A. M. Lingga, "Salamat Hashim's Concept....," 50. Emphasis added.

[132] "Leader of Moro. . . in *Crescent*, 1.

to the modern Philippine nation state. Thus, for Salamat and the MILF, the first objective is to win back the territorial integrity of the Bangsamoro. Salamat asserts that the natural progress of the development of the Islamic political institutions in Moroland in the 16th century was interrupted by the coming of the Western colonizers. The MILF wants to continue the development "in order to establish an authentic Islamic government in accordance with the Qurʾān and the *sunna*."[133] Accordingly, the model of government to be followed by the Bangsamoro is the government organized by the Prophet of Islam in Medina. Non-Muslims who would like to remain in the Bangsamoro state upon independence will be protected like the *dhimmis* during the time of Muhammad, and will "have the right to participate in government affairs, except to be elected as head of state and to occupy positions directly in charge of the promotion, preservation and defense of the Islamic ideology."[134] The way to win back the Bangsamoro homelands is through *jihād* which Salamat has described as follows:

> Genuine *jihād* is the might or military force of *ḥaqq* [truth, rightness] which will surely prevail when it becomes pure. Our *jihād* has been passing through this period of purification. The MILF is prepared and determined to pursue the struggle against colonial rule or *bāṭil* [falsehood] to achieve one of two objectives: victory or martyrdom.[135]

Asked to assess the ongoing Islamic revolutionary struggles not only in the Philippines but also in many other countries, Salamat says:

> I believe that the promise of Allah in the Qurʾān as well as that of the noble Prophet, upon whom be peace, that Islam

133 "Leader of Moro. . ." in *Crescent*, 1.

134 A. M. Lingga, "Salamat Hashim's Concept.....", 57.

135 "Leader of Moro..." in *Crescent*, 3.

> will certainly prevail over all other religions and ideologies and that the world will be ruled by Allah's System through a righteous Muslim *umma*, is now gradually taking place. The Qur'ān says: "It is He who has sent His messenger with Guidance and the religion of Truth, to cause it to prevail over all religions. . .(9:33)"[136]

Salamat's vision of the *umma* in the Philippines is indeed radical in the sense that it goes back to the original Islamic sources for its form and content. It does not intend to revive the pre-colonial period form of the *umma* (i.e., the sultanate) in the Philippines but to purify it according to the teachings of the Qur'ān and the *sunna*. It goes back to the roots, fundamentals of Islam because it sees any adoption of western ideas and institutions as un-Islamic, i.e., it sees any westernization of Islam as contrary to the Qur'ān and the *sunna*. Thus he considers as "either un-believers or ignorant of Islam" those Muslims who would fall under our classification of "modernist."[137] The views of Salamat are similar or indeed are patterned on or following the ideas that we have encountered in our study of Mawdūdī and Quṭb. Accordingly, Salamat himself cites Mawdūdī and Quṭb as the two contemporary Muslim thinkers who have made a lasting impression on him and that Quṭb's writings especially shaped his Islamic outlook and political beliefs which "inspired him to plant the seeds of Islamic revolution in the Bangsamoro homeland"[138] as part of the mission of the *umma* which is to rule the whole world and be the

---

[136] "Leader of Moro. . ." in *Crescent*, 3.

[137] In particular, Salamat blasted at those Muslims, among whom were a number of *ʿulamāʾ*, who openly said that "there is no more need for *jihād* in the Bangsamoro homeland because Muslim autonomy in the form of the Autonomous Region in Muslim Mindanao has already been established and is even guaranteed by the 1986 Philippine Constitution." Ibid.

[138] A. M. Lingga, "Salamat Hashim's Concept.....", 52.

leader of humankind.[139]

2.3.4.2 The Modernist Trend

While the fundamentalist trend, especially the radicalist one, advocates that only by secession or full independence from the modern nation state can Islam and the *umma* exist, the modernist bridges the gap between the two. If the fundamentalist limits himself to an inward look upon Islam in order to discover the ideal stance of the *umma* in today's world, the modernist applies the Islamic ideal to present-day conditions by learning from the example of the West.

In the context of the present Philippine situation, the modernists do not advocate secession from the Republic. They recognize the existence of certain West-oriented governmental institutions and the minority status of the Moros in a predominantly Christian country. Two types of modernist trends are discernible, depending on how they see their participation in the Philippine state. The first group considers working within the established system as not a hindrance to the authentic practice of their religion,[140] and thus to the existence of the *umma* in the

---

139 On the whole, Salamat sympathizes with any Moro group with different objectives as long as the final goal contributes to the realization of the Islamic ideal. Thus when asked his opinion regarding Muslims who support military operations against an independent small Moro group called Abbu Sayyaf that claims to be an Islamic group without a clear manifesto or ideology but is instead known for acts of terrorism, Salamat says that the Abbu Sayyaf group is nevertheless "a unit of the global Islamic movement. Whoever approves, explicitly or tacitly, of that brutal act [military operations] against a Muslim group is among the followers and supporters of *bāṭil*." "Leader of Moro..." in *Crescent*, 3.

140 See Alunan C. Glang, "Modernizing the Muslims" in *The Muslim Filipinos*, eds. P. G. Gowing and R. D. McAmis, 277-283.

Philippines. This group

> reveres Islam but it rejects a return to the old system of the *datu*. It is wary of the interrelationship between religion and the traditional system, especially because the former has been used to legitimize the latter. Although this inter-relationship per se is not illegitimate. . . it does not amply represent the aspirations of the Moro masses. To amend the situation, these modernists advocate the utilization of opportunities and resources that are available by working within the established institutions. But at the same time, they maintain, the government would be well-advised to understand the Moros' psychology and create conditions for their greater participation in the affairs of government. These steps are essential in order for the Moros to begin to share a common identity with other Filipinos.[141]

The first group of modernists consists of many Muslim intellectuals - mostly lawyers - who are knowledgeable about Islam and Philippine civil law. They advocate reforms in Islamic thought and institutions, reforms which they claim do not go against the Šarīʿa. At the same time, they also advocate the need to reform the existing legal framework of the country in such a way that laws of a particular community are respected[142] while legal dualism or the creation of a "state within a state" is avoided. Such a danger is avoided with the distinction between the "law of

---

[141] K. Bauzon, *Liberation and the Quest for Islamic Identity*, 82.

[142] In 1977, Presidential Decree No. 1083 was signed into law. It provided for the Codification of Muslim Personal Laws of the Philippines as part of the law of the land, and the creation of a special Šarīʿa court system as part of the machinery of the judicial branch of the government. Shortly afterwards, judges were appointed to Šarīʿa courts. For further information and discussion regarding the codification of these laws, see Atty. Hamid Aminoddin Barra, "The Šarīʿa Law in the Philippines: An Introduction" in *Dansalan Quarterly* 13/1-4 (January-December 1993) 2-107.

the land" and "personal law." This distinction, they contend, is also present and guaranteed to minorities living in an Islamic state.[143] The codification of Islamic law and its incorporation into the Philippine legal system, Majul contends,

> . . . will go a long way in the Islamic education of the Muslim masses. Hopefully also, the application of more Šarīᶜa elements will reduce the influence of some old customs which tend to strengthen kinship relations in such a manner that makes possible nepotism. It might also create more consciousness of the community as such that one will emancipate himself from purely personal or family interests and be able to conceive of a greater good - that of the *Umma*.[144]

Also belonging to this group are Filipino Muslims of various age groups whose conviction that Islam and the *umma* can be and should be realized in any historical context, has led them to propagate Islam by the witness of their lives. The same conviction has also made them open to work together with people from other religious traditions of faith in the One God (i.e., with believing Christians) in a common mission to let God be God in this modern age. This is exemplified, among other common Muslim-Christian endeavors, by the Silsila movement of Muslims and Christians based in Zamboanga City. This movement is a call for all Muslims and Christians to establish a chain (*silsila* in Arabic) of unity in God as inspired by the teachings of their respective faiths. Many Muslim and Christian Filipinos who work together on the basis of their faith in the One God have found the collaboration a spiritual

---

[143] M. Mastura, *Muslim Filipino Experience,* 15.

[144] C. A. Majul, *Some of the Social and Cultural Problems of the Muslims in the Philippines*, Paper presented at a seminar sponsored by the Persatuan Mahasiswa Universiti Kabangsa-an-Malaysia, July 25-28, 1986.

journey, a deepening of their respective faiths.[145]

This modernist view thus advocates Filipino nationhood for the Moros in such a way that they do not lose their Muslim identity but, instead, enhance their *umma*-consciousness.

The second group of modernists is led by a younger generation of Muslims who repudiate the leadership of the traditional elites, do not advocate secession from the Philippine nation, but advocate that the Muslim problem can be solved only by granting autonomy to the Bangsamoro, an autonomy to be patterned on the federal democracies of the West. This second group is best represented by the MNLF-Nur Misuari faction since the signing of the Tripoli Agreement in 1976 in which Nur Misuari[146] changed the MNLF objective from full independence to autonomy for the Bangsamoro (Moro nation). The Bangsamoro nationals, as defined by the MNLF-Misuari, are "natives of the territory (13 provinces) who profess the Islamic religion, as well as natives of the territory who are not Muslims, including their

---

145 *Ugnay-Diwa*, no. 10 (July-December 1993) 1.

146 Nur Misuari was born in Cabingaan, a small island in the Sulu archipelago inhabited by Tausug-Samal people. He does not hail from the traditional Muslim elites. Though of humble origins, he managed to pursue his studies in the University of the Philippines in Quezon City where he took up Political Science. After graduation, he taught in the same university. While in UP, Nur Misuari became one of the founding members of the Kabataang Makabayan - known to be a Maoism-Marxism oriented student organization. Later, he went back to Sulu to teach at the Muslim College of Jolo. One of the reasons for the collapse of the original MNLF was the accusation against Misuari by some fellow Muslims that "the MNLF leadership was being manipulated away from Islamic basis, methodologies and objectives and fast evolving towards Marxist-Maoist orientations." M. Mastura, *The Filipino Muslim Experince, A Collection of Essays* (Manila: Ministry of Foreign Affairs, 1984) 115. Cf. also S. K. Tan, *Internationalization of the Bangsamoro Struggle* (Quezon City: The Center for Integrative and Development Studies, 1993) 34.

offspring and those who reside elsewhere as refugees, and Christian settlers and their descendants who came to the territory on or before 1970."[147] These different groups are referred to by Misuari as "tribes," of which he pointed out that,

> After 18 years of struggle, the people who once upon a time suppressed the tribalistic in their consciousness have now come to realize that they must put aside, as they are putting aside, their tribalistic tendencies and they are now advocating a national consciousness based on the recognition that they belong to one nation, that they belong to one common homeland which is Mindanao, Basilan, Lupasug, Tawi-Tawi, Palawan, including the continental shelves and the historic seas and the airspace.[148]

At the same time, however, the MNLF-proposed Bangsamoro autonomous region is also described as the autonomous region for the Muslims in southern Philippines. There the Muslims shall have the right to set up their own Courts which implement the Islamic Šarīʿa laws and where they shall be represented in all other courts in the autonomous region as well as in the Supreme Court of the Philippines.

In a consultation meeting among Muslims held in 1995 at the

---

[147] Quoted in Federico V. Magdalena, *Ethncity, Identity, and Conflict: The Case of the Philippine Moros* (Singapore: Institute of Southeast Asian Studies, 1996) 34.

[148] Tape recorded speech during a consultation in Iligan City on 7 October 1986. Quoted in Ibid. The prevailing use of the term "Moro" limits it to the Muslims and never includes the Christians. However, since the time Misuari gave his new definition of the Moro nationality, two Christians - Fr. Florio Falcon and Rev. Absalon Cerveza, respectively a Catholic priest and a Protestant pastor - have considered themselves Bangsamoro nationals and have sat in the MNLF-Misuari panel during negotiations with the government since 1986. Ibid., 52, note 22.

Mindanao State University, Marawi city campus, the MNLF further clarified its vision of southern Philippines as a Bangsamoro. The opening speech by Duma Sani, an MNLF spokesman, was a clarification of the view of the MNLF leadership. He emphasized that the attitudes of "prejudice, distrust and hatred" belonged to the medieval times. He described the Spanish and American colonial rulers, together with the Filipinos in the past, as creatures of their time, and of their historical conditions of "prejudice, distrust and hatred" towards other people.[149]

> . . .In this modern world of increased convenience in communication, travel, trade and education, they [Muslims], together with the Christians, have increasingly recognized, day by day, that the person on the other side is, after all, a human being just like themselves. That person, they each found, is someone with the same feelings and failings as they have . . . . someone who can share with them the same meaningful experiences, someone who can show them the same kindness, hospitality and generosity that they show someone that they can even love. They are, of course, aware of their differences, but they are more intrigued by the similarities of their belief in goodness. . . We are at the crossroads of our history. At this point of our mental and cultural illumination, we are still torn between the instinct of the old tradition of prejudice and dislike -- for indeed tradition dies hard inside a person -- and the instinct of reaching out to the new experience and adventure of friendship with a former enemy.[150]

The MNLF vision of a Bangsamoro is one in which the Muslim *umma* exists side by side and in harmony with the other religious

149 From Duma Sani's speech of introduction of the main speaker (Nur Misuari) on July 26, 1995, Mindanao State University, Marawi City. The copy was given me by Duma Sani himself, during my interview with him and other MNLF spokesmen in July 1996, in Marawi City.

150 Ibid.

communities - each of them following their respective particular laws - in an autonomous region to be headed by a Muslim.

For twenty years since 1976, the Philippine government and the MNLF were engaged in a series of peace talks, ceasefires, breakdown of peace talks, and renegotiations accompanied by reformulations of objectives and demands. A peace agreement was finally reached and signed in the Malacañang Palace by President Ramos and Nur Misuari on 2 September 1996. Since then, the MNLF forces have been integrated into the Philippine military. Nur Misuari was appointed chairman of the Southern Philippine Council for Peace and Development (SPCPD) and later was elected governor of the Autonomous Region for Muslim Mindanao.

It should be noted that the above-outlined classification of the trends is not a hard and fast one. It represents the immediate present. Within Philippine contemporary Islam, individuals or groups identified with one trend may shift to another trend under given circumstances, or a particular trend may altogether disappear. The main classification would be the opposition between the fundamentalists (especially the radical ones) and the modernists whose acceptance of Western values is seen by the former as one in which little of Islam is left except the name.

3. Recapitulation and Conclusion

We are now in a position to summarize the main points that we have seen in our survey of *umma* as it has been translated or understood in Islam as it is found in the Philippines.

In the context of the Philippines, the *umma* concept was expressed in an Islamized indigenous ideology of authority, manifested in the form of an accommodation between the Islamic institution of the *ḫilāfa*/ caliphate and the local pre-Islamic social institution called the *barangay*. The pre-Islamic *barangay* consisted of several families headed by a *datu.* Several *barangays* would form a confederation which would be headed by the most powerful *datu* among them. Adherence of the *datus* and their followers to Islam transformed the institution into an Islamic state called the sultanate with the chief *datu* assuming the title of Sultan. The legitimacy of the rule of the Sultan was secured by his being able to show that he descended from the Prophet of Islam. His position then legitimized the sultanate as the expression and guardian of the *umma* in the Philippines with its geographical demarcation and its own internal coherence and self-sufficient structures. It thus also maintained the traditional stratification of society into the chiefly class (to which belonged the *datus* and religious personages), the nobility class (who had no actual power but shared the prestige of and supported the chiefly class), and the dependent class (who had no ascribed status or political power but had to depend on the upper classes for their well-being in exchange for service and loyalty). As God's representative and the one who succeeded the prophet *(halip tul rasul),* the sultan became the political and religious leader or *Imām* at the same time. He was the main Islamizing factor for the laws and practices of the community. The sultanate was basically a closed community but the consciousness of belonging to the wider *umma* was expressed in its attitude of inclusiveness towards fellow believers from other lands. The relative facility with which Islam was accepted by the Filipinos is to be explained in part also by the indigenous Filipino (and Southeast Asian) holistic view of reality in which diversities and differences are seen not as oppositions to be suppressed but as complementing elements to be integrated. Islam's manner of entrance suited the indigenous Filipino mind's manner of reception.

The coming of the Spaniards with the intention of reshaping the Muslims' way of life through the imposition of Christianity only served to strengthen the *umma* consciousness of the Muslim Filipinos, especially their consciousness of being part of a wider *umma.* They could count on the help and compassion of Muslims from other sultanates. With their subjugation by the Americans, for the first time the Filipino Muslims experienced being thrown into a system with values and secular concepts of politics and society most unfamiliar to them. Nevertheless, to a great extent, the *umma* was still preserved, the sultanate system still functioned. When historical developments finally put the Muslims together with the rest of the Filipinos into one independent nation state called "The Philippines," the identity crisis of the Filipino Muslims began. With the introduction of a system of government based on the values and secular concepts of politics and society which the Americans had introduced, the sultanate system with its own internal coherence and self-sufficient superstructure collapsed. Gone was the defined geographical boundaries of the *umma*. The lands which used to be exclusively *dar ul-islam* were now inhabited by Muslims and non-Muslims alike. Muslims found themselves governed by laws totally foreign to them. Thus until the present time, Filipino Muslims have been struggling with the problem of how to realize or preserve the *umma* in the present Philippine situation. Filipino Muslim views on how this realization is to come about have not been the same.

The revivalist fundamentalist view rejects as un-Islamic the West-derived socio-political structures of the Philippine state. It advocates the revival of the sultanate and its structures for the Filipino Muslims as the only political-religious system that can allow the Šarīʿa to be the supreme law of the Bangsamoro and thus preserve the *umma* in the Philippines. This view of the *umma* interlocked with the sultanate political structure is most manifest among traditional leaders who have felt displaced in the modern Philippine state and have since longed for a restoration of their glorious past. The radical fundamentalist view also rejects any West-derived ideas or customs as something that can only dilute the purity of Islam. However, it also rejects the revival of the sultanate as un-Islamic. Instead, it envisions the *umma* in the Philippines as an Islamic state of the Bangsamoro homelands, patterned on the one established by Muhammad in Medina, where the Šarīʿa was implemented to the letter. This view is most manifest among the younger generation of *ʿulamāʾ*, especially those who did their Islamic studies in Cairo and other centers of Islamic learning in the Muslim world.

On the other hand, the modernist view is characterized by its repudiation of traditional Moro leadership and by its openness to the Philippine nation state. The first group of modernists considers the present established system as no hindrance to the authentic practice of Islam and the preservation of the *umma* in the Philippines. This view is exemplifed by Filipino Muslims who work for a place of Muslim personal laws within the legal framework of the country and/or work together with people of other religious traditions of faith in the One God (Christians, in particular) in endeavors for a common mission of letting God be God in this modern age. The second group of modernists insists that the realization of the *umma* within the context of the Philippines can be achieved only if a Bangsamoro autonomous region is created, one which is patterned on the federal democracies of the West. This trend is best represented today by the group led by Nur Misuari, a Tausug (Ṣulu) who does not come from the elite class of their society, and whose education and consequent teaching stint of political science at the University of the Philippines exposed him as well to ideologies other than Islamic. Notwithstanding this particular classification of the trends in the re-formation of the *umma* in the Philippines, the main opposition within Philippine Islam today is between the fundamentalists who are trying to restore an idealized past and the Westernizing Muslims or modernists whose openness to Western values and concepts would be seen by the fundamentalists as jeopardizing the purity of Islam.

What then is *umma* in the context of the Philippines? Our study has shown that *umma* as it was communicated and received in Philippine Islam has been understood first and foremost as a socio-political concept and reality. What came was the *umma* based on the Qurʾān but contained in its application to a particular historical situation in the past. It was *umma* as "it had meant" to the Muslim community in a particular historical situation which was not much different from the one that existed in the Philippines when it came. In other words, *umma* came as the spirit and soul of the caliphate institution, which consequently found its expression in the Philippine sultanates. The caliphate or the sultanate was seen as the visible form best suited for the actualization of the *umma* as a religious/spiritual community, under the conditions prevailing everywhere in the world at that time.

Filipino Muslims today, like the rest of the Muslims in today's world, have realized that the prevailing conditions in today's world are totally new to Islam. How is the *umma* in today's world or in today's Philippines to be expressed or realized? We have seen that Filipino Muslims have varied answers to this question. Those whom we have described as modernist exhibit the attitude of "facing squarely" the modern situation. They realize that the *umma* spirit must be lived in the context of today. Those whom we have described as revivalist fundamentalist exhibit the attitude of "turning back" on the modern situation. They cannot see the *umma* outside of the sultanate context, (i.e., devoid of the form or "clothing" in which it came). Those whom we have described as radicalist exhibit the same attitude of "turning back" on the modern situation. They cannot see the *umma* outside of its historical application in the beginning of Islam.

The concept of *umma* in the Qur'ān together with what we have learned from the commentaries, provides an important clue to the realization of the Islamic *umma* in today's world.

CONCLUDING REMARKS

Our reading of the Qurʾān has shown us that the central meaning of *umma* in the Qurʾān is "a religious community." As such it refers, first of all, to the one religious community *(umma wāḥida)* of all of humankind which existed in the beginning of human history. Every human being then followed the basic disposition to submit to the One God, which disposition God Himself created in every person. This was the original situation obtaining until people started going different ways, the ways of unbelief and worship of other gods. Then God sent prophets to different peoples and nations at different times, with the identical message and mission of calling people back to the worship of the One God. The prophets therefore preached one religion and thus one religious community (*umma*) of believers in the One God. The various groups following the tradition of their respective prophets constituted the various dimensions of the one community of the prophets; they recognized the equality of the various prophetic traditions. When the last of the prophets came, i.e., Muhammad, the various groups had developed attitudes divisive of the one community of the prophets. Soon they became not just divisive groups within the one *umma*, but separate, exclusivist communities, thus rupturing the one *umma* of the prophets. Each of these groups is now recognized as an *umma* if it is characterized basically by submission to the One God and the ordering of that which is *maʿrūf* and the forbidding of that which is *munkar*. It is in the context of a multi-religious community world that God, through this last of the prophets, established the Muslim *umma*, a religious community in a special sense.

The Muslim community is an *umma*, just as the other religious communities are each an *umma* too. The specialness of the Muslims does not necessarily consist in their submission to the One God because the other religious communities are precisely each an *umma* too because of this basic submission to the One God. Neither does their specialness lie in their having a particular way of worship because God has provided for each religious community a proper rite. What makes the Muslim community an *umma* in a special sense is its *ḥanīf* way, i.e., submission to God which includes or which results in the recognition of the equality of all revelations. It is in its being *ḥanīf* that the Muslim community becomes the preserver of the original religion of humankind as well as the *umma wāḥida* of the prophets. Thus in a world of various *umam*, the Muslim community is The *Umma*. The Muslim community in the world vies with the other religious communities in acts of goodness and justice, in calling back to the worship of the One God all unbelievers and worshippers of idols. The existence of the Muslim community is at the same time a constant invitation to all religious communities, to adopt the *ḥanīf* way of submitting to God, so that they may recognize the equality of all revelations, while they continue with the worship or rituals particular to their respective communities. The first historical application of this concept of the *umma* in a special sense obtained in the context of 7th century Medina, realized by the community founded by Muhammad. Such a community has been described by the Qurʾān as *wasaṭ*, as the best.

On the other hand, our study of the representative commentaries has shown us how this qurʾānic concept has been translated or understood by the Muslims in the particular historical contexts throughout the centuries. Up until the late 19th century, the world conditions were basically the same. The prevailing mentality among various communities and civilizations everywhere in the world was one of exclusivism, one in which to consider other peoples as equal was not a virtue. In the face of such world conditions, the Muslim community was secure in itself, with Islam embracing every aspect of the life of its members. The geographical extension of the *umma* was defined, self-sufficient with its superstructure. The world was physically divisible into the abode of Islam or *dār al-islām,* and the rest of the world as the abode of war or *dār al-ḥarb.* In this period, each commentary on the *umma* reflected the general mentality of "exclusivism" and the particular situation of a generation of the Muslim community. The pluri-dynamic term *wasaṭ,* as a description of the Muslim *umma,* was the common stem, the point of departure from which the various interpretations have sprung up in the particular contexts in this period, and in which they all continued to share.

The last three commentaries on the *umma* verses that we considered, reflected the prevailing conditions in today's world, unprecedented in Islamic history. The *umma* vis-a-vis modernity is the main question addressed by these commentaries. This is the same question faced by many Filipino Muslims today. And their answers have not been the same. We will now consider the various Filipino Muslim perspectives of the *umma* in the Philippines in light of the qurʾānic concept of *umma* as well as the remarks of several Muslim scholars of today that corroborate our own findings.

1. The Qurʾānic Concept of *Umma* and the Fundamentalist Trend

The first group of fundamentalists advocates the restoration of the sultanate with its internal structures and defined geographical boundaries as a continuation of the caliphate, while the radical fundamentalists through their main spokesman Hashim Salamat advocate the realization of the Medinan pattern of an Islamic state in southern Philippines. In this trend, we see the *umma* concept interlocked with the idea of Muslim religious and political rule together with defined geographical boundaries. This view implies that the concepts and principles revealed in the Qurʾān cannot be divorced from the historical foundational context of the qurʾānic revelation. It follows from this reading that the *umma* in whatever period in history can be authentic only by strict adherence to the *umma* as defined in the Qur'ān together with its application in its foundational phase, which for the mainstream Sunnis includes the age of the four rightly-guided caliphs.

We have seen in our study of *umma* in the *tafsīr* that this view was spearheaded by the Muslim Brotherhood of Egypt which was founded by Al-Banna in 1928 and later with Sayyid Quṭb as the chief expounder of its qur'ānic basis. Quṭb expounded especially on the need of power or might (سلطان) in order to accomplish the mission of actualizing the *umma*. We have also seen that this interpretation came about as a reaction to what was seen as the decline of the *umma* due to western innovations beginning with the disintegration of the caliphate. In its non-distinction between the eternal message of the Qur'ān and the historical context to which it was first applied, this view then does not see any positive value in historical change. In this view, "human development and progress and new insights do not exist."[1] Progress is achieved by a restoration of the foundational historical context of the qur'ānic *umma*. This view, however, is not shared by many modern Muslim scholars.

Fazlur Rahman[2] of Chicago (formerly of Pakistan) does not have much sympathy with those who put the blame on external considerations for the crisis of the *umma*. He emphasizes that the source of Islamic decadence is to be traced all the way back to the original institutionalization of Islam. The *umma* which was supposed to have been an inspiration for the rest of the world, became a dynastic institution of power politics, the ensuing main characteristic of which turned out to be the desire for self-preservation. Hussein Ahmad Amiṇ of Algeria is among those who express basically the same view but he emphasizes that the

---

[1] Christian W. Troll, "The Qur'ānic View of Other Religions: Grounds for Living Together" in *Encounter*, no. 140 (December 1987) 10.

[2] Fazlur Rahman, *Islam and Modernity*, 26.

crisis became all the more serious as a result of the now widespread influence of Western civilization. He agrees with the fundamentalists in their claim that in order to move in the right direction, Muslims must return to the past. Such a return, however, must not be aimed at restoring the historical past but at searching for the true essence of Islam, which will necessarily lead to

> first, the admission on our part that the purely theoretical thought underlying our faith, as well as all other faiths, assumes, whenever it appears in a certain place, at a certain time, and in a society that has its particular characteristics and limitations, certain temporary aspects that are related to these particulars. Therefore, it is legitimate for those who live in other ages and places and who are concerned with the teachings of the faith to start by distinguishing between what is eternal in them and what is temporary and merely a matter of politics and, secondly, between what was originally there and what was added later through the centuries.[3]

Amin concludes his critique of the fundamentalist view by citing a Chinese proverb which says; "He who gives me a fish provides me with food for one single day. But he who teaches me fishing provides me with food for the rest of my life." It is by being guided by the spirit of Islam that Muslims can find the right way wherever and in whatever circumstances they live. It is in the light of this spirit that Muslim views become Islamic. "Only thus can their faith be as valid and as effective as that of *al-salaf al-ṣāliḥ*, the Prophet's companions, and *al-tābiʿūn*."[4]

---

[3] Hussein Ahmad Amin, "The Present State of the Muslim *Umma*" in *The Muslim World*, vol. LXXIX, nos. 3-4 (July/October 1989) 230.

[4] Ibid.

2. The Qurānic Concept of *Umma* and the Modernist Trend

The modernist way of realizing the *umma* in the Philippines has been branded by the fundamentalists as one of unbelief or ignorance of Islam. The modernist trend exemplified by the post-Tripoli agreement MNLF, headed by Nur Misuari, shows an openness to some modern ideas. This group of modernists insists that the realization of the *umma* within the context of the Philippines can be achieved only if a Bangsamoro autonomous region is created, one which is patterned on the federal democracies of the West. It wants to learn from the West in the context of a nation governed by Muslims. This view thus reflects Muhammad ʿAbduh's idea of bridging the gap between Islamic and Western cultures. The Bangsamoro nation advocated by this trend may be seen as the Philippine translation of the *qawmiyyat-l-ʿarabiyya* of Egypt especially during the time of Nasser. The fundamentalist Muslim Brotherhood initially supported Nasser in the hope that the latter would transform the *qawmiyyat-l-ʿarabiyya* into an *ummat-l-islamiyya*. The MILF's breaking away from the MNLF shows that it has learned from the sad experience of their Egyptian model, (i.e., the Muslim Brotherhood).

On the other hand, there are modernists who see the present established system as no hindrance to the authentic practice of Islam. They affirm that the incorporation of Muslim personal laws into the Philippine legal system as well as the experience of working together with people of other religious traditions of faith in the One God (i.e. with believing Christians), has deepened their Islamic faith and their *umma* consciousness. The *umma* that may be discernible in this trend is not a political community; neither is it one with clearly demarcated geographical boundaries. It is a spiritual reality. This trend implies an understanding of the *umma* in the Qurān which distinguishes between the *umma* as a concept or spiritual reality and its foundational historical contextualization. It is not a restoration of the past historical context but an application of the concept to the present historical situation.

This modernist trend, therefore, far from being one of unbelief or ignorance, is a return to the purest spirit of the *umma* which we saw in our study of the *umma* in the Qur᾽ān.

3. The Imperatives of the Qur᾽ānic Concept of *Umma*, Today

It cannot be sufficiently emphasized that the present historical reality in which the *umma* concept is to be actualized, is an exceptional one, unprecedented in Islamic history. In our survey of the *umma* in the Philippines, we have described this historical situation as the struggle of the *umma* vis-a-vis the modern Philippine nation state. It is a situation marked by the loss of the geographical and political boundaries which used to indicate the visibility of the *umma* as well as the loss of the main Islamic validator, whether in the person of the Muslim ruler or the Šarī῾a as the main law of the land. This situation is really the Philippine dimension of a worldwide phenomenon brought about by modernity and its secularizing spirit. Though the process of modernization started in certain definite parts of the world, it now concerns the whole world, i.e., all peoples and countries. Modern technology, especially the unprecedented growth in the intensity and extent of communication and mass production, has made the world become small, so to say. "The world has become, as it were, a large pool; if a stone is flung in at any point, the ripples from it spread over the whole pool."[5] In the past, different civilizations were clearly demarcated by historical, geographical and ethnic factors. Foreign influences, despite their fecundity, only helped to shape and consolidate specific internal realities. Today, the barriers are tumbling down. The modern forces of science, technology and industry have caused the movement of civilizations to what has been described as one world. In this world, people of different religions find themselves mingling with one another.

---

[5] W. Montgomery Watt, *What is Islam?* (Frome and London: Butler and Tanner Ltd., 1968) 210.

The other aspect of modernity is its accompanying or resulting spirit of secularization. In the past civilizations, religions integrated economics, politics and society in such a way that these followed the social goals laid down by religion. With modernity came the growing autonomy of social institutions like economics, politics, religion, with each of them having its own structure and goals. In the present situation the Muslim *umma* finds itself without defined boundaries and mingling with adherents of other religious beliefs (religious pluralism) in a society/nation where religion is losing its role as the main provider of an overall meaning system for everything.[6] Modernity thus is a problem or a challenge not only to Islam but also to all other religions. Mushir-ul-

---

[6] The impact of modernity on Islam may be demonstrated by the following observations by Fazlur Rahman: "With the exception of the official attitude of Turkey.... everywhere in the Muslim world both the peoples and the governments have been saying that Islam is a "complete way of life" rather than being either merely a set of religious rites or pertaining exclusively to the private relationship between the individual and his God.... The curious paradox, however, is that in most Muslim countries Islam is not actually treated as the basis of state policies - either socio-economic or external policy or in any field directly touching public life except personal law; for all practical purposes, Islam is treated as a narrow religious sphere in official policies which either leave it to itself or, at best, have established 'departments of religious affairs' - which in itself shows that officially these countries actually believe in a bifurcation of life into the religious and secular domains whether they admit or dare to admit it or not. .. The main reason for the official double-mindedness cannot but be the difficulty of working Islam in a modern nation state particularly in face of the stark opposition of the *ʿulamāʾ* to modernism and the intellectual failure of the official classes to re-present or re-formulate Islam in consequential modern terms." Fazlur Rahman, "The Impact of Modernity on Islam" in *Islamic Studies,* vol. 5, no. 2 (June 1966) 123-124. Cf. also A. A. Roest Crollius, "God, Man and Community in Islam" in *Islamic Spirituality,* ed. Augustine Thottakara (Bangalore: Dharmaram Publications, 1993) 151.

Haq expresses the mounting challenge as follows:

> Ours is perhaps the only age in the recorded history of man when not this or that religion but the institution of religion itself is being denigrated. The very *raison d'etre* of religion is being questioned. It is being claimed that man has outlived religion, and will be well advised to cast off for good this outmoded garment. The time has come now when the followers of various religions must work out a common strategy to fight against the forces of atheism and irreligiosity. . . This challenge must be accepted unitedly by all religions, if they do not want to be wiped out one by one.[7]

Each community of faith must assess anew its place and mission in this new universal order that is emerging. The urgency of applying the qurʾānic concept of *umma* to the present historical situation has been advocated, with varying nuances, by Mushir-ul-Haq and some other modern Muslim thinkers like Muhammad Talbi of Tunis, Syed Vahiduddin of India and Fazlur Rahman of Chicago (formerly of Pakistan).[8] We confine ourselves here to some pronouncements of Mohammed Talbi on the *umma*. The *umma* is a religious community. In the past it used to be geographically situated. Now it has lost the one in whom it was in-

---

[7] Mushir-ul-Haq, "Towards World Community" in *Islam and the Modern Age*, vol. 7, no. 4 (November 1976) 56-57.

[8] Cf. Mohammed Talbi, "A Community of Communities: The Right to be Different and the Paths to Harmony" in *Encounter* (Rome) no. 77 (August/ September 1981) 1-14; Fazlur Rahman, *Islam and Modernity* (Chicago: The University of Chicago Press, 1984); Syed Vahiduddin, *Islamic Experience in Contemporary Thought* (Delhi: Chanakya Publications, 1986); and Mushir-ul-Haq, "Towards World Community" in *Islam and the Modern Age*, vol. 7, no. 4 (November 1976). Their ideas are also discussed in C. W. Troll, "The Qurʾānic View of Other Religions: Grounds for Living Together" in *Encounter*, no. 140 (December 1987).

carnated, the Caliph. *Umma* is no longer one nation and there is no longer a nation whose citizens are all Muslim. *Umma* no longer corresponds to geographical realities.

> One thing is certain today, and there can be no going back on it: the frontiers of the *umma* are not marked out in the world. From now on they are to be found only in the hearts of those who pray, whether those hearts be in Sweden or in China, in Cairo or elsewhere. A German or a Malay may belong, while a Tunisian or an Egyptian is excluded of his own free choice.[9]

Talbi says that this great change that is taking place is not a bad thing. The superimposition for a long time of the *umma* as a community of faith and the *umma* as a political community paved the way for "illusions and confusion difficult to escape from" and for the concept of *umma* to be "manipulated for all sorts of purposes." The present situation should pave the way for the rediscovery of the distinction between "Islam-conviction" and "Islam-culture." The former supposes the latter but not vice-versa.

> "Islam-conviction" is not a nation but it is lived out in the nation. It is a community of faith *[umma]*, i.e., of the heart, within a geo-political community.[10]

Talbi then concludes that a Muslim believer can belong to any political community of his choice and live his faith at the same time. The traditional division of the world into the *dār al-Islām* and *dār al-ḥarb* has lost much of its meaning. It is no longer possible for the *umma* (or any other community of faith, for that matter) to become isolated within its own system. Isolation will forever be equivalent to suicide.

---

[9] Mohammed Talbi, "A Community of Communities, 4.

[10] Ibid.

What remains forever valid and to be applied to the present is the concept or ideal of the *umma* which we have seen in our study of the Qurʾān: a single community of brothers "loving God with their whole heart, and loving one another in God."[11] It is an invitation to faith in the One God and the promotion of what is *maʿrūf* or just and the forbidding of what is *munkar* or unjust (3:104). This task of invitation entrusted to the Muslim *umma* for humankind presupposes the freedom of the individual to accept or reject it. Ultimately what matters is faith in God and the works that one does. God sanctioned a pattern for humankind that allows for differences in belief and behavior. "For each We have appointed a divine law and a traced-out way. Had God willed He could have made you one community. But that He may try you by that which He has given you (He has made you as you are). So vie with one another in good works" (5:48).[12] The universality of the perfect community then is to be merited by the Muslims' witness of exemplary faith and practice among the rest of humankind (cf. 2:143). To actualize the qurʾānic *umma* in the context of today's world then is, first of all, to realize and accept the fact that this universe is necessarily pluralistic, that it has to be constructed together with others.

> to live in a community of communities, to respect differences and bring them into harmony, is a return to the purest spirit of Islam.... The aim here is for each community to safeguard its own identity without blocking the way to a device of harmony in which the inner freedom of each individual and of each group is respected.[13]

---

[11] From the sermon of Muhammad on the occasion of his entry into Medina, recorded in Ibn Hisham, *Sīra,* vol. II (n. d.) 348. Quoted in Mohammed Talbi, "A Community of Communities...," 7. Cf. Sūra 3:103-104.

[12] Cf. 11:118, 16:93.

[13] Mohammed Talbi, "A Community of Communities...," 5-6.

The most famous precedent of an application of this principle is to be found in the Constitution of Medina,[14] promulgated by the prophet of Islam himself. This Constitution brought both Jews and Muslims into association, in a spirit of harmony. It provides a foundation in theory and practice for the right of the other to be different, a right inscribed in the Constitution. The principle of collaboration was laid out and applied in the historical context of Medina.

Today, the community-state no longer exists. Islamic legislations which have a foundation in the Qurʾān, interpreted in a traditional way, will have to be revised in the context of today. The *umma* today is in the hearts of Muslims who live the Islamic faith in the context of the various political communities to which they belong. It is a globally indivisible community. As a witness of God in a pluralistic and questioning world, the attitude of the Muslim believer is one of listening to *al-ġayb,* to God, of acceptance and respect for each person's loyalties and being other, and of dialogue and collaboration with others with the aim of achieving a maximum of justice in the world as well as of eliminating injustice in the world, i.e., of promoting what the Qurʾān calls *maʿrūf* and opposing what the Qurʾān calls *munkar*. The Muslim *umma* is to be in dialogue and collaboration, first of all with other religious communities with whom it shares the same faith in the one God,

---

[14] On this Constitution, see, among others, M. Hamidullah, *Le Prophète de l'Islam,* vol. I (Paris: n. p., 1959) 133-137. For studies on this Constitution by non-Muslims, see, among others, F. Denny, "Umma in the Constitution of Medina" in *Journal of Near Eastern Studies,* vol. 36 (January 1977) 39-47; and the following articles by R. B. Serjeant: "The Constitution of Medina" in *Islamic Quarterly,* vol. 8 (June 1964) 3-16 and "The *Sunnah Jāmiʿah,* Pacts with the Yathrib Jews, and the *Taḥrīm* of Yathrib: Analysis and Translation of the Documents Comprised in the So-Called 'Constitution of Medina'" in *Studies in Arabian History and Civilization* VI (London: Variorum Reprints, 1981) 1-42.

like the Jewish and the Christian.[15] They are in the same predicament. They live in the exile of faith in a world dominated by interests (materialistic and selfish) other than religious. Together they have to face the *ummiyyūn* of today's world. Together they face the challenge posed by modernity to religion itself. Thus "people of faith today are one people, regardless of their religious affiliation."[16] This dialogue, however, is not limited to only those who believe in the One God. For true believers in God who created all things, the mystery of creation and the dignity of the human being constitute an inexhaustible source of inspiration which sustains them in the sincere effort at undertaking and carrying on a dialogue with all.[17]

In the end, the challenge of the *umma* as an institutionalized

---

[15] Muhammad Talbi ("Religious Liberty: A Muslim Perspective" in *Encounter* (Rome) no. 126-127 (June/July 1986) 1-17) points out that the status of *ḏimmī-s* was based on the Qur'ān's principle of religious freedom but interpreted "in the Medieval contexts of wars, hostilities and treacheries," at the time when "it was not then a virtue - according to the Medieval mentality prevailing everywhere in the world and inside all communities - to consider all human beings as equal." Thus, because of the prevailing circumstances of the time, "traditional theology did not remain faithful to the true spirit of the Qur'ān. This theology abridged seriously the liberty of choice of one's religion." True religious liberty as advocated in the Qur'ān can no longer be interpreted as in Medieval theology since "religious liberty is today, as a matter of fact, definitely and for good rooted in our social life. Since the Declaration of Human Rights in 1948, this concept is henceforth an essential part of international law." The same applies to the case of the apostate *(murtadd)* where traditional theology also did not remain faithful to the spirit of the Qur'ān due to prevailing circumstances of the time.

[16] M. M. Ayoub, "Roots of Muslim-Christian Conflict" in *Muslim World,* LXXIX/1 (January 1989) 44.

[17] See A. A. Roest Crollius, "Il Risveglio dell'Islam in un Mondo Pluralista" in *La Civiltà Cattolica,* 131 (1981) 132.

community of Muslims is the inner *umma*, the pure spiritual *umma* that can be found only in the hearts of true Muslim believers. It is that *umma* which is a surrender of all things to God, which in the context of every age lets God be God in the individual lives of believers, in society, in local, national and world affairs. It is that *umma* which can adopt the *ḥanīf* attitude which recognizes the validity and the equality of all communities of believers in the One God.

In the particular context of the Philippines, the realization of the *umma* is facilitated by two things: 1) the return to the pure spirit of the *umma* in the Qur'ān which is applicable to any particular historical context, 2) coupled with the indigenous Filipino holistic view of reality in which diversities and differences are seen not as oppositions to be suppressed but as creative elements to be integrated - a holistic view which in practice finds its realization in, among other things, the pursuit of peace and harmony. These two elements provide a growth in the understanding of, and the consequent response to, the clarion call sounded out by Cesar Adib Majul, which provided us the impetus to choose *umma* as the theme for our doctoral study.

> The fundamental question now facing individual Muslims in the Philippines is whether they still desire to have or preserve a Muslim community in the country - a community that will testify to the Oneness of Allah and the Prophethood of Muhammad and who will adhere to the fundamentals of Islam. This question is not the same as that as to whether the Muslims want to exist as individuals or not. The question, to be repeated, is whether the Muslims want to preserve their existence as an *umma*.... It is inconsistent and not canonically possible for an individual to claim that he can still be a Muslim and not advocate the existence of a Muslim community.... Moreover, Allah has commanded the believers to act as a community.... [18]

---

[18] As quoted on page 1 of this thesis.

BIBLIOGRAPHY

Only those works that have directly served in this study are mentioned here.

1. The text of the Qurʾān

Al-Qurʾān al-Karīm. Edition of Cairo, 1342/1923.

2. The commentaries

Abū Jaʿfar Muḥammad b. Jarīr al-Ṭabarī. *Jāmiʿ-al-bayān fī tafsīr-al-Qurʾān*. 30 vols. Cairo 1954.

Abū-l-Qāsim Maḥmūd b. ʿUmar al-Zamaḫšarī. *Al-Kaššāf ʿan ḥaqāʾiq-al-tanzīl wa ʿuyūn-al-aqāwīl*. Cairo 1308.

Abū-ʿAbd-Allāh Muḥammad b. ʿUmar al-Rāzī. *Mafātīḥ-al-ġayb*. Cairo 1352/1933.

ʿAbd-Allāh b. ʿUmar al-Bayḍāwī. *Anwār-al-tanzīl wa asrār-al-taʾwīl*. Cairo (n. y.).

Ismāʿīl b. ʿUmar abū-al-Fidāʾ b. Kaṯīr. *Tafsīr Ibn Kaṯīr*. Cairo: Dār al-Kutub1393 AH.

Abū-l-Faḍl ʿAbd-al-Raḥmān b. Abī-Bakr Jalāl-al-Dīn al-Suyūṭī and Al-Maḥallī Jalāl-al-Dīn. Abbr.: Al-Jalālayn. *Tafsīr al-Qurʾān*. Cairo: Dār al-maʿrifa, 1412/1992.

Riḍā, R. *Tafsīr-al-Qurʾān al-ḥakīm al-šahīr bi-Tafsīr-al-Manār*. 12 vols. Cairo edition, 1972.

Mawdūdī, Sayyid Abul Aʿlā. *Towards Understanding the Qurʾān*. Leicester: The Islamic Foundation, 1988.

Quṭb, Sayyid. *Fī Ẓilāl al-Qurʾān*. Beirut: Dar al-Shuruq, 1982.

3. Translations of the Qurʾān

Arberry, A. *The Qurʾān Interpreted*. Oxford: Oxford University Press, 1983.

Asad, M. *The Message of the Qurʾān*. Gibraltar: Dar Al-Andalus, 1980.

Bell, R. *The Qurʾān: Translated, with a Critical Re-Arrangement of the Sūras*. 2 vols. Edinburgh: T. and T. Clark, 1937.

Blachère, R. *Le Coran III*. Paris: Maisonneuve, 1950.

Dawood, N. J. *The Qurʾān*. London: Penguin Books, 1956/1974.

Jullundri, A. A. K. *The Glorious Holy Qurʾān*. Lahore: Ripon Press, 1962.

Mawdūdī, Sayyid Aʿlā. *Towards Understanding the Qurʾān*. 5 volumes. Translated from its Urdu original and edited by Zafar Ishaq Ansari. Leicester: The Islamic Foundation, 1988.

Pickthall, M. *The Meaning of the Glorious Qurʾān*. New York: Mentor Books, 1953.

Zafrulla Khan, M. *The Qurʾān*. London: Curzon Press, 1991.

4. Studies related to the interpretation of the qurʾānic notion of *Umma*.

Adams, C. C. *Islam and Modernism in Egypt*. London: Oxford University Press, 1933.

Aḥmad, Rashid. "Qurʾānic Exegesis and Classical *Tafsīr*." *The Islamic Quarterly* 12/1-2 (1968)71-119.

Ahmad, Syed Barakat. "Non-Muslims and the *Umma*." *Studies in Islam* 17/2 (1980) 80-118.

Ahmed, Manzooruddin. "*Umma*: The Idea of a Universal Community." *Islamic Studies* 14/1 (1975) 27-54.

Al-Ahsan, A. *Umma or Nation? Identity Crisis in Contemporary Muslim Society*. Leicester: The Islamic Foundation, 1992.

Al-Ahsan, A. "The Qurʾānic Concept of 'Umma'." *Journal Institute of Muslim Minority Affairs* 7/2 (July 1986) 606-622.

Al-Bazzaz, Abd al-Rahman. "Islam and Arab Nationalism." *Arab Nationalism, An Anthology*. S. G. Haim, ed. Berkeley: University of California Press (1976) 172-188.

Al-Bukhari. *Šaḥiḥ al-Buḫārī*. 3 vols. Beirut, 1978.

Al-Haq, Mushir. "Towards World Community." *Islam and the Modern Age* 7/4 (1976) 54-65.

Al-Haq, Mushir. "Inter-Religious Understanding." *Christian-Muslim Dialogue. Broumana 12-18 July 1972.* S. J. Samartha and J. B. Taylor, eds. (Geneva: WCC, 1973) 32-40.

Al-Moussalli, Ahmed Salah. *Radical Islamic Fundamentalism: The Ideological and Political Discourse of Sayyid Quṭb.* Beirut, 1992.

Al-Moussalli, Ahmed Salah. "Two Tendencies in Modern Islamic Political Thought: Modernism and Fundamentalism." *Hamdard Islamicus* 16/2 (1993) 51-78.

Al-Muʿjam al-mufahras li-alfāẓ al-qurʾān al-karīm. Cairo, 1411/ 1991.

Al-Suyūṭī, Jalāl al-Dīn. *Al-Itqān fī ʿulūm al-Qurʾān II.* Cairo: Maṭbaʿa Ḥijāzī, 1318/1900.

"Am Ha-arez." *Encyclopedia Judaica.* vol. 2. Jerusalem: Keter Publishing House Ltd. (1973) 834-836.

Amin, H. A. "The Present State of the Muslim *Umma*." *The Muslim World* 79 (1989) 217-231.

Anawati, G. C. "Fakhr al-Dīn al-Rāzī." *Encyclopedia of Islam.* New edition. 2 (1965) 751-755.

Athamina, Khalil. "'Al-Nabiyy al-Umiyy': An Inquiry into the Meaning of a Qur'anic Verse." *Der Islam* 69:1 (1992) 61-80.

Ayoub, M. M. "Roots of Muslim-Christian Conflict." *Muslim World* 79/1 (1989) 25-45.

Ayoub, M. *The Qurʾān and Its Interpreters.* vol. 2. New York: State University of New York Press, 1992.

Baljon, J. M. S. *Modern Muslim Qurʾān Interpretation.* Leiden: E. J. Brill, 1968.

Barclay, H. "Sectarian Theory and the Muslim Community." *Studies in Islam* 17/3 (1980) 165-175.

Bell, R. "Who Were The Hanīfs?" *The Moslem World* 20/1 (1930) 120-124.

Bell, R. *The Origin of Islam in its Christian Environment.* London: Frank Cass and Co. Ltd., 1968.

Bijlefeld, W. "A Prophet And More Than A Prophet?" *The Muslim World* 59 (1969) 1-28.

Birkeland, H. "The Lord Guideth: Studies on Primitive Islam." *Skrifter* (1956) 1-140.

Blachère, R. *Introduction au Coran.* Paris: Maisonneuve, 1950.

Bravmann, M. M. *The Spiritual Background of Early Islam.* Leiden: E. J. Brill, 1972.

Brockelmann, C. "Al-Zamaḫšarī." *Shorter Encyclopedia of Islam.* H. A. R. Gibb and J. H. Kramers, eds. Leiden: E. J. Brill (1991) 656-657.

Brohi, A. K. "Mawlānā Abū-l-Aʿlā Mawdūdī, The Man, The Scholar, The Reformer." *Islamic Perspectives: Studies in Honor of Mawlānā Sayyid Abū-l-Aʿlā Mawdūdī.* K. Ahmad and Z. I. Ansari, eds. Leicester/Jeddah: The Islamic Foundation/ Saudi Publishing House (1979) 289-311.

Buhl, "Ḥanīf." *Shorter Encyclopedia of Islam.* Leiden: E. J. Brill (1991) 132-133.

Buhl, F. "Zur Ḳurānexegese." *Acta Orientalia.* 3 (1924) 97-108.

Buhl, F. "Milla." *The Encyclopedia of Islam.* New edition. 7 (1993) 61.

Caldarola, C. (ed.). *Religions and Societies: Asia and the Middle East.* Berlin/New York/ Amsterdam: Mouton Press, 1982.

Calder, N. "The *Ummī* in Early Islamic Juristic Literature." *Der Islam* (1990) 111-124.

Carra de Vaux, B. "Djahannam." *Shorter Encyclopedia of Islam.* H. A. R. Gibb and . H. Kramers, eds. Leiden and New York: E. J. Brill (1991) 81-82.

Chaumont, E. "Salaf." *Encyclopedia of Islam.* New edition. 8 (1993) 899-900.

Choudhury, G. W. *Islam and the Modern Muslim World.* London: Scorpion Publishing Limited, 1993.

Choueiri, Y. *Islamic Fundamentalism.* London: Printer Publishers, 1990.

Cooper, J. *The Commentary on the Qur'ān by Al-Ṭabarī.* Oxford: Oxford University Press, 1987.

Cragg, K. *Counsels in Contemporary Islam.* Edinburgh: University Press,1965.

Cragg, K. *Readings in the Qur'ān.* London: Collins Religious Publishing, 1993.

Cragg, K. *The Call of the Minaret.* London: William Collins Sons & co. Ltd., 1985.

Cragg, K. *The Event of the Qurān: Islam in its Scripture*. London: George Allen & Unwin Ltd., 1971.

Cragg, K. *The Pen and the Faith*. London: George Allen and Unwin, 1985.

Crone, P. and Michael Cook. *Hagarism: The Making of the Islamic World*. Cambridge: Cambridge University Press, 1977.

Dawn, C. E. *From Ottomanism to Arabism*. Chicago: University of Illinois Press, 1973.

Denffer, Ahmad von. *ʿUlūm al-Qurʾān*. Leicester: The Islamic Foundation, 1994.

Denny, F. "Some Religio-Communal Terms and Concepts in the Qurʾān." *Numen* 24 (1977) 26-59.

Denny, F. "The Meaning of *Umma* in the Qurʾān." *History of Religions* 15 (1975) 34-70.

Denny, F. "*Umma* in the Constitution of Medina." *Journal of Near Eastern Studies* 36 (1977) 39-47.

Donahue, J. and John Esposito, eds. *Islam in Transition, Muslim Perspectives*. New York: Oxford University Press, 1982.

El-Affendi, A. *Who Needs an Islamic State?* London: Grey Seal Books, 1991.

Esposito, J. *The Islamic Threat: Myth or Reality?* Oxford: University Press, 1992.

Fahd, T. "Nār." *Encyclopedia of Islam*. New edition. 7 (1993) 957-960.

Faris, N. A. and Glidden, H. W. "The Development of the Meaning of the Koranic *Ḥanīf.*" *The Journal of the Palestine Oriental Society* 19 (1939-1940) 1-13.

Faruqi, I. H. Azad. "The Qurʾānic View of Other Religions." *Islam and the Modern Age* 18/1(1987) 39-50.

Firestone, R. *Journey in Holy Lands: The Evolution of the Abraham-Ishmael Legends in Islamic Exegesis.* Albany: State University of New York Press, 1990.

Fleischer, H. L. *Kleinere Schriften.* Leipzig: Verlag von S. Hirzel, 1888.

Gardet, L. *La Cité Musulmane.* Paris: Librairie Philosophique J. Vrin, 1954.

Gardet, L. "Djahannam." *The Encyclopedia of Islam.* New edition. 2 (1965) 381-382.

Gätje, H. *The Qurʾān and its Exegesis.* London: Routledge & Kegan Paul, 1976.

Geagea, N. *Maria nel messaggio coranico.* Roma: Edizioni del Teresianum, 1973.

Geiger, A. *Judaism and Islam.* New York: KTAV Publishing House, Inc., 1970 edition.

Gimaret, D. "Muʿtazila." *The Encyclopedia of Islam.* New edition. 7 (1993) 783-793.

Goldfeld, I. "The Illiterate Prophet *(Nabī Ummī):*" "An Inquiry into the Development of a Dogma in Islamic Tradition." *Der Islam* 57 (1980) 58-67.

Goldziher, I. *Muslim Studies* 2 vols.. London: George Allen and Unwin Ltd., 1967/1971.

Goldziher, I. "Ahl." *The Encyclopedia of Islam*. New edition. 1 (1986) 257.

Grunebaum, G. E. von. *Medieval Islam*. Chicago: University of Chicago Press, 1962.

Guillaume, A. *The Life of Muhammad* (A translation of Isḥāq's *Sīrat Rasūl Allāh*). London: Oxford University Press, 1970.

Guillaume, A. "The Meaning of Amānīya in Sūra 2:73." *The World of Islam: Studies in Honor of Philip Hitti*. J. Kritzeck and R. B. Winder, eds. London: Macmillan and Co. Ltd., (1960) 41-46.

Haddad, Y. "Sayyid Quṭb: Ideologue of Islamic Revival." *Voices of Resurgent Islam*. J. Esposito, ed. (New York/Oxford: Oxford University Press, 1983) 67-98.

Haffner, A. "Āl." *The Encyclopedia of Islam*. New edition. 1 (1986) 345.

Haim, S. (ed.). *Arab Nationalism*. Berkeley: University of California Press, 1962.

Hallaq, W. B. and D. P. Little, eds. *Islamic Studies Presented to Charles Adams*. Leiden: E. J. Brill, 1991.

Hodgson, M. *The Venture of Islam*. vol. 1. Chicago: The University of Chicago Press, 1974.

Horovitz, J. *Koranische Untersuchungen*. Berlin: Walter de Gruyter and Co., 1926.

Horovitz, J. "Jewish Proper Names and Derivatives in the Koran." *Hebrew Union College Annual* vol. 2. Hildesheim: Georg Olms (1964 edition) 145-227.

Horovitz, J. "Nabī." *Shorter Encyclopedia of Islam.* H. A. R. Gibb and J. H. Kramers, eds. Leiden/New York: E. J. Brill (1991) 427-428.

Hovannisian, R. and Vryonis, S. Jr., eds. *Islam's Understanding of Itself.* Malibu, California: Undena Publications, 1983.

Ibrahim, A., Siddique, S., and Hussain, Y., compilers. *Readings on Islam in Southeast Asia.* Singapore: Institute of Southeast Asian Studies, 1985.

Ibrahim, L. "Al-Bayḍāwī's Life and Works." *Islamic Studies* 18 (1979) 311-321.

Ibrahim, L. "Al-Zamaḫšarī: His Life and Works." *Islamic Studies* 19 (1980) 95-110.

Izutsu, T. *Ethico-Religious Concepts in the Qurʾān.* Montreal: McGill University Press, 1966.

Izutsu, T. *God and Man In the Koran.* Tokyo: The Keio Institute of Cultural And Linguistic Studies, 1964.

Jansen, J. J. G. *The Interpretation of the Qurʾān in Modern Egypt.* Leiden: E. J. Brill, 1980.

Jansen, J. J. G. "Sayyid Quṭb." *The Encyclopedia of Islam.* New Edition. 9 (1997) 117-118.

Jeffery, A. *Materials for the History of the Text of the Qurʾān.* Leiden. E. J. Brill, 1937.

Jeffery, A. "The Qur'ān as Scripture." *Muslim World* 40 (1950) 41-55 & 106-134.

Jeffery, A. *ISLAM: Muhammad and His Religion*. New York: The Liberal Arts Press, 1958.

Jeffery, A. *The Foreign Vocabulary of the Qur'ān*. Baroda: Oriental Institute, 1938.

Juynboll, G. H. A. *Muslim Tradition*. Cambridge: Cambridge University Press, 1983.

Ka-ka Khel, M. N. "The Rise of the Muslim 'Umma' at Mecca and its Integration." *Hamdard Islamicus* 5 (Autumn 1982) 59-74.

Karpat, K. *Turkey's Politics*. Princeton: Princeton University Press, 1959.

Katsh, A. I. *Judaism in Islam*. New York: New York University Press, 1954.

Kazi, Abdul Khaliq. "The Meaning of *Īmān* and *Islām* in the Qur'ān." *Islamic Studies* 5/3 (1966) 227-237.

Kerr, M. *Islamic Reform*. Berkeley: University of California Press, 1966.

Kettani, M. Ali. *Muslim Minorities in the World Today*. London/New York: Mansell Publishing Ltd., 1986.

Khurramshāhi, Bahā' al-Din. "The Qur'an as Its Own Interpreter." *Ḥikmat* 1/1 (1995/1416) 3-25.

Kramers, J. H. "Al-Rāzī." *Shorter Encyclopedia of Islam* (Leiden: E. J. Brill, 1991) 470-471.

Lane, A. "What is Radical Islam? One Answer." *Encounter* (Rome) no. 216 (June-July, 1995) 1-27.

Lane, E. W. *Arabic-English Lexicon.* 2 vols. Cambridge: The Islamic Texts Society, 1984.

Lazarus-Yafeh, Hava. *Intertwined Worlds: Medieval Islam and Bible Criticism.* Princeton, New Jersey: Princeton University Press, 1992.

Leemhuis, F. "Origins of the Tafsīr Tradition." *Approaches To The History Of The Interpretation Of The Qurʾān.* Andrew Rippin, ed. New York: Oxford University Press, (1988) 13-30.

Levy, J. *Wörterbuch über die Talmudim und Midrashim* vol. I. Berlin/Wein, 1924.

Lyall, Charles. "The Words *Ḥanīf* and *Muslim.*" *The Journal of the Royal Asiatic Society of Great Britain and Ireland* (1903) 771-784.

MacDonald, D. B. "Ḥizb." *The Encyclopedia of Islam.* New edition. 3 (1971) 513-535.

Madigan, Daniel SJ. "Reflections on some Current Directions in Qurʾānic Studies." *The Muslim World* 85 (1995) 345-362.

Makdisi, G. *Ašʿarī and the Ašʿarites.* Paris: G. P. Maisonneuve, 1962.

Margoliouth, D. S. "On the Origin and Import of the Names *Muslim* and *Ḥanīf*." *The Journal of the Royal Asiatic Society* 35 (1903) 467- 493.

Martin, R. C. "Understanding the Qurʾān in Text and Context." *History of Religions* 21 (1981-1982) 361-384.

Massignon, L. "L'umma et ses synonymes: Notion de 'communauté sociale' en Islam." *Revue des études islamiques* (1947).

Massignon, L. "Ṭarīqa." *Shorter Encyclopedia of Islam*. Leiden: E. J. Brill (1991) 573-578.

"Mawlānā Mawdūdī's Autobiography." Translated with an introduction by Seyyed Vali Reza Nasr. *The Muslim World* 85 (1995) 49-62.

McAuliffe, J. D. "Qurʾānic Hermeneutics: The Views of al-Ṭabarī and Ibn Kaṯīr." *Approaches to the History of the Interpretation of the Qurʾān*. A. Rippin, ed. Oxford: Clarendon Press (1988) 46-62.

Mir, M. *Dictionary of Qurʾānic Terms and Concepts*. New York and London: Garland Publshing, Inc., 1987.

Nettler, Ronald. "A Modern Islamic Confession of Faith And Conception of Religion: Sayyid Quṭb's Introduction to the Tafsīr, Fī Ẓilāl Al-Qurʾān." *The British Journal of Middle Eastern Studies* 21 (1994) 102-114.

Nöldeke, T. and F. Schwally. *Geschichte des Qorans*. Leipzig: Dieterich'sche Verlagsbuchhandlung, 1909.

Nyberg, H. S. "Al-Muʿtazila." *Shorter Encyclopedia of Islam*. Leiden: E. J. Brill (1991) 421-427.

Paret, R. "Al-Ṭabarī." *E. J. Brill's First Encyclopedia of Islam*. Vol. 7. Photomechanical Reprint. Leiden and New York: E. J. Brill (1987) 578-579.

Paret, R. "Umma." *Shorter Encyclopedia of Islam*. H. A. R. Gibb and J. H. Kramers, eds. Leiden and New York: E. J. Brill (1991) 603-604.

Paret, R. "Ummī." *Shorter Encyclopedia of Islam*. H. A. R. Gibb and J. H. Kramers, eds. Leiden/New York: E. J. Brill (1991) 604.

Paret, R. *Der Koran, Kommentar und Konkordanz*. Berlin: Verlag W. Kohlhammer, 1986.

Pearson, J. D. "Al-Qurʾān." *The Encyclopedia of Islam*. New ed. 5 (1986) 400-432.

Piscatori, J. *Islam in a World of Nation-States*. Cambridge: Cambridge University Press, 1986.

Powell, A. J. "The Qurʾānic View of Other Scriptures: A translation of sections from writings by ʿAfīf ʿAbd al-Fattāḥ Ṭabbāra and al-Ustād al-Ḥaddād." *The Muslim World* 59/2 (1969) 95-105.

Rabin,C. *Qumran Studies*. Oxford: Oxford University Press, 1957.

Rahbar, D. "The Tradition of Qur'anic Exegesis." *The Muslim World* 52 (1962) 296-307.

Rahman, F. "The Impact of Modernity on Islam." *Islamic Studies* 5/2 (1966) 113-128.

Rahman, F. "The People of the Book and the Diversity of Religions." *Christianity through Non-Christian Eyes.* P. J. Griffiths, ed. New York: Orbis Books (1990) 102-110.

Rahman, F. *Islam and Modernity: Transformation of an Intellectual Tradition.* Chicago and London: The University of Chicago Press, 1984.

Rahman, F. *Islam.* Chicago and London: University of Chicago Press, 1979.

Reissner, H. G. "The *Ummī* Prophet and the Banū Israel." *Muslim World* 89 (October 1949) 276-281.

Ringgren, H. "The Pure Religion." *Oriens* vol. 15 (1962) 93-96.

Rippin, A. "RḤMNN and the Ḥanīfs." *Islamic Studies Presented To Charles Adams.* W. B. Hallaq and D. P. Little, eds. Leiden/ New York: E. J. Brill (1991) 152-168.

Rippin, A. (editor). *Approaches to the History of the Interpretation of the Qurʾān.* Oxford: Clarendon Press, 1988.

Robinson, F. "Mawdūdī." *The Encyclopedia of Islam.* New edition. 6 (1991) 872-874.

Robinson, N. *Discovering the Qurʾān: A Contemporary Approach to a Veiled Text.* London: SCM Press, Ltd., 1996.

Robinson, N. *Christ in Islam and Christianity.* London: Macmillan Press, Ltd. 1991.

Robson, J. "Al-Bayḍāwī." *Encyclopedia of Islam*. New edition. 1 (1960) 1129.

Roest Crollius, A. *The Word In The Experience of Revelation In Qurʾān and Hindu Scriptures*. Roma. Università Gregoriana Editrice. 1974.

Roest Crollius, A. "God, Man and Community in Islam." *Islamic Spirituality*. A. Thottakara, ed. Bangalore: Dharmaram Publications (1993) 125-157.

Roest Crollius, A. "Il Risveglio dell'Islam in un Mondo Pluralista." *La Civiltà Cattolica* 131 (1981) 117-132.

Roest Crollius, A. "The Prayer of the Qurʾān." *Studia Missionalia* 24 (1975) 223-252.

Roest Crollius, A. A. "Mission and Morality." *Studia Missionalia* 27. Roma: Università Gregoriana Editrice (1978) 257-283.

Rubin, U. "Hanifiyya and Kaʿba." *Jerusalem Studies in Arabic and Islam* 13 (1990) 85-112.

Rubin, U. "The Kaʿba." *Jerusalem Studies in Arabic and Islam* 8. Jerusalem: Hebrew University Magnes Press (1986) 97-131.

Rudolph, W. *Die Abhängigkeit des Qorans von Judentum und Christentum*. Stuttgart: W. Kohlhammer, 1922.

Said, Hakim Muhammad. "The Islamic Community." *Hamdard Islamicus* 5/2 (1982) 33-41.

Sale, G. *The Koran*. London: Frederick Warne and Co., 1893.

Schacht, J. *An Introduction to Islamic Law*. Oxford: Clarendon Press, 1991.

Schacht, J. *The Origins of Muhammadan Jurisprudence*. Oxford: Clarendon Press, 1950.

Schacht, J. "Muhammad ʿAbduh." *The Encyclopedia of Islam*. New edition. 7 (1993) 418-420.

Serjeant, R. B. "Haram and Hawtah, The Sacred Enclave in Arabia." *Mélanges Taha Husain*. Cairo: Dar Al-Maaref (1962) 41-57.

Serjeant, R. B. "The Constitution of Medina." *Islamic Quarterly* 8 (1964) 3-16.

Serjeant, R. B. "The Sunnah Jāmiʿah, Pacts with the Yathrib Jews, and the Taḥrīm of Yathrib: Analysis and Translation of the Documents Comprised in the So-Called 'Constitution of Medina.'" *Studies in Arabian History and Civilization* VI (London: Variorum Reprints, 1981) 1-42.

Sezgin, F. *Geschichte des Arabischen Schrifttums*. Volume I. Leiden: E. J. Brill, 1967.

Sharon, M. "Ahl Al-Bayt." *Jerusalem Studies in Arabic And Islam* 8 (1986)169-184.

Siddiqui, A. *Christian-Muslim Dialogue in the Twentieth Century*. London: Macmillan Press Ltd., 1997.

Smith, J. I. *An Historical and Semantic Study of the Term 'Islām.'* Missoula, Montana: Scholars Press, 1975.

Smith, W. C. *The Meaning and End of Religion.* Minneapolis: Fortress Press, 1991.

Smith, W. R. *Kinship and Marriage in Early Arabia.* S. A. Cook, ed. London: Adam and Charles Black, 1907.

Speight, R. M. "The Function of Ḥadīṯ as Commentary on the Qurʾān, as Seen in the Six Authoritative Collections." *Approaches to the History of the Interpretation of the Qurʾān.* A Rippin, ed. Oxford: Clarendon Press (1988) 63-81.

Sprenger, A. *The Life of Muhammad.* Allahabad, 1851.

Surty, Muhammad Ibrahim H. I. "The Qurʾān in Islamic Scholarship." *The Muslim World Book Review* 7/4 (1987) 51-65.

Talbi, M. "A Community of Communities: The Right to be Different and the Paths to Harmony." *Encounter* (Rome) no. 77 (August/September 1981) 1-14.

Talbi, M. "Religious Liberty: A Muslim Perspective." *Encounter* (Rome) 126-127 (June/July 1986) 1-17.

Tauber, E. "Rašīd Riḍā as Pan-Arabist Before World War I." *The Muslim World* 79 (1989) 102-112.

Tibi, B. *Arab Nationalism. A Critical Inquiry.* London: The Macmillan Press, 1990.

Torrey, C. C. *The Jewish Foundation of Islam.* New ed. New York: KTAV Publishing House, 1967.

Troll, C. W. "The Qurʾānic View of Other Religions: Grounds for Living Together." *Encounter* (Rome) 140 (Dec. 1987) 1-16.

Ursinus, M. O. H. "Millet." *Encyclopedia of Islam*. New edition. 7 (1993) 61-64.

Voorhoeve, P. "Djinn." *Encyclopedia of Islam*. New ed. 2 (1965) 546-550.

Wansbrough, J. "Arabic Rhetoric And Qur'ānic Exegesis." *The Bulletin of the School of Oriental And African Studies* 31 (1968) 469-485.

Wansbrough, J. *Qur'ānic Studies*. Oxford: Oxford University Press, 1977.

Wansbrough, J. *The Sectarian Milieu.* Oxford: Oxford University Press, 1978.

Watt, W. M. "Pre-Islamic Arabian Religion in the Qur'ān." *Islamic Studies* XV (1976) 73-79.

Watt, W. M. "Ḥanīf." *Encyclopedia of Islam*. New edition. 3 (1971) 165-166.

Watt, W. M. *Bell's Introduction to the Qur'ān*. Edinburgh: University Press, 1977.

Watt, W. M. *Companion to the Qur'ān*. London: George Allen and Unwin Ltd.,1967.

Watt, W. M. *Islamic Political Thought: Basic Concepts*. Edinburgh: University Press, 1968.

Watt, W. M. *Muhammad at Mecca.* Oxford: Clarendon Press, 1953.

Watt, W. M. *Muhammad At Medina*. Oxford: Oxford University Press, 1962.

Watt, W. M. *Muhammad, Prophet And Statesman*. London: Oxford University Press, 1961.

Watt, W. M. *What is Islam?* Frome and London: Butler and Tanner Ltd., 1968.

Welch, A. T. "Muhammad's Understanding of Himself." *Islam's Understanding of Itself*. R. G. Hovannisian and S. Vryonis, Jr., eds. Malibu, California: Undena Publications (1983) 15-52.

Wellhausen, J. *The Arab Kingdom and its Fall*. London: Curzon Press, 1927.

Wensinck, A. J. *A Handbook of Early Muhammadan Tradition*. Leiden: E. J. Brill, 1960.

Wensinck, A. J. "Qawm." *Encyclopedia of Islam*. New edition 4 (1971) 780-781.

Wensinck, A. J. "Qibla." *Encyclopedia of Islam*. New Edition 5 (1986) 82-84.

Wensinck, A. J. *The Muslim Creed: Its Genesis and Historical Development*. Cambridge: Cambridge University Press, 1932.

Wensinck, A. J., and J. Jomier. "Kaʿba." *Encyclopedia of Islam*. New edition. 4 (1971) 317-322.

Widengren, G. *Muhammad, the Apostle of God, and his Ascension*. Uppsala/Wiesbaden, 1955.

Wright, W. *A Grammar of the Arabic Language.* Cambridge: University Press, 1991.

Zeine, Z. *The Emergence of Arab Nationalism*. Beirut: Khayats, 1966.

5. Studies related to Islam and the *Umma* in the Philippines

Ahmad, I. *The Rise and Decline of the Muslim Umma.* London: Ta-Ha Publishers Ltd., 1992.

Al-Attas, S. M. N. "Indonesia." *The Encyclopedia of Islam*. New Edition. 3 (1971) 1213-1234.

Alonto, Ahmad Damocao. *Conspiracy to Liquidate Islam in the Philippines.* A Paper read at the 7th Islamic Conference of the Azhar Academy Institute of Islamic Research. Cairo, Egypt. September 9 - 15, 1972.

Arnold, T. W. *The Preaching of Islam*. Lahore: Ashraf Publication, 1979.

Asani, A. "The Bangsamoro People: A Nation in Travail." *Journal Institute of Muslim Minority Affairs* 6/2 (1985) 295-314.

Baltazar, R. "Islam and Secession." *Solidarity* 6/9 (April 1971) 68-69.

Barra, H. "The Šarīʿa Law in the Philippines: An Introduction." *Dansalan Quarterly* 13/1-4 (1993) 2-107.

Bauzon, K. *Liberalism and the Quest for Islamic Identity in the Philippines.* Manila: Ateneo de Manila University Press, 1990.

Bin Bakar, Osman. "Sufism in the Malay-Indonesian World." *Islamic Spirituality* vol. 2. Seyyed Hossein Nasr, ed. London: SCM Press, 1991.

Blair, E. and James Robertson, eds. *The Philippine Islands, 1493-1898*. voi. 4. Cleveland, Ohio: A. H. Clark Company, 1903-09.

Bruno, J. *The Social World of the Tausug: A Study in Culture and Education*. Manila: Centro Escolar University Research and Development Center, 1973.

Buto, Hajji "Traditions, Customs and Commerce of the Sulu Moros." *The Mindanao Herald* (February 3, 1909).

Capalla, F. "The Role of Religious Groups in Modern Pluralistic Societies - Ideals and Realities; Traditions of Harmony in Southeast Asia as a Basis for Christian-Muslim Dialogue." *Notre Dame Journal* 24 (October 1994) 27-34.

Constantino, R. *The Philippines: A Past Revisited* vol. 1. Manila: Renato Constantino, 1993.

Cutshall, A. *The Philippines: Nation of Islands*. Princeton: Van Nostrand Searchlight Books, 1964.

Drewes, G. W. J. "New Light on the Coming of Islam to Indonesia?" *Bijdragen tot de Taal-, Land- en Volken-kunde* 124 (1968) 433-459.

Ellen, R. F. "Social Theory, Ethnography and the Understanding of Practical Islam in Southeast Asia." *Islam in Southeast Asia*. M. B. Hooker, ed. (Leiden: E. J. Brill, 1983) 64-70.

Francisco, J. R. "Selected Essays on Mindanao Art and Culture." *Mindanao Journal* 14/4 (1988) 1-237.

Geertz, C. *Islam Observed.* Chicago: The University of Chicago Press, 1975.

Glang, A. C. "Modernizing the Muslims." *The Muslim Filipinos.* P. G. Gowing and R. McAmis, eds. Manila: Solidaridad Publishing House (1974) 277-283.

Gowing, P. G. *Mandate in Moroland.* Quezon City: New Day Publishers, 1983.

Gowing, P. G. *Muslim Filipinos - Heritage And Horizon.* Quezon City: New Day Publishers, 1979.

Harrison, F. B. *The Cornerstone of Philippine Independence.* New York: The Century Co., 1922.

Hooker, M. B. *Islam in Southeast Asia.* Leiden: E. J. Brill, 1983.

Hooker, M. B. "The Trengganu Inscription in Malayan Legal History." *Journal of the Royal Asiatic Society - Malaysian Branch* 49/2 (1976) 127-131.

Hooker, M. B. *Islamic Law in Southeast Asia.* Singapore: Oxford University Press, 1984.

Johns, A. H. "Islam in Southeast Asia." *The Religious Traditions of Asia.* J. Kitagawa, ed. New York: Macmillan Publishing Company (1989) 165-191.

Johns, A. H. "Islam in Southeast Asia." *The Encyclopedia of Religion.* 7 (1987) 404-421.

Kiefer, T. W. *The Tausug: Violence and Law in a Philippine Muslim Society.* New York: Holt, Rinehart and Winton, 1972.

"Leader of the Moro Islamic Front Outlines His Vision for the Future From His jungle Base. An interview of Salamat Hashim." *Crescent* (August 16-31, 1994) 1-3.

Lingga, A. M. "Salamat Hashim's Concept of Bangsamoro State and Government" in *Dansalan Quarterly* 15/3-4 (1995) 49-60.

Lingga, A. M. *The Political Thought of Salamat Hashim. An unpublished M. A. thesis.* Quezon City: University of the Philippines, 1995. 82 pp.

Madale, N. "The Resurgence of Islam and Nationalism in the Philippines." *Islam and Society in Southeast Asia.* Singapore: Institute of Southeast Asian Studies (1986) 282-314.

Magdalena, F. *Ethncity, Identity, and Conflict: The Case of the Philippine Moros.* Singapore: Institute of Southeast Asian Studies, 1996.

Majul, C. A. "Islamic and Arab Influences in the South of the Philippines." *Journal of Southeast Asian History* 7/2 (1966) 61-73.

Majul, C. A. "Muslims and Christians in the Philippines: A Study in Conflict and Efforts at Reconciliation." *The Vatican, Islam and the Middle East.* K. C. Ellis, ed. Syracuse, New York: Syracuse University Press (1987) 309-336.

Majul, C. A. "Muslims in the Philippines: An Historical Perspective." *The Muslim Filipinos.* P. G. Gowing and R. D. McAmis, eds. Manila: Solidaridad Publishing House (1974) 1-12.

Majul, C. A. "Succession in the Old Sulu Sultanate." *The Muslim Filipinos.* P. G. Gowing and R. D. McAmis, eds. Manila: Solidaridad Publishing House (1974) 61-73.

Majul, C. A. "The Genealogy of Sulu." *Readings on Islam in Southeast Asia*. A. Ibrahim, et. al., compilers. (Singapore: Institute of Southeast Asian Studies, 1985) 48-57.

Majul, C. A. "The Moro Struggle in the Philippines." *Third World Quarterly* 10/2 (April 1988) 897-922.

Majul, C. A. *Muslims in the Philippines*. Quezon City: University of the Philippines Press, 1973.

Majul, C. A. *Muslims in the Philippines: Past, Present and Future Prospects*. Manila: Converts to Islam Society of the Philippines, 1971.

Majul, C. A. *Political and Historical Notes on the Old Sulu Sultanate*. Paper No. 30, International Conference on Asian History. University of Hongkong, 1964.

Majul, C. A. *Some of the Social and Cultural Problems of the Muslims in the Philippines*. Paper presented at a seminar sponsored by the Persatuan Mahasiswa Universiti Kabangsa-an-Malaysia, July 25-28, 1986.

Majul, C. A. *The Contemporary Muslim Movement in the Philippines*. Berkeley: Mizan Press, 1985.

Mastura, M. *Muslim Filipino Experience, A Collection of Essays*. Manila: Ministry of Muslim Affairs, 1984.

May, R. J. "The Philippines." *The Politics of Islamic Re-assertion*. Mohammed Ayoob, ed. London: Croom Helm Ltd. (1981) 211-232.

Mednick, M. "Some Problems of Moro History and Political Organization." *The Muslim Filipinos.* Gowing, P. G. and Robert D. McAmis, eds. Manila: Solidaridad Publishing House (1974) 13-26.

Mednick, M. *Encapment of the Lake: The Social Organization of a Muslim Philippine (Moro) People.* Chicago: University of Chicago, 1965.

Mercado, E. "The Moros of the Philippines." *MIDEO* 16 (1983) 275-288.

Mercado, L. *Elements of Filipino Philosophy.* Manila: Arnoldus Press, 1974.

Mercado, L. *The Filipino Mind.* Manila: Divine Word Publications, 1994.

Michel, T. *Islam in Asia.* Estella, Spain: Editorial Verbo Divino, 1991.

Milner, A. C. "Islam and the Muslim State." *Islam in Southeast Asia.* M. B. Hooker, ed. (Leiden: E. J. Brill, 1983) 39-42.

Misuari, Nur. *Moro National Liberation Front.* Unpublished speech of Nur Misuari at the 9th World General Assembly of the World Muslim Congress. Karachi, March 30 - April 2, 1988.

Moore, R. L. P. *Women and Warriors: Defending Islam in the Southern Philippines.* San Diego, California: University Microfilms International, 1986.

Muslim, M. A. *The Moro Armed Struggle in the Philippines.* Marawi City: University Press and Information Office, 1994.

Nimmo, H. A. *The Sea People of Sulu: A Study of Social Change in the Philippines*. San Francisco: Chandler Publishing Co., 1972.

Phelan, J. L. *The Hispanization of the Phlippines: Spanish Aims and Filipino Responses, 1565-1700*. Madison: University of Wisconsin Press, 1959.

Redfield, R. *Peasant Society and Culture*. Chicago: University Press, 1956.

Rixhon, G. "Tausug Literature: An Overview." *Sulu Studies* 3 (1974) 1-86.

Roest Crollius, A. "The Source of Life at the Meeting of the Two Oceans: Reflections on the Majmaʿ-al-baḥrayn of Dara Shukoh." *Islam in India* vol. 1: 43-51.

Rothermond, D. (ed). *Islam in Southern Asia*. Wiesbaden: Franz Steiner Verlag, 1975.

Saber, M. "Darangen: Epic of the Maranao." *The Journal of History* X/3 (1962).

Saleeby, N. M. "Studies in Moro History, Law and Religion." *Notre Dame Journal* 6/1 (April 1975) 1-63.

Saleeby, N. M. *Studies in Moro History, law and Religion*. Manila: Bureau of Public Printing, 1905.

Saleeby, N. M. *The History of Sulu*. Manila: Filipiniana Book Guild, 1963.

Santos, J. Jalal-ud-din de los. "Towards a Solution of the Moro Problem." *Dansalan Quarterly* 1/4 (1980) 217-230.

Spoehr, A. "An Archaeological Approach to Ethnic Diversity in Zamboanga and Sulu." *Sulu Studies* 2 (1973).

Stewart, J. C. "Maguindanao." *Muslim Peoples: A World Ethnographic Survey*. Weekes, R. V., ed. Westport, Connecticut: Greenwood Press (1984) 462-466.

Supreme Executive Council. The Bangsa Moro Liberation Organization, a policy statement (n.p., May 1978) 22 pp.

Tan, S. K. *Internationalization of the Bangsamoro Struggle.* Quezon City: UP Center for Integrative and Development Studies, 1993.

"The Moro People: Is Destiny Finally in their Hands?" *Mindev.* A bi-annual journal of the Managing Alternatives Group, Inc. (1995) 1-39.

Tiamson, A., ed. *Papers on the Tripoli Agreement.* Quezon City: International Studies Institute of the Philippines, 1986.

Ugnay-Diwa 10 (July-December 1993).

Winstedt, R. O. *A History of Malaya.* Singapore, 1935.

Zaide, G. F. *Philippine Political and Cultural History. vol. 1: The Philippines Since Pre-Spanish Times.* Manila: Philippine Education Company, 1949.